D1518227

Emperor of Culture

University of Pennsylvania Press
MIDDLE AGES SERIES
Edited by EDWARD PETERS
Henry Charles Lea Professor
of Medieval History
University of Pennsylvania

A complete listing of the books in this series
appears at the back of this volume

Emperor of Culture

Alfonso X the Learned of Castile and His Thirteenth-Century Renaissance

Robert I. Burns, S.J., Editor

uɲɲ

University of Pennsylvania Press
Philadelphia

Partial funding for the publication of this book has been provided by The Program for
Cultural Cooperation Between Spain's Ministry of Culture and United States' Universities.

Library of Congress Cataloging-in-Publication Data
Emperor of culture: Alfonso X the Learned of Castile and his thirteenth-century
  Renaissance / Robert I. Burns, editor.
      p. cm. — (Middle Ages series)
    Includes bibliographical references.
    ISBN 0-8122-8116-0
      1. Alfonso X, King of Castile and Leon, 1221–1284. 2. Spain—Intellectual life—
711–1516. I. Burns, Robert Ignatius. II. Series.
DP140.3.E47 1990
946'.02—dc20   89-40395
                                                                    CIP

Contents

List of Illustrations

Abbreviations

AHDE	*Anuario de historia de derecho español.*
Alfonso, Emperor	*Alfonso X the Learned: Emperor of Culture, 1284–1984,* special issue of *Thought* 60 (239), December 1985.
BAE	*Biblioteca de autores españoles,* 203 vols. to date (Madrid: 1846 et seq.).
Ballesteros, *Alfonso X*	Antonio Ballesteros-Beretta, *Alfonso X el Sabio* (Madrid: C.S.I.C., 1963, repr. Barcelona: El Albir, 1984).
BHS	*Bulletin of Hispanic Studies.*
BNM	Biblioteca Nacional, Madrid.
BRAH	*Boletín de la (Real) Academia de la historia.*
CAX	*Crónica del rey D. Alfonso X,* in *BAE,* vol. 66.
CLC	*Cortes de los antiguos reinos de León y Castilla,* 5 vols. (Madrid: Real Academia de la Historia, 1861–1903).
LWAX	*The Legislative Works of Alfonso X, el Sabio: A Critical Bibliography,* comp. J. R. Craddock (London: Grant and Cutler, 1986).
MHE	*Memorial histórico español: colección de documentos, opúsculos y antigüedades,* 50 vols. (Madrid: Real Academia de la Historia, 1851–1963).
MLR	*Modern Language Review.*
NRFH	*Nueva revista de filología hispánica.*
RABM	*Revista de archivos, bibliotecas y museos.*
RCEH	*Revista canadiense de estudios hispánicos.*
RFE	*Revista de filología española.*

Studies on the   *Studies on the "Cantigas de Santa Maria": Art, Mu-*
Cantigas   *sic, and Poetry,* ed. I. J. Katz, John E. Keller, et al.
                         (Madison, Wisc.: Hispanic Seminary of Medieval
                         Studies, 1987).

Worlds of Alfonso   *The Worlds of Alfonso the Learned and James the*
                         Conqueror: Intellect and Force in the Middle Ages, ed.
                         Robert I. Burns, S.J. (Princeton: Princeton Uni-
                         versity Press, 1985).

Preface

The seventh centennial of Alfonso the Learned's death in 1284 occasioned an outburst of international congresses, conferences, and celebrations. The earliest of these, at the University of California, Los Angeles, I designed to display the talents of the burgeoning American school of medieval Hispanists. Two separate books resulted. *The Worlds of Alfonso the Learned and James the Conqueror: Intellect and Force in the Middle Ages* appeared in 1985 from Princeton University Press and under the auspices of UCLA's Center for Medieval and Renaissance Studies. It focused on Alfonso's social and political context, his ruinous financial policies, the municipal militias supporting his crusades and bellicose adventures, and his cycle of contributions to Roman law, all in a comparative perspective with his rival and neighbor, James of Aragon, with parallel date-charts to synchronize Alfonsine activity with wider European history. As a companion volume that same year, I presented *Alfonso X the Learned: Emperor of Culture, 1284–1984* in the form of a special issue of *Thought*.[1] Its contributors were not from the American school of medieval Hispanist history but from the literary-cultural Alfonsinists.

The historical book was widely reviewed in both the professional and popular press; the cultural book, by reason of its journal format, inevitably received less formal attention—all of it, happily, welcoming. The need for a wider and more accessible exploration of the cultural themes inspired the present book. Its scale and range are larger. The number of studies has increased from eight to thirteen. Of these thirteen, however, eight are entirely original and formed no part of the *Thought* volume. Three more are so radically revised as to constitute new, and newly titled, contributions. The remaining two, including my own introduction, remain substantially the same as in *Thought*. Of the wholly new articles, two are by contributors to the original journal volume. This means that six new authors appear, and eleven new articles of the present thirteen chapters are new. To emphasize the novelty of content while indicating some continuity, the book's title is reversed and it now has a subtitle.

The present set of scholarly studies is designed to advance our knowledge of important aspects of El Sabio's contributions to Western culture. At the same time, the studies are broadly conceived and designed so as to be accessible to and interesting for the educated general reader. None of the studies is a general synthesis or popularized essay, however; these are serious and focused original works, useful to specialists and requiring the general reader's careful attention. The combined authors, as a glance at the list of contributors will indicate, constitute a representative roll call from the major literary and cultural Alfonsine scholars in this country. Had more space been available, the number of distinguished senior and junior medieval Hispanists might easily have been tripled. The chapters afford a wide vista of Alfonso's own achievements, treating his ruler-image, his role in the evolution of language, his Jewish translators/collaborators for Arabic science, his art in its European context, his chancery-scriptorium interchange, his influence on Dante and on contemporary Italy and France, and his new historiography as well as his music, legal contributions, and connections with drama. An essay by the king's most indefatigable bibliographer appropriately closes the sequence, pointing the reader toward further search and discovery.

In presenting the Learned King's achievements, this book follows the practice widespread among medievalist Hispanists of usually omitting modern accents and tildes from the titles of the king's books. It does not adhere to this policy slavishly. The word *crónica* has particularly kept its accent, since many Hispanists are disconcerted to encounter it in the nude. The same is true of the familiar *Espéculo.* The *Cantigas,* which appears here so frequently, would have had its accent on the first syllable; a fair number of Hispanists incorrigibly mispronounce this fine Galician word in Castilian mode. No apology is needed for Englishing cortes, as even American newspapers do, but several other Spanish terms have been similarly appropriated where it seemed a sensible expedient. A few kings also appear in English garb, because they either are more familiar in that guise (Frederick II of Germany-Sicily) or ambiguously have more than one alien form (Jaume/Jaime of the Realms of Aragon and his son Pere/Pero, here as James and Peter, respectively).

I must thank here, once again, the granting bodies that funded the original international congress—the National Endowment for the Humanities, the Ahmanson Foundation, the Del Amo Foundation, the Spanish Consulate, the Institute for Medieval Mediterranean Spain, and the University of California at Los Angeles.

Robert I. Burns, S.J.
University of California, Los Angeles

Robert I. Burns, S.J.

I. *Stupor Mundi:* Alfonso X of Castile, the Learned

In 1984, many countries celebrated the seven-hundredth anniversary of the death of the most remarkable king in the history of the West, Alfonso X of Castile. The prototypical philosopher-king, he is aptly named El Sabio— "the Learned" or "the Scholar." Half of his greatness lay in the man himself, in his polymath hunger to absorb all beauty and learning, to codify and reshape it, and to propagate it throughout his somewhat backward society with a missionary fervor. By the great creations he presided over and participated in, he intended more: nothing less than to reshape and elevate that society in its future generations. The other half of his greatness lies, as with any great man, in the extrinsic historical accidents down to the present day. For example, he is rightly called the founder of Castilian as a proper language, but he could not have foreseen that the language he helped fashion would by the commemorative year 1984 rank fourth in the number of native speakers on the planet. He created a vast encyclopedia of life and society, in the guise of a closet or literary code of law, but he could not have imagined how it would spread to Africa, Asia, and the New World and achieve "the widest territorial force ever enjoyed by any law book" and to become "one of the outstanding landmarks" not only of Spain's actual law but "indeed of world law." His code is vital even to the legal life of the United States; "civilized law began" with Alfonso's code "in a considerable group of jurisdictions" here and can still be cited from Louisiana and Louisiana Purchase states to California and the Mexican War acquisitions.[1] Alfonso's contributions to science, music, historiography, poetry, fiction, and art were each unique, but they also became lasting and endlessly influential.

All of this has been on public record and in restricted circles well enough known. Our English heritage has been impatient with Spanish history, however, and the historiography which prevailed from its nine-teenth-century Romantic-nationalist origins until World War II glorified

instead the dominant northern countries of Europe producing that historiography. Alfonso was never wholly neglected outside of Hispanic countries, and for a generation now interest in him by outsiders has widened
until it is reaching flood tide. The new balance, mostly on the literary and
cultural side, was evident in the recent centennial celebrations in the United
States, beginning at UCLA in 1981, culminating during the main year 1984
with symposia at universities such as the University of California at Berkeley, Catholic University, Colorado, Harvard, Houston, Kentucky, Western
Michigan, Ohio State, Old Dominion in Virginia, Plymouth State in New
Hampshire, and Wisconsin, and receding in 1985 with a flurry of belated
academic festivities. The books and articles emerging from such exercises
continued to appear throughout the late 1980s. The celebrations in Washington D.C., attended by the Spanish ambassador, were illustrated by an
Alfonsine exhibit at the Library of Congress. In the Modern Language
Association's general meeting in December 1984, Joseph Snow reviewed
the phenomenon with his "The Alfonsine Year: A World Survey."[2]

In 1221, the year of the great king's birth, his country seemed an
unlikely garden for so exotic a plant as this man who saw himself as king or
even emperor of all Spain and who struggled for most of his reign to
validate his claims as Holy Roman Emperor over Christendom. Castile was
then an upland frontier, far from the international maritime lanes of the
urbanized Mediterranean, landlocked except for the Bay of Biscay to its
north, backward and feudal, but good cattle country. It was "a society
organized for war," in Elena Lourie's phrase, especially along its advancing
south whose frontier confronted the great Islamic civilization occupying
half the peninsula. Castile itself was only one of several kingdoms sharing
the peninsula's north—little entities straggling in a line along the Atlantic
and Pyrenees, each recently grown into an oblong stretching south as the
Muslims had yielded their less valuable borderlands to these unreasonably
fierce warriors. From left to right stood Portugal, León, Castile, Navarre
(blocked by the others from much advance), Aragon, and Catalonia (the
last two yoked under one dynasty). This geography had just changed
radically, as Alfonso's father, St. Fernando III, began his epic conquests
against Spanish Islam, matched by the march of Arago-Catalonia down
Mediterranean Spanish Islam. One by one, the great Islamic centers fell to
Castile and Aragon—the Balearics, Córdoba, Valencia, Murcia, Jaén, and
Seville—until only the rump-state Granada remained, enclaved between
the mountains and the sea and tolerated as a vassal of Castile. When Alfonso
was nine, his father had also inherited the kingdom of León, joining this

neighbor definitively into a superkingdom twice the size of Castile and more variegated. St. Fernando, now the hero of Christendom, was preparing to invade Africa when he died just after midcentury.

Growing up in the shadow of this intimidating saint and conqueror, Alfonso might have retreated into a quieter existence, like the obscure sons of so many great men. He passed his childhood in the rough Celtic countryside of Atlantic Galicia, with surrogate parents as was then the custom for royalty. When he was a teenager, his mother died. His education, which we can only conjecture from his later proficiencies, must have been solid and wide-ranging. He married at twenty-three, beginning a large family of six sons and three daughters. No saint himself, he also had mistresses and illegitimate children. Shortly after his marriage, Alfonso led the army that conquered for his father the Mediterranean Islamic kingdom of Murcia. He fought at his father's side too during the siege of Seville. Alfonso was already thirty, a minor patron of law, literature, and Islamic science, when he finally inherited the throne.

His country now was enormous, from the Atlantic to the Mediterranean, with the beginnings of a proper navy and merchant marine. Metropolises like Seville (his favorite) now flew his Christian flag, and wealth from Spanish Islam filled his treasury. The three million people scattered over these spaces included a large minority of Muslims as well as an increased Jewish community; Alfonso had become, in effect, like his namesake Alfonso VI, "ruler of the three religions." As a German from his mother's side, he soon maneuvered his election as Holy Roman Emperor, beginning a twenty-year effort to move from title to reality, a doomed and endlessly expensive enterprise. His first decade on Castile's throne was bellicose, with armed adventures against Portugal on the west, Navarre and English Aquitaine on the north, and Morocco on the south (which he invaded at Salé in 1260). Against resurgent Islam, he clung to his father's conquests, painfully reconquering rebellious Murcia, taking the Atlantic holdout Cádiz, and stemming general countercrusades from North Africa and Granada in the 1260s and 1270s.[3]

Alfonso was not a popular king. His attempts to act as a proper sovereign rather than a feudal suzerain alienated the nobility. His inordinate expenses at home and abroad alienated every taxpaying stratum of society. His championship of Roman law did not recommend him to a customary-law people. His adventurism irritated and disturbed his neighbors. The successful closing of the Iberian frontier of conquest against Islam left many of his knights without their lifestyle and source of ready

Figure 1-1. Alfonso as king, receiving a delegation from the community of conquered Muslims of Murcia. *Cantigas de Santa Maria,* Patrimonio Nacional.

wealth. At the same time, past Islamic wars had long inhibited the development of a Castilian middle class. Alfonso managed to alienate even his churchmen. There are paradoxes here: wars, but not the right kind for his barons; wealth, but an inability to channel it effectively or to live within the limits of the king's share; exalted titles and a high profile elsewhere in Europe, in contrast to the rooted inclination of his people for a more parochial existence.

Historians have generally considered Alfonso a poor manager, despite his effective innovations in administration. They stress that his title El Sabio should not bear any echo of one possible translation, "the wise." And they ratify the judgment of the seventeenth-century Jesuit historian Mariana that he pondered the heavens but lost the earth. That judgment may be modified, as historians now begin to give to the historical side of his reign the manuscript and contextual attention that literary scholars have long given to his creative works. Perhaps his failures were less personal than they were the product of circumstance. At any rate, he ended his life afloat on a very sea of troubles, repudiated abroad as emperor and dethroned at home in a civil war led by his son, all the discontents of his people and of neighboring lands converging. His major ally now ironically Morocco, Alfonso died suddenly in April 1284 in the city he had helped his father conquer, Seville.[4]

I have focused on Alfonso and his Castilian background. What of the wider world of which he formed an integral part? The thirteenth century was remarkable for its glories, to the degree that some have too exuberantly claimed for it the title "the greatest of centuries." It saw the culmination and most notable protagonists of many movements on which the high civilization of the West was built. In philosophy, this was the age of scholasticism and Aquinas; in art, of Gothic and Giotto; in religion, of the Mendicants and the imperial papacy (with Innocent III and Francis of Assisi); in poetry, of the vernacular and Dante; in commerce, of the Mongol imperium and the world traveler Marco Polo; in medicine, of the new surgery and Arnau de Vilanova; and so in other spheres from music and mathematics to technology and mysticism. Truly great kings filled the age. St. Louis IX created France out of his native northern Francia together with the alien Occitania he took over down to the Mediterranean. Frederick II Hohenstaufen, the Holy Roman Emperor, ruled from a pluriethnic Sicily while enemies whispered that he was half-Muslim in his lifestyle and beliefs; his cultural achievements and patronage won for him the sobriquet *Stupor mundi*, "wonder of the world." James the Conqueror in Aragon and his son Peter the Great (Dante's hero) built a Mediterranean "empire," and presided over troubadours and such institutions as the great medical university at Montpellier and the Dominican schools of Arabic from Barcelona to Tunis. These kings also have claims to be called founders of their peoples' greatness and culture, with few peers in that context before or after. All these kings were patrons and active in their culture. None of them, however, can boast the range and depth of achievements of Alfonso the Learned. They and their contemporaries in every field do give a clue to the dynamism of the age itself, to its ambition, complexity, and energies.

Alfonso did not merely preside over his Castilian renaissance but was both instigator and personal participant in its multiple manifestations. Nor did he merely plunge into cultural activities as an aesthete, indulging a voracious appetite; he proposed by those activities to reshape society, to bring Castile itself into the mainstream of high civilization and to set afoot a process that would produce a united, educated, artistic, and religious people. The vision here is as remarkable as the means. Alfonso himself can be seen, therefore, more in his mighty works than in his routine political history; even his portrait is several times depicted in them realistically. A major component of his work, indeed the indispensable tool, was intensive further absorption of Islamic culture by translation, adaptation, and influences. Another dominant tool was Roman law, at that time occupying elsewhere in Western culture the status and ubiquity that science was to boast in the nineteenth century.

An overview of Alfonso's work may suitably start with the several individual projects most highly prized today. The *Siete partidas,* or *Seven Divisions,* of his Roman law code (the number seven held powerful symbolic meanings for Alfonso) makes as good an entry as any. It is like no other law code but is unique in intention and nature, monumental in size and scope, with an influence even today that is incalculable. Its present shape includes further developments in Alfonso's name for a half-century after his death, though their number and importance have been exaggerated by Alfonso García Gallo and others during a recent polemic. Even had the *Siete partidas* evolved considerably, Alfonso's other legal works would serve as guide to his intentions and vision. Though it has been a working public code since 1348, Alfonso himself apparently had no hope of imposing it generally upon his custom-law people. Their society would eventually need such a system, he knew, as its level of political and commercial sophistication was raised. For the time being, he would create an instrument for appeals, a closet code or work of literature, and a program. It would become familiar and be at hand. Alfonso was also responsible for five legal treatises (as distinct from lesser bodies of actual regulations), whose interrelation, partial authorship, practical intent, and sequence in appearing continue to be subjects of debate. He promulgated only one of these legal works, and only as supplementary law. All five seem to have been stages or echoes of the monumental *Siete partidas* itself, a kind of encyclopedia of medieval man's institutions and values as viewed by university jurists and through legal concepts. Basically, Alfonso directed the construction by his legal experts of an ample code, much as Justinian and Napoleon did (though Alfonso's presence in his wonderfully literary production is far more personal). The schools and lawyers then improved his product for over fifty years until its present form was ready to promulgate.

The first division, or partida, discussing the church under twenty-four headings and some five hundred subheadings, includes among its chatty little essays such topics as burial—why near a church, how to measure off a cemetery, who can be buried within a church, why knights killed in tournaments are excluded, the expenses of funerals, and that valuables must not be buried with the corpse. The second division, on public law and government, includes among weightier matters little talks on how a king should dress, stand, sit, hunt, act toward his wife, and how he should educate his children and relate to his female relatives. This section includes a small handbook on castles—their kinds, repair, provisioning, surrender, and defense. On knights, it tells us how to become one and how they should ride, dress, and eat (two pages on this) as well as train and talk. Warfare of all kinds gets multiple treatises for nearly a hundred pages, covering cavalry, infantry, and naval warfare, drill, tactics, flags, logistics, artillery, spies, sentries, and ranks. This partida's long discussion of universities is itself worth the price of admission: where to build one, teachers and salaries, student bookstores, labor unions, tax exemptions for teachers, and the students' need for fresh air, good food, and resting the eyes.

The essays of the *Siete partidas* do not resemble the terse law codes promulgated by Frederick II and James the Conqueror in this century; both codes are now landmarks in European legal history. The *Partidas* are instead reflective historico-moral disquisitions such as one might expect from Plato's philosopher-king. Like Aquinas's *Summa* or a Gothic cathedral, this vast structure is an exhaustive and systematic interweaving of age-old wisdom. Alfonso's code is an integral component of United States law today, and the only English translation is the exact and painstaking volume commissioned a half-century ago by the American Bar Association. It was not for this linkage, however, that the United States House of Representatives commissioned a high-relief bust of Alfonso to grace the gallery doors of its chambers. Alfonso is present there, among some twenty renowned heads, simply as one of the greatest legislators in world history.[5]

More remarkable as a creative achievement, though less well known, was Alfonso's own favorite work, the *Cantigas,* or *Canticles of Holy Mary.* A collection of over four hundred lyric and narrative poems, set to as many musical compositions, the songs accompanying and enlivening its nearly 1,300 realistic miniature paintings of daily life, the book defies categorizing. Some see it as an encyclopedia of art forms, others as the most impressive trove of medieval secular music, and others as a great work of literature. It is more than all of these because it combined these elements into a unity, to be "performed" on feasts of the Virgin in the cathedral of conquered Seville. Jealously guarded in its main codex at the Escorial palace-museum, the

Cantigas has moved into general modern awareness only in our own day—
its musical code broken, its corpus of pictures just recently reproduced in
full color, and its poetical text given both a critical edition and (soon to be
published) an English translation from the troubadour-Galician of the
original. Each page captivates the reader by showing its narrative in a
picture series like a modern comic strip; the technique is cinematic and
lively. Had Alfonso done nothing besides the *Cantigas,* his fame would still
be established; this unique production ranks with Dante's *Divine Comedy* or
with the best Gothic cathedral. These "sacred" canticles overshadow Alfonso's other major body of poetry, the *Profane Canticles* of troubadour
bawdry, satire, and love.[6]

A major contribution to Castilian prose, and a strong contribution to
the self-definition of Alfonso's enlarged Castile, was his history projects. A
staff working under his direction produced two seminal works, a history of
Spain down to his father's reign, and a far larger history of the world
through antiquity almost to the time of Christ. Their titles can be confusingly similar: the first, *General Chronicle of Spain* (*Crónica general de
España,* or *Estoria de Espanna,* or more often today *Primera crónica general*);
and the second, *General Chronicle* (*Crónica general* or *Gran e general estoria*
or *Historia universal*). These two became the foundation stone of Spanish
historiography, previously a feeble growth. Their use of sources—Christian, Arabic, and ancient—was exemplary for their day, though epics and
other literary productions were incorporated. This new history was distinguished not only by its vernacular style but by a concern to include social
and cultural as well as political history. Again we see Alfonso bringing his
Castile into the European mainstream, projecting his task on a monumental
scale with a team to sort through and analyze the sources, and by the moral-
educative tone of these histories both elevating public taste and reinforcing
a protonational identity. Here again, he left a legacy that would continue to
be cherished and to work like a leaven toward his vision of a new society.

Alfonso continued a grand tradition of Spanish monarchs by his
scientific activity, specifically in translations from Arabic astronomy, with
its accompaniment, astrology. The staff here was largely trilingual Jews.
Unlike the famed translators in Spain during the previous century, such as
Gerard of Cremona, Mark of Toledo, and Robert of Chester, these men
produced Castilian rather than Latin works. Scientific translation was a
lifelong preoccupation with Alfonso, resulting in five major works. The
Alfonsine Tables was perhaps the most original, transmitting and updating
the charting of the movements of the heavens by al-Zarqālī. The work

involved painstaking observations by teams of scientists for a decade at Toledo, a government project both expensive and, for science itself, stimulating. The *Tables* would spread over Europe and serve astronomy for several centuries. As part of this enterprise, Alfonso's scientists translated over a dozen crucial treatises from the heritage of Spanish Islam, collected as *The Books of the Wisdom of Astronomy (Libros del saber de astronomia)*, revising Ptolemy's astronomy; and *The Book of the Judgments of Astrology (Libro de las cruzes, or Libro de los juicios de las estrellas)*. These and his other astrological works shade off into pseudoscientific works, such as his *Lapidary (Lapidario)*—a brilliantly illustrated treatise on medical and other properties of gems and stones. In technology, Alfonso joined contemporaries like Louis IX of France and Emperor Frederick II in the search for a perfect clock—in Alfonso's case, a mercury-controlled, weight-driven mechanism. Such clocks primarily forecast the movements of heavenly bodies and only incidentally told time.

Translations of various kinds formed a daily backdrop to the king's other creative projects. His nephew Juan Manuel describes how Alfonso had "the whole sect of the Moors" (taken today to mean the Qu'rān) translated, "and the whole Jewish law and even their Talmud, and another very secret science the Jews have which they call cabala."[7] Alfonso also had the most celebrated book on games—*Chess, Dice, and Backgammon (Libro de ajedrez, dados y tablas)*—translated, bountifully illustrated, and revised to improve it over the original and even over the genre in Islam or the West. He is credited also with a translation of *Muhammad's Ladder,* whose detailed trip through heaven and hell influenced Dante's otherworldly cosmos. Among these translations, a collection of oriental tales, called *Calila e Digna* after the protagonists of one story, had a large popular impact and influenced the development of fiction in Europe. Other Alfonsine works are now lost. Though we have one book on hunting, for example, another codex on hunting animals has only recently turned up.

All of Alfonso's work demonstrates his determination to advance the Castilian language, at that time a rough instrument struggling to achieve literary form. Eschewing the Latin which was then the language of academe, business, diplomacy, and the educated classes in general, the king had his scientific, literary, historical, juridical, and other works, both originals and translations, put into Castilian. This lessened their universal influence, thus contrasting with the more famous translators of twelfth-century Spain. But it helped achieve the elevation of Castilian society and culture which was Alfonso's aim. He also decreed that most documents, of the thousands from his chancery, be drafted in Castilian instead of Latin. Together with his legal productions, this spread his encouragement of the vernacular over a broad, grassroots range.

Francisco Márquez Villanueva has noted that Alfonso's choice of Castilian was related to the lamentable state of Latin schools and study in Castile. But Alfonso could readily have overcome that obstacle by employ- ing Latinate Jews or importing more Italians. Other scholars have sug- gested that the example of his father-in-law, James the Conqueror, in Catalonia, inspired his opting for the vernacular; in his advanced Catalan society, James had ordered official versions of his pioneering Valencian code both in Catalan and in Latin and was preparing his autobiography in Catalan. The examples of Occitania and Italy may also have influenced Alfonso as his now enlarged kingdom related ever more to their affairs. In any case, the impact Alfonso had on language alone has won him the epithet "father of Castilian."

Though scholars will continue to argue the precise participation of Alfonso personally in each of his works, it is clear that he not only presided as patron but organized as editor, and often directly took part. For some books, we have revealing descriptions; speaking in the third person, for example, Alfonso says that "he corrected it and ordered it written, and he struck out the words which he understood to be superfluous and of doubt- ful meaning and which were not in pure Castilian," and in general "set the entire writing in order." Alfonso tells us, in the case of his universal history, how "I had caused to be assembled" the various sources, and then "I selected from them the most reliable and the best that I knew," and "made this book" and "commanded" the contents to be written.[8] He was a gifted poet and, because of that profession at that time, therefore also a musician. He did not merely encourage the scholars and artists at his court but recruited them, set grand projects afoot, and financed, directed, and sus- tained them in teams. This farsighted, indefatigable king was a one-man renaissance.

How shall we finally explain this great man? The many-sided studies proliferating during the decade before his seventh centennial and now during these years of celebration are already offering clues and hinting at solutions. It is no longer enough to dismiss him as an artist-intellectual, unsuitable like all intellectuals to the practical business of government. One interesting thesis recently proffered by Cayetano Socarras[9] rejects the argu- ment that Alfonso neglected political affairs, escaping into the cultural sphere; on the contrary, he plunged enthusiastically into politics and even led Castile onto the central stage of European history. Many believe that he lacked the managerial skills necessary for success in his various political situations. Further study and reflection, I suspect, may reveal him as a better manager than certain crises or failures indicate and that perhaps he was a victim of intrinsically unmanageable situations arising from Castile's stunning expansion, its altered and pluriethnic demography, its destabilized power balances within society, and the problems of a Europe entering more general crises from midcentury to 1300.

Socarras himself sees a man caught between two personally interiorized traditions, so incompatible as to make him at first seem "a dual personality." In the creative sphere of his life, "he was moved by a desire to recreate the brilliant intellectual world of the Muslim Caliphate of Córdoba," so that he boldly organized "a gigantic *Summa* of the best of two worlds that came into contact in Spain." He had no such freedom in the world of politics, or at least could not break out of the "great political tradition" which dictated his responses and options but which was no longer "appropriate for his own times." The result of his failure was "almost two centuries of civil strife and turmoil."

The clue for Socarras here is "imperialism." In its cultural expression, Alfonso "wanted to give a final form and unity to all disciplines: law, history, astronomy and other sciences, to the meters of poetry according to the different themes," and to language as the instrument for unifying Spaniards under Castilian predominance—in short, "dominating everything, centralizing everything around himself" as an "emperor of Culture." In its political expression, however, "this same imperialism" drove him to attempt to validate the peninsular "empire," which his forebear Alfonso VII of Castile and León had dreamed of when he took the title Emperor a century before, and to widen it and link it to the Holy Roman Empire of Christendom—a Mediterranean unity of Christians and conquered Muslims, a new Roman Empire. Unlike his cultural imperialism, for which the time was uniquely ripe, his political imperialism was untimely and impossible—"in complete disregard of the actual conditions" in Spain. Alfonso resembled in this his contemporary Dante, who dreamed ineffectively of a Holy Roman Empire under Henry VII leading all Christendom, but whose reality and accomplishment was his own creation of a transcendent empire of the artist-intellectual in his summa, the *Divine Comedy*.[10]

Within this larger framework, inner patterns can be discerned. Joaquín Gimeno sees the turmoil and civil war from Alfonso onward, for example, as a process of radical changes gripping Castile. This period "of incredible dynamism, of incessant clash of ideas, of audacious innovations" now "changed Castile, changed its system of government, [and] changed in a very special way the powerful institution of the nobility." Nobles, cities, and kings had entered a new world of possibilities because of the situation Alfonso inherited and presided over. The interests, expectations, and ideas of these incompatible, "bellicose antagonists" pointed anarchistically to "three quite different Castiles" in the future. As Alfonso tried to transform himself from feudal suzerain to Roman-law king, to change the very "image of the monarch," he provoked his nobles to resist on the battlefield. On all sides—in taxes, laws, city privileges, and the very vision of Spain—radical innovation and radical conservatism clashed. By this view, Alfonso's political failure was inevitable from the domestic situation alone, and it was less a failure than an inescapable confrontation and dialogue of values in a changed world.[11]

A final reflection must be offered, on Alfonso's incorporation or adaptation of Islamic learning and culture. This is too often seen, after the fashion of Américo Castro, as uniquely Castilian, so that Alfonso's great projects arose in a non-European context and "remained obscured, like an eccentric recluse," in their own language and culture, with Alfonso "not interested in including contemporary Europe in the panorama of his culture."[12] Castro's position here seems extreme. Alfonso's country was indeed a special mix of Muslim, Christian, and Jew; and its underdeveloped and ruralized context had just absorbed the main cultural centers of Spanish Islam. Alfonso did see the need to create and stimulate a high culture for his newly aggrandized people, to elevate them as proper colleagues for their Mediterranean Christian neighbors. And from long tradition he appreciated both the necessity of some borrowing from the Islamic high culture at hand and the special opportunity of doing so at this moment of conquest-conjuncture. It was Alfonso, after all, who had entombed his warrior-father in conquered Seville with burial inscriptions in Latin, Arabic, Castilian, and Hebrew. The mixture of cultures was more grossly apparent in Alfonso's Castile, precisely because the leap of cultural elevation was so much higher, within so much shorter a time, and with so powerful an assist from the alien culture now conveniently resident within. Nothing so drastic happened in King James the Conqueror's massive conquests, for example, where a Catalan culture had already reached the point of producing (from 1250 to 1350) its high culture with a real but not so pronounced and artificial Muslim component. The architecture, crafts, and language of Valencia would profit from and be marked by Islam; the medical advances of Arnau de Vilanova and the philosophical-literary outpourings of Ramon Llull are inconceivable without Islam; but they form part of a balanced Mediterranean Christendom.

Alfonso's fusion of some Islamic influences into European patterns (stronger in some works such as the translations, useful and innovative in others such as the law code or the histories, and feeble or absent in others such as music) did not separate Castilian culture from its neighbors, however, in any but a manneristic or superficial sense. The Holy Roman Emperor Frederick II had enjoyed a pluriethnic court and translations from the Arabic; the troubadour literature in Provence-Languedoc and the medical learning at the University of Montpellier had living roots in Islamic invention; universities themselves and their scholastic methods, as George Makdisi has instructed us, were profoundly influenced by Islamic schools;[13] the contemporary mathematics of Fibonacci of Pisa, the mysticism of Francis of Assisi, and the metaphysics of Thomas Aquinas (not the least in his collaboration with Ramon Martí on the Islamic-Catalan frontier) owed a debt to Islam. Commerce linked the Islamic and Christian worlds more closely than we previously realized, with commercial colonies of Italians and other Christians as privileged enclaves in the North African cities, and fonduks or hospitality centers for Muslim merchants in the Christian ports. King James, when he was not conquering Muslims, rented armies to Islamic rulers. The interchange was constant, at formal and informal levels, deliberate as well as subconscious, in technology, trade, mutual absorption of slave populations, entertainment, learning, and art. But all these regions, including Castile, were solidly established in the general European culture, and borrowed out of that position of strength.

Thus, Alfonso is not a freak or a break with European tradition, however idiosyncratic the Castilian model seems on the surface. It is more true to say that we moderns broke with him, when the northern industrial countries of the early nineteenth century invented a nationalist historiography that moved Europe's medieval center north to jibe with its more modern center and marginalized the heartlands of its earlier Mediterranean-centered self. As we recapture our wider history in our own day, Alfonso the Learned can be seen as a major actor in a widely based transfer of learning and letters from Islam to the West, particularly but by no means exclusively for his own country in that universal transfer. When we add his role as transformer of Castilian society, language, and law and his world role as father of Spanish law in all its many countries including our own, we recognize how richly he deserves his titles "El Sabio" and "emperor of Culture." Much more than his contemporary, the Holy Roman Emperor Frederick II Hohenstaufen, he is the true *Stupor mundi*—a royal wonder of the world.

Joseph F. O'Callaghan

2. Image and Reality: The King Creates His Kingdom

Alfonso X of Castile and León is commonly known to Spanish historians as El Sabio, variously translated as "the wise" or "the learned." That appellation is well deserved; as everyone knows, Alfonso X was an erudite man, probably without peer among contemporary monarchs. A poet and scholar, he brought together an equipage of poets, jurists, musicians, painters, scientists, historians, and others, who collaborated with him in the production of a body of literature and scholarship unparalleled in thirteenth-century Europe. One cannot doubt that, in this respect, he merits the title El Sabio.[1]

Alfonso's achievements as a king, however, have not won high praise. His unsuccessful quest to rule the Holy Roman Empire and the unfortunate denouement of his reign, when his son Sancho deprived him of the powers of government and thus effectively deposed him, have prompted historians to render a negative judgment of his abilities as a ruler. That judgment can and should be nuanced to some extent.[2]

My purpose is to focus attention upon Alfonso X as ruler of a thirteenth-century kingdom and to assess his work. In doing so, I will address the following themes: (1) the government of Castile and León, (2) relations with the other peninsular states, (3) the affair of the Holy Roman Empire (*fecho del imperio*), and (4) the crisis of the succession. I cannot presume to treat each of these themes in the depth that it deserves, but an overview will provide a coherent understanding of Alfonso's activities and will assist in forming a judgment of his accomplishments as a ruler and a statesman.[3]

In beginning this process, certain aspects of the legacy he received from his father, Fernando III (1217–1252), ought to be considered. Fernando won extraordinary renown because of his conquest of most of Andalusia and Murcia. Alfonso evidently admired him and may always have measured himself against his father's achievement; perhaps he ultimately felt somewhat less successful. In the *Estoria de Espanna,* he recorded the words spoken to him by his father on his deathbed:

> My son, you are richer in lands and good vassals than any other king in Christendom. Strive to do well and to be good, for you have the wherewithal. My Lord, I leave you the whole realm from the sea hither that the Moors won from Rodrigo, king of Spain. All of it is in your dominion, part of it conquered, the other part tributary. If you know how to preserve in this state what I leave you, you will be as good a king as I; and if you win more for yourself, you will be better than I; but if you diminish it, you will not be as good as I.[4]

By speaking in this manner, Fernando III, unconsciously or not, placed a burden on his son's shoulders, as he implied that his worth as a king would depend on his pursuing an expansionist policy. This should be understood in the light of Fernando's expressed desire, reported in Alfonso's *Setenario,* to assume the imperial title of the old Hispanic Empire, which had lapsed upon the death of Alfonso VII in 1157. The Hispanic imperial tradition considered the kings of León as heirs of the Visigoths and, as such, responsible for reconstituting their kingdom by the reconquest of the whole of Spain and also of North Africa, regarded as having once been part of the Visigothic realm. The goals that Fernando III set for his son therefore were clear: the completion of the reconquest of Spain and North Africa and, by implication, the assumption of the title of emperor of Spain.[5]

These ideas ought to be borne in mind if one is to understand Alfonso's policies. So also must his conception of monarchy as set forth in the *Espéculo* and the *Partidas.* Comparing king and people to the human body, he emphasized that the king was the head and the people the members. As such, they formed a unity under the guidance and direction of the head, the king. The king was God's vicar on earth in temporal affairs, placed here to rule the people in justice, rendering to each man his due. The king wielded the same powers in his kingdom as did the emperor in his empire.[6] Although Alfonso acknowledged the supremacy of the pope in spiritual affairs, he stressed that "we have no superior in temporal matters." By affirming two notions common among the jurists of the thirteenth century, namely "a king is emperor in his kingdom" (*rex in regno suo imperator est*) and "a king recognizes no superior in temporal affairs" (*rex non recognoscat superiorem in temporalibus*), the king was proclaiming his independence of all other rulers, while also declaring his direct dependence on God, whose vicar in temporal matters he professed to be. Although he did not use the word sovereignty, Alfonso was effectively asserting his sovereign position.[7]

The Government of Castile and León

As a king, Alfonso's first task was to govern effectively the kingdoms that he had inherited. Although he pronounced the unity of king and people in one body, the fact is that he did not rule over a unified state. Rather, his monarchy included several different kingdoms, as the royal intitulation makes clear: king of Castile, Toledo, León, Galicia, Seville, Córdoba, Murcia, Jaén, and the Algarve.[8] By listing all these titles, Alfonso was indulging in a bit of braggadocio, suggesting that his power and prestige were greater because of the many states subject to his rule. At the same time, however, the list also emphasized the historical fact of expansion by conquest, as well as the disparities existing among his dominions. Not only were the legal and institutional differences between Castile and León significant but so were the differences between these two together and the kingdoms to the south. Toledo, Seville, Córdoba, Murcia, Jaén, and the Algarve had once been petty Muslim kingdoms. Toledo, captured in 1085, was listed second after Castile and before León because it was the ancient seat of the Visigothic monarchy. To create a unity from such diverse elements was a staggering task that could not be accomplished in a generation, but Alfonso made certain efforts in that direction.[9] His purpose was not to obliterate all differences but to make them work in a coherent harmony.

Juridical unity could not be said to exist as long as a significant segment of the population was not subject to a common law. A Muslim and Jewish population of significant proportions was incorporated into the kingdom, particularly as a consequence of the conquest of Andalusia and Murcia. These populations were not easily assimilated because they continued to be assured of the right to worship freely and to be governed by their own laws and officials.[10]

The presence of a non-Christian population was closely linked with the task of settling and repopulating Andalusia. If the region were to remain under Castilian control, a substantial Christian population had to be established there. The emigration of thousands of Muslim workers who preferred to live in an Islamic state opened land for colonization, but it also weakened the economy. The distribution of lands to bishops, abbots, nobles, military orders, and others was carried out systematically; within a few years, however, many settlers, finding life on the frontier too arduous or dangerous, opted to return to their previous homes.[11] Coupled with the 1264 revolt of the Mudejars (as Muslims living under Christian rule were known), this situation required that the work of settlement be undertaken once again. For two years, the Mudejars of Andalusia and Murcia, spurred on by Ibn al-Aḥmar, king of Granada, resisted Alfonso's efforts to reduce them to submission; but at length, Alfonso's superior strength prevailed. As a consequence of the rebellion, the Moors of Andalusia were expelled from their lands and moved either to Granada or to North Africa, and the king endeavored to induce Christian settlers to occupy the abandoned lands.[12] After the pacification of Andalusia, Alfonso X spent the years 1270–1272 resettling Murcia, where the Mudejars were allowed to remain though segregated from their Christian neighbors.[13] The retention of these conquered areas was one of the most important tasks that Alfonso had to undertake. Even at the time of his death, the frontier was still not entirely secure, and the settlement of Andalusia was not yet complete.

Alfonso also strove to strengthen the institutions of monarchy as instruments of effective government.[14] Not only did he seek to exalt the person of the monarch and to elaborate standards of court etiquette that stressed the king's unique status, but he also shaped the administrative branches of the royal court.[15] The role and functions of the chancellor, notaries, scribes, and other subordinate personnel responsible for drafting, registering, and sealing royal documents were defined. The proper forms for different types of royal documents and a schedule of fees to be charged were set down. Alfonso's successors often cited his ordinance concerning this.[16]

The king also restructured the royal tribunal and described the qualities and duties of royal justices. The ordinance enacted at Zamora in 1274 outlined the functions of the royal court in more explicit detail and also specified the *casos de corte* or cases that pertained exclusively to royal jurisdiction. Ordinary royal justices heard suits in first instance, as well as appeals from municipal courts; but their judgment could be appealed to other justices especially designated for that purpose. As the one ultimately responsible for the administration of justice, the king himself sometimes sat in a judicial capacity, promising to do so at least three times a week.[17]

The king's most far-reaching action in the legal sphere was his compilation of a code of law to be applied in the royal court. This was the *Espéculo de las leyes,* a mirror of laws, according to which all other laws would be judged. Probably promulgated in the cortes of Toledo in the spring of 1254, it was intended to serve the justices of the royal court.[18] All litigation brought before that court would be adjudicated in accordance with the *Espéculo*. Founded essentially upon Roman law, the new code required that the king's justices should have an expertise in that law. As a consequence, the administration of justice was entrusted to professional jurists, thus excluding amateurs, such as the nobles. This was a fundamental reason for their protest against the king in the cortes of Burgos in 1272. Work on the *Siete partidas* began soon after the completion of the *Espéculo*, because of Alfonso's election as Holy Roman Emperor and his desire to have a code that would reflect his new status. Though probably finished in 1265, the *Partidas* apparently was not promulgated until Alfonso XI gave it legal force in 1348.[19]

The regrettable disappearance of so many of the original records of the monarchy makes it difficult to say to what extent the financial arm of the royal court was modified. No doubt the treasury assumed a more professional cast because of the greater complexity of the king's finances and the increase in personnel that it necessitated. The amount of the royal revenue was substantially greater than in any previous reign. Aside from the traditional sources of income cited in the municipal codes, or *fueros,* Alfonso collected the septennial coinage-tax called *moneda forera,* the *tercias reales* or crown share of the ecclesiastical tithe, customs duties, and *servicios* or subsidies granted by the cortes. Added to them was the tribute paid annually by the king of Granada, ranging from a third to a half of his yearly income. Though payment of that sum was interrupted from time to time, it deluded Alfonso into believing that he was wealthier than he was. A continuing inflation often wiped out gains on paper and reduced the purchasing power of royal income.[20]

Alfonso probably had more to do with the development of extraordinary taxation than any of his predecessors. Extraordinary taxation was a common novelty throughout Western Europe in the late thirteenth century, because the business of monarchy had become more complex and more ambitious, and the ordinary revenues of the crown were insufficient to meet new needs. At the same time, Alfonso X incurred exceptional expenses beyond those of most of his contemporaries. For this reason, he aroused intense hostility that eventually contributed to his downfall.

The levying of extraordinary taxes was one reason why the king summoned the cortes into session. The evidence for the existence of the cortes as an assembly of prelates, nobles, and representatives of the towns can be traced back to the late twelfth century; but it was during the reign of Alfonso that it began to meet regularly, on the average of about every two and a half years. His description of a *curia generalis* or cortes in 1254 as consisting of "archbishops and bishops; barons and great men of our court; [and] the procurators of cities, fortresses, and towns designated for this by their communities," aptly placed this new body in the institutional framework of the combined Castile-León. In the course of his reign, he convened the cortes concerning such varied issues as the succession to the throne, the regulation of the economy, the projected invasion of North Africa, his claim to the Holy Roman Empire, and the levying of taxes.[21]

Whereas the king believed that the convocation of the cortes had certain advantages for him in winning support for his policies, it also gave each of the estates an opportunity to express its concerns and grievances. In his dealings with the clergy, Alfonso presented himself as the defender of Christendom against Islam. On the supposition that what he was doing was for the well-being of the church and of the Christian world in general, he claimed the right to nominate the bishops and to take the *tercias reales,* or a third of the church tithe, for his purposes. Though generally submissive to the royal will, the bishops occasionally challenged him.[22] The king made fair promises to them in 1255, in response to their complaints about royal encroachments on ecclesiastical jurisdiction, the *tercias,* and the goods of deceased bishops which he claimed; but he did not substantially modify his policies. Nor does he appear to have observed his pledge, in return for the grant of a subsidy, to ask the consent of the prelates before levying it in the future.[23] When some of the prelates, emboldened by the nobles' challenge to him in the cortes of Burgos in 1272, decided to protest royal policies, Alfonso threatened to expel them from the realm. Two years later, his son Fernando de la Cerda, acting on his father's instructions, endeavored to placate the bishops, but nothing really changed. Pope Nicholas III in 1279 sent a legate to confront the king with a long series of charges of abuse and of oppressing the church. Alfonso's failure to provide any real satisfaction, or to show any sign of modifying his attitude toward the church, prompted some of the prelates to join the movement against him in 1282.[24]

Alfonso enhanced the position of the nobility, but instead of giving their allegiance, they chose to challenge him directly and even to rebel against him. With the intention of encouraging their service to the crown, he doubled their stipends (*soldadas*), but this increase was dependent upon the tribute from Granada and ultimately required new taxes. The king's action was a bad precedent, as it aroused greediness among the nobles that could never be satisfied. They also profited from the distribution of lands in Andalusia. The king's modification of their *fueros* by reason of the *Espéculo,* as well as his imposition (with their consent) of six *servicios* upon their vassals in 1269, eventually stirred their ire.[25] Under the leadership of his brother, Felipe, they confronted him in the cortes of Burgos in 1272. Perhaps influenced by the dispute between James I and his Aragonese nobility, over the appointment of the *justicia* as arbiter of noble litigation in the royal court, the Castilians demanded the appointment of *alcaldes fi-josdalgo* or noble judges to adjudicate their disputes in accordance with their customary *fueros.* Alfonso protested that he had always dealt fairly with them and that this demand was a novelty, because none of his predecessors had had such judges in the court. Circumstances had changed, however, as the influence of Roman law in the law codes and in the royal court was paramount. Royal judges were trained in the new law; and even though they might be knowledgeable in the old *fueros,* they were not inclined to apply them since the king had ordered the exclusive use of the *Espéculo* in his court. The nobles, in effect, were demanding judgment by their peers according to the old laws. Alfonso had to bow to them, confirming their *fueros* and also limiting the taxes due from their vassals. Some of the more intransigent nobles led by Infante Felipe rejected any compromise and went off to the kingdom of Granada; but within two years, the controversy had been settled, and most of them had returned to their allegiance.[26]

Alfonso effected long-range changes in the government and social structure of the towns. By summoning the towns regularly to the cortes, he gave them the opportunity to participate directly in the highest councils of the realm. The obvious importance of the municipalities, as centers of administration and as sources of military forces and revenues, prompted his action. He attempted to overcome the diversity of municipal laws by granting the *Fuero real* to the towns of Castile and Extremadura. This code, based in some measure on the *Espéculo* and probably promulgated with it in 1254 rather than conceded to individual towns over a long period of years, was intended to bring about some uniformity in municipal law. Appeals could be carried from it to the royal court, where final judgment would be rendered according to the *Espéculo.* Although the towns grumbled and complained, compelling the king to confirm their traditional codes in the cortes of Burgos in 1272, the *Fuero real* continued in use in many towns.[27]

Royal measures also significantly altered the social structure of the towns. The towns of Extremadura especially had supplied a substantial part of the urban militias for the wars of the reconquest. Now that the frontier was removed to some distance, and the possibility of getting rich by a quick foray into Muslim territory was lessened, many townsmen were not readily inclined to respond to royal demands for military service. Concerned about defending Andalusia, Alfonso in 1256 tried to make military service more attractive by granting exemption from taxes to many mounted warriors in the Extremaduran towns who maintained horses and arms suitable for battle. The exemption was also extended to their widows, minor children, and dependents under certain conditions. The king thereby hoped to assure himself of an urban cavalry always ready for war. His action, on the other hand, served to emphasize the social and economic distinction between the *caballeros villanos,* or mounted warriors of the towns, and the *peones* or footsoldiers. Not only were the former privileged and exempt, but they also tended to control the principal offices of municipal government and probably were the usual representatives of their towns in the cortes. Ironically, though exempt from taxes themselves, they were called upon to consent to taxes that would be payable by others less privileged. The *caballeros villanos* were duly grateful and in the long run tended to become allies of the crown against a turbulent nobility.[28]

Alfonso's economic measures—some innovations, some carryovers from his father's time—affected all classes but especially the townsmen. The policies he established would be continued by his successors. Specifically, he condemned guilds of merchants and artisans unless they were of a purely spiritual or social nature. Merchants were forbidden to join together to fix prices; but in 1252 and again in 1268, the king published both price and wage schedules. Exports were closely controlled, and the export of certain goods (the so-called *cosas vedadas*—namely, horses, livestock, gold, and silver) was forbidden outright. Royal customs officials were appointed at specific locations to control traffic and to collect customs duties. For the first time, customs duties became a regular and important part of the royal revenue. Alfonso also set down uniform weights and measures and fixed the rate of interest at $33\frac{1}{3}$ percent. He failed to maintain an acceptable coinage, unfortunately, issuing debased coinage that drove good money out of circulation and caused prices to rise. His privileges granted to the Mesta in 1273 and 1278 apparently were intended to bring litigation between the sheepmen and the townsmen and others under royal control and also to enable him to tap the resources of the sheepherding industry more efficiently by levying the livestock subsidy *servicio de los ganados*.[29]

The modifications of the municipal *fueros,* the debasement of the coinage, regulation of the economy, imposition of fines, and levying of extraordinary taxes in the form of subsidies granted by the cortes were causes of irritation and eventually drove the towns into the arms of the Infante Sancho. Before considering the dispute between the king and his son, however, attention must be directed to Alfonso X's external policies, first with respect to the peninsula itself and then to the Holy Roman Empire.

Relations with the Peninsular States

Alfonso X was acutely conscious of the Hispanic imperial tradition which regarded the entire peninsula as the legacy of the Visigoths, to be brought under the rule of their heirs, the kings of León. Toledo, the city where Alfonso was born and baptized, had been the seat of the Visigothic monarchy where, as he explained, "the emperors and kings whence we descend were buried." Toledo was the "*cabeza de España,* where anciently the emperors were crowned." Alfonso may have crowned himself there during the cortes of 1254.[30] Early in 1259, he convened the cortes there concerning the affair of the empire—that is, the business of making good his recent election to the Holy Roman Empire.[31] Perhaps he also wished to use that occasion to proclaim his hegemony over the entire peninsula, thereby resurrecting Leonese pretensions. The political realities had changed significantly since the eleventh and twelfth centuries, when Alfonso VI and Alfonso VII could claim to be emperors of Spain; but Alfonso X probably still aspired to gain recognition of his dominant position, perhaps by persuading the other peninsular rulers to become his vassals as the king of Granada was.

That his peninsular ambitions were not mere fantasy is indicated by the reaction of James I of Aragon-Catalonia. He appointed a procurator to oppose any assertion that Alfonso "should be a Hispanic emperor [*imperator hispanus*] and that we and our kingdoms and lands should be in any subjection to him by reason of empire" (27 September 1259).[32] James evidently saw Alfonso's election to the Holy Roman Empire as a threat to his own independence. Whether his reaction was prompted by a suggestion that Alfonso's supremacy be acknowledged cannot be ascertained.[33]

If the likelihood of gaining ascendancy over Aragon was quite remote, Alfonso clearly hoped to be able to reduce Navarre to submission. Since the twelfth century, the kings of Castile and Aragon had planned to partition Navarre; but now James I, fearful that Alfonso X might gain control there, lent his support to King Thibault II (1252–1270). One source reported that Thibault came to Alfonso's court at Vitoria early in 1256 and became his vassal. If that be so, it is curious that Alfonso, in the subscription to his charters, did not mention Thibault among his vassals. Alfonso threatened to invade Navarre again in 1274, but the widow of King Henry I (1270–1274) took her daughter Jeanne, heiress to the Navarrese throne, to France, seeking the protection of King Philippe III. Jeanne's betrothal to the heir to the French throne, the future King Philippe IV, made Navarre an appendage of the French monarchy for many years. Even so, Alfonso X and Peter III of Aragon in 1281 renewed plans for a partition of Navarre, though these were never carried out. In sum, Alfonso gained nothing substantial from his intervention in Navarre, but he drove the Navarrese into the arms of the French and thus furthered the aggrandizement of the French monarchy.[34]

In the middle of the twelfth century, the kings of Castile and León had also proposed the partition of Portugal, though Alfonso X seems to have been content with an acknowledgment of his suzerainty in the Algarve. In 1253, he made an agreement with Afonso III of Portugal (1245–1279), who married El Sabio's illegitimate daughter, Beatriz, and received the usufruct of the Algarve. When the Mudejars revolted in 1264, Alfonso X sought help from his son-in-law, yielding effective authority in the Algarve in exchange for the service of fifty knights. After the suppression of the Mudejar uprising, he agreed in February 1267 to cancel the service as a favor to his Portuguese grandson Dinis and to cede the Algarve to Afonso III. Although Alfonso X continued to call himself king of the Algarve, that may reflect the conservative practice of the chancery rather than an attempt to keep alive some vestigial claim to suzerainty. The boundaries of the two realms were also delimited along a line from Elvas and Badajoz to Ayamonte on the Atlantic Ocean. Some further modifications were made during the reign of King Dinis. In the long run, Alfonso X opted for a valuable alliance on his western frontier in return for territorial concessions.[35]

Although Gascony was not part of the peninsula or of the Visigothic legacy, Alfonso X put forward claims to it based on his descent from Alfonso VIII and Eleanor Plantagenet, whose dowry it was. When the unruly Gascon nobility turned to Alfonso X for help against King Henry III of England, the latter decided to negotiate. By the treaty of Toledo signed in the spring of 1254, Alfonso's sister Leonor married Prince Edward, heir to the English throne. When their union was solemnized at Burgos in November, Alfonso ceded whatever claims to Gascony he had to

the newlyweds. For his part, Henry III promised to aid Castile in a projected invasion of North Africa. Alfonso probably never expected to take
possession of Gascony but considered an alliance with Henry useful. As
events were to show, Henry's promises proved worthless, and Alfonso
gained nothing other than the goodwill of his English brother-in-law
Edward I (1272–1307).[36]

The invasion of North Africa, a region once regarded as having been
part of the Visigothic realm, had been planned by Fernando III. At the
beginning of his reign, Alfonso X sought papal approval of the enterprise as
a crusade and built shipyards at Seville for that purpose. In 1260, he
appointed a sea lord (*adelantado de la mar*), "because we greatly desire to
carry forward the work of the crusade overseas for the service of God and
the exaltation of Christianity." The only consequence of all this activity was
a brief Castilian occupation of the port of Salé, Arabic Salā, on the Atlantic
coast of Morocco. Pleased with the apparent success of that raid, Alfonso
summoned the cortes to Seville in January 1261, to seek counsel "concerning
the affair of Africa that we have begun." No further action in Africa was
taken, although the Islamic kingdom of Niebla to the west of Seville was
conquered in February 1262. Quite possibly, the king concluded that,
before undertaking any other ventures in Africa, it would be advisable to
gain control of all the ports giving access to the peninsula.[37]

With that in mind, he demanded from Ibn al-Aḥmar, king of Granada,
the cession of the ports of Gibraltar and Tarifa. Knowing that this would
effectively cut his realm off from the possibility of help from North Africa,
Ibn al-Aḥmar refused. As a diversion, the Granadan encouraged the Mudejars of Andalusia and Murcia to revolt in the spring of 1264, thereby
preventing Alfonso from intervening further in North Africa. The king of
Granada returned to his obedience, but Alfonso continued to interfere in
his kingdom, lending support to Muslim lords there who sought greater
independence. That antagonized Ibn al-Aḥmar, who eventually summoned
the Marinids of Morocco to his aid.[38] Their arrival in the peninsula came at
a most inopportune time for Alfonso, who was returning from his journey
to southern France to place his case for the crown of the Holy Roman
Empire before Pope Gregory X.

The *Fecho del Imperio*

Among Alfonso's most consuming passions was his quest for the crown of
the Holy Roman Empire. His claims came from his mother, Beatriz,

daughter of Emperor Philip of Swabia (1198–1208) and granddaughter of the famous Emperor Frederick Barbarossa (1152–1190). Alfonso became actively involved in imperial affairs after the death of the anti-emperor William of Holland in January 1256. The republic of Pisa, a Ghibelline town, sent a deputation to Soria in March to recognize Alfonso as king of the Romans. No doubt flattered, he sent envoys to Germany to persuade the electors to vote for him. Much to his chagrin, Richard of Cornwall, brother of King Henry III, was chosen by several electors in January 1257. Alfonso X was elected by another faction on April 1, and German representatives offered the crown to him at Burgos in August 1257.[39]

While Richard went to Germany to be crowned, Alfonso pressed his claims from afar, appointing Duke Henry of Brabant as imperial vicar and sending money to various German princes. Alfonso also sought an alliance with Norway and found support in northern Italy with Ezzelino da Romano, one of the extreme partisans of Emperor Frederick II. Although Alfonso did not directly claim the kingdom of Sicily, he did object to the marriage in 1260 of James I's son and heir, Peter, to Constanza, daughter of King Manfred of Sicily. Both the royal chronicle and Jofre de Loaysa emphasize that the imperial quest was expensive, bringing great poverty to Castile and León.[40]

From the outset, Alfonso realized that papal recognition of his rights was essential. Perhaps with that in mind, he paid the ransom of Philip of Courtenay, son of Emperor Baldwin of Constantinople, hoping that this gesture would enhance his reputation as a munificent ruler and so win papal favor. *El fecho del imperio*—the affair of the empire—was the principal business prompting the king to summon the cortes to Toledo early in 1259, but what precisely was determined there is unknown. His negotiations with several pontiffs were inconclusive, and the distraction of his Africa expedition, the revolt of the Mudejars, and then the revolt of the Castilian nobility compelled him to postpone any departure for Italy or Rome.[41]

The death of Richard of Cornwall in April 1272 gave Alfonso reason to hope that at last he could secure an undisputed right to the empire. The Castilian nobility chose to confront him in the cortes of Burgos in September, unfortunately, and their quarrel was not resolved until the following March. Meanwhile Pope Gregory X encouraged the German princes to elect Rudolf of Habsburg on 1 October 1273. Rudolf's promise to lead a crusade to liberate the Holy Land—a promise that was never kept—won him papal approbation.

Alfonso stubbornly refused to accept this new situation. After inducing the nobles to return to their allegiance, he summoned the cortes to

Burgos in 1274 to consider "sending knights to the empire of Rome." The main business of the cortes was to appoint the Infante Fernando as regent during his father's projected absence from the realm and to arrange a retinue of knights to accompany the king. Alfonso reminded the assembly that the Lombards had often entreated him to come to them; now that the realm was at peace, he could do so. Setting out on his quest for the empire (*ida al imperio*), he went not to Italy but to Beaucaire in southern France, where he vainly pleaded his case before the pope in May 1275. Perforce he had to accept the reality of events and abandon his imperial pretensions once and for all, although thereafter he occasionally used the title King of the Romans. In practical terms, nevertheless, his imperial quest was finished.[42]

The Crisis of the Succession

Returning in great disappointment from his interview with the pope, Alfonso heard even more dismaying news of events that had transpired in the peninsula during his absence. The Marinid emir of Morocco, Abū Yūsuf, invited by the king of Granada, invaded Spain in the summer of 1275. At first news of the invasion, the regent Fernando de la Cerda hastened to the frontier but died suddenly at Villarreal on 25 July. The Marinids gained a victory over the Castilians near Ecija on 7 September, but the king's second son Sancho assumed command and regrouped his disheartened troops. Thus, when Alfonso reentered his kingdom, he found himself faced with two problems. The more immediate one was to prepare for the renewal of hostilities with the Marinids in the spring. The other was the question of the succession. The Marinids were persuaded to accept a truce for the time being; the succession was a more difficult matter.[43]

Essentially, the issue was this: should the king designate as his heir Alfonso de la Cerda, the oldest son of the dead infante, even though he was under age, or Sancho, now aged seventeen? In the spring of 1276, Alfonso summoned the cortes to Burgos to consider the problem. While Juan Núñez de Lara urged the claims of Alfonso de la Cerda, Lope Díaz de Haro and many other nobles, prelates, and townsmen supported Sancho. Ballesteros believes that the king did not make a decision at this time, but the Marinid threat and the king's own infirmity and increasing age put him under great pressure to act resolutely. That Sancho was acknowledged is indicated by his appearance in charters of October 1277 as *fijo mayor et heredero,* and by his generally faithful and assiduous service to his father during the next several years. This behavior is evidence of Sancho's assurance and confidence in his position as the king's designated heir. The rejection of Alfonso de la Cerda's claims was also confirmed by the withdrawal of his chief supporter, Juan Núñez de Lara, to France, where he became a vassal of King Philippe III in September 1276. Given the French king's insistence on upholding his nephew's rights, Alfonso nevertheless agreed in November 1276 to allow the issue to be adjudicated before his own court, but Philippe failed to ratify that agreement. In giving his consent, Alfonso probably was confident that Sancho's supporters would not abandon him and that if the issue came to trial it would be resolved in his favor.[44]

The Moroccans invaded the peninsula again in June 1277, waging war all along the frontier until a truce was concluded in February 1278. As the defense of the frontier preoccupied the king, he apparently decided to entrust Sancho with greater responsibility for the governance of the northern regions of Castile and León. Convening the cortes to Segovia in the spring of 1278, Alfonso not only confirmed Sancho's rights as heir but also conferred even greater authority upon him. In his will of November 1283, Alfonso remarked that he had given Sancho "greater power than any king's son had in his father's lifetime." Fray Juan Gil de Zamora, Sancho's tutor, also noted that Spain was ruled by many noble kings until the time of "King Alfonso, elected king of the Romans, and his son the illustrious Sancho who began to reign together [*corregnare*] with him in the year of the Lord 1278." In taking this step, Alfonso would seem to have rejected once and for all the claims of his grandson. That may have been the reason for the flight to Aragon of Queen Violante with her daughter-in-law Blanche and her two children, the infantes de la Cerda.[45]

In spite of that contretemps, Alfonso X had to concentrate attention upon the continuing threat of the Marinids. In the hope of shutting off the invasion route from North Africa, he laid siege to Algeciras, but lack of funds caused him to abandon the project in October 1278. In the interim, he tried to exploit every source of income, imposing fines on Christian usurers and on merchants who violated the laws concerning weights and measures and the export of prohibited goods. He also plundered the Jews, manipulated the coinage, and demanded ever larger *servicios* from the cortes. Tensions in the king's relations with nobles, prelates, and townsmen steadily mounted. The townsmen vented their grievances by appealing to Sancho and the king's brother Manuel to intercede for them. Philippe III of

France, moreover, demanded that some provision be made for the infantes de la Cerda. As a consequence, Alfonso proposed granting the kingdom of Jaén to Alfonso de la Cerda, to hold in vassalage of Castile. That was unacceptable to Philippe as too little, and to Sancho as too much.[46]

The climax came when the king convoked the cortes to Seville in the fall of 1282. In order to press the war against the Moors, he proposed an innovation in the coinage, to which the assembly consented "more out of fear than love." The king made a grave mistake, however, when he indicated his intention to allow Alfonso de la Cerda a share in the inheritance. Sancho objected strenuously to any diminution of the realm, insisting that unity must be preserved. Harsh words were exchanged, and Sancho decided to appeal to the realm for support.[47]

The assembly summoned by Sancho for Valladolid in April 1282 brought together the principal estates of the realm, including Queen Violante (who had returned from Aragon in 1279) and Infante Manuel. The decision was taken to deprive Alfonso of the essential powers of government and to entrust the administration of justice, the collection of taxes, and control of royal fortresses to Sancho. Alfonso was left with the empty title of king. This was a fundamentally conservative action, in that Alfonso was not deposed. The leaders of the opposition, chiefly the king's brother Manuel, evidently taking into account the powers already given to Sancho in 1278, proposed giving Sancho full authority throughout the kingdom but not the royal title. In that way, Alfonso retained the honors of kingship, while his responsibilities were transferred fully to Sancho.[48] While the assembly was in progress, several bishops and abbots, chiefly from León, as well as the towns of León and Castile, formed leagues (*hermandades*) in support of Sancho. As a means of defending their liberties against both the king and Sancho, should either intrude upon them, the leagues proposed to meet annually.[49]

Following the assembly of Valladolid, Sancho still had to persuade his father to accept the new situation, but the king retained the loyalty of Seville and Murcia. Abandoned by his wife, his sons, his brother, and many of his subjects, Alfonso denounced Sancho's actions in scathing language and disinherited him. He found it necessary, nevertheless, to borrow money from his erstwhile enemy, the emir of Morocco, who landed troops in the peninsula and plundered the regions around Córdoba, Toledo, and Murcia, ostensibly on the king's behalf. As a stalemate developed, proposals for a reconciliation were made but came to naught. In his last will, drawn up in January 1284, Alfonso affirmed his rejection of Sancho, bequeathing his realms to Alfonso de la Cerda and creating vassal kingdoms at Seville and Murcia for his younger sons, Juan and Jaime, who had returned to their former allegiance. Should Alfonso de la Cerda have no heirs, the kingdoms of Castile and León would pass to the king of France. That can only be regarded as a final expression of a father's spleen against a rebellious son. This time of turmoil came to an end shortly thereafter when the king died at Seville on 4 April 1284.[50]

A Final Assessment

In weighing the accomplishments of Alfonso, one must bear in mind that there is little in history that can be stated starkly in black and white terms. A merely mechanical calculation of successes or failures is an inadequate method of assessment. As light blends into shadow and shadow into light, pierced at times by flashes of brilliance and clouds of darkest gloom, so too Alfonso's more than thirty years on the throne were marked by extraordinary triumphs and grave calamities, but also by steady and substantial achievements. One thing is certain: Alfonso was an activist king who sought to advance his people and his kingdom beyond the point where they were when they first became his charge. As a student of Roman law and of the writings of St. Isidore of Seville, he knew that a monarch's principal responsibility was to render to every man his due and to merit the title of king by ruling properly. As head of the body politic, he recognized his duty to give guidance and leadership to his people. Aside from his personal accomplishments as a scholar and poet, he strove to educate his people, a role that many other scholars have discussed.

As an activist king, he consciously built upon the foundations established by his predecessors, but he transformed them as well. His impact upon the institutional development of his realm was profound and the consequence of a deliberate policy. By exalting, strengthening, and expanding the idea of kingship, he ran the risk of raising questions about the extent of royal authority in matters of justice, legislation, and taxation. Convinced of his duty to see that justice was done to every man, he endeavored to establish the *Fuero real* as a uniform municipal law and the *Espéculo* (and later the *Partidas*) as a common law for the royal court. He challenged the separate jurisdiction of church courts and, by means of the special judges of the Mesta, brought litigation involving the sheepmen under royal control. In this way, he strove to achieve a semblance of juridical unity, without which only a limited political unity could exist. His efforts roused opposition among nobles, clergy, and townsmen, but his innovations eventually triumphed and became the basis for the laws of modern Spain. This surely was his greatest achievement as a ruler. One might add that if he had ordered the *Partidas* written in Latin, it would have probably been accepted as the basic code of law for all of Western Europe.

His restructuring of royal administration, particularly the chancery and the tribunal, similarly had long-term significance. The development of the cortes, convoked at frequent intervals, also owes much to him. Aside from its value as an instrument of royal government, the cortes allowed the estates, especially the townsmen, an opportunity to voice their opinions on matters of public policy. Although Alfonso continued the tradition of his predecessors in successfully curbing the independence of the clergy, his concessions to the nobility ultimately worked to his disadvantage and to that of his successors. He gained short-term benefits from the privileges granted to the non-noble urban cavalry (*caballeros villanos*), but this was detrimental to the towns and society as a whole in that it created another privileged class and emphasized social distinctions so as to encourage social conflicts.

The king's activist bent also led him to regulate the economy and to attempt to bring the problem of inflation under control. Many of the measures he took, such as the establishment of customs posts and regular customs duties, became the foundation of later governmental policy. His manipulation of the coinage, unfortunately, had a destructive effect and roused intense hostility. His request for subsidies from the cortes established the basis for extraordinary taxation in the future but provoked the outcry that he was reducing the kingdom to poverty. Inasmuch as we do not possess the royal budget with information about his ordinary and extraordinary income and expenses, we cannot say whether the charge rested upon a substantive basis. While the plea of poverty may be regarded to some extent as a rhetorical response to the king's expressed needs, I am inclined to think that it did reflect reality.

Alfonso was unable to resuscitate the Hispanic Empire as he and his father had probably hoped to do. His relations with Aragon and Portugal, despite some controversies in his earlier years, on the whole ultimately proved to be friendly. His one misstep was his attempt to browbeat Navarre into submission, with the result of allowing France to extend its influence and power into that kingdom.

In dealing with the Muslim world, he realized that the conquest of

Granada, already tributary to Castile, was not an immediate necessity and that the wisdom of attempting to absorb its thousands of Muslims was doubtful. He recognized that the consolidation of Castilian control over Andalusia and Murcia with its substantial Moorish population was of paramount importance, though it greatly strained the resources of the kingdom. His repopulation and retention of these regions, in the face of their concerted effort to throw off the Castilian yoke and of later Moroccan offensives, was an achievement of great significance.

His preparation for an invasion of North Africa was in response both to ideological presuppositions and to strategic considerations. The Visigoths, whose heirs the kings of Castile-León claimed to be, were thought once to have ruled Morocco; thus, its subjugation seemed logical to many. Of more practical concern was Alfonso's recognition of the necessity of gaining control of the ports giving access to the peninsula. His planned campaign in North Africa came to naught, though his conquest of Niebla completed his control of the coastline from the Algarve to the frontiers of Granada. Though he was unable to capture Algeciras or to persuade the king of Granada to surrender Gibraltar and Tarifa, his efforts to close the invasion route from across the Straits pointed the way for his successors to follow.

Alfonso's greatest disappointment perhaps was his unsuccessful quest for the crown of the Holy Roman Empire. Because of his pursuit of the imperial throne, historians have described him as an unrealistic dreamer and his reign as a failure politically. Roger Merriman, for example, remarked that "he aspired to be emperor, though he was not even able to play the king."[51] In light of what has been said thus far, that judgment is erroneous. To expect that Alfonso would have refused the imperial crown when offered, given his ties to the Hohenstaufen family, would be unrealistic. It is hardly likely that any other thirteenth-century ruler would have spurned it. If one were to fault Alfonso, it would be for not having been more aggressive in seeking the empire, but that would have required sending troops to Germany and Italy or going there personally. He chose not to abandon Spain or to neglect his responsibilities there, I believe, because Spain was always paramount in his thought and he hoped to link the universal claims of the Holy Roman Empire to the peninsular aspirations of the Hispanic Empire.

The reign of Alfonso ended badly, because of the unforeseen controversy that developed over the succession. I doubt that Sancho would have succeeded in depriving him of royal authority if Alfonso had not already antagonized significant elements in society. In the heat of conflict, and feeling a keen sense of betrayal by his son, Alfonso proposed the partition of his realms for the benefit of his grandson Alfonso de la Cerda and for his own younger sons. While one may understand and perhaps even sympathize with the king's decision, it ran counter to the thrust of thirteenth-century political theory, which was beginning to emphasize the notion of the state and the inalienability of its territory. The principle was stated clearly in the *Partidas:* "Anciently they made a *fuero* and statute in Spain that the dominion of the king should never be divided nor alienated."[52] Alfonso's decision was a political misjudgment of the gravest sort; if implemented, it could only have been disastrous.

To conclude: Alfonso was not a frivolous man, not an idler or a fool, not dissolute or dissipated, but a hard-working monarch who took his responsibilities as king seriously. His exaltation of kingship; his organization of royal government; his development of the tax system, of the law, of the judicial administration, and of the cortes; and his consolidation of his father's conquests rank him as one of the greatest medieval kings of Spain and a distinguished contemporary of Emperor Frederick II, Louis IX of France, and Edward I of England. If he suffered the ignominy of rejection by his son and by many of his people, that was perhaps because he attempted to do too much and to move his kingdom forward too quickly.

3. Alfonso el Sabio and the Thirteenth-Century Spanish Language

In several respects, Alfonso el Sabio was a pioneer. Well-educated, intelligent, keenly aware of the value to his nation of the maintenance of learning and culture, he employed his position and his wealth in the furtherance of goals which have justified his designation as "the wise" or more properly "the learned" during succeeding generations. Ambition for his nation extended to himself as well. He dreamed of larger things, which undoubtedly played an important role in the less fortunate aspects of his political life. As the son of a great and saintly father and of a mother with an illustrious political heritage, his vision of himself in a greater than Spanish context helped to bring both him and his cultural dreams to a sad end. His final troubled days could well have been an object lesson of the vanity of ambition. His actions in later life made his sobriquet "the wise" quite inappropriate. But he was definitely learned, and in a cultural context he still looms large. Further study of what he left Western civilization has, bit by bit, served to raise his stature.

In the cultural sense, he was, of course, primarily a patron. Quite aside from his activities as a poet of both religious and profane songs and his sponsorship of music, he still remains, if not through total physical participation, the guiding spirit of a monumental enterprise. The royal patronage extended beyond financial support, and it is clear he shared in the great cultural tasks that he sponsored and supported, assuming an active role in some of them. The aspects of Latin and Arabic culture which he made available were in his opinion personal contributions, as is attested by his well-known statement to the effect that this was his own work although the carrying out of his ideas was entrusted to others. This was by necessity, of course, for his plans were so great and the available royal time so little. He recognized himself as the architect, and like a good architect, he con-

cerned himself with even small details in the total structure, while entrust-
ing his overall plan to execution by others.

The scope of Alfonso's concept of his cultural mission is pertinent to
the general consideration of the language in which his work was preserved.
His activities at the royal literary court, both in his translations and in the
more original compilations, are reminiscent of several similar activities
located in the Iberian peninsula during the Middle Ages. In breadth of
activity and in the use of translation as a source of information, the group is
similar to the twelfth-century so-called Toledo school of translators. These
earlier activities had centered around translations from Arabic into Latin,
however, thus providing European contemporaries with some knowledge
of the Eastern learning that had long been in the possession of the Arabs
and was drawn from varied sources, including ancient Greece. They were
an important component of the renaissance of learning which is associated
with the twelfth century in Western Europe. Yet, that group of translators
of many national origins was by comparison to Alfonso's an amorphous
body, whose primary accomplishment was transferring the knowledge
locked up in Arabic manuscripts to the universal Latin of the scholar. The
operations of these translators were on a high intellectual level.

Another similar but much later venture, quite possibly inspired by the
Alfonsine example and resembling it in its choice of the vernacular instead
of a scholarly language, was the huge corpus of translation and compilation
left by the grand master of the knights of St. John of Jerusalem, Juan
Fernández de Heredia, whose histories and translations provide precious
linguistic material on the state of the Aragonese language in the fourteenth
century. His work filled in certain gaps, such as translation directly from
Greek and from French, but there was a utilitarian aspect to his activity
which removed it from the more intellectual approach of both the Toledo
group and Alfonso el Sabio. Living both in the eastern Mediterranean
region and at the papal court in Avignon, the grand master seems to have
conceived of the products of his scriptorium as a means of assisting in a
passage to the Holy Land, a crusade against the infidel. By learning to know
the enemy, the Muslims, better, he appeared to believe that they could be
pushed back more effectively. Thus, his scriptorium issued a series of texts
informative of the eastern Mediterranean area and beyond.

On the other hand, Alfonso el Sabio was, as Antonio Solalinde
pointed out so perceptively, oriented toward a study of human nature—
man as conceived of in the thirteenth century. Historical man, revealed
through his acts throughout the centuries since the creation, would show

what he had been, where he erred, and what he could teach individually and collectively. Then there was moral man, whose ideal type should be revealed by law. Law would teach him how he should act. Finally, man not only lives through earthly influences but also is affected by heavenly bodies. These influences were of the utmost importance and could be revealed by astrology and related sciences, primarily astronomy. This triple concept of mankind seems to lie at the core of the Alfonsine efforts at the literary court, and there his scholars planned, compared, translated, paraphrased, and commented.

Perhaps little original work was accomplished, but at a time when authority was stressed, it must not seem surprising that authority is constantly cited for everything. On those occasions when there was a conflict in the authorities, it was incumbent upon the scholars to reconcile if possible, to explain away the differences, and even occasionally to venture their own opinion. This attitude served to keep the Alfonsine work close to the source text, of course, whether it was in Arabic or in Latin. And translation is one way to stick close to authority.

It would be advantageous indeed if the actual source manuscripts employed by the translators were known, but the identity of any surviving texts has not been established as those actually used at the royal scriptorium. In a close comparison, it would be interesting to know whether what now appear to be deviations in the text were the result of erroneous readings or even of punctuation in the source, which would make a difference in modern editorial procedures. This might also explain why a translation from classical Latin would be flawless and a section derived from a simpler medieval Latin text would be hopelessly garbled. Close comparisons occasionally yield unexpected bonuses. They have demonstrated, for example, that the readings in Alfonso's translations of the letters in Ovid's *Heroïdes* are not errors on the part of the Spanish translators but represent a family of manuscripts whose existence had been suspected by textual critics but which apparently have now disappeared. Alfonsine readings agree with the hypotheses of the editors—a triumph for textual criticism. It appears that in general the Alfonsine collaborators were rather good Latinists, being able to handle classical authors like Ovid and Lucan adequately and with genuine feeling for the original readings. Yet, in a much simpler text such as the Vulgate, translations are presented in a meaningless garbled fashion, as in the literal translation of the Psalms in part three of the *General estoria*. Since the earliest manuscript of this part dates back to the thirteenth century, one must posit a defective original biblical text or a very early scribal deformation in the Spanish version, since the manuscripts of both surviving families are untrustworthy.

It is a rare thing to possess a manuscript from the Middle Ages which is identified as undoubtedly the one produced by the author himself. In this respect, Spain is most fortunate, for a good number of the original Alfonsine manuscripts have been preserved. These include such long texts as parts one and four of the *General estoria,* the *Estoria de Espanna* (also known as the *Primera crónica general*), and a set of astrological and scientific works. The codex containing the astronomical works has also been preserved in the library of the University of Madrid; but over the years, it has been mutilated through vandalism, not the least of which was its employment in building the barricades in University City during the civil war in the 1930s. Nonetheless, the prewar text had been preserved on Photostats at the University of Wisconsin and on microfilm at the Biblioteca Nacional of Madrid, which can now be of help to those working on the original codex. All in all, an enviable amount of unquestioned authoritative material is available for a study of the language used by Alfonso el Sabio. Only in the case of the many preserved texts of Fernández de Heredia is there anything similar found in Spain.

The possibility of studying the language employed at the royal scriptorium, with absolute faith in its authenticity, is guaranteed by the availability of these manuscripts. It is true that some questions have arisen about the authenticity of several of the Alfonsine texts as the original product of the royal scriptorium, but their dating as belonging to the thirteenth century has not been disproved. There exists, then, a range of historical texts which have in part a literary background, a series of pseudoscientific texts with their specialized technical vocabulary, a book on games, and a legal text. The loss of slightly more than three parts of the original manuscript of the *General estoria* and six parts of the *Siete partidas* will always be regretted, but as it is, the amount of authoritative material to illuminate Castilian of the second half of the thirteenth century is overwhelming. An idea of its extent can be had by consulting the microfiche version of those texts and the concordances thereto, which occupy a total of approximately 20,000 pages.[1]

So far as the methods of work at the royal scriptorium are known, these texts presumably bear the approval of Alfonso, who as architect and general editor prescribed procedures and standards. The scribes were clearly trained with great care in the use of the French Gothic minuscule script, which characterizes all of the manuscripts produced at the royal scriptorium. Standards of language were set, a clear necessity in such a varied group as the one Alfonso had working around him. It consisted, as is well known, of Christians, Jews, and Muslims, men from various parts of the peninsula. The cultivation of Castilian was de rigueur, as the language of the court and of the most rapidly expanding sector of the kingdom. But scribes did have occasional problems, and other linguistic forms did manage to creep in. There were slips, as in the *Libro de las cruzes,* where Catalan words crept in; the translators of this work identify themselves as Jhuda Fy de Mosse al Choen, and Maestre Johan dAspa, apparently from eastern Spain. At other times, there were variations in form and spelling that clearly reflected language in the process of change. As could be very well expected, there appear to have been difficulties with new and unfamiliar words, particularly in the case of transcription or adaptations of Arabic words in the technical treatises. Finally, adhering to the rule that there is no error-free copy, it is reasonable to expect scribal errors even in the process of transferring the text from the *borrador* or rough draft to the splendid royal codex. Thus, the texts do not reflect absolute accuracy or uniformity, but frequently they are more interesting because of what the defects reveal.

The specific contributions that these prose texts made to the Spanish language and its expression would at this point be very difficult to pin down. To make such a determination, of course, it would be necessary to analyze previous prose and then prose subsequent to Alfonso's in great detail and then compare them with the products of the royal scriptorium. This has not been done for very good reasons. Until recently, sufficient data were not readily available to assess even the prose of Alfonso's works alone, without reference to anything else. But the analysis of prose previous to 1250 offers considerable difficulty. The identification of literary prose before that time gives scholars very little on which to base a judgment about the type of prose employed then. Even in some of the early works represented by much later manuscripts, there has been a tendency to associate their original date with the time of Alfonso if not actually with the activities of the monarch himself. Extensive works preceding him are nonexistent. It is supposed that the translation of the *Fuero juzgo* may have antedated him, but perhaps it did not. If it is anterior to 1250, it might be used for comparison with Alfonso's legal works; strictly speaking, in such a case one should employ the legal texts exactly as composed by Alfonso and not some corrupted reworking of later centuries, but those are unfortunately not available. Thus, there is little concrete material with which to compare the huge mass of data in the Alfonsine manuscripts. The picture is sketchy at best. It is almost as if prose was born full-fledged like Minerva, with Alfonso assuming the role of Jupiter.

The insistence on using only the original texts in studying the language of Alfonso X is a luxury that cannot be duplicated with other authors, but as long as these manuscripts are available, the unique opportunity should not be passed up. Certainly, the transcriptions of royal scriptorium manuscripts provide a sufficient body of text to afford a broad and detailed view of Alfonsine prose in general. It makes sense to reject later manuscripts of Alfonso's works. Experience in editing the *General estoria* and in studying variants has put scholars on guard concerning the many alterations and distortions that exist in later manuscript copies and has raised doubts concerning the trustworthiness of "restored" readings. Nor do edited texts inspire confidence, for the process of editing in itself admits of various solutions, and it has even been used to force texts into patterns to suit the editor's bias. The result is unsatisfactory for strict analyses. In making the most significant comparisons with Alfonsine prose, it would be necessary to accumulate from later authors and works the type of data that is now available for the royal scriptorium texts, using a good manuscript that originates as close to the date of its composition as possible.

The Alfonsine lexicon is of special concern at the moment, particularly in establishing special meanings current at that time. Another point of interest is the identification of the earliest use of words in Castilian; on the basis of available data, there seem to be a goodly number of such cases in Alfonsine prose. It is not surprising that terms not normally used in poetry should appear first in texts which so often are technical in nature. Even with a word at hand in the Castilian text, it may be questionable as to whether it should be counted as truly Spanish. It can be argued that, in the eye of the translator, they were loanwords of the period and that, during the time of their currency, they may not have been preserved in any texts that have survived. Often a word, the name of a stone in the *Lapidary,* for example, appears to be merely the transliteration of an Arabic term which the translator did not recognize as anything familiar. The question of how to treat such words is not easy to answer.

The determination of first appearances, or the earliest date when a word makes its entrance into the written language, is a tricky matter. Until every text in Castilian has been checked, scholars cannot be certain that a given word was first used at any particular time and not before. With the Alfonsine language in mind, I used a survey of words of Arabic and Persian origin in the works of Alfonso el Sabio which was compiled by the late Hispano-Arabist A. R. Nykl. This list included as well some words of other origins, mostly Greek, which were transmitted through Arabic. (Regrettably, this work has remained unpublished because of defects in treatment and presentation.) Despite the problem words in the list which were discarded, the number of terms that could be regarded as first appearances was naturally large.

A check on the words beginning with *A* in the new edition of Corominas's etymological dictionary,[2] in order to determine whether any of the words in the Nykl list were designated by Corominas with a chronologically later "first usage," yielded a number of surprises. In some instances, the discrepancy is insignificant, as when a date such as 1295 or 1300 is given, often without any indication of the work in which the word is found, yet the word appears on the earlier folios of the *Estoria de Espanna* which is of a somewhat earlier date—words such as *almohade* [Almohad], *azagaya* [javelin], or *alfaqui* [a scholar versed in Islamic law]. Slightly greater is the time difference in words such as *algalia* [musk] (in Alfonso's *Picatrix* as opposed to the Corominas lexicon entry of 1328–1335); *albur* [a kind of fish] (in Alfonso's *General estoria II* as opposed to the later author Juan Ruiz); *alamin* [a market judge] (in Alfonso's *Judizios* as opposed to a notice of 1313); and *alhayd, alhoyd,* or *alhaite* [a string or necklace] (in his *Astronomia* as opposed to a notice from the fourteenth century). More striking are the gaps in *alamud* [bolt, bar for a door] (in his *General estoria IV* as opposed to a fifteenth-century reference), *alquice* for *alquicel* [cloak] (in both his *Lapidario* and *Picatrix* as opposed to a notice from 1611), or *albait* or *albaida* [egg] (in his *Astronomia* as opposed to the year 1884).

Most of these are far from common words, but they do indicate the possibility of a greater choice in vocabulary from the Alfonsine period onward than the Corominas dictionary indicates. It is much easier to spot first appearances with tools such as the now difficult to obtain Oelschläger *Wordlist*[3] and the Alfonsine concordances. In the meantime, the number of lexical items contained in these works leaves no doubt that the royal scriptorium had already established on a literary basis a very large body of words sufficient for any normal expression.

Orthography was a matter that Alfonso could have taken into account, but the practice in the various texts he sponsored has not been consistent. For example, the word mentioned above which Corominas finds as *alloza* appears in the astronomical texts variously as *allauce, allauza,* and *alleuce*. This inconsistency constitutes today one more hurdle for the lexicographer who seeks to subordinate all these errant forms under the proper lemma. The reader with imagination and with a sense for the sound of a word may scarcely be bothered. Spelling appears not to have been a matter of deep concern to medieval people.

If spelling was no problem to Alfonso, there was deep concern about the meaning of words. In some areas, exactness of definition was of utmost importance. In order that there should be a clear transmission of meaning from author to reader, he deemed it advisable in a number of instances to define the words that he used. Often they were terms used in legal works, where the need for a definition did not result from unfamiliarity with the term but was needed to establish boundaries to its meaning and to prevent quibbling. But there were other definitions that explained scientific terminology, medical terms, obsolete words, special usages, and gems. They range from precise scientific explanations to a mere statement of lexical equivalents. In some instances, Alfonso has recourse to the etymon in establishing meaning. These definitions have a special appeal to lexicographers, as representing contemporary opinions about the meaning of a word or a phrase and as substantiation or correction to what has been determined by them through other methods. A few examples of Alfonsine definitions, given in Appendix 1 at the end of this chapter, illustrate the various means used to clarify the meanings of terms.

Comparable to the lack of uniformity in orthography is the deviation within morphological patterns. This is possibly in part a reflection of regional differences or an indication of the uncertainty present during a time of linguistic change. The morphological field presents a large and complicated area of study, but the status of the problem may be illustrated with several examples. The strong preterite which developed mainly from the Latin third conjugation did not always result in the forms that might be expected. The form *traer* [to bring] (with its compounds *atraer* and *maltraer* following suit) displays four stems in use. Because of the nature of the Alfonsine works the first and second persons are infrequent; but in the third-person singular and plural, the variant forms *troxo* and *troxieron* are by far the most used, followed by the forms *trexo* and *trexieron*, then by *traxo* and *traxieron*, and finally by the rare form *trogo*. The statistics are surprising, and the philologically inclined will be interested in seeing that the *troxo* type, singular and plural, appears 95 times, the *trexo* type 25, the *traxo* type 6, and *trogo* only twice. Ultimately, it was *traxo* that won out, with *trujo* succeeding *troxo* in substandard speech.

The presumably dialect forms with the preterite third-person plural ending in *-oron* were very nearly eliminated in the Alfonsine writings. They are found occasionally, but if they were heard in other parts of Spain, Alfonso's scribes did a good job in regularizing the first conjugation ending *-aron* in scriptorium use. The total forms in *-oron* (only twenty-two, of which six are in the latter portions of the *Estoria de Espanna* and another six in the *Libro de las cruzes*) are indeed few, when for example compared with 273 cases where the reduction of the *ie* diphthong in the preterite third-person plural of the second and third conjugation verbs resulted in the ending *-iron*. From bits of evidence such as this, it is clear that a good deal of uniformity was operative among the scribes and that the best examples of writing and language that the age could offer as worthy of emulation were indeed these. The problem of deviations from the preponderant usage in these texts deserves full examination.

Literary translation, as opposed to translation of didactic materials, begun by Alfonso el Sabio and later carried on by the humanists of the fifteenth century, put the capabilities of the young Spanish language to a test. It is unlikely that Alfonso's primary aims were at all literary. After all, he was writing history. It was a history that concerned itself most with human exploits and individual acts, however, and that could serve to reinforce the moral lessons to be derived from the past. With the idea of drawing profitable lessons and guided by other medieval moralization, he incorporated all the details that the poets provided concerning the deeds of even mythological figures of the ancient world, precisely at those points where the chronological tables of Eusebius and Jerome specified that they had taken place. In this way, the *General estoria,* which depended so much on the historical portions of the Bible as the framework on which to hang other information, became a mosaic in which literature periodically elbowed aside the Bible and the historians to permit the purely literary Roman poets and the French cycle of antiquity to take over. Collectively, these authorities were referred to as the *sabios antiguos,* whose writings all appear to have been considered authoritative.

Treatment of pagan sources was the same as in the case of biblical material. If the Bible quotes a speaker verbatim, Alfonso gives the exact Castilian equivalent. When Ovid quotes his characters, Alfonso translates their words as if they were historical utterances, even down to the exclamations. In general, the classical material is more or less paraphrased, as are the more historical sources. When direct quotations arise, however, a careful translation is given. One of the finest examples of consistent translation appears in the utilization of Ovid's *Heroïdes,* whose epistles are rendered in long passages in which the wording is respected as historical evidence. Although the translation as such is generally accurate, there are many occasions when the spirit of the situation carries the writer along so that he does more than an adequate job on his material. A happy choice of words and sentence rhythms makes for a moving presentation in prose. Thus, the ability to interpret the spirit of a situation argues for a knowledge of writing far beyond any primitive stage. An example is given in Appendix 2 at the end of this chapter.

Historical narrative with action generally depicting the individual even amongst the most bizarre backgrounds (as in the case of Alexander the Great), interest in the various aspects of the creation and nature (as seen by such diverse eyes as those of biblical commentators and the classical Pliny), and the depiction of human emotions all found a place in the various productions of the Learned King. Whether they were history or not, at numerous points they crossed over into the purely literary realm of the ancients. For several centuries in their Castilian form, they provided a possibility of getting acquainted with the themes of classical antiquity, for readers without the capability of enjoying the originals. Did many take advantage of this possibility? The multiple manuscripts remaining of the Alfonsine histories are indicative of their extensive circulation and availability.

Their influence on various aspects of medieval forms and themes, both in style and in subject matter, is an intriguing possibility to examine. Olga Impey of Indiana University is currently engaged in the study of courtly love and the sentimental novel of the fifteenth century, as related to the Alfonsine histories. In all present and future work, the availability of these histories to medieval scholars is a problem that may be close to resolution. The first, second, and fourth parts of the *General estoria* are now available; the third is edited but not yet printed. Transcription of the fifth part, which derives from Lucan and the Bible, has been completed in the Netherlands, where Wilhelmina Jonxis-Henkemans is cooperating most effectively with the Wisconsin project. Various signs of interest in doing a careful edition of the legal works give hope that soon the entire body of work ascribed to Alfonso will be available and will provide the possibility of definitive studies of their place in Hispanic culture. Finally, the remaining texts of the astronomical or astrological group are being worked on by Anthony Cárdenas. In these years marking the septencentennial of Alfonso's death, it would be appropriate to observe the occasion with the editing and scholarly investigation needed to see him on all scores in the proper light.

Appendix 1: Definitions from Alfonso's Works, in Translation[4]

"*Lector*. There is another rank [in the clergy] which is called 'lector,' which signifies reader." (*Libro de las leyes*)

"1. *Febrero*. 2. *Hebrero*. 1. The second month was given the name 'febrero,' from *februa*, which they say in Latin for purification. 2. The second month is 'hebrero,' which in the ordinary year has 28 days and in leap year has 29." (*Astronomia*)

"*Bigamia*. 'Bigamia' is having two wives, for we say *bis* in Latin for two, and in Greek we say *gamos* for woman, and by joining these two words *bis* and *gamos*, the men learned in Latin grammar composed this noun *bigamis*; wherefore bigamy means one man having two wives together at the same time." (*General estoria I*)

"*Planeta*. 'Planeta' is the same as 'wandering star,' and they gave it this name from *planos*, which is what Greek calls such wandering." (*General estoria I*)

"*Astrologia*. 'Astrologia' is the science of the stars, and astrology derives its name from *astris*, which they say in Latin for stars, and *logos* in Greek for discourse, wherefore 'astrologia' is equivalent to discourse or science of the knowledge of stars." (*General estoria I*)

"*Argent*. The stone which is commonly called 'argent' or silver, and the Moors call *feda*, can be hammered or smelted the same as other metals. And if its filings are mixed with medicines for the inflammation which they call 'uitreun,' it is beneficial. And likewise for all illnesses which involve inflammation. . . . And the color of this stone is white, and the more it is polished, the shinier it gets." (*Lapidario*)

Special curiosities are the definitions of the tiger and unicorn. Surely the latter would scarcely be recognized as the mythical animal discussed in medieval bestiaries, for here it is clearly a description of the rhinoceros.

"*Thigre*. The tiger is a very fierce and brutal beast by nature. Its body is large, like a big deer, and it is as strong and fierce as the most savage beast in existence. It has the feet, the legs, and the tail of a lion. Its face is long, similar to that of a bald man." (*General estoria II*)

"*Unicornio*. The unicorn is a very large and very strong beast; and it has two horns: one on its forehead and the other on its nose, and the one on its nose is longer than the one on its forehead. This unicorn has a large body like ivory of an ashen hue, and its legs are like ivory, and its ears like those of a pig." (*Ajedrez*)

The originals read:

"*Lector.* Otro grado y ha a que llaman lector, que quier tanto dezir cuemo leedor."

"1. *Febrero.* 2. *Hebrero.* 1. Al segundo mes pusieron nombre febrero, de februa, que dizen en latin por alimpiamiento. 2. El segundo mes es hebrero, el qual en el anno simple es de xxviii dias et en el anno bissiesto de xxix."

"*Bigamia.* Es bigamia auer dos mugieres, ca dezimos en el latin bis por dos e en el griego dizen gamos por mugier, e ayuntado estas dos palabras bis e gamos, conpusieron ende los sabios en la gramatica en latin este nombre bigamis; onde quier dezir bigamia tanto como un varon auer dos mugieres en una sazon e en uno."

"*Planeta.* Planeta tanto quier dezir como estrella andadora, e dieron le este nombre de planos, que dize el griego por tal andar."

"*Astrologia.* Astrologia es el saber de las estrellas, e ende a la astrologia este nombre, de astris que dizen en el latin por estrellas, e logos en el griego por razon; onde astrologia tanto quiere dezir como razon o scientia del saber de las estrellas."

"*Argent.* La piedra a que llaman comunal miente todos argent o plata, e los moros feda . . . sufre martiello e fundicion, assi como las otras que son metales. Et si las limaduras della con las melezinas que son contra la flema a que llaman uitreun metiere, presta. Et otrossi a todas las enfermedades que son de flema. . . . Et la color desta piedra es blanca e quanto mas la pulen, mas resplandece, mas no que la passe el uiso."

"*Thigre.* Es la thigre bestia muy brava e muy bruda de natura. Es grant de cuerpo como un grant cieruo e fuerte e brava assi como la bestia mas salvage que y a. A pies e piernas e rabo de leon. El rostro a luengo a semeiança de ombre caluo."

"*Unicornio.* Ell unicornio es bestia muy grant e muy fuerte, e ha dos cuernos: ell uno en la fruente e ell otro en la nariz, e el de la nariz es mas luengo que el de la fruente. E este unicornio a el cuerpo grant como marfil e la color como de ceniza e las piernas tales como el marfil e las oreias commo de puerco."

Appendix 2

The reader may judge from the following passages translating from the *Heroïdes*—the epistle of Ariadne to Theseus as found in the *General estoria*.5

"Aquel tienpo de la noche era en que la elada comiença primero a esparzer se por la tierra e parescer reluzient e uidria como uidrio, et quando las aues que estan por los aruoles cubiertas de la foia se querellan e murmurian. Et yazia yo a aquella ora, e esto podrie seer a los primeros gallos, que nin uelaua nin yazia espierta. Et atal qual estaua sonnolienta, moui las manos por el lecho pora poner las en ti, Theseo, e non falle nada; e leue las manos aluen e desi trox las a todas partes por ueer si te fallaria, e non falle nada.

"Alli oue el miedo tan grant que todo el suenno perdi, e leuanteme muy espantada, e derribeme luego del lecho que falle bibdo sin marido. Et assi como fuy en tierra, eche las manos en los uestidos, e rompi me toda, e feri me los pechos, e messe los cabellos assi como me leuantaua e los tenia bueltos. E fazie estonces luna, e sabes lo tu, e cate yo a la luz della si ueria otra cosa si non las riberas. Mas los mios oios non uieron otra cosa si non la mar e la ribera; et yo, mesquina e desamparada, comence a correr por la ribera a todas partes e sin todo ordenamiento.

"Et era aquel lugar grand arenal, commo tu sabes; e quando corria por ueer por uentura si te fallaria entrando aun en el nauio e me recibries, tardaua me el arena los pies que fuye con ellos. Et pues que ningun recabdo non fallaua nin ueya nada, comence a llamar a grandes uozes 'Theseo' por toda la ribera. Et las pennas que estauan y socauadas rescibien la mi boz, e retennien e dizien otra uez el tu nonbre. Et quantas uezes te yo llamaua, tantas uezes te llamaua aquel logar: assi que semeiaua que querie fazer su ayuda a mi, mesquina e desamparada."

Ellen Kosmer and
James F. Powers

4. Manuscript Illustration: The *Cantigas* in Contemporary Art Context

The *Cantigas de Santa Maria,* produced for Alfonso X el Sabio around 1280, is one of the most spectacularly illustrated manuscripts of the period.[1] Its 212 full-page illuminations, each divided into six compartments, are amply impressive; but its greatest significance resides in the fact that most of these miniatures, though illustrating hymns of praise to the Virgin, present a compendium of scenes from daily life. Wars are waged, merchants trade, seafarers cross perilous oceans, craftsmen practice their mysteries, games are played, births and deaths occur both peacefully and violently, and over this panoply of medieval life the Virgin presides, now watching, now interceding in the lives entrusted to her maternal care. In the number of illustrations of genre scenes and in the carefully detailed observations of life recorded in them, the *Cantigas* manuscript is unique among late thirteenth-century illustrated books. This manuscript also offers an unparalleled opportunity to study pictorial narrative techniques and relationships among text and image, particularly revealing in that the newly created text required an original visualization that could rarely rely on an earlier, established pictorial tradition.

Despite its significance, this manuscript has received relatively little attention from the point of view of its art-historical importance and its stylistic relationships with other late thirteenth-century manuscripts. John Keller's commentaries on the *Cantigas* focus on the literary more than the art-historical point of view.[2] The miniatures of the *Cantigas* need to be seen in their art-historical context, so that the place of this manuscript not only in the court of Alfonso el Sabio but in the cultural milieu of late thirteenth-century Europe may be better understood.

This period witnessed a dramatic rise in the growth of European towns. As urban economies prospered, so too did craftsmen, whose numbers increased dramatically in the late thirteenth century. The book trade, which by around 1250 had largely become a lay rather than monastic enterprise, mirrored the changing society of the late Middle Ages. The growing use of the vernacular in written texts, and the rise of literacy among the laity, stimulated manuscript production all over Europe. Royal courts gave the major impetus to the production of luxury manuscripts; kings and nobles became major patrons of the visual and literary arts.

Thus, Alfonso's commission of this literary work written in a vernacular, the Galician dialect, with its lavish illustrations, puts him in the company of other great thirteenth-century royal patrons—Louis IX of France and his sons Philippe III and Philippe IV, the southern Italian court of the Hohenstaufen emperor Frederick II and his son Manfred, and in England Henry III and Edward I.[3] The *Cantigas* is distinguished from the works commissioned by these other royal patrons by the length of its text and the extensiveness of its pictorial program. The abundance of literary and visual material in the *Cantigas* prevents, in this relatively brief discussion, any consideration of more than a few examples. The focus will be on a small selection of illustrations, some of which are characteristic of the manuscript as a whole (for example, cantigas 9, 28, 34, 185) (see Figs. 4-1 and 4-2), and on a few exceptions against which to measure them (for example, cantigas 29 and 80).

Only exceptional miniatures here rely on traditional illustrative formulae, such as the Tree of Jesse in number 80, and on the use of traditional formats, as in number 29 in the last two compartments on the page, which show highly formalized compositions: on the left Mary between two angels, and on the right a typical annunciation scene. The standard illuminations in this manuscript are remarkably liberated from conventional pictorializations. Examples are the unusual composition with seated figures amidst an architectural frame in number 185, illustrating the story of Mary's protecting the castle of Chincolla from the Muslims (and see numbers 46, 65, 126, and 185), as well as the numerous examples of extensive landscape representations of a highly realistic nature. Lively representations of commerce, detailing carefully observed scenes of buying and selling, occur in numbers 108 and 172. Perhaps the most unusual glimpse of medieval life occurs in a miniature that recounts the story of a Jew who disposed of the Virgin's image in a latrine; believers rescued the statue which then performed many miracles (number 34).

Figure 4-1. A woman requests that a monk buy her an image of the Virgin during his pilgrimage to the Holy Sepulcher. The image subsequently saves the life of the monk during encounters with a lion, some thieves, and a storm at sea. *Cantigas de Santa Maria,* cantiga 9, Patronato Nacional.

Figure 4-2. While Constantinople is under siege by a sultan, Saint Germanos prays for Mary's protection. Mary saves the city from the sultan's catapult stones with her mantle. The sultan, awe-struck, gives generously of his wealth to Mary and is baptized a Christian. *Cantigas de Santa Maria*, cantiga 28, Patronato Nacional.

Since the Gothic style began in a clearly defined geographical area, northern France, and then spread from there, the French style in European manuscript illumination was the universal Gothic norm, which by midthirteenth century was dominated by Paris. By the time the *Cantigas* appeared, Parisian manuscript illumination had attained heights of technical excellence and pictorial elegance which resulted in widespread admiration and imitation. The manuscripts produced for the Capetians' sainted king, Louis IX, are among the most brilliantly executed of the period.[4] The style resulting from Louis's patronage came to be known as the Court Style, and Parisian manuscripts became the standard of excellence by which other books were judged.

It is not surprising therefore to find a significant amount of French influence in the *Cantigas* miniatures. The French manuscript that comes immediately to mind for its stylistic affinities with the *Cantigas* is the so-called *Shah Abbas Picture Bible,* the greater part of which is in the Pierpont Morgan Library in New York (MS 638).[5] This Bible is a fine example of a wandering manuscript; although its miniatures are definitely of Parisian origin, around 1250–1260, its script and decorated initials are Italian, around 1300. Pope Clement VIII presented it to the Persian Shah Abbas the Great in 1608, at which time Arabic inscriptions were added to explain the biblical subjects.

Its full-page miniatures are divided into three or four compartments; the organization of the page into many compartments was a long-standing tradition of northern European manuscript illumination, especially in the large Romanesque Bibles produced in the twelfth century, as for example, the Morgan, Erlangen, and Lambeth Bibles.[6] Although the subject matter in the *Shah Abbas Bible* is ostensibly that of the Old Testament, the visualizations, as was typical of all historical representation in the Middle Ages, present the scenes as if they were contemporary events.

Thus, when the city of Hai is captured (fol. 10v) the figure of Joshua is represented as a splendid knight in a golden helmet. Indeed, in its battle scenes, we receive a picture of medieval warfare as vivid as that found in the *Cantigas.* Battle scenes and soldiers on the way to combat are far more frequently encountered in the *Shah Abbas Bible,* where one observes some thirty-six of these combats in the ninety-two full-page illustrations, as compared to approximately twelve battle scenes contained in the 212 full-page illustrations in the *Cantigas.* One must allow for the frequency of opportunities for military illustration in the *Shah Abbas Bible,* especially in the Book of Kings, as compared to a book on the miracles of the Virgin. A strong tendency existed on the part of the illustrators of the *Shah Abbas Bible* to select military subjects from the many other themes available, nonetheless, considering that over a third of this material is not in reality devoted to warfare as the ration of illustrations might suggest. A number of other illustrations, not considered in this count, depict military garb and weapons in both manuscripts, but again, the tendency to picture such figures is far stronger in the *Shah Abbas Bible* than in the *Cantigas*. As with so many other aspects of the comparison, one forms the impression that the *Cantigas* manuscript offers a closer representation of everyday life with regard to the military presence in its society—interesting in the light of the intensive militarization of society which historians tend to presume regarding Reconquest Iberia.

The presentation of military accoutrements and equipment offers a basis for both comparison and contrast. A wider variety of helmets appear in the *Shah Abbas Bible,* for example, as compared to the *Cantigas.*[7] Round-topped helmets atop mail coifs dominate the *Cantigas* depictions, with head-enclosing casks rather less frequently pictured. The *Shah Abbas Bible* offers round-tops, casks, helmets with wide base-rims that move out from the side of the head, and even some older-style conical helmets with nose pieces, the origins of which predate the *Shah Abbas Bible* by two centuries. While swords, spears, and chopping weapons are similarly depicted in the two manuscripts, the *Shah Abbas Bible* presents a predominance of conventional bows in the hands of its warriors, in contrast to the *Cantigas*'s numerous well-drawn crossbows. If the evidence offered by these illustrations fairly represents the actual situation, both Spanish Christian and Muslim armies presented more advanced firepower than did the French of the period. Interesting also is the depiction of shields. In the *Cantigas,* the Christian armies carry only the kite-shaped shields, while the Muslim forces bear kites and also the heart-shaped shield (*adarga*) which had appeared in the thirteenth century. The *Shah Abbas Bible* invariably shows the Israelites bearing kite-shaped shields, while their opponents usually carry circular shields with an occasional kite. This may refer back to an earlier twelfth-century tradition, where kite shields identify the morally good or Christian forces versus the circular shield indicating the morally evil or Muslim side. An earlier preference of the Muslims for the circular shield in actual battlefield use did in fact exist in Spain.[8]

The pictorial narrative reaches beyond men and their personal equipment in its display of military endeavors. Field tents appear in both the *Cantigas* and the *Shah Abbas Bible.*[9] Especially interesting is the appearance of the trebuchet, the great stone-throwing machine which employed a heavy counterweight to obtain its hurling power. The *Cantigas* displays only one (where it appears in two frames of number 28) (see Fig. 4-2); but in this set the trebuchet plays a central part in the narrative, in that the Virgin will use her cloak to repel its stones in frustrating a Muslim siege of Constantinople. The *Shah Abbas Bible* displays two dramatically drawn examples in sieges of towns (fols. 23v, 46v). This would have been a comparatively new weapon in midthirteenth century Western Europe, and it caught the attention of both manuscript workshops.

Horses play a large role in both manuscripts and provide a fine indication of the use of naturalism by the artists. The knights seem smaller in proportion to their horses in the *Shah Abbas Bible* compared with those of the *Cantigas*. This conforms to our evidence that the Spanish barb horse was smaller than its contemporary French competitor. The *Cantigas* artists also depict another known reality of the epoch, namely that the Christian Spanish tended to ride with a long-stirrup style called *a la brida,* while the Muslims rode with a short-stirrup strap which required bending the knee, a style called *a la ginete.*[10]

In the *Shah Abbas Bible,* there is not only an abundance of graphically portrayed battle scenes but also human interest stories, such as David's adultery with Bathsheba (fol. 41v) presented in a mode comparable to the lively scenes in the *Cantigas*. The narrative techniques are similar in both, with the visual narration following the text closely, even when minor episodes are represented. This expansive treatment makes it impossible for either the *Bible* or the *Cantigas* to represent every textual episode; in both manuscripts, the solution is to omit some stories altogether rather than compromise the close visualization of the text.

Both manuscripts make use of Gothic architectural framing, but there is a major difference in the way each uses the outer border. The *Cantigas* borders are visually busier and more obtrusive than those in the *Shah Abbas Bible*. In both, the entire miniature is circumscribed with a flat, ornamented bar border, which in the *Shah Abbas Bible* is confined to the rectangular outline of the page. In the *Cantigas,* the border also bisects the page vertically, however, and is highly decorated with quadrilobed and other geometric patterns resembling the colorful cloisonné metalwork of the Mosan region. Ramón Menéndez Pidal has suggested ivories as a source of inspiration for the six-part division of the page and for the borders, but in fact, carved ivory borders are not commonly found with the kind of geometric patterns used in the *Cantigas*. The more usual type of carved ivory border is a three-dimensional stylized acanthus leaf of Gothic architectural framing. The very flat geometric quality and clear-cut compartmentaliza-tion of the colors in the borders of the *Cantigas* strongly suggest an enamelwork source in which the metal strips mark out color boundaries.[11]

Another difference between these manuscripts concerns the relation-ship between the border and the space around it on the page. An unusual feature of the *Cantigas* miniatures is the inviolability of the borders. Noth-ing is allowed to intrude in their space. In the *Shah Abbas Bible,* on the other hand, the illustration of David and Bathsheba breaks the frame in the upper border, where a roof line extends into the margin of the page, and again in the lower-right corner where Joab's feet protrude into the border. Another well-known example of this kind of interaction between the border and the surrounding page occurs on folio 23v, depicting Saul's battle against the Ammonites, where a man on the left, completely outside the border on the miniature, clings valiantly to a rope on a catapult while an archer shoots from the top margin. Examples like these abound in the *Shah Abbas Bible,* where the border often seems too small to contain the force and vitality of its figures or the magnificence of their architectural setting.

In the *Cantigas,* the integrity of the border is never breached, on the other hand, and all its elements are tightly confined. In the scenes of the Moors besieging Constantinople in number 28, nothing breaks the integ-rity of the outer border, and only unobtrusively does a piece of siege machinery extend across the central border strip (see Fig. 4-2). Yet within individual scenes in the Spanish work, there is a great deal of spatial experimentation. Thus, in number nine, the placement of objects and figures in the vaulted room in the upper-right compartment indicates a large degree of spatial sophistication and awareness (see Fig. 4-1), as does the scene in the central compartment on the right, the selling of the Virgin's image. In both scenes, the figures interact spatially with the architecture: they move both in front of and behind columns and pillars. This type of spatial experimentation is extensive in the *Cantigas* and allies it with the *Shah Abbas Bible* where similar innovation abounds.

A significant difference between the *Cantigas* and the *Shah Abbas Bible* is the marked quality of elegance and refinement in the French work and its conspicuous absence from the Spanish manuscript. In the *Cantigas,* the figures are short and blocky; they move with a studied deliberation rather than with mannered grace. The gestures of the *Cantigas* figures are clearly delineated and convincingly represented, but they do not convey the bal-letic charm of the French work. The Spanish figures instead have a down-to-earth stolidity and earnestness which lends them an appealing quality of slight awkwardness and the immediacy of reality. Proportions are heavier in the *Cantigas,* whereas the French figures are more attenuated. The drapery in both is well-shaded, giving a sense of three-dimensional solidity to the forms. In the *Shah Abbas Bible,* cloth characteristically falls in casually elegant folds, as for example in Saul's surcoat and his horse's trappings (fol. 27v). Throughout the French work, the drapery flows around the figures in a manner suggesting that the artist took great delight in enriching his miniatures with linear playfulness and charm. In the *Cantigas,* the drapery is volumetric and convincingly reveals the body within, but its flow and pattern are commonplace.

Many of these specific non-French qualities are found in late thirteenth-century Italian manuscripts, especially those produced in southern Italy for Frederick II's son Manfred. Another connection with southern Italian manuscript tradition is exemplified by the careful observations and delineations of birds in the *Cantigas,* as for example in numbers 124 and 142, which bear very close resemblance to the illustrations in Frederick II's hunting manuscript, *De arte venandi cum avibus.* A particularly telling stylistic relationship exists between the *Cantigas* and a manuscript in Rome's Biblioteca Angelica, Peter of Eboli's poem on the baths of Pozzuoli.[12] The illuminators of both manuscripts faced the same challenge to create illustrations for a newly written text without an existing pictorial tradition.

Unlike the *Cantigas,* the Angelica illustrations are single full-page miniatures which are not subdivided into a series of compartmentalized narrative episodes. The Angelica artist does not use architectural framing, but he does employ architecture within each miniature to provide a sense of setting and space. He also makes serious attempts to integrate figures and architecture in a way very similar to that used in the *Cantigas.* The architecture in the Pozzuoli pictures, however, makes no pretensions to the Gothic; rather, it is resolutely Romanesque, solid, earthbound, and secure.

An important point of similarity between the *Cantigas* and the *Pozzuoli Baths* is the concern both share for representing, or attempting to grapple with, depictions of landscape space. In this area, both are far more sophisticated than the French work, which simply continues to use the old convention of a slightly wavy ground line to indicate outdoor scenes. Both the Italian and the Spanish illustrations show complex landscape settings with figures and architecture integrated into them, thereby achieving a kind of spatial actuality even though the pictures are not realistic in the sense of

Figure 4-3. Thieves attack and behead a young man traveling through the forest. Two friars hear a cry for penance and see the young man's head and body joined together requesting confession. He is confessed before many people. One of the friars preaches on the blessings of the Holy Virgin Mary. *Cantigas de Santa Maria*, cantiga 96, Patronato Nacional.

Figure 4-4. David sends Joab after Amasa. Joab feigns friendship for Amasa and then treacherously slays him. Joab lays siege to Abel-beth-maacah, setting his soldiers to the undermining of its walls. A wise woman beheads Sheba and passes his head over the wall to Joab, who abandons his siege. 2 Samuel 20. *Shah Abbas Bible*, New York, Pierpont Morgan Library, MS 619, f. 46v.

Figure 4-5. Peter of Eboli, *The Baths of Pozzuoli*, "Balneum Raynerius." Rome, Biblioteca Angelica, MS 1474, f. 12.

three-dimensional illusionism. Of these two, the *Cantigas* is by far the more developed in landscape representation. The Italian manuscript makes extensive use of conventionalized formulae, such as regularly rippling lines for water, repetitious broccoli-like trees perched on conical mountains, and shading that is more linear than tonal. The *Cantigas* presents landscapes that, though stylized, achieve a sense of reality not matched elsewhere until the fourteenth century. Cantiga 9 shows a delightful landscape in which a monk is confronted by a lion, while in cantiga 96 the Virgin miraculously restores a severed head in a landscape that is equally miraculous in its representation of hills, flowers, and trees (see Figs. 4-1, 4-3, 4-4, and 4-5).

It is in the treatment of figures, however, that the relationships between the Italian and the Spanish work are the most marked. In the illustration on folio 12 of the *Pozzuoli Baths,* for example, the figures walking through the landscape at the top of the miniature share many characteristics with the robbers in the first panel of cantiga 96 (see Figs. 4-3, 4-5). Heads are slightly too large in proportion to their bodies, movements are stiff and angular, facial features are bold and simplified, and the drapery is shaded in a linear fashion. Similarly, the nude representations, of which by the nature of its subject matter the *Pozzuoli Baths* manuscript has a great many, are done in both books in a direct, forthright, and well-observed manner (as in cantigas 60 and 96) (see Fig. 4-3).

This discussion is not meant to suggest that there was direct influence from the *Shah Abbas Bible* or the *Pozzuoli Baths* manuscripts upon the *Cantigas*. The intention rather is to compare a major Spanish work with two other major works of a slightly earlier date, and to suggest the strong possibility of influence from similar French and Italian work upon the *Cantigas* pictures. One might be tempted to explore the possibility of German influence, considering that Alfonso el Sabio had a Hohenstaufen mother, and considering the existence of strong Hohenstaufen connections to the king of Aragon contemporary with the completion of the *Cantigas* manuscript. The likelihood of influence from German work ought nonetheless to be discounted because the German manuscript tradition of the second half of the thirteenth century was *retardataire* and heavily dependent upon French models. It seems therefore unlikely that it would have provided any major stylistic stimulus to the *Cantigas,* which is itself very advanced for the period.[13]

Norman Roth

5. Jewish Collaborators in Alfonso's Scientific Work

Just as in the Middle Ages, when it was imagined that there was an international "congress" of Muslim, Jewish, and Christian scientists, so popular modern mythology has assumed that a "school" of translators existed at Toledo, already under the patronage of the twelfth-century archbishop and then later in the reign of Alfonso X. Less romantic consideration shows that no such school actually existed and that translation activity was taking place all over Spain and was by no means centralized in Toledo.[1]

What is remarkable about the Jewish translators whose work was sponsored by Alfonso, following an already old tradition of Jewish translation activity, was their concentration almost exclusively on scientific literature and their significant contribution to the development of the Spanish language. While Jewish scholars, with the exception of the pioneer Moritz Steinschneider, have totally ignored this aspect,[2] Spanish scholars have demonstrated an increasing awareness of the importance of Alfonso's Jewish "collaborators" in the scientific corpus. Thus, José Muñoz Sendino has remarked: "The Hebrew element was the group of the greatest scientific value because of its great intellectual discipline [and its] mastery of both languages—Arabic and Spanish—[which] guaranteed a faithful reflection of the original thought" of the works translated.[3] This view of the fidelity of the translation, fully substantiated by the careful analysis of J. M. Millás Vallicrosa,[4] invalidates the claim of earlier scholars like Gonzalo Menéndez Pidal, who conjectured that a second translation into Latin from Spanish was necessary because Jewish translators rendering Arabic texts into Spanish used "a very peculiar and archaic dialect, which was barbarous to Castilian ears."[5]

Américo Castro also has commented on the significance of Alfonso's choice of Castilian rather than Latin for the writings he sponsored—historical, legal, and scientific. (This Castilian form is the reason why some of the works were retranslated into Latin for use in other European countries, of course, and not because of any barbarism which supposedly exists in the medieval Spanish versions.) "This interest the Jews, above all, would feel," Castro wrote. "The innovation of writing historical and scientific books in Romance appeared to be sponsored by a monarch compared by the Jews with Alexander and Caesar, and who recompensed with splendid favors their services and praises."[6] Of particular importance are the remarks of Alfonso's nephew Juan Manuel; after mentioning Alfonso's translation of *toda la secta de los moros* (which may refer to all or part of the Qu'rān), he wrote,

> Furthermore he ordered translated the whole law of the Jews, and even their Talmud, and other knowledge which is called *qabbalah* and which the Jews keep closely secret. And he did this so it might be manifest through their own Law that it is all a [mere] representation of that Law which we Christians have; and that they, like the Moors, are in grave error and in peril of losing their souls.[7]

In spite of the concluding dogmatic pietude, which need not be taken too seriously in light of both Alfonso's and Juan Manuel's personal friendship with Jews, it is significant that Alfonso apparently arranged for the translation of the entire Talmud and certain cabalistic works. There is no trace of the existence of such translations, but this testimony is certainly reliable.

The reign of Alfonso X was an extremely productive and generally beneficial period for the Jews, marred only occasionally by some restrictive actions (the laws, such as the *Siete partidas,* were entirely of a theoretical nature). There was great independent literary, scientific, and philosophical activity among the Jews of Spain at this time, and it is significant that a very large percentage of the work of "Jewish collaborators" in the Alfonsine scientific corpus consists, in fact, of original writings and not just translations from the Arabic.

The first of the translated works, which together with the literary work *Calila e Digna* was done when Alfonso was still infante, was the book on gems and stones called the *Lapidary* by an unknown author identified only as "Abolays."[8] The translation was done sometime between the conquest of Murcia in 1243[9] and the conquest of Seville in 1250, according to the prologue:

> He [Alfonso] obtained it from a Jew who held it hidden, who neither wished to make use of it himself nor that any other should profit therefrom. And when

he [Alfonso] had this book in his possession, he caused another Jew, who was his physician, to read it, and he was called Yhuda Mosca *el menor* and he was learned in the art of astrology and understood well both Arabic and Latin. And when through this Jew his physician he understood the value and great profit which was in the book, he commanded him to translate it from Arabic into the Castilian language.[10]

From this prologue, it is clear that Yehudah was the physician to Alfonso while the latter was not yet king. It is not entirely clear whether the title *alfaquim* which appears after his name in all of the other translations he did (except in the *Tablas astronomicas* and the *Libro de las estrellas fixas*) meant literally that he was a physician, or was merely an honorary title.[11] He was "helped" in the translation of *Lapidario* by a priest named Garcí Pérez.

José Amador de los Ríos refers to Yehudah as Yehudah ha-Qaton ("the small" in Hebrew), which is perhaps the explanation of the appellative *el menor* found only in the prologue of *Lapidario*.[12] The term is not satisfactorily explained, however, either by the previous attempts mentioned by Gerold Hilty or by his own suggestion of "junior, younger," which would only make sense if his father's name had also been Yehudah (instead of Moshe). If the title has any significance at all, and is correctly assumed to correspond to the Hebrew suggested by Amador, then the meaning is most probably "insignificant," a term used by the poet and philosopher Solomon Ibn Gabirol, among others.

There is, however, another possibility. Hilty has convincingly argued that Yehudah b. Moses ha-Kohen and Yehudah Mosca are one and the same, and that Mosca is not a corruption of Moses (Moshe), but rather a family name identical to that of the astronomer Yehudah b. Solomon Ibn Mosca.[13] If this is correct, then *el menor* in the sense of "the lesser, the other" could have served to distinguish him from his relative who lived at the same period of time. This suggestion would not invalidate, but rather strengthen, Hilty's surmise as to why the title is found only in the first work translated by Yehudah. As his fame increased, Hilty argues, it was no longer necessary to distinguish him from the other Yehudah; the latter by 1247 was already in Italy, where he engaged in scientific discussion with Frederick II. Furthermore, if Yehudah in fact was related to that Yehudah b. Solomon, then he was a member of the famous Ibn Susan family, members of which were officials of Alfonso.[14] This might explain how such a young man came to the attention of the then infante and became his physician.

Even before the *Lapidario*, however, Yehudah made a Latin translation of the *Azafeha* (*Ṣafīḥa*) of Azarquiel (the correct form of this name is noted below) together with Guillelmus Anglicus, between 1225 and 1231. The prologue refers to him as "Iuda filius Mosse Alchoen, professione t____, ex merito sciencie astronomus dictus." Hilty suggests *tabib* for the missing word (Arabic *ṭabīb,* or "doctor"). If so, Yehudah was a physician even at this early period; that is not impossible, but the peculiarity of an Arabic word in an otherwise Latin text needs explanation.[15]

Hilty accepts the theory proposed by Millás Vallicrosa that the discrepancy between the Biblioteca Nacional manuscript, which ascribes the translation of the *Azafeha* to Yehudah, and the two European manuscripts, which ascribe it to Guillelmus, is to be explained by Yehudah's making the original adaptation which was then put into polished Latin by Guillelmus. The final resolution of this problem will depend on detailed analysis of the translation and on comparison with other known translations by Yehudah, for such elements as terminology. Yet it is clear that the reference to six years spent in study of the work, and the professions of "doctor" (?) and astronomer, which are attributed to *both* Yehudah and Guillelmus in the manuscripts respectively, must refer originally to Yehudah alone. This leads to the speculation that European copyists merely substituted the name of the better known Guillelmus for the Spanish Jew.

Hilty considers as unproven the suggestion of George Sarton and Millás Vallicrosa that Yehudah was also the translator of Ptolemy's *Tetrabiblon* (*Quatripartito*). Muñoz Sendino, however, accepts this suggestion as definite.[16] This discrepancy also could profit from detailed textual/comparative analysis.

The *Libro conplido en los iudizios de las estrellas,*[17] begun on 12 March 1254, is a translation of Abu'l-Ḥasan ʿAlī b. al-Rijāl, *Kitāb al-bāriʿ fī ahkām al-mujūm.* Here Yehudah is described as "su alfaquim e su mercet," which means that he was granted a privileged status or received special favors from Alfonso.

The *Libro del saber de astrologia* (as Anthony Cárdenas has shown, this is the correct title) was composed approximately during the years 1256 to 1280 in the final redaction. Altogether there are sixteen treatises that make up the *Libro del saber.*[18] Table 5-1 shows the treatises that were either written by Jews or translated solely by a Jewish translator, with the correct title of each book in the order of its appearance, together with the corresponding pages of Rico's edition.

The *XLVIII figuras de la VIII espera,* or *Libro de la ochava sphera* for short (which Hilty insists on calling *Libro de las estrellas fixas*), is based on a work by Abu'l-Ḥusayn ʿAbd al-Raḥmān b. ʿUmar al-Ṣūfī,[19] but greatly

TABLE 5-1.   Treatises Written by Jews or Translated Solely by a Jewish Translator

Yehudah b. Mosheh and Samuel ha-Levi	*XLVIII figuras de la VIII espera*	Rico I, 1–145
(Yehudah b. Moshe?)	*Espera redonda (Alcora)*	I, 153–206
Xosse (Mosse?)	*Cuemo se deuen fazer las armillas del atacyr*	I, 113–222
Çag (author)	*Astrolabio redondo*	II, 206–8
Çag (?)	*Astrolabio llano*	II, 225–92
Çag	*Libro dell ataçir*	II, 295–309
Çag	*Lamina universal*	III, 1–135
Yehudah b. Mosheh	*Azafeha*	III, 135–237
Çag (author)	*Libro de las armellas*	II, 1–79
?	*Laminas de cada una de las siete planetas*	III, 241–84
Çag (author)	*Libro del quadrante*	III, 287–316
?	*Relogio de la piedra*	
Çag (author)	*Relogio de agua*	
Çag (author)	*Relogio del argent vivo*	IV, 3–118
Samuel ha-Levi (author)	*Relogio de la candela*	
Çag (author)	*Palacio de las horas*	
Çag (author)	*Cuemo se debe fazer . . . atarçir*	II, 295–309

revised and with additions by Yehudah.[20] The translation was begun in 1256, and the final redaction completed in 1276. Abraham Zacut, the fifteenth-century Jewish astronomer of Spain whose tables were used by Columbus, mentions this translation by Yehudah in his chronicle (where he also refers to the "wondrous" historical composition of Alfonso).[21]

Great caution is needed in referring to the direct participation of Alfonso himself in these astronomical works, as well as in all of the works composed during his reign. Hilty himself, who discusses this direct participation, seems too naive in accepting it at face value and in assuming that the entire group of translators at Toledo followed the king from Burgos to Victoria, and that the king had the time on these journeys to concern himself with the translation of this book. Alfonso certainly had more important things on his mind in 1276.[22]

The *Alcora*[23] is a translation by Yehudah of a work by Qusṭa Ibn Lūqā.[24] The prologue states: "And he made this book in Arabic, and later the king don Alfonso ordered it translated from Arabic into the Castilian language . . . by Master Johan Daspa his cleric and Hyuda el Cohem his *alfaquim.*" The translators (Yehudah was probably among them) added four introductory chapters not found in the original, on the making and use of the "*espera.*" There is an additional problematic chapter (fol. 38r) on making the *armillas* of the sphere, by "don Xosse nuestro alfaquim." Anthony Cárdenas, who corrected the text to "Mosse," claiming that Manuel Rico y Sinobas erred in reading "Xosse," dismissed the chapter as a later interpolation.[25] Never doubting its authenticity, Hilty argues that the author is the same as Yehudah b. Moses.[26] He holds that the calculations in the chapter reflect the period of astronomical observations between 1263 and 1272, which would seem to prove the authenticity of the chapter (Cárdenas does not disagree on this but still denies the authenticity).

Tentatively, it seems to me arbitrary to challenge the authenticity of the chapter and to consider it a later interpolation. The identification of "Xosse" (as all who have read the text have cited it) or "Mosse" with Yehudah b. Moses ha-Kohen is also problematic. It fails to explain why Yehudah's name is given correctly in the prologue and indeed in all the other works that bear his name, whereas only his father's name is given here in a chapter in the same book. If only one name were used to identify him, why not his own name (Yehudah) instead of that of his father?

Baer conjectured that "Xosse" is the same as the "Yuçaf" (actually Juçef in the text), *su alfaqui* (of Alfonso), mentioned in a document of grants of land by Alfonso to various Jews in Seville in 1253.[27] This is etymologically impossible, however, since in medieval Castilian *x* always represents either *s* or *sh*. The most plausible identification for our "Xosse," therefore, seems to me don Ziza *su alfaquim* in the very same document. This is none other than Ziza Ibn Susan mentioned above. In any case, it is quite clear that he is completely distinct from Yehudah b. Moses ha-Kohen. The grant to Xosse was a substantial one, too, not likely to have been made to the young Yehudah b. Moses. That same document of grants of land, as well as an earlier such charter, also mentions other well-known Jewish officials of Alfonso: don Çuleman [Solomon Ibn Sadoq], don Todros [Abulafia], and Çag el Maestro.[28] Note also that the list uses only first names.

The *Libro de las cruzes* by one "Oueydalla," whom Sarton identifies as Abū Saʿīd ʿUbayd-Allāh, an identification which is problematic,[29] was the next work translated by Yehudah, in 1259. This work affords a better insight into the work of the "collaborators" in Yehudah's translation; the prologue states that it was translated from Arabic into Castilian by Yehudah— "Hyuhda fy de Mosse alChoen Mosca"—and that "Maestra Johan"

(Daspa) arranged it in chapters, since the original work was not so arranged.[30] Certainly in this case, at least, the work of the Christian "collaborator" was obviously minimal.

It is possible also that Yehudah took part in the translation of the *Liber picatrix*. The Spanish manuscript is mutilated, as A. G. Solalinde indicates, but the Latin manuscripts should be examined for possible evidence of Yehudah's participation.

Very valuable is Hilty's conclusion that Yehudah did *not* orally translate the works but rather wrote them out.[31] Hilty calls attention to the marginal notes in the manuscript of *Libro conplido* which prove the collaboration, in that work at least, of a group of translators and an *emendador* (corrector, or editor). In spite of his interesting conjectures about the meaning of this latter term, scholars are still in no position to decide with any certainty what his exact function was, or to determine whether Yehudah wrote the prologues himself (I am inclined to doubt this), or to be certain what parts of any given work come directly from his pen and what from that of others.

Hilty claims that since the Latin translation of the *Azafeha* was done between 1225 and 1231, and since it was the first of Yehudah's works, he must have been born before 1205.[32] This is a faulty conclusion, based on the arbitrary assumption that he must have been at least twenty years old at the time he began his work. The usual age for having completed one's studies (including science and medicine) among Muslims and Jews in Spain was much earlier, however, at least by age eighteen. On the other hand, the fact that Yehudah was still actively working in 1276 renders suspect such an early date (1205) for his birth. It would seem more likely that he was born *after* 1205 than before. Possibly the fact that a second translation of the *Azafeha* was ordered by Alfonso in 1277, and was made by Abraham rather than Yehudah, as discussed below, indicates that Yehudah was either dead or retired from his work in that year. Hilty is probably correct in saying that Yehudah was a resident of Toledo, but his attempt to identify Yehudah's father as the "Rabbi Moses ha-Kohn" of various documents remains unconvincing—not only because of the chronological problems which he himself recognized, but because both the names Moses and ha-Kohen were very common among Jews.[33]

Finally, Hilty's table showing Yehudah's work is reproduced here as Table 5-2.

The famous *Tablas alfonsies*[34] were composed by—not translated but the original work of—Yehudah and the Rabbi Çag who appears below.

TABLE 5-2.   Yehudah's Work*

Date	Title	Author/Translator	Collaborator
1225–1231	*Azafeha* (Latin tr.)	Iuda filius Mosse Alchoen, professione t____, ex merito science astronomus dictus	Guillelmus Anglicus
1243–1250	*Lapidario*	otro su judio que era su fisico Yhuda Mosca el menor	Garci Perez, un su clerigo
1254	*Libro conplido*	Yhuda fi de Mosse Alcohen, su alfaquim e su mercet	Other translators and *emendador*
1256	*Libro de la ochava sphera*	Yhuda el Cohen, so alhaquim	Guillen Arremon Daspa, so clerigo
1259	*Libro del alcora*	Hyuda el cohem so alhaquim	Mestre Johan Daspa, so clerigo
1259	*Libro de las cruzes*	Hyuda fy de Mosse Alchoen Mosca, su alfaquim e su merced	Maestre Johan
1263–1272	*Tablas [astronomicas]*	Yhuda fi de Mose Mosca	Rabiçag
1276	*Libro de las estrellas fixas* (final redaction)	Yhuda sobredicho	Maestre Joan de Mesina, Maestre Joan de Cremona, Samuel

*Revised from Hilty.

The prologue of the Spanish manuscript gives their names as "Yhuda fi de Moses fi de Mosca, e Rabiçag Aben Cayut."[35] Noting that the manuscript is a late fourteenth- or early fifteenth-century copy, Hilty is convinced that an error has been made in both names. The first should be simply Yhuda fi de Moses Mosca, he proposes; the second, Cayut, he correctly assumes is Arabic Sīd and should therefore probably be Cayd. These suggestions appear acceptable.

The exact date of the composition of the *Tablas* is conjectural; Hilty dates it between 1263 and 1272.[36] In fact, those are the dates of the astronomical observations, not necessarily the dates of the composition of the work. The year 1272 is suggested by both Sarton and Millás.[37] In addition to the Spanish manuscript, there is at least one other manuscript of the Latin version, and an extant Hebrew translation which has never been examined. The whole work definitely needs a new edition, taking these problems and findings into consideration.[38]

Many of the tables are dependent upon those of Azarquiel (the correct form of that name apparently should be al-Zarqāllah, not al-Zarkālī).[39] The tables appear to have had an influence also on later Jewish astronomy, and this should be a subject for further research.[40]

About Rabiçag, the author of at least seven of the treatises in the *Libro del saber* collection and the translator of another, we know almost nothing. In the prologue to the *Libro del quadrante* (see below), he is also called Rabiçag Aben Cayut; this raises some doubt as to whether this form of the name in the *Tablas* is, as Hilty thought, erroneous.[41]

Isaac Israeli, a student of Rabbi Asher b. Yehiel of Toledo, composed an astronomical treatise in 1310 in which he briefly mentions Çag. "I examined [calculations of] three eclipses, which Rabbi Isaac *ha-hazzan* b. Sīd prepared and arranged in the city of Toledo at the command of the king don Alfonso, according to what was available to me, [saw] how he prepared them, and [saw them] in his own handwriting." There follows a detailed description of three lunar eclipses of 1266 and 1267, and also a solar eclipse of 1263.[42]

More information is reported by Abraham Zacut in his Hebrew chronicle:

> Then [in the reign of Alfonso] the scholar Rabbi Isaac b. Sīd, *hazzan* of Toledo, prepared tables of the host of the heavens with great precision at the [command] of the king, and their like had not been in precision in the tables and books of astronomy, for Rabbi Isaac Israeli and Rabbi Levi b. Gerson [Gersonides] and all who came after them found in him no fault with them . . . and they are called *zīj* [Arabic for "tables"] *Alfonso,* and from the east to the west, Germany, France, England, all Italy, and Spain, they broke all the former tables and kept these tables to this day.[43]

In the first version of this study, I mistakenly suggested that Zacut may be the don Çag referred to in a letter of Alfonso dated 15 July 1278. I have since discovered that this is not so and that the reference there was to Çag de la Maleha.[44]

Table 5-3 shows the works written and/or translated by Isaac b. Sīd. Unfortunately, dates cannot be definitely assigned to any of these, except 1277 for the *Libro del quadrante*.

The prologue of the *Libro del astrolabio redondo* (fol. 40r to fol. 66r) reads:

> And since there are facts in the aforesaid science, and since we do not have a book in which is told how [an astrolabe] is made, therefore I, the king don Alfonso, order Rabbi Çag to make this, well and clearly done.[45]

The book is divided into three parts: the making of an astrolabe, the nature of the "firmament" of the heavens and its movements, and the use of the astrolabe. Each part is composed of several chapters. This is a major scientific treatise, which deserves careful analysis of topics such as sources utilized and influence on later works.[46]

An interesting feature in the *Libro del astrolabio llano* (fol. 66r) is the use of the letters "a,b,*g*,d" to locate points on a circle. This betrays the Jewish origin of the author, for this series is explicable at this time and place only in terms of the Hebrew alphabet (and not, of course, the Latin or Arabic). Note also his reference to the custom of some Christians (*algunos delos cristianos*) in the marking of their astrolabes (fol. 73v). In the *Libro de lamina universal,* he has already corrected the system of lettering to "a,b,*c*,d."[47]

The *Libro de lamina universal* (fol. 80r) consists of two sections. The first, written by Çag, is the theoretical portion. The second (fol. 83v) is on the use of the *lamina,* as translated by Çag.[48] The prologue reads:

> We wish to speak of how to make the universal table which was done in Toledo, where the table [*açafeha*] of al-Zarqallah was produced. . . . Therefore I, don Alfonso, order my learned Rabbi Çag of Toledo to make this.

The part on the use of the instrument was written by "Aly el fijo de halaf," whom earlier authorities erroneously identified as Abu'l-Ḥasan ʿAlī b. Khalaf Jālib al-Ansārī.[49] José Sánchez Pérez even attributed it to Azarquiel.[50] Cárdenas conjectures that the author may have been Abu'l-Qāsim Khalaf b. Ḥusayn b. Marwān Ibn Ḥayyān (such is the correct spelling); but the name ʿAlī is missing here altogether. In fact, the author was Abu'l-Ḥasan ʿAlī b. Khalaf b. Aḥmad, astronomer of the Banū Dhu'l-Nūn of Toledo, as Millás had already observed.[51]

The *Libro del quadrante con que rectificar* consists of two parts, one on the construction of the quadrant and the other on its use.[52] (Cárdenas

TABLE 5-3.   Works Written and/or Translated by Isaac b.
Sīd

1.   *Tablas alfonsies [astronomicas]* with Yehudah b. Moshe
2.   *Astrolabio redondo**
3.   *Astrolabio llano**
4.   *Lamina universal* (translated)*
5.   *Libro del quadrante**
6.   *Libro de las armellas**
7.   *Libro del ataçir**
8.   *Relogo de la piedra* (?)*
9.   *Relogo del agua**
10. *Relogo del argent vivo**
11. *Palacio de las horas**
12. *Libro (del) quadrante sennero*
13. *Canones* of al-Batānī (? translated)
14. Tables of Almanach of "Azarquiel" (translated)

*Asterisks indicate inclusions in the *Libro del saber.* Question marks
indicate uncertainty.

suggests *rectifican* in the title, but Millás and others read *rectificar*.) To
divide the treatise into two such parts seems to have been the established
pattern of Çag's works. The *Libro de fazer las armellas* (or *armillas*)[53] is on
the construction and use of an instrument of Ptolemy called *dett alhalac*
(Arabic *dat al-ḥalaq,* "sphere of rings") or *armillas* in "Latin"—that is,
Romance, perhaps betraying the Arabic and Jewish use of *latino* to mean
"Romance."[54]

   The *Libro del ataçir* is unfortunately missing several folios at its beginning, including the prologue—the text begins at the end of chapter one. It
is impossible to be sure, therefore, but the attribution of the work to Çag is
probable.[55] The same is true of the *Relogio de la piedra,* which lacks the first
three folios.[56] I am unaware of anyone else who has attributed this work to
Çag; and I would hesitate to be so bold as to suggest it, except that it comes
in order in the manuscript with other works by him and all of the other
treatises on clocks except one are by him. Perhaps here as well, careful
linguistic analysis and comparison would solve the problem. The other
treatises on clocks by Çag are the *Relogio del agua,* the *Relogio del argent vivo,*
and the *Palacio de las horas.* The last is in many ways the most interesting,
being a sun clock with twelve windows, one for each daylight hour.[57]

   Because of the insight and diligent research of Millás Vallicrosa, without whom our knowledge of the Jewish culture of medieval Spain would be considerably diminished, we now know of Çag's composition of the *Libro que es de saber como puede omne rectificar el quadrante sennero*, or *Book for knowing how a man can verify the solitary quadrant*.[58] The same manuscript contains the translation of the *Canones* of al-Battanī (the authenticity of its attribution is now in doubt), and Çag's translation of the astronomical tables of Azarquiel.[59] Neither of these important manuscripts has yet been edited. David Romano has challenged the attribution of the translation of al-Battanī, perhaps on good grounds, though he does not mention Millás's study cited here. Romano's claim that Isaac did not know Arabic at all, however, has absolutely no merit.

The least-known of the Jewish collaborators in the *Libro del saber* is Samuel ha-Levi. Steinschneider, usually a reliable source of information even when all others fail, seems in this case to be the cause of the erroneous name Abulafia for Samuel, which is still repeated by scholars.[60] There was one and only one eminent Abulafia family in Spain, which numbered among its ranks several ministers and officials of Alfonso, as well as rabbis and the great poet Ṭodros.[61] There is no evidence for a Samuel in this family, however, and it is incorrect to assume that every Jew named ha-Levi, an extremely common name, was automatically Abulafia. We may conjecture—but it is only that and hardly worth serious consideration— that our Samuel was an ancestor of the famous Samuel ha-Levi of Toledo, *tesorero mayor* of Pedro I and patron of the famous synagogue of Toledo.[62] Samuel translated, with Yehudah b. Moses ha-Kohen, the *Libro de la ochava sphera* discussed earlier under Yehudah. In addition, he composed—not translated as Steinschneider said, followed by Sarton—the *Relogio de la candela*.[63] There he is called simply "Samuel el levi de Toledo nuestro iudio."

We come finally to Abraham, *alfaquim* (physician, in this case) of Alfonso. Once again, Steinschneider has caused confusion, by identifying him with Abraham Judaeus Tortuosensis (actually Abraham b. Shem Ṭov b. Isaac of Tortosa, active around 1254–1264), who translated Abu'l-Qāsim Khalaf b. ʿAbbās "al-Zahrawi" (for Ibn Sarābī), the court physician of al-Ḥakam II of Córdoba.[64] The most probable identification of our Abraham, almost certainly correct, was made by Evelyn Procter, who conjectured that he is identical with "don Abraham fisico," later the court physician also of Alfonso's son Sancho IV.[65] (Romano erroneously identifies him as Abraham b. Susan.) He is therefore Abraham Ibn Waqar, member of another eminent family of Jewish diplomats, courtiers, physicians, and officials, whose activities extended over a long period of time in the courts of Spain. He was not only physician to both Alfonso and his son Sancho but also a close personal friend of the latter. Together with his brother "don Zag" (Isaac), he was present at the deathbed of Sancho and received the king's last will and testament. The scene is movingly described by Alfonso's nephew Juan Manuel.[66] Baer claims that Abraham was captured and held hostage by the rebels in the struggle between Sancho and his father, but he cites no source for this, and I have not been able to verify it.[67]

The most famous work for which Abraham was responsible, although the original is unfortunately lost, preserved now only in Latin and French translations from his Spanish, is the translation of *al-Miʿrāj* (based on Sura 70 of the Qu'rān) called *Escala de Mahoma,* done in 1263.[68] His second known work, produced sometime after 1270 at the order of Alfonso, is a cosmography (*Kitāb fī hayʾat al-ʿalam*) by Ibn al-Haytham.[69] Finally, in 1277 at the command again of Alfonso, Abraham made a new translation of the *Azafeha* of Azarquiel, revising and correcting the translation by the Christian Fernando of Toledo; it appears in the *Libro del saber.*[70] There is no justification, incidentally, for the claim of Castro that Fernando was a *converso.* Nor is it necessarily true that, merely because Alfonso was in Burgos when he commissioned the translation by Abraham, we should conclude that Abraham was born in Burgos, as Procter has claimed.[71]

Millás has concluded that Abraham's translation of the *Azafeha* is more faithful to the original Arabic text than either the Hebrew translation done by Profiat (Judah b. Makhir) Ibn Tibbon or the Latin one by Guillelmus Anglicus and that it is "absolutely in harmony with the Arabic source."[72] This judgment coincides generally with Millás's positive view of all the Alfonsine translations made by the Jewish translators.

It is good to end this brief summary of the contributions of Jewish scientific translators and authors to the Alfonsine corpus on such a positive tone. The influence of both the translations and the original compositions upon later Jewish and non-Jewish scientific treatises, the significance of the Jewish contribution to the development of the Spanish language, and the relationship of these translators and authors to the broader picture of Jewish translation and literary activity prior to and during the period of Alfonso el Sabio remain to be considered in more detail.

John E. Keller

6. Drama, Ritual, and Incipient Opera in Alfonso's *Cantigas*

What may be regarded as a peculiar flaw, a mysterious lacuna, and a downright puzzle as concerns medieval Spanish culture is the apparent absence of drama in either Latin or Castilian in the thirteenth and fourteenth centuries, except in Catalonia. Can it be true of Castile, a kingdom ruled in the thirteenth century by an enlightened monarch, Alfonso X el Sabio, that only one piece of drama existed? Dramas flourished elsewhere in Europe, particularly in France, writes Ernst Curtius, due to the unbroken continuity running from classical times through the Renaissance.[1] Why not in Spain? I believe that the same continuity of drama also existed there. Yet our greatest scholars still maintain that no medieval drama in Latin, and only one in a vernacular, was available. Alan Deyermond, whose scholarship all respect, states that "the only vernacular play before the fifteenth century is that known as the *Auto de los reyes magos*."[2] I must respectfully disagree with him, even in the face of a definite lack of extant plays between the twelfth-century *Auto* and Gómez Manrique's *Representacion del nacimiento de Nuestro Señor*. (The latter dramatizes the same subject matter as the *Auto,* each poet following the gospel account in Matthew 2:1–12.)

Scholars have made it clear that in other cultures premedieval and medieval dramatic activity was present—Clifford Davis, William Tyedeman, Bernadette Rey-Flaud, Richard Trexler, and O. B. Hardison, the last of whom has taken so much interest in the *Drama de Elche*.[3] The wisdom of such experts is comforting as I begin this treatment of drama in Spain which is based upon what can be regarded as a combination of intelligent speculation and plausible observation of drama, as depicted in some of the illuminations of the *Cantigas de Santa Maria* produced under the patronage of King Alfonso.

If one is to provide some background for this king's interest in drama, he must begin with the survivals of Roman drama after the fall of Rome. Some of the plays of Terence, Plautus, and Seneca survived in written form (and perhaps also in oral tradition) into the Middle Ages.[4] Uneducated mimes must have inherited the traditions of late Roman theatre and acted in what may be considered to have been a kind of folk drama. When Christianity replaced paganism in the period erroneously called the Dark Ages, the clergy quickly realized the value of drama as a didactic tool for implanting and strengthening religious lessons. The church seems to have depended upon profane drama then, since it may have been the only drama it could use as a model. The time came when pietistic drama superseded the profane, of course, leading to the production of those tropes which some experts regard as the beginnings of European theatre. Some even see in the Mass the influence of earlier non-Christian rituals and believe that, without those rituals, the Mass could not have developed along the lines it did. Since Curtius's theory of continuity surely included Spain, and since sufficient proof can be marshaled of drama's continuity in the peninsula, I cannot accept that drama was unknown in Castile—or that, if known, it was stifled.

Before treating the possibilities of drama in thirteenth-century Castile, it is well to ask what Alfonso must have gleaned about drama from the past. The best references to drama in Latin would have been St. Jerome's adaptation of Eusebius's *Universal Chronicle,* but Jerome did not produce a systematic use of chronology for a Christian theory of literature. It was St. Isidore's *Etymologies,* finished in the seventh century before Spanish vernaculars had emerged from Vulgar Latin, which offered the best explanations of drama of the past and quite possibly of the survival of Roman theatre still extant in southern Spain. Seville and considerable territory in the south preserved close ties with the eastern empire, and Constantinople periodically sent troops to keep at bay the incursions of Visigothic rulers.[5] Isidore sent his brother St. Leander to Athens for books. In the *Etymologies,* Isidore described the theatre, the orchestra or stage, and how a narrator (often called an *auctor*) recited or read lines while mimes silently acted. This form of drama, the theatre of mimes, survived from the classical period through the so-called Dark Ages into medieval and renaissance Europe, surely including Spain. And some varieties of such drama, read or recited by a narrator, added original touches. Some mimes did not continue the age-old silent form of theatrical presentation: they began to speak or sing their parts.[6]

Alfonso had the knowledge imparted by Isidore and Isidore's sources, then, and he demonstrated a great deal of interest in various aspects of theatre. His great code of laws, the *Siete partidas* or *Seven Divisions* of law—

the most widely disseminated code, since it affected law in all parts of Spain's possessions, including regions that eventually became part of the United States—dictated certain restrictions and permissions regarding the presentation of plays. Some researchers argue that Alfonso and his legists were translating or paraphrasing rules regulating drama from books not written in Spanish—for example, from ecclesiastical decretals. To some extent this may be true; but even so, it is obvious that the *Partidas* were aimed at a Spanish audience. Would the Learned King have cluttered his legal code with prohibitions against nonexistent varieties of drama? Would he have employed a Spanish designation to identify such plays as the *juegos de escarnio,* which his subjects knew were farces—plays, that is, which were often obscene and even blasphemous? Surely he condemned such dramas because he saw in them a present and active means of disseminating not only bad taste but even dangerous ideas.

The *Partidas* treat secular drama, of which Alfonso disapproved, and went so far as to suggest penalties for clerics who acted in such plays. These laws also offer considerable comment regarding religious drama—nativity plays, shepherd plays, and resurrection dramas. These were to be presented only in cities, under the jurisdiction of the higher clergy. Plays not monitored by such authorities were apparently forbidden. After warning priests against playing dice, entering taverns, and any association with gamblers, Alfonso continues:

> Nor should they be involved with farcical plays [i.e., *juegos de escarnio*] so that people may attend them and hear them. If other men perform these things, ecclesiastics should not be present, because many evil speeches are uttered and indecencies committed there; nor should any such things take place in churches, for we have previously declared that those who act in this manner should dishonorably be ejected from them, since the church of God is made to pray in, and not for the purpose of uttering farcical speeches.

The king then recommends some drama as beneficent:

> There are certain representations, however, which ecclesiastics have a right to perform, for instance that of the birth of Our Lord Jesus Christ, in which is shown how the angel appeared to the shepherds and told them that Jesus Christ was born; and also that of his appearance, and how the three kings of the Magi came to adore him; and the one relating to his resurrection, which shows that he was crucified, and on the third day arose. Representations of this kind, which induce men to do good and have devotion for the faith, ecclesiastics can perform; and they are also beneficial, for they cause men to remember

that the other events actually happened. These things should be done in an orderly way, and with great devotion, and should take place in large cities where there are archbishops or bishops, and either by their command, or by those of others who occupy their places; and they should not take place in villages, or in vile places, or for the sake of earning money by means of them.

Such prohibitions of secular drama, and to some extent of religious drama when the latter were unmonitored, would not have been written into the king's important code of law, unless such plays existed.[7]

The *Partidas* were not promulgated until the reign of Alfonso's grandson, between 1310 and 1350, and not printed until 1491. Thus they did not become the law of the land during Alfonso's lifetime. Many communities may not have been aware of the prohibitions against drama or even aware that the higher clergy were to regulate it. Although the *Partidas* (which we now believe Alfonso produced as a guide for future laws) were studied in university law schools to the extent that they were becoming law without formal promulgation, not even this would have made such unpromulgated laws known and accepted everywhere.[8] There is reason to doubt, therefore, that the *Partidas* did much to smother drama in far-flung parishes in which no higher clergy or their representatives were present. Nor can it be that the ubiquitous *juglares* and actors in *juegos de escarnio* could have been monitored or would have surrendered their means of earning a living. Illegal forms of entertainment have always been integral parts of all cultures and, in spite of prohibitions, have prospered.

Commenting upon the early lack of drama in Latin or in Spanish, Deyermond states that the regulations against drama by the monks of Cluny tended to smother medieval drama in Spain.[9] But Cluny's influence was strong mainly in northern areas of Alfonso's kingdom. Moreover, Cluny in its homeland of France did not curtail the rise, development, and flourishing of great dramatic activity either secular or pietistic; nor was Cluny's influence great in Catalonia. The scholar must search for better reasons than Cluny's disinterest in or antagonism toward plays, in order to explain satisfactorily the dearth of drama in most of medieval Spain before the fifteenth century.

Dramas have usually been created for living audiences, and those who composed them in the Middle Ages were interested surely in live drama rather than in plays written to be read. Plays, whether clerical or secular, were not composed by great authors whose works would have been preserved. It is probable that most plays, in both oral and written form, were learned by rote by actors, many of whom could not have read a play if a written script had been available; and most of what is not written tends to disappear. If the *Auto* had not survived by some fortuitous circumstance, some scholars would opine that there was not even one vernacular drama in Spain before the fifteenth century, only plays written in Latin in Catalonia. Aside from the lack of extant drama, other factors should be taken into consideration: the abandonment or destruction of those churches with dramatic traditions, the loss of written dramas when these had existed, and the death or removal of priests who favored drama and their replacement by others who had no interest in plays (perhaps a sign of the influence of Cluny).

As to the *Auto,* Deyermond states, with good reason, that a Gascon living in Toledo may have translated it from his own French dialect. He suggests that since the play seems to be a translation, one might prefer to think of it as not true Spanish literature. But *Calila e Digna,* and the *Libro de los engaños* translated from Arabic, and *Barlaam e Josafat* translated from Latin along with Berceo's *Milagros* and *Vidas,* have always been regarded as genuine Spanish literature.[10]

My own theories concerning medieval Spanish drama have not been influenced greatly by previous scholarship, since there is so little of it. Aside from what Isidore and Alfonso's *Partidas* reveal, I have relied upon the suggestions of only a few scholars with regard to drama depicted in the miniatures of the *Cantigas de Santa Maria* and upon my own suppositions concerning these illustrations. Alfonso, always avant-garde, seems to have arranged for portrayals of drama, ritual, and incipient opera to be painted in many of the miniatures, especially in those of the Códice Rico, manuscript T.I.1 at the Escorial library. This monarch's originality and innovativeness concerning art has been stressed by José Guerrero Lovillo and concerning drama and art by Ana Domínguez Rodríguez, each of whom is a renowned art historian.[11] Ana Domínguez particularly inspired me to expand my studies of art and drama in the miniatures illustrating the *Cantigas* miracles into a study of those illustrating the cantigas *de loor* or songs of praise. She states (my translation): "In these representations of the troubadour king [Alfonso], we see him standing, kneeling, pointing to the evangelical scene, always in the presence of the docile group of courtiers who listen attentively to him; are perhaps some of these scenes a graphic testimony of dramatic presentation, in which the king and his courtiers act in the palace's own chapel or in some of its annexes?" I shall attempt to answer her question affirmatively through detailed interpretations of certain pages of miniatures, relating these to the texts that accompany them.

I am equally grateful to Maricel Presilla, with whom I have exchanged ideas on drama in the miniatures. Her insights into Alfonso's political ideology, as she sees it demonstrated in the *Cantigas* as to text and miniatures, may serve as an important link between drama and Alfonso's intent in producing this remarkable work.[12] She believes that Alfonso intended to broadcast his message—that is, his ideology—insofar as possible, and to attempt to reach the entire social structure of his realm. And what better way than the use of drama, the most apt tool for indoctrination, aided by the pleasure obtained through the threefold impact of presentation—visual, verbal, and musical? After all, large audiences might have seen some of the cantigas staged, while the number of viewers of the precious codices must of necessity have been limited to a few favored individuals.

Richard Kinkade states convincingly that a kind of theatre-in-the-round accompanied sermons. He and I have also taken exploratory steps in the investigation of drama in some of the *Cantigas* miniatures that illustrate miracles. From these studies, it is clear that Alfonso and his collaborators brought staging techniques into book illustration, especially in the form of "dramatic arches" so convincingly treated by Otto Pächte, which can be seen in such pages of miniatures as those illustrating cantigas 13, 18, 20, 42, 59, and 63, to cite only a few.[13] The device of the arches, often used outside Spain in manuscripts, in triptychs, and on stage, could make a scene enclosed by arches in a book acquire the characteristics of a *tableau vivant*. This concentrates the viewers' attention and leads them to feel that they are actually observing a dramatic event, or even participating in it. The viewers of Alfonso's miniatures would have known that arches were used to frame theatrical tableaux or scenes in medieval staging. If indeed Alfonso's viewers had not observed such arches in their own Castile—and surely they did observe them there—those who traveled abroad, especially to France, would have seen them in dramas.

The device of the dramatic arches in Alfonso's miniatures may with reason be regarded as an adaptation of stagecraft to the art of illumination. Quite probably, those who viewed the miniatures were well aware of such adaptation, savoring therefore various typological elements modern viewers have not observed. Since the miniatures are perforce static representations, whose dynamism depends upon the intrinsic properties of book art and drama to stimulate viewer imagination, one can believe that the creators of these pictures, through the conscious application of dramatic stratagems or theatrical techniques, strove to enhance their vitality and animation, of which arches would be one of the most important devices.[14]

In connection with the miniatures illustrating miracles and not songs
of praise, I elsewhere mention another factor, which suggests dramatic
presentation. "If so much French influence is felt in other Spanish artistic
manifestations, why not in drama based upon the miracles" in the *Cantigas
de Santa Maria?*[15] Nor is it difficult to imagine the *Miracle de Théophile*
staged in Spain. Many other miracles might just as well have been adapted
to drama. In fact, any might have been dramatized, except those whose
miniatures depicted events and scenes too vast for staging—ships at sea in
cantiga 36, a hunt in 142, or an entire city under siege in 99. Nor has it been
pointed out previously that the statues of the Madonna and the Child in
certain miniatures assume different positions in separate panels or scenes on
the same page. These differences are not due to the fact that the images are
supposed to have moved, because in a case such as cantiga 18 the images are
no more than parts of the background scene. And yet in this cantiga both
figures move, in the sense that they change position. If an artist were
sketching, as he watched a dramatic presentation, he might have caught the
actress who served in the play and the child who portrayed the infant Jesus,
as they shifted positions in order to rest.[16]

When I began to study the cantigas *de loor* in the *Cantigas* for traces of
the visualization of drama, guided by the observations of Ana Domínguez,
I realized how correct she was in her suppositions and how helpful it would
have been had she discussed this matter in more detail. Since her primary
interest lies in art history, however, it is understandable that she did not
elaborate upon ideas concerning drama as it may be depicted in Alfonso's
miniatures. Songs of praise appear in far fewer numbers than do miracles.
Every tenth cantiga is a cantiga *de loor;* but sometimes overlooked is the fact
that, toward the end of the manuscript, the number of such songs increases.
After number 399, which is a miracle, there are twenty-six additional numbers and, of these, eighteen are songs of praise.

We know that the *Cantigas* were to be sung to the accompaniment of
some sixty musical instruments—trumpets, finger cymbals, drums, bag-
pipes, recorders, and others which (though illustrated in the Escorial
manuscript B.I.2) have not been identified. Alfonso in his last will and
testament decreed that on feast days of the Virgin in the church in which his
remains would lie—the cathedral of Seville—cantigas were to be sung,
presumably to the accompaniment of instruments. To this day, these instructions are occasionally carried out.[17]

Singing, especially when more than one singer performs and when
dialogue is present, can result in a production not far removed from opera.

Modern groups of professional vocalists and instrumentalists, such as the Waverly Consort and the Trio Live Oak, which often feature the *Cantigas,* present both miracles and songs of praise in a fashion which may parallel that employed under Alfonso's patronage. One singer narrates the miracle or song of praise while one or more repeat the refrain to the accompaniment of music.

This leads back to earlier remarks about intent, a question that has never been settled to the satisfaction of all researchers. Alfonso, it was noted, desired to make all his works known to his subjects. He seems to have been exceptionally anxious to do so in the case of the *Cantigas.* Presilla asserts that Alfonso wanted to use the *Cantigas* as a form of propaganda, through which he could bring to all his people certain aspects of life and belief not supported by the church. Perhaps, she suggests, Alfonso depicts the Blessed Virgin as a kind of iconoclast who enabled her devotees to rise above or circumvent various ecclesiastical regulations that people found difficult to obey—prohibitions against signs of excessive grief, the Virgin as panacea against the terrors of purgatory and hell, and her willingness to save her devotees from damnation even when their sins were virtually unpardonable, as for example with incest, murder, and theft.[18] In other words, Santa Maria offered salvation and comfort to her devotees; and even though these people realized that she could not, or would not, come to the aid of everybody, she had done so for many, leaving each devotee with the hope that he or she out of many might be the lucky one. Presilla's convincing suggestion is that Alfonso, through the Virgin of his *Cantigas,* hoped to draw his subjects from under the complete influence of ecclesiastical rule.

To return to drama, as depicted in some of the cantigas *de loor* as well as in some of the miracles, it will be necessary to see how the king injected himself into his work. Joseph Snow has written extensively on the troubadour persona of Alfonso in the *Cantigas,* adding to our understanding of Alfonso's own intensely intimate connections with his work.[19] Snow derived his findings from a study of the text of both varieties of cantigas, but he did not relate what the text states to what the miniatures illustrate. What follows can make even more evident Alfonso's human and personal ties with his miracles and hymns.

In some of the miniatures illustrating songs of praise, Alfonso can often be seen playing the role of narrator or troubadour, enabling the viewer to visualize dramas in progress. It would seem that the avant-garde king brought the attributes and presentation of the theatre of mime into the miniatures and even changed the mimes into singers. He had no need to invent such varieties of drama; the continuity extolled by Curtius had carried such plays across the centuries from Roman times.[20] Curtius even states that in some plays not only the narrator but also the actors spoke or sang. Ana Domínguez writes:

> The king seems to act before his public, simply to recite the poems, or rather to explicate them. This pertains, in all cases, to every tenth cantiga or song of praise, more complex than the miracles as to being understood by the ignorant public. Their originality is great, and I believe I can affirm that it is a case unique in medieval art: the presence of a king in pictures which show him reciting or explicating his poems for the Virgin to a group of courtiers and even acting as though in an authentic religious or liturgical theatre in the palace.[21]

One might respectfully add two concepts. The first is that Alfonso is not always playing the role of narrator, explicator, or troubadour with courtiers. In some of the miniatures, he speaks to people who, by their costume, are not of the nobility—to women in number 90, to men not dressed as noblemen in 80, to clergy and physicians in 40, and to the clergy and nobles in 180. Secondly, the statement that the cantigas *de loor* might have been too complex for comprehension among the general public contradicts Presilla's and my own opinion that the king was attempting to reach all strata of his subjects. Intent again must be taken into consideration.

Specific pages of miniatures must now be considered, and it will be necessary therefore to describe detailed aspects of their composition. Each page that illustrates a miracle or a song of praise is divided into six parts, or panels (all except the first cantiga, which contains eight). Much has been written about the influence of six-paneled triptychs upon the miniatures.[22] These are not the only models Alfonso's artists might have seen and utilized. Urban T. Holmes mentions that, in a French *jeu* dealing with the resurrection, the *décor simultané* was arranged so as to appear in six scenes to be viewed from left to right, as is true in the miniatures of the *Cantigas*.[23] This offers further support for drama's influence and how Alfonso and his artists utilized it.

The page of miniatures that visualizes cantiga 1 will now be studied in detail (Fig. 6-1). Viewed as a whole as one might see a multifaceted tapestry or dramatic presentation, in eight scenes or tableaux which present important incidents in the Virgin's life, this page shows the annunciation, the nativity, the visit of the angels to the shepherds, the Magi and their gifts, the Magdalene's report to the Virgin that Jesus has risen, the ascension of the

Figure 6-1. The first cantiga of praise of Holy Mary, depicting the seven joys she had from her son.

Lord, Pentecost, and the coronation of St. Mary in heaven. Every panel, as is the case with all but a few pages of miniatures, is captioned by a brief statement as to what is illustrated; and these captions may well be what a narrator, in many instances Alfonso himself, recited. Alfonso simply *is* the narrator or troubadour; this is made manifest not only by the king's appearance, but also by the first-person wording of the poem. This indicates strongly that such presentations—verbal, musical, and visual—are modeled upon drama. Since each of the eight panels visualizes what is reminiscent of a dramatic tableau, it seems worthwhile to explicate the contents of each panel, so as to compare and contrast visualization and verbalization and to relate how these pictures seem to illustrate staging. I translate the wording of each caption and remind the reader that all captions and all pages in the manuscript, together with a transcription of all the cantigas and their translations into Spanish, can be found in José Filgueira Valverde, and that Kathleen Kulp-Hill has translated all of the cantigas— text and captions—into English.[24]

If readers think of Alfonso as the narrator or troubadour, who states (might not Alfonso have sung?) what each panel explains in its caption, they will sense the dramatic quality. Panel 1 (*How the Angel Greeted St. Mary*) clearly tells what the viewer of the miniature is to see. Dramatic arches play a significant role, just as arches did in actual dramas outside Spain and possibly within her borders. The central arch encompasses a large jardiniere in which grows a five-blossomed lily, the flower symbolic of Mary's virginity and of her five joys. Ana Domínguez writes:

> It is the typical iconography of the thirteenth century. The only Alfonsine peculiarity lies in the stage setting [*escenario*] with its huge flower container. Here also we can accept a theatrical setting. This is not certain, but that it is different from such French representations is certain.[25]

It will be recalled that the account of the annunciation in Scripture (Luke 1:26–38) states that Gabriel visited the Virgin in Nazareth of Galilee. Alfonsine artists usually painted the city mentioned, so one is easily persuaded that, when they did not do so in this miniature, they were painting a theatrical setting.

The words of the cantiga expand upon the statement in the caption. Speaking in the first person, the narrator (surely Alfonso) in stanza 2 puts words into the mouth of the angel.

> Therefore, I wish to begin
>   with how She was hailed

By Gabriel when he went to summon her:
  "Oh, Blessed Virgin, beloved of God,
  You now bear within you him
Who will save the world,
  and your kinswoman,
  Elizabeth, who doubted,
  is thereby proven wrong."[26]

The threefold impact intended by Alfonso and his collaborators—verbal, visual, and melodic—must have been impressive to those who were present when the cantiga miniature was viewed by a group, while singers and instrumentalists rendered the hymn.

Panel 2 (*How St. Mary Gave Birth to Jesus Christ and Placed Him in a Manger*) presents a simple nativity scene of the kind presented in churches in accordance with the regulations of the *Partidas*. Its setting on stage would have been feasible. The arches lead the eye from left to right, offering a dramatic succession of events or incidents. Under the left-hand arch, St. Joseph sits, gazing into the central arch which frames the manger placed beside the Virgin's bed. The luxurious quality of the Virgin's bed in that humble stable, with its fine covers and its canopy, leads me to believe that the miniaturist was copying a scene in a drama or ritual in the palace, in which Alfonso ordered the Virgin to be portrayed not in the bed of straw she would have had to use in Bethlehem but in a bed worthy of the future Queen of Heaven.

The two animals, the ox and the ass often seen in nativity scenes, are also presented in a fashion uncharacteristic of cantiga miniatures. Alfonso's artists were accustomed to paint human and animal bodies in their complete forms, unless for some reason some of their parts were concealed by a wall or other object. In this panel, the artist could easily have depicted the entire animals, following the usual habit of depicting everything in great detail, since there is space for both creatures. Why are only their heads portrayed? I suggest that in dramatic scenes indoors the presence of living farm animals would have been impractical, not to mention the inconvenience and impropriety. In stage settings, where animals were needed, painted animals or parts of animals may well have been utilized by those who set stages. Having viewed such stage props, the artist would have sensed the connection between drama and book-art, and would have accepted the convention and savored it. Indeed, he may have painted the scene just as Alfonso had staged it.

The words of the hymn itself narrate more than the scene in the panel; even so, they describe the most important concepts of the Holy

Family's arrival at the stable. The narrator speaks in the first person again in stanza 3:

> Then I wish to relate to you
>   how She arrived in Bethlehem,
> being weary. She took shelter
>   in the gates of the city
>   and thereafter gave birth
> to Jesus Christ, like a poor woman.
>   She laid him in a manger,
>   where they provide the barley,
> and they place him
>   among the beasts of the field.

Panel 3 (*How the Angel Appeared to the Shepherds*) is another *tableau vivant* and shows similarities to a staged scene. There is a conventionalized landscape. Why did the artists limit themselves, painting so little of the landscape, when characteristically the out-of-doors was painted more realistically? Were they copying a staged scene? In this panel, there are no arches. Only one angel appears—not in the sky but standing on a ridge. The angel holds an unrolled scroll. The two shepherds gesticulate, as would actors on stage. The two dogs, the goat, and the rather numerous flock of sheep convey a rural atmosphere. On a stage, the animals would have been represented by artificial ones or by pictures of animals. The wording of the stanza that matches this illustration relates more than the picture reveals, as was the case in panel 2. Neither the shepherds nor the animals are mentioned, but we read words familiar to all Christians, which the angels sang, as the first-person narrator here voices them:

> Also I must not forget
>   how the angels sang a hymn
> of praise to God
>   and "peace on earth,"
>   nor how the star showed
> the way to the three kings
>   from far away
>   by which they came
> to offer their gifts
>   precious and rare.

Panel 4 (*How the Three Kings Gave Their Offering to Jesus Christ*) reminds one of the church tableaux also. Dramatic arches are important stratagems here, since they divide the panel into two separate incidents in time. Framed by the arch at the left, a man holds the reins of the horses belonging to the kings. The central arch encapsulates the kings. All are white men, without the African king so popular later. The two blond kings stand near one another and seem to converse, as one holds up his offering and with his other hand points to the Virgin and the Child in the central and right-hand arches, providing one of the types of visual transition so prevalent in medieval narrative art. The oldest king, white-haired, kneels and extends his gift into the right-hand arch, emphasizing transition from arch to arch. In that arch, the Virgin is seated on the bed, and the Child, no longer depicted as an infant, stands in his mother's lap and extends a hand as though to receive the gift. The verbalization, as seen in the stanza above, includes the events of this panel also.

Panel 5 (*How the Magdalene Tells St. Mary that Her Son Has Risen*) contains elements that come closest of all to the depiction of staging, since what the miniature depicts, as well as what the verses relate, is reminiscent of a *Quem quaeritis* play. In tropes, as is well known, a coffin or sometimes nothing more than a small chest represented the tomb in which the Lord was laid to rest. The concept of a coffin, rather than a tomb, had become an accepted staging device. A tomb of the dimensions described in all four Gospels would have been too difficult to provide on stage; hence, the coffin in lieu of it. Recall that in Scripture Jesus' tomb had been sealed by a great stone, so heavy that it required several men to roll it aside. It was on this stone that the Magdalene and the other Mary saw the angel seated (Matthew 28:1–10). The miniaturist could easily have painted a tomb large enough to contain several people; if he had so depicted Jesus' burial place, however, he might have confused the viewers, since those who knew *Quem quaeritis* plays would have been accustomed to seeing the open casket with the angel seated on its lid. And so the scene was painted, a scene possibly taken from the living drama mentioned in the *Partidas* and played in much of Christendom.

The angel seated on the coffin's lid appears in the left-hand arch. The right-hand arch frames three women with halos, one of whom is the Magdalene who kneels with her hands steepled in devotion before the Virgin; the Magdalene delivers to the Virgin the message that her Son has risen. The words of stanza 5, told in the first person by the narrator who puts the words into the angel's mouth, is very reminiscent of drama:

Another event I wish to relate,
   which was told by the

Magdalene, of how she
  perceived the stone
    rolled away from the sepulcher
and guarded by an angel,
  who spoke to her and said:
  "Unhappy woman, be comforted,
for Jesus, whom you come to seek,
  arose this morning."

Panel 6 (*How Jesus Christ Ascended to the Skies in a Cloud*) would have needed little staging. Nothing would have been required beyond eleven kneeling apostles and an actress or statue to portray the Virgin—with, of course, artificial clouds and paintings of two angels flying between them with their scrolls.

Panel 7 (*How the Holy Spirit Came Above the Apostles*) contains three arches. The left-hand arch shelters six apostles; the central one frames the Virgin; and the right-hand one contains the other six disciples. The Holy Ghost is portrayed as a white dove, from whose beak crimson streams of light fall upon the apostles. The miniaturist may have modeled the panel upon a dramatic tableau or may have simply depicted Pentecost from his own imagination. In the sky above the human figures, three clouds appear. The one in the center represents the ascension, but the Lord is not seen in it. Between the clouds, which appear at the right and the left of the central cloud, fly two angels carrying scrolls which announce the event. Stanza 6 matches very well what the miniature displays. The first-person narrator directly addresses his hearers:

And I also wish to tell
  the great and wondrous joy
She had when She saw
  the luminous cloud lift up
  Her son, and when he had
ascended, angels appeared
  walking among the crowd
  of bewildered people, saying
"Thus he will come to judge.
  This is a proven thing."

Panel 8 (*How Jesus Christ Crowned St. Mary in Heaven*) might have been sketched from a dramatic piece, but it is more likely that the miniaturist used as a model some picture or tapestry or else created it from his own imagination. The poem parallels what is visualized:

And, in God's name, I must
   not fail to mention
how She was crowned. When She
   had passed from this world,
   He took Her to be united with
Him in heaven to sit at His side
   and be called Queen, Daughter, Mother
   and Handmaiden. Hence
She must help us
   for She is our Advocate.

Ana Domínguez was the first to describe this panel. "Heaven is represented in a scientific manner: we see the successive spheres, not the nine mentioned to us in the *Libros del saber de astronomia* of Alfonso X but only two, filled with a series of angels, and the great sphere with Christ and the Virgin seated on their thrones at the moment of the Coronation."[27]

Another of the most interesting pages of miniatures is that which illustrates cantiga 90 (see Fig. 6-2). It is here, along with the illustrations of cantiga 1, that the probability of drama is best represented. The page is unusual also in that the spaces normally occupied by captions are blank. This is a great pity, since not all experts agree as to what the six panels represent. The narrator-troubadour, definitely Alfonso since he is clearly depicted, speaks directly to the Virgin, telling her, "You were alone, Virgin, without a companion." The first stanza relates that she was alone when Gabriel spoke to her and that she conceived alone—that is, by herself, with no companion—and that she destroys the devil. But the illustration shows her holding the Child in her arms, and one wonders why this panel was not given second place, since in panel 2 we see the angel speaking to her and telling her that she has conceived. In this second panel, he stands under the left-hand arch as he speaks to the Virgin, who occupies the entire central arch. It is in the right-hand arch that we see the devil. Stanza 1, then, is illustrated by two panels. Connie Scarborough treats the matter of such differences between text and miniatures.[28]

What appears to be staging is seen in panel 3 which is divided into two parts by a band of alternating castles and lions *rampant*. The right-hand division is separated into two dramatic arches. The Virgin is under the right-hand arch, seated with seven women, each with a halo. Ana Domínguez believes that this scene represents "St. Mary, now an adolescent, in the temple in which she is being educated with her companions."[29] The women seem not to be adolescents, however, and the Virgin, though

Figure 6-2. Cantiga 90, hymn of praise.

young, is a mature woman. Why, too, is she accompanied by so many women, when the poem repeatedly states that she was always alone? What seems to be a stage appears in the left-hand division of the panel. On this stage the women sit. A stairway leads up to the stage, and underneath the steps appear three closed doors. To Ana Domínguez these seem to be the trapdoors placed beneath stages to provide entrances and exits for devils and other actors. It is difficult to imagine what else these doors could represent—leading one to suppose, with reason, that the artist had a stage before him as he painted or that he had a stage in mind.

The right-hand side of this panel may also depict a stage setting. It too is divided into two arches. Both appear to contain the depiction of a stage with doors beneath. In the left-hand arch sits a Jewish priest who looks into the right-hand arch under which the Virgin is seated while she embroiders. It would be possible to continue to develop the thesis that the cantigas *de loor* were staged or that the artists had staging in mind when they painted the miniatures. What has been stated thus far, however, should suffice.

In summation, Alfonso was familiar with the extant types of drama from his knowledge of what was customarily played in churches, from what he learned about drama from Isidore's *Etymologies,* and from what he had seen in Spain as well as abroad. He knew the theatre of mime, then, and also that theatre which Curtius mentions as having existed, namely the kind of drama in which a narrator spoke and in which actors sang or spoke as they played their parts. Alfonso caused these kinds of drama to be illustrated in his *Cantigas de Santa Maria*. It is likely too that, not content with playing such dramas in the royal chapel for courtiers, he may have had such plays presented in more public places, even if he himself did not appear in these as narrator. It seems possible that he allowed his miniaturists to copy his stage settings and even his drama in action, as models for their work. It is logical to believe that Alfonso had drama on his mind, as the *Partidas* indicate. And it makes sense to suppose that he produced drama bordering upon opera, or perhaps it might better be termed dramatic ritual set to music and sung. In this way, through book-art and through the drama used as models for that art in the form of miniatures, the Learned King was able to bring his message to his subjects.

Anthony J. Cárdenas

7. Alfonso's Scriptorium and Chancery: Role of the Prologue in Bonding the *Translatio Studii* to the *Translatio Potestatis*

The depiction of Alfonso X as a bumbling astrologer king who lost his throne because of his preoccupation with the stars is a fabrication that, while cleverly connecting Alfonso's cultural zenith with his political nadir, is more harmful than helpful inasmuch as it deviates from an accurate presentation of historical fact. This study examines the hitherto unexplored relatedness of two aspects of this nadir and zenith—namely, the connection between Alfonso's chancery, that writing chamber from which issued his statute law, and his royal scriptorium, that writing chamber from which issued his cultural legacy, his various treatises on astronomy-astrology, history, and law, his *Cantigas de Santa Maria,* and his treatise on board games. Rather than two chambers, what actually may have existed was a dual chamber or possibly, and more simply, a single chamber.

The Alfonsine prologue—the prologues found in his royal scriptorium treatises produced under his aegis and surviving today in several extant royal scriptorium codices—offers an important bit of evidence on how Alfonso viewed his work. As Margo Ynes Corona de Ley has observed, "The prologue can be seen as the point of contact of the author, the text, and the audience."[1] Although the question of audience is important too and is discussed later, the first two elements of this triad, showing the relationship between the author Alfonso and his text, form the special interest of this study. An examination of this author/text duality, combined with information from recent studies treating his historical texts (as well as

Figure 7-1. King Alfonso el Sabio dictating in his court, with choir and musicians. *Cantigas de Santa Maria,* Patrimonio Nacional.

from another study in which I establish a nexus between the royal scrip-torium prologue and a foral or local statute document known as the *privilegio rodado*), permit observations that tie the studies together. These observations also suggest motives for Alfonso's more than thirty years of sustained scholarship, which produced what might be viewed as his cultural journey toward empire.

The question of authorship in Alfonsine royal scriptorium redactions has a long history. Despite the more than seventy years since Antonio Solalinde's seminal article on Alfonsine intervention,[2] however, we are far from a comprehensive picture regarding the monarch's personal interven-tion as author. This assessment does not belittle what has been done, but rather signals the great amount remaining to be done before we have a complete understanding of Alfonso's specific role in the production of his works. Solalinde's findings merit repetition. The first passage he cites hails from the *General estoria* and explains how Alfonso viewed regal authorship:

> Regarding the redaction of these words, you have heard in the beginning of this chapter how Our Lord stated that he would write them; and here he states in the twenty-fourth chapter of *Exodus* that he ordered Moses to write them; and you also will have heard in the book called *Deuteronomy* . . . that says that Our Lord himself wrote them. And it seems that these statements are contra-dictory. Concerning this contradiction Master Peter speaks and explains thus:

he says that all is correct, and that we can understand and say that Our Lord composed the content of the commandments, and that he had authorship and credit therefrom, because he ordered them to be written, although Moses wrote them; thus we have said many times: *a king makes [writes] a book, not because he wrote it with his own hands, but because he composes its arguments, and emends them, and makes them uniform, and rectifies them, and shows the way they should be done, and thus he whom he [the king] orders writes them, but we say for this reason that the king writes the book.* Also, when we say the king makes a palace or some work, this is not said because he himself makes it with his hands, rather because he ordered it made and provided the things necessary for it. And he who does this, that person receives credit for doing the work; and we thus, I see, are accustomed to speak.[3]

Alfonso not only presents here his view on regal authorship but also provides an example of the kind of revelatory gloss lurking within all of his prose.

Francisco Rico notes in the last nine words a contrast between the use of the regal first-person plural "we" (*nos*) and the first-person singular of the verb "I see" (*veo*) and suggests that this may be a specific example of Alfonsine dictation.[4] I would add as more evidence of direct Alfonsine intervention a passage, one of several possible, from the *Libro del saber de astrologia,* or *LSA,* which I am currently editing. Although this passage is less remarkable because it lacks the contrasting features as seen above, it nevertheless shows that Alfonso goes beyond his source, even in his scientific treatises, and adds a very personal element in these nonliterary works. The treatise on the construction of the *Açafeha* in the *LSA* compendium offers the following:

> We the king, the aforesaid don Alfonso, seeing the usefulness of his *saphea* which is generally for all latitudes, and how this instrument is very complete and perfect, and how it is difficult to calibrate, and that many men could not fully understand the manner in which it is made according to the words that the sage who composed it spoke, we ordered it to be illustrated in this book. And we ordered that all those circles called *almadarat* be done in black ink . . . And also so that these circles may be better recognized and more distinct from the others, we had the space between them tinted in saffron. And we also ordered the circles that are called *almamarrat* in Arabic, that go from one terrestrial pole to the other, [done] in vermilion, and the circles of longitude that are parallel to the zodiac and in a direct line with it, and also the circles of the latitudes that go from one pole of the signs to the other. And these two kinds of circles are to the zodiac as the other two are to the equator. And these four kinds are all the circles drawn on the surface of the lamina. And because there are many and they resemble one another, we distinguished them with different colors as stated.[5]

Solalinde takes his second passage, one long known, concerning Alfonso's editorial intervention, from the same *LSA*. The passage does not survive in its royal scriptorium form since that portion of the *LSA* codex has been lost. Its actual existence, however, is attested by its survival in three variant copies. Solalinde cites the following passage from the first edition:

> And afterward the above-mentioned king rectified it and had it fixed. And he removed the words he thought were superfluous and duplicated and that were not in true Castilian [*castellano drecho*]. And he put those others which he thought completed the work. And as for the language, he himself corrected it.[6]

This evidence and that previously cited suffice to show the accuracy of Evelyn Procter's summary regarding Alfonso's role as author:

> If taken together, the prologues of all these astronomical and astrological works show that Alfonso was more than a mere patron: that he sought for books, initiated projects, allotted work among his collaborators, gave them their instructions, and to some extent revised their work; finally he was a scholar who could appreciate the results of their labours.[7]

This stance is distinct from and much more acceptable than George McSpadden's unsubstantiated claim that Alfonso was author of all his prologues,[8] or George Sarton's pronouncement, also unsubstantiated, that Alfonso was author of ten prologues.[9] Even Alberto Porquera Mayo's hypothesis that "Alfonso X's prologues are probably his own work"[10] is unacceptable to the extent that it stresses probability.

The most thorough treatment of the Alfonsine prologue occurs in the study cited above by De Ley, "The Prologue in Castilian Literature between 1200 and 1400," which asserts nothing concerning Alfonso's role as author of the prologue. For our concerns, it is more important that her examinations of topics, techniques, and terms reveal little uniformity among the various prologues. Because of the non-belletristic nature of the Alfonsine treatises, creative variety is not an expected quality as it might be in works of a more literary nature. The lack of uniformity, thus, suggests absence of a fixed plan for his prologue, and possibly that more than one author composed them. One prologue constant from De Ley's point of view is Alfonso's preoccupation with the transfer of learning (*translatio studii*): "Insistence on this is so frequent and so emphasized in his prologues that it amounts to an obsession on his part."[11] This transfer, that is, the handing down or the preservation of knowledge, is important, for the motive behind it is consistent with nearly all aspects of the literary activity espoused by the king.

Antonio Ballesteros Beretta muses over the plausibility of the idea that Alfonso developed a bent for the Galician lyric, the medium of his profane and Marian poems, as a youth raised in northwestern Spain.[12] Similarly, Alfonso's infatuation with knowledge and letters must have begun at an early age under the guidance of the best tutors, as John Keller and E. N. van Kleffens claim.[13] Charles Faulhaber indicates that the *Epistolarium,* an *ars dictaminis* or rules of letter-writing by Ponce of Provence, points toward the possibility that "Alfonso himself studied *dictamen* with one of the best-known teachers of that art."[14] Even Alfonso's claim that he finished the *Setenario* at his saintly father's request is in keeping with what must have been his father's interest in his preparation.[15] Van Kleffens even claims that one of Alfonso's tutors was the Bologna-trained jurisconsult Jacobo de la Junta, ultimately known as Jacobo de las Leyes,[16] though the information provided by Jean Roudil would appear to make this unlikely.[17]

Alfonso's own education may—and I stress that I am conjecturing here—be reflected in his *Siete partidas.* The second partida states that kings and queens should teach their royal offspring, besides the decorum detailed in previous laws, other things:

> and this is reading and writing, which is very advantageous to the one who knows how, for learning more easily the things he wants to know, and to better safeguard his secrets.[18]

Another passage explains why a king should be eager to know how to read and learn everything possible:

> The king should be eager to learn the arts because by them he will understand the basis of things and will better know how to work with them, and also by knowing how to read he will better know how to guard his secrets and be lord of them, which in any other manner he would not be able to do well, because by the inability to know these things he would necessarily have to involve another who knows how. And it could come to pass to him what King Solomon said, that he who places his secret in another's power makes himself that person's slave; and he who knows how to keep it to himself is lord of his heart, which is very appropriate for a king.[19]

These laws certainly could explain in part Alfonso's interest in knowledge, and might well mirror his own youthful experiences. As such, they reflect a part of the influence that Fernando III had on his son.

This paternal influence manifests itself in other areas and is worth noting because it provides valuable insights for the raison d'être of Alfonso's royal scriptorium legacy. To begin with, Alfonso inherited not only his father's chancery but also the use of the vernacular in chancery documents. Although Spanish became the norm in Alfonsine documents,[20] Fernando had used Spanish in documents as early as 1 January 1214,[21] more than two years before Alfonso was born. When Alfonso ascended the throne, his chancery was essentially that of his father. Van Kleffens writes:

> The labours, in the field of law, of Kings Ferdinand the Saint and Alfonso X his son, have to be seen as a continuous creative process, borne along by that single preoccupation these monarchs shared: to bring about more legal unity and uniformity, and to improve the law generally.[22]

If they shared a common goal, it was a goal initiated by Fernando III and inherited, albeit perhaps expanded, by his firstborn.

The benefit that educated men provide the commonwealth is no secret, and thus, in a charter dated 6 April 1243, Fernando III wrote: "Because I understand that it is to the benefit of my kingdom and of my land, I grant and order that there be schools in Salamanca."[23] Eleven years later, in a charter dated 8 May 1254, Alfonso continues this favor:

> And with the great desire that I have that the university [*studium*] be more advanced and improved, I heeded those things they asked of me; and I took my counsel and my accord about those things with the bishops and archdeacons and with other good clergy who were with me; and having that counsel that understood the benefit and honor to me and to my kingdoms and to the scholars and to all the land, I followed it and ordered it and held it as good.[24]

The founding of an institution of higher learning (*studium*) in Salamanca promotes Fernando's "benefit of my kingdom and of my land," whereas favoring the same *studium* becomes Alfonso's "benefit and honor to me and to my kingdoms." I discuss elsewhere other echoes found between Fernando's 1243 charter and Alfonso's.[25] Not only did Fernando's influence go from charter to charter, however; since those charters constitute a source for the *Siete partidas,* that influence extended directly into Alfonso's *lex legum,* and specifically into his so-called Educational Code,[26] as partida II, title 31, laws 1–11.[27]

Law 11 of that title holds particular interest for this discussion of Alfonso's attitude toward education, for in it he provides for a stationer (*stationarius*), so that the university might be complete. The stationer's main responsibility was to provide good, true, and legible books so that students could copy from them, emend the ones they had, and so on. The rector of the university was responsible for choosing a qualified stationer and for insuring that the texts the stationer provided met the stated criteria—good, true, and legible. The rector, in consultation with the university people (the masters not the students),[28] set the price.

The great detail given in the matter of the stationer points to what had to be a major problem for any medieval university, the accessibility of texts. And it raises the question why Alfonso, given his interest in education, did not confront the problem of texts directly. He had at his disposal, in the scholars assembled for his scriptorium, the wherewithal to produce "good, true, and legible" texts for the university. Valeria Pizzorusso has edited, for example, an *Ars dictandi* for rhetoric, which Alfonso had apparently commissioned and destined for use at the university at Salamanca.[29] Procter adds the following information:

> The Castilian translations of the *Quadripartitum* and of the compendium of Ibn-al-Haitam have perished, but are known from Latin translations made from the Castilian, and the *Libro de los juicios de las estrellas* was also twice translated into Latin by Alfonso's command under the title *Liber magnus et completus de iudiciis astrologiae*.[30]

Were the texts to which Procter refers translated for the university as well? Alfonso, it appears, could have supplied it with official texts, but chose not to when he opted for use of the vernacular in his royal scriptorium texts.

Did he choose the vernacular as his medium, as Juan Gil de Zamora states, "so that all could very clearly observe, and in every way understand, things which appear even to the erudite [only] under the embellishments of the Latin language and in a closed and recondite form"?[31] Procter, from whom I cite, affirms that Latin was not at a low level, but rather:

> It is probable, indeed, that Alfonso aimed at reaching a wider audience, composed of laymen as well as clerics, than was possible through the medium of a classical language, but the use of the vernacular seems also to have had behind it national pride and a definite element of propaganda.[32]

I leave Alfonso's reasons for using the vernacular to those who care to speculate. It is not unlikely, however, that the example set in his father's chancery initiated the momentum toward the vernacular. As Julio González has noted:

> By the time Fernando III began to reign, the vernacular was vigorously on its way; it appeared with growing frequency and more or less integrity in private

documents and was appearing in royal commands; during his [Fernando III's] period, it would end up by dominating in the last decade.[33]

Use of the vernacular provides a link not only between Fernando's and Alfonso's chanceries, but also between Alfonso's chancery and scriptorium.

Another bond between father's and son's chanceries, again extending to Alfonso's chancery and scriptorium, is a type of foral document known as the *privilegio rodado*. This document corresponds to the French *diplôme*[34] and is characterized by its "principal sign of validation . . . the royal signum—the *rueda* or *signo rodado*,"[35] namely the large polychrome wheel dominating usually the interior third of its lower half and "incorporating the king's signum and heraldic devices in a blaze of color."[36] Procter describes the wheel in more detail; she makes clear that its use in Castilian and Leonese chanceries predated Alfonso X by nearly a century, and that those chanceries probably based their *rueda* on the papal *rota*.[37] Indeed, Julio González presents in his "evolution of the *signo rodado*"[38] four samples of Fernando's signum from 7 November 1217 to 30 November 1248. His last sample reveals the greatest similarity to the Alfonsine wheel as described by Procter and seen, for example, in the fifth and eighteenth plates at the end of Ballesteros Beretta's monumental *Alfonso X el Sabio*.[39] The significance of the wheeled charter is that Alfonso was not merely content to continue its use in his chancery; instead, he incorporated its formula into the prologue of his royal scriptorium texts.

Procter has examined the formula in such a privilege in light of its description in the *Siete partidas* (III.18.2), and has listed constituent elements of the formula and frequency of occurrence.[40] I divide these formulaic elements into the following twelve components:

1. Invocation (a short phrase, such as *In dei nomine*) or a chrismon (both unusual).

2. Preamble (exceptional).

3. Formula of Notification (primarily "let it be known" [*conoscida cosa sea*] until 1260 and predominantly "let all . . . know" [*sepan cuantos*] afterward).

4. Royal Superscription consisting of (a) a personal pronoun (singular until 1258 and plural afterward), (b) Alfonso's name and title, (c) a listing of his dominions, and (d) the statement that he reigns with his wife and children.

5. Prefatory Statement to the Seal.

6. Date and Place with (a) place, (b) day of the month, (c) year (according to the Spanish era), and frequently (d) day of the week. For (e) see 8.

7. Indication that the document was drawn up at the king's Command, which may be added to the date or to the redactor's Subscription.

8. Subscription of the redactor, after which we usually find the (6e) regnal Year.

9. Signal events (seldom found).[41]

10. Corroboration formula following the date, consisting of (a) the king's name, (b) mention of his wife and children, and (c) a list of dominions (not identical to that of the Superscription).

11. Royal Signum.

12. List of Cosigners, that is, *confirmantes* (a pro forma requirement, in that the persons named were not necessarily present or witnesses).

Reproducing the corresponding portion of a charter dated at Burgos, 28 December 1254, not only illustrates Procter's analysis but also shows the theoretical nature of the *Siete partidas*,[42] in that the charter does not conform exactly to the prescribed formula from partida III.18.2:

> [3. Notification] Let it be known to all men who see this letter [4. royal Superscription] that [a. personal pronoun] we [b. name and title] Don Alfonso by the grace of God king [c. dominions] of Castile, León, Toledo, Galicia, Seville, Córdoba, Murcia, Jaén, and lord of all Andalusia [d. reigning with wife and children] together with the queen Doña Violante my wife, and with my daughters the princess Doña Berenguela and princess Doña Beatriz . . . [corpus] . . . [6. Place and Date] Charter done [a. place] in Burgos [7. at king's Command] by order of the king, [6b. day of the month] the twenty-eighth day into the month of December [6c. the year according to the Spanish era] in the era 1292. [10. Corroboration] and I the aforesaid [a. king's name] king Don Alfonso [b. mention of wife and children] reigning together with the queen Doña Violante my wife, and with my daughters the princess Doña Berenguela and the princess Doña Beatriz [c. dominions] in Castile, Toledo, León, Galicia, Seville, Córdoba, Murcia, Jaén, Baeza, Badajoz, and in the Algarve, grant this privilege and confirm it and order that it prevail—[9. Signal event] [in] the year when Don Edward the first son and heir of King Henry of England received knighthood in Burgos from King Don Alfonso the aforesaid . . . [12. list of Cosigners follows] . . . [8. Subscription of redactor] I, Juan Pérez of Cuenca, wrote it, [6e. regnal year] the third year that the king reigned.[43]

Items lacking in this charter are the Invocation (No. 1) and the Preamble (No. 2) which, as noted, were usually absent; the Prefatory Statement to the Seal (No. 5); the day of the week (No. 6d), a minor omission; and the royal Signum (No. 11). Absence of the royal Signum may be a question of modern editorial fancy rather than an actual absence in the original document. All in all, this document can be considered a typical wheeled charter.

Alfonso uses a very similar formula in every genuine royal scriptorium prologue. The Invocation and Preamble occur infrequently in the privilege and in these prologues. Vestiges of an Invocation appear in two prologues. In *Libro del fuero de las leyes,* we read, "We begin this book in the name of the Father and of the Son and of the Holy Spirit."[44] Does this come from its source? The *Iudizios* states: "Let us render praise and thanks to God the Father,"[45] and later "in the name of God."[46] These two works constitute the exception rather than the norm, and one has to question whether or not presence of the Invocation derives from their source. The *Albateni,* for example, attributes such custom precisely to its source: "Mahomat, son of Gerber Albatheni, said that the first thing a man should do in beginning a book is to praise God and extol Him."[47] Similarly, *Cruzes* appears to be citing its source in the rubric for its first chapter, which reads: "In the name of God. This is the book of crosses in the judgment of the stars that Oueydalla explained."[48] Whatever may account for an Invocation in the prologue of *Leyes* and *Iudizios,* it simply does not form an integral part of either Alfonso's privileges or his royal scriptorium treatises. If *preamble* means the introductory part of a constitution or statute that usually states the reasons for and intent of the law, little room exists for such in the prologues to the various treatises. If *preamble* means simply an introductory statement of what is to follow, however, something like that manifests itself in nearly all the prologues under consideration.[49] In some instances, it is a brief one-line synopsis as in *EE I;* in others, it is substantially more, as in Alfonso's *Lapidario.*

Although Procter is not specific with regard to the use of the pronoun in the Corroboration, the Superscription and the Corroboration seem essentially identical and can thus be discussed jointly. As Procter points out, the basic difference between the two is that the list of dominions differs slightly in the Corroboration: "*En el Algarbe* ends the list from the first year of the reign, and *Badajoz* and *Baeza* are sometimes included."[50] This can be seen in the Burgos charter of 28 December 1254 reproduced above. For the Superscription the last dominion mentioned is *Jaén* "until 1260, when *y del Algarbe* is added."[51] With the exception of *Cruzes,* it would appear that Alfonso derives the list of dominions in his prologue from the Corroboration rather than from the Superscription, since his earliest texts, even those prior to 1260, include *y del Algarbe.* The Superscription and the Corroboration offer the strongest parallels between chancery documents and royal scriptorium treatises. The personal pronoun occurs in five of the thirteen prologues examined (*QS, Acedrex, GE I, EE I,* and *Q*). Only in *GE I* is it singular. Name and title are evident in all prologues except in the treatise on the *Quadrante sennero,* which contains name only: "And thus, we Don Alfonso the aforesaid, ordered Rabiçag."[52] This results from its being an interior or intratextual prologue, and occurs in others of this kind. Combined with the line "we have spoken thus far in this book on the manners of planetary equations, and by what computation each was done,"[53] this suggests strongly that the *QS* should be dealt with as a part of a larger compendium, rather than as an independent treatise as all of its editors have done.[54] Only three of the thirteen prologues lack a listing of the dominions: the two treatises on quadrants, by virtue of the fact that they are intratextual prologues, and *Albateni,* an oddity which will be examined subsequently. It should be stressed that *Cruzes* does not list the dominions either, but alludes to them in a novel fashion: "the very noble king, Don Alfonso of Spain."[55] *Iudizios* adds "and of Badajoz"[56] after the traditionally last phrase "of the Algarve."[57] Procter indicates a similar occasional inclusion not only of Badajoz but also of Baeza.[58]

Finally, rather than mentioning his wife and children in the prologues, Alfonso names his parents—the most common formula being "son of the very noble king, Don Fernando and of the queen Doña Beatriz." Mention of his predecessors, however, is wanting in four prologues (*Albateni, Iudizios,* and the two intratextual treatises on the quadrants). The term "family" in the prologues denotes progenitors, whereas in the chancery documents it signifies wife and progeny. The reason for this difference may be that the prologues look toward the noble lineage from which Alfonso is descended, perhaps for added prestige, perhaps to honor them, or again, perhaps because they and in particular Fernando III initiated Alfonso into the world of knowledge. The foral (local statute) documents, on the other hand, look toward the future, toward regal heirs, thereby assuring the stability of that legal authority.

Unlike chancery documents, only seven of thirteen Alfonsine prologues contain a Date of compilation, and three of these are from interior prologues of the *Libro del saber.* In general, minimal chronological information occurs in the prologues, consisting of the year in the form of the era, plus either the anno Domini or the regnal year (and sometimes both, as in *Formas*). *Cruzes* also presents the dates, in Arabic terms.[59] Even less commonly found in the prologues, perhaps influenced by its invariable absence in the wheeled privilege, is the date of actual completion, a date perhaps more appropriate for the concluding colophon than for a prologue. Its omission is inconsequential for the latter; nevertheless, a date of completion would be very welcome and useful for the bulky treatises, which indubitably required more than one sitting for their scribing. Only three prologues give dates of completion: *Leyes* (28 August 1265), *Cruzes* (26 February 1259), and *Lapidario* (1250). On the last folio of text, the *Acedrex* offers the date 1283 and the place Seville, but it is unclear whether this date signifies the time of inception or completion or both. The only prologue to indicate place (Burgos) is that of the *Açafeha*. The prologue to the *Espera* offers the day of week, Thursday. Day and month can be found in all but the *Formas, Lapidario, Açafeha,* and *Quadrante*. The *Lapidario* uniquely dates itself with a signal event: "It was concluded in the second year that the noble king Don Fernando won the city of Seville," 1250.[60] *Cruzes* alone provides the Arabic chronology. Only two provide the anno Domini: *Formas* as 1276–1279 and *Quadrante* as 1277. Here too, there exists a general mirroring of the formula used in the wheeled charter—although to a significantly lesser extent, since dating is explicit in only five distinct texts (of seven explicit dates, three are found in treatises of the *Libro del saber*). While a date was imperative for legal effectiveness, unfortunately no similar need existed for the dating of Alfonso's scriptorium treatises.

The seventh element of the wheeled charter indicates that the document was drawn up at the king's command. As one might expect, every Alfonsine prologue so indicates. This appears most commonly in the third-person singular (employed twenty times), as in "he had it done"[61] or "he had it translated."[62] First-person plural follows as a distant second, used five times, as in "we had this book done"[63] or "we ordered it compiled."[64] First-person singular occurs in only one text, the *GE I*.[65] Finally, two texts, the *Iudizios* and the *Açafeha,* use the phrase "by order of,"[66] duplicating the formula used in the charter to state that a document was drawn up at Alfonso's behest. This listing strongly suggests that at best Alfonso himself wrote perhaps six detailed prologues—those using the first person pronoun, singular or plural. Since the choice of the formula employed can be accounted for in a number of ways, only further detailed analysis of these six compared with the others may determine whether this was in fact the case. The Alfonsine prologues offer no information regarding the names of the scribes who actually sat down to write the texts. The names of Alfonso's collaborators do, however, appear in the prologues and have been studied by several scholars.[67] The only Signal event (No. 9) has been treated with the Superscription.

The introductory passage to the *Canones de Albateni* is worth examining. It reads: "Here begins the book of the *Canones de Albateni* which the very noble king don Alfonso, to whom may God give life and health for much time, ordered written";[68] and it is followed immediately by chapter rubrics. Examination of a facsimile copy of the codex of the *Albateni,* housed in the Seminary of Medieval Spanish Studies, suggests that it lacks a listing of dominions because the first folio is a later replacement, written in a Gothic script much rounder than that of subsequent folios, which display the square, compact, squat Gothic script present in all genuine Alfonsine codices. Folio 2r, which is genuinely Alfonsine, contains 47 lines per column, whereas folio 1 v, the apparent addition, contains 51 lines in the first column and 52 lines in the second. This is not the Alfonsine way. Reconstructing the chapter rubrics on this folio would have been a simple matter of retrieving them from subsequent folios; but reconstructing the prologue according to the formula presented above was another matter, for it would have required: (1) awareness that such a formula existed and (2) access to another royal scriptorium text from which to copy it. Not even the headings that occur on either side of the second folio were copied onto the first folio in the *Albateni.*

It is not clear when the treatises contained in the Paris Arsenal MS 8322 were completed. Bossong in his edition of the *Canones de Albateni* merely, but prudently, states that the text hails from the second half of the thirteenth century.[69] A matter worth considering at this point concerns the similarity between the script found in an Alfonsine foral document dated 1260,[70] on the one hand, and the script in that Paris codex in a portion titled *Las tablas d'Albatheni* and beginning at folio 28v. The scripts are substantially similar but not identical. It nevertheless seems plausible that an Alfonsine scribe trained in the cursive hand seen in the 1260 document could be responsible for penning the text beginning on folio 28v and continuing on in that style in the Paris Arsenal manuscript. If so, the *Albateni* offers plausible evidence for contact between chancery and scriptorium. Juan Manuel del Estal provides many plates[71] displaying a Gothic minuscule very comparable to the squat, square, compact style found in bona fide royal scriptorium codices. Again, this script is similar and not identical, being somewhat less compact and less squat. Did Alfonso employ the scribes of his chancery in the production of his royal scriptorium texts? Procter has uncovered evidence that encourages an affirmative answer, in the persons of Juan de Cremona and Gil de Tibaldos (Egidius de Tebaldis), who seem to have collaborated in both chancery and royal scriptorium.[72] That there were others as well must remain conjectural, a conjecture that is nevertheless plausible and not unreasonable to maintain. One other bridge between chancery and scriptorium exists: the obvious connection provided by the legal documents issuing from Alfonso's chancery and the royal scriptorium legal documents, notably the *Siete partidas*. Recall that in some instances chancery documents provide the basis for portions of the *Partidas*.

That Alfonso inherited the chancery from his father, that Alfonso essentially inherited his legal program from his father, that the father commissioned the historical treatise *De rebus Hispaniae* which Alfonso used as one of the main sources for his *Estoria de Espanna*,[73] and that Alfonso continued using the vernacular, a practice begun by his father—all make clear that Alfonso essentially continued the impetus provided by his father, and that his royal scriptorium found many of its roots in the chancery which, again, was inherited from Fernando III.

Alfonso's choice of the formula found in the *privilegio rodado* as a constant in his royal scriptorium prologue was not due to chance, for both Francisco Rico and recently John Dagenais[74] show clearly that Alfonso was aware of what was called an introduction to the authors (*accessus ad auctores*). Rico cites a passage from Alfonso's *General estoria* which states:

> Many of the masters, when they want to read their books in the universities, require at the beginning of them a certain number of things and others more, some five things, and others six, and there are others (who require) even more.[75]

Alfonso describes here what Edwin Quain calls "the custom of medieval commentators on classical authors of prefixing to their works a *schema* generally called an *accessus*. . . . In such a prefatory note they treated of items such as the following": the author's life, title of the work, purpose of the writer, matter, utility, and branch of philosophy to which it pertains.[76] Alfonso X does not use such an introduction, obviously because he does not view himself as glossing an author. Gloss he does and refer to authors, too, but to a different end. There is no question that he treats his sources in much the same way that a master at any medieval university would. He presents his material (in writing—at the university, it would be read); he then glosses (the masters did the same). Regarding this, Rico accurately states: "The *General estoria*—I believe—does not offer as much a translation as it does an *enarratio* [interpretation] of the *auctores*."[77] Alfonso's procedure is the same, but his intention is different.

De Ley's observation concerning Alfonso's "obsession" with the transfer of learning is worth recalling, for that *translatio* is intimately related to another, the *translatio potestatis* or *translatio imperii* (transfer of power or of empire) that Rico has pointed to in his chapter titled "Alfonso X y Jupiter."[78] Rico appropriately finds it significant

> that of all the great modern kings that could have been named, Alfonso (who if not he?) mentions explicitly only his great grandfather Barbarossa and his uncle Frederick II: that is, the two great emperors of the house of Swabia, from which emanated his own imperial rights and ambitions.[79]

In a brilliant study, Charles Fraker treats the *Estoria de Espanna* with three problems hitherto unexamined: (1) the chronologies of the later chapters employing the regnal year of the Roman emperor, (2) the favorable portrait of Charlemagne not found in Alfonso's sources, and (3) the stress on the Roman section in this work "with its largely 'Gothic' emphasis."[80] Fraker also convincingly points to a solution in an imperial theme: "that the *Cronica* was to have ended sounding loudly the note of Alfonso's Roman and imperial heritage."[81] In another excellent study, Fraker shows how the *Estoria de Espanna* and the *Fet des Romains* are both "vernacular works . . . in part translations *with commentary* of ancient texts; they are not simply amplified versions of Lucan or Sallust, but have the look of a text plus gloss or scholia."[82] The transformation is from "history as spectacle" to "history as *example*":

> Different Latin texts are combined, details added, changes made, at times schemes of motivation are supplied, all to create virtually new narratives which yield these various emphases, these patterns of exemplarity.[83]

Fraker clarifies how the exemplarity makes clear to "the great of this world the practical art of leadership, in peace and especially in war."[84] Similarly Rico, in his usually perceptive manner, states regarding a portion of the *GE:*

> Of course, it is a fact that a good portion of those that could be treated as "digressions" (glosses, meditations and incidental remarks that do not strictly constitute an explicatory note of the account) allude to themes that would fit wonderfully in any treatise on the education of princes.[85]

The practical purpose of history is stated in the prologue of the *GE:* "so that from the deeds of the good, men would take example in order to do good, and from the deeds of the evil that they would receive a lesson to know what to refrain from doing."[86] Despite or perhaps in addition to that practical purpose, the lesson Fraker extracts from the *EE* as well as the lesson seen in the *GE* by Rico is not appropriate for everyone. Such is the case for the audience of Alfonso's scientific treatises. The *Lapidario* (his earliest work, if the date provided is trustworthy) claims on its first folio that Alfonso had it translated "from Arabic into Castilian so that men would understand it better and better know how to take advantage of it."[87] The requisites for understanding this text, however, make it clear that *los omnes,* or men, are not everyone. Rather they are the select few: (1) who knew astronomy (which included astrology), (2) who knew how to distinguish between the subtlety of stones, and (3) who knew the art of medicine.[88] An interesting study by John Nunemaker, "Obstetrical and Genito-Urinary Remedies of Thirteenth-Century Spain,"[89] treats remedies for these types of ailments and points to the practical reason for having such a work translated. It is no accident that Yhuda Mosca el Menor, Alfonso's own physician,[90] was the man selected to translate this work. Even Alfonso's latest and most scientific text, the *LSA,* is replete with references to *omnes entendudos,* or intelligent, learned men for whom such knowledge is intended. Again the audience is not everyone. Three other early codices translated from Arabic—the *Canones de Albateni,* the *Iudizios,* and the *Cruzes*—are astrological and thus eminently practical.

If knowing the past was important, how much more practical would be predicting the future? José Sánchez Pérez's remarks concerning the *Cruzes* are appropriate: "The *Libro de las cruzes* is an astrological work with the deliberate intention of gathering only those judgments of judicial astrology that can most affect the person of a king and the politics of his kingdom."[91] The *Iudizios* falls into a similar category. The *Albateni,* on the other hand, seems more astronomical in a modern sense; but astronomy was merely the handmaiden of astrology, a necessary means to the end, since astrology constituted a major cultural fiber in the tapestry of Alfonso's cultural milieu when "the rise and fall of the Christian west were subjects of earnest calculation."[92] Alfonso stayed within Christian orthodoxy by making the stars the servants of God, since, according to Alfonso, God made

> these figures [the constellations] all and in such a manner, and placed them there where He understood it would be best. And He gave them virtue and power so that by them men would be able to help themselves in their deeds and in the things for which they had great need, also for knowing the past as well as the future. Because this—knowing things that are to be before they are—is something that man's soul greatly desires.[93]

Thus, history and science, one looking backward for exemplarity, the other looking forward, constituted a potential Janus of knowledge that any prudent king would want to utilize, especially one living in Alfonso's bellicose era. Not only did the infidel constantly threaten, but Alfonso also had to contend with an unruly nobility and the complications of his claim to Holy Roman emperorship.[94] For Alfonso *not* to have connected a *translatio studii* to a *translatio potestatis*—learning and power yoked—both from his ancestors to him and especially a *translatio* from him to his progeny, would have been impractical if not foolhardy. From Alfonso's viewpoint, as evident in the *Partidas,* the practicality of centralized Roman law over the fractured and partisan foral statutes in effect needed no elaboration.

Even two works that seem to stress delight rather than utility, the *Cantigas de Santa Maria* and the *Libro de acedrex & dados & tablas,* take on practical characteristics. Joseph Snow has elucidated perceptively two supremely practical motives for the *Cantigas:* on the one hand and ultimately, Alfonso's own quest for salvation, but on the other hand, the more earthly and immediate assistance from the Mother of God.[95] The basic formula in each miracle is that the Virgin provides succor to her devotees. John Keller has noted twenty-eight miracle accounts that "relate miracles performed by the Holy Virgin for King Alfonso or for members of his family."[96] Alfonso's last commissioned work, his treatise on games, also takes on a utilitarian appearance as manifested in its beginning words:

> Because God wished that men have every kind of joy for its own sake, so that they might be able to bear cares and labors when they happened, therefore men sought many ways by which they might fully secure this happiness.[97]

This is "recreation" to enable man better to endure the hardships of this world. It was commissioned in Seville, which had maintained its fidelity during Alfonso's troubles with his usurping son Sancho. Completed apparently in the first half of 1283, in the thirty-second year of his reign, when Alfonso was 61 and about one year before his death, it describes various kinds of pleasures—equestrian pastimes, fencing, wrestling, batting a ball, and other games that can be played day or night by

> women who do not ride horseback and are enclosed . . . and also *those men who are old and weak,* or those who wish to take their pleasures privately in order to avoid disturbances or worry; or those who are in foreign power such as prison or captivity or who travel on sea.[98]

Even this final work, a treatise on games, rises from a foundation of practical motives.

The question of Alfonsine authorship is a major puzzle that welcomes any piece that any scholar can possibly add. Pragmatism certainly characterizes Alfonso's relationship to his text. His interest in knowledge no doubt began with the education his father afforded him as a prince. His interest in the Galician lyric appears to have been the result of youthful experience. His interest in law is directly attributable to Fernando III. He inherited from his father the use of the vernacular in his chancery documents, as he did his signum in the wheeled charters. The possibility that his royal scriptorium rises from his chancery also seems likely, and certainly his use of the formula of the wheeled charter in his royal scriptorium treatises derives from his chancery. Using that formula implies an attitude toward the treatises that is much more practical, perhaps political, than if, for example, he had used a standard introduction to the authors (*accessus ad auctores*), of which he was aware.

Finally, his audience: who could this audience have been? Is it the Latinate *ipsi sapientes* of Juan Gil de Zamora or Alfonso's universal *los omnes*? Is it the wider audience of clerics and laymen, as Procter suggests on the basis of Alfonso's own words? The messages and the kinds of knowledge contained in his treatises, except perhaps for the *Cantigas,* do not seem entirely appropriate for everyone. In the case of all his treatises, especially the *Cantigas,* the largess required to produce these lavish volumes must have been enormous. The *Lapidario,* the *Libro del saber,* the *Acedrex,* the *Cantigas,* indeed nearly all his codices, even the unillustrated *Iudizios* or the *Cruzes,* would have made and do make wonderful display books. For whom were these books intended? Certainly not the universities, as we have seen. If these texts "were deposited in the king's chamber," as Procter claims,[99] who besides members of the royal family and immediate nobility would have had access to them? The one scientific treatise that was copied ad infinitum,[100] it would seem, was the *Alfonsine Tables.* Emmanuel Poulle argues that it circulated in the form provided by fourteenth-century Parisian astronomers;[101] even so, its practical and utilitarian nature and its Latin form provided the impetus for this dispersion. The only vernacular texts that spawned myriad copies were the histories; their interest as records of a *translatio potestatis* and as guides for princes may account for this. For obvious reasons, the *Siete partidas* also survives in many codices; the vernacular scientific treatises, the *Acedrex,* and the *Cantigas* certainly do not.[102]

In conclusion: content, form, and housing seem to belie the notion that Alfonso in fact "set out to reach a wider audience in his own country than he could have reached through the medium of Latin."[103] Instead they argue for a very practical motivation for his cultural endeavors, a bonding of *translatio studii* with the *translatio potestatis*. All this combines to argue in favor of considering Alfonso's chancery and scriptorium ideologically, if not physically, one.

Julia Bolton Holloway

8. The Road Through Roncesvalles: Alfonsine Formation of Brunetto Latini and Dante—Diplomacy and Literature

In the *Inferno,* Dante sees giants, whom he mistakes for towers (XXXI.31), and Satan, whom he mistakes for a windmill (XXXIV.5–7). Translated by Enrique de Villena, that text was in turn to influence Miguel de Cervantes and his Don Quixote, who mistook windmills for giants. This essay discusses such reciprocal literary games between Spain and Italy as partly originating in intensely serious political diplomacy between republican Florence, the Florence of the Primo Popolo, by means of her ambassador, Brunetto Latini, and the imperial candidate in Spain, Alfonso X el Sabio of Castile. The Florentine scholar and diplomat Brunetto Latini was present at the court of Alfonso X in 1260 and then in exile in northern France, before his return to Florence in 1266 or perhaps 1267. A number of scholars have asked whether Brunetto's embassy and exile might have transmitted from Alfonso to Brunetto's student Dante Alighieri a translation of *The Ladder of Mahomet,* a work that has striking parallels to Dante's *La Divina commedia.*[1] Brunetto's literary activity in Castile and northern France, however, really ought to be considered in terms of a larger body of works than simply *The Ladder of Mahomet.* Through an examination of Brunetto's literary activity, and a study of several important manuscript traditions, it should be possible to suggest at least a textual framework for the question of Arabic-Castilian literary influences on Latini's *Tresor* and Dante's *Commedia.*

In 1260, the *anziani* of the *comune* and *popolo* of Florence—their republican senate modeled on that of ancient Rome (*senatus populusque romanus,* or SPQR)—chose Brunetto Latini as ambassador to the regal and almost imperial court of Castile. Brunetto had already served his republic in drawing up peace treaties between Florence and Siena and between Florence and Arezzo; fine holograph documents exist of both these treaties.[2] The radical Florentine commune, which had ousted the landowning aristocracy from government in 1250, an event followed by the death of the opposed Ghibelline leader Frederick II in 1251, had at first experienced a decade of great energy and prosperity. Now war clouds were gathering. In 1257, Pisa was treating with Alfonso el Sabio, proposing his election as emperor, in return for his support against Lucca, Florence, and Genoa. That nomination was successful; he was elected at Frankfurt in April 1257, in opposition to the already elected Richard of Cornwall.[3] Brunetto Latini was later to write his account, in his chronicle section of *Li livres dou tresor:* "A division [arose] among the the princes of Germany, for some supported the king and emperor His Highness Alfonso king of Castile and of Spain, [while] others supported the count Richard of Cornwall, brother of the king of England."[4]

Ghibelline and aristocrat Farinata degli Uberti, exiled to Siena, was treating with Manfred of Sicily, Frederick's illegitimate son and heir, against Florence.[5] The rival city-states were playing dangerous power games leading up to the disaster that would be the battle of Montaperti. In desperation, Guelf Florence decided to dispatch two statesmen, both of them also poets. They sent Guglielmo Beroardi first to Richard of Cornwall, Alfonso's rival imperial candidate, at Worms, and then to the eight-year-old Conradin, grandchild of Frederick and nephew of Manfred in Bavaria. They sent Brunetto Latini to Alfonso el Sabio. Florence thus hoped to gain the support of one or all of these imperial candidates against Ghibelline Siena and Manfred of Sicily.[6]

Electing Alfonso as emperor was insufficient. The next part of the gamble would be the imperial candidate's coming to Italy at the head of his army, running the gauntlet of the feuding city-states and their factions, to be crowned emperor by the pope in malarial Rome. Alfonso was wise to dally with the idea but not swallow the bait. It is most probable that Latini's instructions as ambassador were to the effect that Florence would aid Alfonso in his coronation journey, if he in turn would wage war against Manfred and Siena. The Guelf republic had turned emperor-maker in desperation. In this it failed. Later the Florentine Guelf bankers were to succeed in colluding with the pope—though they were in exile and under papal interdict for the murder of the Ghibelline abbot Tesoro of Vallom-brosa—in making Charles, the count of Provence and Anjou, senator of Rome (June 1265) and then king of Sicily (6 January 1266).

So important was the embassy in Florentine history that Giovanni Villani, in his *Cronica di Firenze,* allotted to it an entire chapter, drawing his narration from archival chancery material, some of which was likely to have been generated by Brunetto Latini himself:

> In that same year, there being such a delay that the electors of the empire out of discord elected two emperors, one party (in which were three of the electors) electing King Alfonso of Spain, and the other party of the electors electing Richard Count of Cornwall and brother of the king of England; and because the realm of Bohemia was in discord, and two of them were made king, each gave their vote to his party. And for many years there was this discord of the two candidates. But the church of Rome more favored Alfonso of Spain, because he could have come with his forces and combatted the pride and control of Manfred; for which reason the Guelfs of Florence sent him ambassadors to persuade him to come, promising him great help if he would favor the Guelf party. And the ambassador was Ser Brunetto Latini, a man of great wisdom and authority; but before he could complete the embassy, the Florentines were defeated at Montaperti, and King Manfred seized control of all Italy, and the power of the party of the church was much diminished, for which reason Alfonso of Spain abandoned the task of the empire and Richard of England did not pursue it.[7]

That is the political context of Brunetto Latini's embassy in 1260 to Alfonso el Sabio. There is also a significant literary context that cannot be separated from the political. Brunetto memorialized his embassy to Alfonso in a dream-vision work he wrote, the *Tesoretto,* a poem that was to be a prototype for Dante's dream vision, the *Commedia.* In it Latini gives this account:

Lo tesoro comincia,	The *Treasure* begins,
Al tempo ke fiorença	At the time when Florence
Fioria e fece frutto	Flourished and bore fruit,
Sì ch'ell'era del tutto	So that she was of all
La donna di toscana;	The Lady of Tuscany;
Ancora che lontana	However, at a distance
Ne fosse l'una parte	One faction was exiled
Rimossa in altra parte,	Into another region,
Quella de' ghibellini.	That of the Ghibellines.
Per guerra di vicini,	Because of civil war,
Esso comune saggio	This wise republic

Mi fece suo messaggio	Made me ambassador
All'alto re di spangna,	To the great king of Spain
Ch'or è re de la mangna	Who now is king of Germany
E la corona attende,	And awaits the crown
Se dio nolglil contende.	If God does not dispute it.
Ché già sotto la luna	There has not yet below the moon
Non si truova persona	Been found such a person
Che, per gentil lengnaggio	Who for noble lineage
Né per alto barnaggio,	Or great baronage
Che sì dengno ne fosse	Was more worthy of it
Com'esto re nefosse.	Than this King Alfonso.[8]

In the *Tesoretto,* in a splendid manuscript of the Laurentian library at Florence, we find not only this text speaking of the political context of that embassy but also a joyous and delicate illumination, in sanguine, of Brunetto at the court of Alfonso in Spain. We can approximately date that embassy from archival material, for Brunetto was deeply involved in the preparations for war, as shown in the 1260 *Libro di Montaperti,* some pages of which are in Brunetto's hand. His dates there are 26 February, then 20, 22, 23, and 24 July.[9] Alfonso's court was at Seville on 27 July, moving to Córdoba on 20 September. The actual battle of Montaperti itself took place on 4 September of that year. Thus, we can even place the embassy (and the *Tesoretto* text and illumination of it) in the magnificent Moorish "Hall of the Ambassadors" of the Alcazar of Seville.

It was customary for ambassadors to be cultured and capable of writing and exchanging poetry and prose. Up until this time, Brunetto seems to have been well acquainted with texts from the axis of Rome—of Cicero, Sallust, Lucan, and Livy—texts concerning the civil war and the republic and concerning the loss of civil liberties with the coming of the Caesars. His translations of speeches made by Cicero, Cato, and Catiline survive in the *cancelleresca* script and are found in collections of chancery letters begun by Frederick's chancellor Pier delle Vigne, continuing through the Florentine republic's chancellor Leonardo Bruni Aretino.[10] It was in Spain that Brunetto likely first truly encountered the Greco-Arabic axis of learning and acquired translations of Aristotle's *Ethics* and *Politics* made there as well as the Alfraganus-Ptolemy *Almagest.* He was to translate these into French as *Li livres dou tresor* and later into Italian as *Il tesoro,* in the latter case using the Ghibelline and Sicilian-endorsed translation of the *Nicomachean Ethics.*[11] He would later teach these texts to Dante, who would eventually use them for the structuring of his own great poem.

Islamic Toledo had fallen to the Christian King Alfonso VI in 1085.

Spain at that time encouraged pluralism; the thirteenth-century kings Fernando III and Alfonso X of Castile retained something of the style of their forebear Alfonso VI, who was called "king of the three religions." To this day, Toledo is a city of mosque, synagogue, and church buildings. Toledo, and Seville after its conquest in turn from the Arabs in 1248, became centers for translations from the Arabic of Islamic and Greek materials into Latin and the Romance languages. The intermediaries for these translations were often Jewish *alfaquines* or physician-savants (the *ḥakīm*). The final form was usually shaped by foreigners at the court, who included Gerard of Cremona for the *Almagest* of Alfraganus, Hermann the German for the *Ethics* of Aristotle, and Bonaventure of Siena for the *Ladder of Mahomet*.[12] Though it is quite probable, as Walter Goetz and Francis Carmody have argued,[13] that Brunetto did not stay in Toledo, he would have been at Alfonso's peripatetic court in either Seville or Córdoba, or both; and he would have encountered Alfonso's translators and seen his chancery at work there, a process of abiding interest to the man who (according to Demetrio Marzi) was Florence's first chancellor.[14] Alfonso's court would also have given Brunetto a pluralistic parallel to the court of Frederick in Sicily. Although hated by freedom-loving Guelfs, Frederick's chancery was also their model, Brunetto copying out the letters of Frederick's chancellor Pier delle Vigne, in order to appropriate that Ghibelline style for Guelf uses.[15]

In encountering Aristotle, the Guelf republican who so consciously modeled his own style upon that of Cicero found the literary means to balance these differences in power structures. Alfonso was himself involved with the text of Aristotle's *Politics* at the time, and he probably talked to Brunetto of that work.[16] Cicero was the staunch Roman republican; Aristotle was the democratic Athenian tutor to the imperial Macedonian Alexander, and Brunetto learned how to compromise, to harmonize these opposites. Both Cicero and Aristotle were now to be Latini's literary and political role models. We find later manuscripts of the *Rettorica* showing, within the two curves of the letter *S,* the two portraits of the Roman Cicero and the Florentine Brunetto.[17] We likewise find, in manuscripts of the *Tresor,* in its different partidas, portraits both of Brunetto teaching his students and of Aristotle. In these, Aristotle may even be garbed as an Arab complete with turban, seated upon a mosque floor, reading from a text in Arabic, and teaching it to his students; Alexander may be shown playing his schoolboy jest of having Aristotle ridden by the beautiful, golden-haired, red-garbed Phyllis about the castle courtyard, while the laughing young prince looks down upon them both.[18]

In Dante's case, exile was to mean the writing of a masterpiece. His teacher preceded him. In the *Tesoretto* (ll. 143–62), Brunetto tells how he learned of his own exile. News traveled slowly in the Middle Ages. As he was making his way home from his failed embassy, he met a student from Bologna in the pass of Roncesvalles who gave him the news:

Venendo per la valle	Coming through the valley
Del piano di roncisvalle,	Of the plain of Roncesvalles,
Incontrai un scolaio	I met a scholar
Sour un muletto baio,	Upon a bay mule,
Che venia da bolongnia,	Who was coming from Bologna,
E sança dir mençogna	And, without telling lies,
Molt'era savio e prode:	He was very wise and brave:
Ma lascio star le lode	But I leave behind the praises
Che sarebbero assai.	That would be great indeed.
E io'l pur domandai	And I also asked him
Novelle di toscana	For news of Tuscany
In dolce lingua e piana;	In the sweet and clear tongue;
Ed e' cortesemente	And he courteously
Mi disse immantenente	Told me immediately
Che guelfi di fiorença	That the Guelfs of Florence
Per mala provedença	Through ill fortune
E per força di guerra,	And through the force of war,
Eran fuori de la terra,	Were exiled from that land,
E'l dannaggio era forte	And the penalty was great
Di pregione e di morte.	Of imprisonment and death.

That setting of the opening of the *Tesoretto*'s dream vision in the valley of Roncesvalles echoes back to the *Chanson de Roland* and forward to the opening of Dante's *Commedia* where that poet, likewise deeply sorrowing, would enter a dream-vision landscape and where later, deep in hell, he would hear Roland's horn reverberate intertextually with visions of dwarfs, giants, and windmills, intertextually reflecting back to John of Salisbury and forward to Miguel de Cervantes.

There is a letter from Brunetto's father, who was similarly a notary, which begins: "Bonaccorsus Latinus of Florence to his beloved son Brunectus, notary, now at the court of the most excellent lord Alfonso, king of the Romans and of Spain, sent by the commune of Florence, greetings and loving paternal affection." The text goes on to speak of the tears that wet and stain the pages of the letter, on the part of both writer and reader. It next narrates the account of the battle of Montaperti on Saturday, 4 September, describing how the Guelf Florentines were now under papal protection in Lucca and how exile had been proclaimed against Brunetto and others: "putting you and other Guelfs and supporters under perpetual banishment."[19] Brunetto's brother Latinus Bonaccursi, later to be a banker and at this time possibly a student at Bologna, brought the letter from Lucca.[20]

In the dream vision of the poem—part fantasy and part fact, as was also to be the case with Dante's *Commedia*—Brunetto then describes himself, deeply sorrowing, making his way to France. The text specifically mentions Montpellier. We also know of his presence in Arras, Paris, and Bar-sur-Aube from important holograph documents (one now in the Vatican, the other in Westminster Abbey), which he wrote for the Florentine Guelf government-in-exile. These letters involve negotiations with the papacy, in which the Florentine banking families raised funds by means of the crusade tithe, to pay Charles of Anjou to fight against Manfred of Sicily.[21]

Because the Florentines despaired of Alfonso's help, they had selected as their champion Charles of Anjou, brother of King Louis IX of France. But they had doubts about Anjou's ability to understand their republican form of government. To make this lesson very clear, Brunetto set to work to write in French a book whose first part contained an encyclopedic history and geography of the world (including a bestiary), whose second part translated Aristotle's *Nicomachean Ethics* as well as treating of vices and virtues, and whose third part discussed the use of Ciceronian rhetoric in a republican city-state or commune. The book concluded with a "politics" section, a complete account of how a commune elected its chief executive or *podestà*, who would take the oath to protect its liberties. It is in this final section that Latini gives the letter to Charles of Anjou inviting him to be senator of Rome, and to swear upon Rome's Capitoline Hill to uphold the constitution and freedom of Rome's republic. It is clear that Latini in the *Tresor* was taking from Alfonso el Sabio the "treasure" of wisdom, Aristotle's *Ethics,* and was attempting to transmit this material to Charles of Anjou, to educate him as Aristotle had educated Alexander. At the same time, Arnolfo di Cambio, architect of Florence's communal Palazzo Vecchio, sculpted the statue of Charles of Anjou as a Roman senator in a toga, constitution in hand, for placement on the Capitoline.[22] Alfonso was envisioned as a Greco-Arabic, democratic philosopher-king; Charles was cast in the role of a Roman republican senator. The material acquired from the one was given to the other.

The literary manuscripts underscore what the political documents have also demonstrated: that Brunetto Latini was in Arras first and then Paris. He would have traveled to the great fair in Champagne at Bar-sur-Aube, where Florentine bankers arranged for major financial transfers, especially the payments to Lucca for its protection of exiled Guelfs residing in its San Frediano district.[23] Many of the *Tresor* manuscripts are in the Picard dialect of the Arras region—the Artois and Picardy mentioned by Chaucer in connection with his *Canterbury Tales'* Squire, a region that had strong associations with both England and the great Florentine bankers. The *Tresor* is widely dispersed throughout Europe; copies are found in the Vatican, El Escorial, Leningrad, Oxford, Arras, Brussels, Paris, Naples, and elsewhere.[24] (These are all cities with which the Florentine bankers had dealings.) The first version is a diplomatic presentation text, written for Charles of Anjou. But Brunetto was able to make generic copies of the *Tresor* and present them also to other major figures the Florentines wished to influence and impress, such as Alfonso el Sabio.

Among other texts Brunetto wrote was the *Tesoretto*. When first editing it, I believed that the dedication was not to a monarch but a friend. There is a charming joking quality (*scherzo* rather than *serio*) to Brunetto's texts, especially in those aspects dealing with his relationships and interactions within the texts to his readers. I now realize, from reading more widely amongst Latini's manuscripts, that his dedications were to monarchs as friends, and also to other friends as individuals whom he could educate and to whom he could dedicate his books in the same manner as he did to monarchs, both addressed with *tu* as his equals. He envisioned the Republic of Letters as a place of laughter combined with wisdom. Besides the Arabic learning Brunetto acquired at Alfonso's court, the *Tesoretto* text also shows the influence of the *Roman de la Rose,* which originated in the Lorris-Meung region to the southwest of Champagne's Troyes and Bar-sur-Aube. He wrote his books on the models of both Cicero and Aristotle, for his commune, for rich bankers, for counts, for kings, for emperors, for popes. Given this evidence, it is now clear that the *Tesoretto* or "little treasure" was originally written as a charming and witty diplomatic thank-you letter to Alfonso el Sabio, perhaps prefacing a translation into French or Italian of the Alfraganus-Ptolemy *Almagest* or of the entire *Tresor* (the dream vision breaks off just as Ptolemy is about to narrate to Latini all of his wisdom).[25] The *Tesoretto* is preface to another text, some manuscripts stating that it is the *Tesoro maggiore* or "greater treasure." There is a reference to a *Tesoretto* having been in the library of the Marqués de Santillana, though it no longer seems to exist in that collection.[26] We know of seventeen manuscripts of the *Tesoretto,* most of them in Italy. One is in Kraków, one at Cornell, and one in Paris, but none today is in Spain; three are bound with Dante's *Commedia.*[27]

Another Latini text that made its way to Alfonso el Sabio is a splendid translation into Italian of Aristotle's *Ethics.* In this instance, it is not the translation of the text from Spain by Hermann the German; instead it translates the text from Sicily by Taddeo d'Alderotti in Bologna.[28] Its exemplar may be the manuscript in chancery script written on a thirteenth-century legal palimpsest at Yale (Marston 28); the Biblioteca Nacional manuscript (10124) in Madrid is written in the Bolognan *libraria* script we see in other contemporary Brunetto Latini manuscripts from his work-shops in France and in Italy. The first translation of Aristotle made by Latini was acquired from Alfonso, then given to Charles of Anjou. This second translation is the official Ghibelline version of Aristotle, now sub-verted and taken over by the Guelf writer, for it was first authorized to be taught at the University of Bologna by Frederick II's Pier delle Vigne and then sent by Manfred of Sicily to the University of Paris to be its authorized text.[29] (An error has crept into scholarship that the *Tesoro* simply copied an *Ethics* that Taddeo had already translated into Italian; Taddeo's version is in Latin.) We can tell from the manuscripts of the texts in Paris that Brunetto had access to both translations while in exile in France.[30] He had earlier made use of the official Ghibelline style, imitating and mocking it in his letter sent by the commune of Florence to the commune of Pavia on the occasion of the murder of Abbot Tesoro of Vallombrosa.[31] Many years later, Dante was to comment that Taddeo's version left much to be de-sired.[32] Is one hearing him repeat a lecture comment made by his teacher, the translator of the text into Italian, and from this does one assume that Latini preferred the text from Spain by Hermann the German to the text at Bologna by Taddeo d'Alderotti? This may well be the case.

In return for these manuscripts, Alfonso el Sabio may have sent to Brunetto Latini (or to the Florentine bankers whom he represented— Florence's Guelf government-in-exile, allies of the pope, and recognized king- and emperor-makers) the splendid *Cantigas de Santa Maria* now in the Biblioteca Nazionale.[33] If so, it was probably a suggestion to them that he would appreciate their further support for his imperial coronation. Already elected in 1257, Alfonso had written to the pope in 1264, making that request.[34] But Bishop García di Silves, carrying that message for the second time, was murdered by the Florentine Ghibelline Rinier dei Pazzi in December 1267. For that violence, Dante would memorialize him in the

Inferno as "Rinier Pazzo, who made such war on the roads" (XII.137: *A Rinier Pazzo, che fecero alle strade tanta guerra*). The Guelfs had been under ecclesiastical interdict from 1258 to 1266 for their murder of Abbot Tesoro of Vallombrosa, a murder used as a "just war" excuse for the battle of Montaperti by the Florentine Ghibellines-in-exile under Farinata and the Sienese commune. Now the Ghibellines, in turn, were placed under an interdict; their murder of a bishop acting as emissary of a king-who-was-almost-emperor canceled out the murder of a treacherous abbot, in this chess game of the politics of violence. But it is clear that neither Guelf nor Ghibelline much desired continuing Alfonso's candidacy. Instructions to Brunetto appear to have been to maintain friendly and literary contact with the Castilian king; actual monetary support was to be for Charles of Provence and Anjou, not as emperor but as senator of Rome, king of Sicily and Jerusalem, and imperial vicar of Tuscany. Neither the popes nor Florence wanted more emperors, after Frederick II.

The splendid French *Tresor,* now in the Escorial, is a second-redaction manuscript, containing the chronicle's continuation through the defeat of Conradin at Tagliacozzo by Charles of Anjou. It is interesting that the section on vices and virtues is much annotated in Latin in its margins, possibly by Brunetto for Alfonso. But the manuscripts that proliferate in Castilian translations are first-redaction manuscripts, concluding with Brunetto Latini's exile because of the Montaperti defeat; this may indicate the presence formerly of an earlier first-redaction *Tresor* in Seville.[35]

After the battle of Benevento on 26 February 1266, it became rather clear to the Florentines that Charles, now senator of Rome and king of Sicily, had no intention of reading or upholding the principles of Aristotelian and Ciceronian government presented to him by Brunetto Latini in *Li livres dou tresor.* Brunetto served as protonotary to Jean Britaud, Charles's vicar in Tuscany, but only for a brief period from 1267 (after his return from Paris) to 1269 or possibly 1270. Then there is a strange silence. One wonders where he was. Brunetto wrote no new literary texts during this period, other than to update the chronicle sections of the French and Italian versions of the *Tresor/Tesoro.* Archival documents in Bologna refer to him twice in connection with family members and bank loans in 1270.[36] He was noted as absent, or his Florentine residency as in the past tense, in two documents of 1275 and 1280. He was mentioned once in 1282 at a council meeting of the Capitani, just after the institution of the priorate.[37] From that time on, he was enormously active in Florentine affairs, constantly mentioned in council meetings and involved in diplomacy from 1283 following the Sicilian Vespers (Charles of Anjou dying in 1285) until June 1292, and acting as prior in 1287. His speeches deal with constitutional matters and diplomacy, with liberty and the freeing of slaves, and with political prisoners. They have about them the flavor of both Aristotle and Cicero.[38] The minutes for these meetings refer to Brunetto as the wise man. He had begun his political career in 1254 as the notary for the Senate or *anziani* of Florence's Primo Popolo government. He was now the distinguished senior statesman of the Secondo Popolo. He is discussed as such at his death, again receiving an entire chapter in Giovanni Villani's *Chronicle,* as well as a vita in Filippo Villani's *Lives of Illustrious Florentines.*[39]

During this last part of Brunetto's life, new versions of *Li livres dou tresor* appear, translated into Italian as the *Tesoro* with historically updated material in chronicle style, through the reign of Charles of Anjou, including the Sicilian Vespers. These versions were earlier thought to have been done by Bono Giamboni and to be Ghibelline, not Guelf. One late paper manuscript has the translation ascribed to Bono Giamboni; the early manuscripts and the first printed edition clearly state they are by Brunetto Latini. Nor should the weather-vane political shift be so polarized. Brunetto was not only a legal colleague of Bono Giamboni but a friend. Even in the worst moments of exile, Brunetto made a point of writing poetry that included Ghibelline with Guelf. His poem *Il favolello* on friendship, for example, was dedicated to the Ghibelline Rusticho di Filippo, who wrote *tenzoni* concerning Charles of Anjou; it also mentions and praises the Guelf poet Palamidesse Belindoti, member of the banking family named in a Westminster Abbey document concerning payment of the tithe by England toward Charles of Anjou's expenses. This capacity to see both sides was typical of Brunetto, who also wrote *Il fiore dei filosafi,* a *tenzone* between Cicero and Cato, whose authorship he claims in the preface to the *Orazioni.* Brunetto's circle of poet friends, both Ghibelline and Guelf, wrote increasingly skillful and witty *tenzoni* about and against Charles of Anjou.[40] It is clear that Brunetto was capable of becoming extremely critical of Charles; it is even possible that he took part in the Sicilian Vespers against him.[41] The *Tresor* texts that Michele Amari edited in *Altre narrazione* exist in a milder version (of which there are several manuscript copies, including the Ambrosian library's G 75 sup.). It also survives in a more extreme version (Magliabechian MS VIII, 1375), consisting of narration interspersed with diplomatic letters concerning the event, including the pope's letter criticizing Charles of Anjou for bad government of his kingdom.[42] The assumption that these chronicle additions to the Italian *Tresor* are Ghibelline is not valid. They are part of Guelf political propaganda, now turned against their former patron who had so bitterly disappointed them. Giovanni Villani is to repeat their material in his Guelf *Cronica*.

These *Tesoro* continuations are of great interest, since not a few of them chronicle the secret cloak-and-dagger diplomacy between the pope, the Byzantine emperor Michael Palaeologus, and King Peter of Aragon through the intermediaries Gianni di Procita and a northern Italian called Accardo Latino; disguised as Franciscans, these agents travel between three rulers and instigate the Sicilian Vespers against Charles of Anjou.[43] These various accounts come replete with secret diplomatic documents. These can be partly retrieved in the Vatican Secret Archives, which mention the embassy and stress the importance of knowing Greek for this purpose.[44] Such documents can also be retrieved in Spanish archival materials, in which letters are found by Gianni di Procita and others to Alfonso el Sabio, explaining that King Peter is unable to aid Alfonso in his campaign against his sons, due to preparations for the invasion of Sicily.[45] Interestingly, this facility in Greek was not in the Renaissance but in the Middle Ages. Brunetto's knowledge of Greek, acquired partly in Arabic Spain, perhaps partly even at Constantinople itself, was greater than Dante's.

If these *Tesoro* continuations represent Brunetto Latini's own thinly disguised "Foggy Bottom" or State Department memoirs, as I suspect, they go far to explain the presence of his manuscripts not only in Castile but also in Aragon. Translated into Catalan and Aragonese, they can be found in Barcelona and Gerona.[46] Again, these are texts designed to teach kings good government and either are the complete *Tesoro* or give its third part, the "rhetoric" section of that text. In one instance, that text is actually bound with an Aragonese chronicle account of the Sicilian Vespers, though the document is admittedly late.[47] After the partial failure of the Vespers revolt and the ensuing deaths of kings Peter and Charles, the kingdoms of Naples and Aragon cultivated close ties, the Aragonese court educating the Angevin King Robert of Naples during his imprisonment by them in Catalonia from 1288 and arranging his marriage in 1297 to Violante, the daughter of King Peter of Aragon and Constance of Swabia. One of Brunetto's sons was later ambassador to King Robert in 1314; another was associated with his court. It appears that Brunetto and the Guelf Bonaccorsi banking family and associates, while continuing to maintain friendly relations with Alfonso of Castile, next backed Charles of Anjou, then turned against him and plotted with Peter of Aragon, and that they finally worked to reconcile the Aragonese and Angevin crowns.

The reigns of both Alfonso and Charles ended in disaster. Alfonso's brother betrayed him, then Alfonso's own sons warred against their father. Pressed for money, Alfonso destroyed the delicate interracial relations in his kingdom by his use of Jews as tax gatherers. The Sicilians likewise finally rose in revolt against overtaxation, in this case against the tithe for Charles's crusades, first with his brother King Saint Louis in the disaster at Tunis and then in Charles's own preparations to capture Constantinople. Had the Florentine bankers aided Alfonso financially instead of Charles, perhaps Spain could have maintained its culturally diverse richness. We know that the pope eventually permitted Alfonso to keep the crusade tithe for his own Spanish wars, supposedly against Muslims.[48]

Certainly the Florentines, through the manuscripts Brunetto acquired when on embassy to Alfonso el Sabio, were able to commence a magnificent tradition which combined the praxis of politics and its theory in philosophy. Brunetto's manuscripts, conveying that material, were used as diplomatic presentation volumes in the thirteenth, fourteenth, and fifteenth centuries throughout Europe. These manuscripts failed to have much of an impact on Charles of Anjou, to whom Florence gave so generously (of others' money); in their own right and in Dante's use of them, however, they reached audiences everywhere, and they especially influenced both Castile and Aragon.

One *Tesoro* manuscript especially needs to be noted. Written in 1287, it is a fine early text. Only the fact that it is mutilated, lacking its beginning and ending, has led to its neglect by scholars other than Helene Wieruszowski.[49] The manuscript is of special interest because it contains Brunetto's *Sommetta,* formulae for notaries in letters between important dignitaries. It includes a form for the pope to use in writing to Alfonso el Sabio: "Bishop Gregory, servant of the servants of God, to the illustrious and beloved dear son, Alfonso king of Castile."[50] Following that formula is the mode of address to King James of Aragon, King Peter having died in a fall from his horse. The text also gives Aristotle's *Ethics* and Brunetto's *Politica*—his material on how a city-state, the *comune,* elects the *podestà,* who swears to protect its constitution. The text was probably dictated by Brunetto, in his customary manner, to a chancery apprentice. In 1287, when Dante Alighieri was twenty years old, Brunetto was shortly to be prior of Florence and was involved diplomatically with Archbishop Ruggieri and Count Ugolino of Pisa; the formulary includes the manner of address between the pope and Archbishop Ruggieri.[51] Roberto Weiss has discussed the relationship between poetry and chancery later in the Renaissance.[52] I believe this relationship is also here, first with the model established by the imperial Ghibelline Pier delle Vigne in Sicily, then in Florence with Guelf republican Brunetto Latini. Verona has a fine *Tresor* manuscript that was a diplomatic presentation copy to a doge of Venice; it is possible that Dante was instrumental in obtaining that manuscript and intended to make use of it diplomatically.[53] Indeed, Latini manuscripts in both French and Italian, including Bergamese, are scattered throughout this region of Italy—in Milan, Ferrara, Verona, Bergamo, Brescia, Venice, and San Daniele del Friuli. Other copies are more predictably in Florence, Rome, Naples, and Palermo. Brunetto's texts, acquired partly from Spain, thus had a far-reaching influence.

Probably because of Alfonso's approval of them, these texts also had a tremendous impact upon Castilian Spain. In this instance, Spanish material, or Greco-Arabic material deriving from Spain, was returning to her in Brunetto's French and Italian translations. The French *Tresor* and the Italian *Ethics* are in the Biblioteca Escorial (L.II.3) and in the Madrid Biblioteca Nacional (10124). These are contemporary productions; in Madrid's Biblioteca del Palacio, the Italian *Tesoro* (II,857) is later, dated 1333 ("This book is called the greater treasure, which was composed by Ser Burnecto Latini of Florence; he wrote [it] in the year 1333"). Translations of these texts were made into Castilian as well as Aragonese and Catalan, as noted earlier. These proliferated throughout Spain; today there is one manuscript in Seville, four at Salamanca (which did not orginate there), six at Madrid, and one at El Escorial; there may well be more.[54] One translation of the *Tresor* was made perhaps by Alfonso el Sabio, according to Ferreiro Alemparte. Manuscripts of the Academia de la Lengua (209,XV), Biblioteca del Palacio (II,3011), Biblioteca Nacional (3380), and Salamanca University (1811 and 1697) make that attribution.[55] The supposed authorship of the French *Tresor* in the Escorial (e.III.8) as by Alfonso X likewise indicates this. Alfonso's son Sancho commissioned a translation by Alfonso de Paredes, the physician-tutor (*alfarqui*) of his own son Fernando; these manuscripts are centered on Seville.[56] Besides the direct presence of Brunetto's texts and translations in Spain, there is also the indirect presence of his work and teaching through the text of Dante's *Commedia,* as translated by the alchemist nobleman Enrique de Villena.[57]

It was Alfonso el Sabio and his work, especially his Aristotelian legal writings in the Castilian vernaculars and his Marian poetry in Galician, which probably gave Brunetto Latini the model for his own writings in the vernacular. These were first in Picard French (in order to educate Charles of

Anjou both in Aristotelian democracy and in Ciceronian republicanism, and thereby protect Florence's communal liberties) and then by translation into his own Italian. That Alfonsine model of the production of books both in texts and miniatures, observed by Brunetto at Alfonso's court, was to be transmitted in turn to the young Dante Alighieri and would result in Dante's *Commedia*. All three men knew how to organize a workshop for the production of books, one that doubled as a chancery for the production of diplomatic letters of state. Brunetto also transmitted the Islamic literary model of teacher and student; this could involve father and son, as when Aristotle wrote his *Nicomachean Ethics* for his child. We see the model in Petrus Alfonsi's writings, where a converted Spanish Jew used the Arabic teaching model in order to convey Islamic learning to the Latin Christian world. That is likewise Brunetto's model, in which a master dictates his lectures to his students ("and then the master said") as in the *Tresor* and the *Tesoro*. That was to be in turn Dante's model, with Virgil as fatherly schoolmaster and Dante as schoolboy. In Dante's encounter with Brunetto (*Inferno*, XV) the text evokes Cicero by the references to Catiline and Fiesole, and Aristotle by the hail of flames from the *Roman d'Alexandre*. And the student looking down upon the master—Dante clothed and dignified, Latini naked and ridiculed—echoes the young Alexander looking down upon Aristotle.[58] We remember that Aristotle's *Ethics* is prefatory to his *Politics;* Brunetto's use of Aristotle is similarly prefatory to centuries of Florentine politics.

It is an intriguing hypothesis that Brunetto Latini's diplomatic exchange of manuscripts with Alfonso el Sabio—including his account in the final partida of the *Tresor* of the election of a city governor as *podestà* to be above corruption—may have shaped in turn Cervantes's presentation of Sancho Panza's ideal governorship of the island. This in turn may have shaped Gonzalo's moving speech in Shakespeare's *Tempest,* and explain why the names there are Spanish rather than the expected Italian. The dream and the reality of these fictional and factual texts, if we can keep translating them into modern idiom, not only shaped the past but may also give us models of constitutional electoral government—a *tesoro* or *tresor*—for the future.

Joseph T. Snow

9. Alfonso as Troubadour: The Fact and the Fiction

The primary purpose of this essay is to explore, principally within the context of Alfonso X's *Cantigas de Santa Maria,* the nuances in the presentation of makers and singers of songs, of troubadours and jongleurs, the process of image-making that takes place in that presentation, and the literary purposes discernable once these nuances and processes are clarified. In carrying out this aim, I shall be positing certain a priori arguments, some of which are the result of previous commentary that I and others have presented in earlier studies and some of which are common knowledge. For example, I often use the designation "Alfonso" to refer to the author of the *Cantigas.* This is, of course, a convention. I do not believe that Alfonso is the author of all of the poems (or the melodies) in this *repertorio marial.* With Antonio Solalinde[1] and many others since, however, I accept the general manner of the king's "making a book." The many roles the king is said to have played make it clear that he was active in almost every phase of book composition, from sourcebook collecting to editing to sponsorship of the large teams necessary in actual production (the miniaturists, the draftsmen, the scribal musicators, and others).

Of Alfonso's known works, the *Cantigas* is the one with which he is most personally identified and which may prove to contain important keys—even at this remove of time—to the kind of person he was or, better yet, the kind of person he wanted to be. Special mention is accorded to this collection and to continued performances from it in both versions of his testament.[2] Alfonso and many members of his family and his court are featured within the precious parchment pages. And although, like many Marian works of the twelfth and thirteenth centuries, the *Cantigas* reflects the wide phenomenon of the efficacy of the Virgin in the affairs of humankind everywhere, the work also reflects the social and political realities of Alfonso's Spain from at least 1257 (when he was elected—albeit never confirmed—emperor of the Holy Roman Empire) to 1281. In addition to

Figure 9-1. Alfonso as prince, receiving a delegation of his Muslim subjects at Murcia (compare this portrait with the older king in Fig. 1-1). *Cantigas de Santa Maria*, Patrimonio Nacional.

this, the miniatures of the twin manuscripts T.I.1. (at the Escorial library and known as the Códice Rico[3]) and the unfinished Banco Rari 20 (at the Biblioteca Nazionale in Florence) portray vividly the full kaleidoscope of changing activity, the hustle and the bustle of daily life in the Iberian peninsula of the mid- to late-thirteenth century. The unfinished nature of the half of the *Cantigas* now at Florence suggests that economic and artistic support for the monumental project terminated with Alfonso's death; in other words, the *Cantigas* was, for the king who styled himself a trou-badour, a work invested with special meaning, meaning that did not tran-scend his own lifespan.

It is the troubadour aspect of the question that fascinates. I have stated this elsewhere, but it bears repeating: Alfonso adds to the notion of the more-or-less standardized anthology of miracles, all of which would have as a common protagonist the figure of Mary, a second protagonist. This protagonist is present in many parts of the *Cantigas* but is preeminent in the *loores* or the songs of praise; and he is seen in the guise, or persona, of a troubadour:

> We see that the *loores* . . . join to tell a story. It is a story which begins in the confessional offering of the first palinode poems (Prologue B.1 and 10 and in which Mary replaces the *outros amores* of the repentent troubadour of profane poetry); develops in the intervening poems with correct troubadouresque vocabulary, conceits, and formulas and personal declarations elevated to the divine plane of love and worship; and concludes in *loor* 400 and the following *pitiçon*. . . . The persona of this troubadour is created out of the emotional patterns that define Alfonso's own feelings for the Virgin, his belief in the efficacy of her protection and the need for solace and refuge in times of great personal need. The *loores,* lyric paeans to a Mary who repeatedly fills these needs, supply us with at least some—albeit not enough—information regarding those emotional patterns.[4]

In transposing the troubadour quest to a divine or spiritual plane, and in identifying this song-making activity with himself as king (as in cantiga 300), Alfonso takes an important step in creating the elements of a spiritual autobiography, a process I have begun tracing in other studies.[5] There is, of course, an organic structure to the story. There is present, at more than one point, a view to a future and a recapitulation of past events. And there are identifiable units that can be treated as chapters in the story. Basically, the tale is the quest for salvation, one in which I have come to see the importance of the prefigural role of Ildefonso, the seventh-century Toledan saint for whom Alfonso was named and who was considered to have gained his salvation through praise of Mary.[6] The tale is updated to Alfonso's time and circumstances, but the parallels are clear. By writing himself into the fabric of the *Cantigas,* however, and having himself represented in the Códice Rico pictorially at those junctures in which pure Marian praise is offered (as by the troubadour to the *domna*), that is, at the *loores,* Alfonso is in effect signing that this is his statement, his story, his offering, his "very small gift" (*don pequen[inn]o,* in cantiga 400: 30). It is clear, too, that it is this gift, these *cantares e sões,* that are designed to be a decisive factor in his *pitiçon* for an entry into paradise where he will be able to gaze for all eternity upon his noble liege lady, as in the conclusion to cantiga 402: "May it be your wish that I see you there, where you are, when I depart from here" [i.e., from this life on earth] (*E querede que vos veja ali / u vos sodes, quando me for daqui*).

Viewing the world about them from the perspective of a troubadour or a jongleur was for many thirteenth-century poets easy to do, for the importance and the impact of this poetic school had long been the dominant lyric mode radiating outward from various courts of southern France. For such as Saint Francis of Assisi, however, who called himself the *giullari di Dio,* or for Gonzalo de Berceo, the *juglar de Santo Domingo,* there is the same sense of distance from the true professional thing as we might find in the *Cantigas* of Alfonso. Like St. Francis and Gonzalo, Alfonso saw the inevitable separation of his own poetizing from that which was traditional or characteristic among the various classes of professionals, even then in manifest decline but welcome always at his court.[7] These poets were all using the term, principally, for its connotation of singer and praiser of a religious figure, a divine presence, without claiming ever to be in reality a member of any group of professionals. It is hardly necessary to belabor this point, except to note that Alfonso did not adduce the comparison without developing it, as did the saint of Assisi and the monk of Berceo for whom the conceit is not extended. As is implied in the extensive quote above, Alfonso's ongoing recourse to the troubadour manner in his own art of poetry in the *Cantigas* requires special study.

I want to elaborate this distinction further, judging it as I do to be vital to Alfonso's design for this work and for its ultimate purpose. For Berceo and St. Francis, direct composition of music does not seem to be a factor in their artistic lives, whereas the opposite is true of Alfonso. We have, in the texts themselves, repeated claims to authorship of both lyrics and melodies. One of many examples is cantiga 401: "Though few songs with music have I finished" (*Macar poucos cantares acabei e con son*). And the independent witness of Alfonso's secretary, the Franciscan Juan Gil de Zamora, supports these statements: "For the praise of the glorious Virgin he composed many beautiful story-songs, [rhythmically] measured with agreeable sounds and musical proportions" (*ad preconium Virginis gloriose multas et perpulchras composuit cantinelas, sonis convenientibus et proportionibus musicis modulatas*).[8] Thus, as a composer of both verse and musical accompaniment, Alfonso was more by way of being a troubadour than others who made use of the metaphor so liberally. Still, one vital distinction remains. The first of the troubadours, William IX the count of Poitiers and duke of Aquitaine, he who did so much to establish the basic archetypes of our views of courtly relationships between men and women, was clearly a troubadour but yet not a professional, one whose livelihood depended on his skill and success as a composer or singer. With time, however, the proliferation of authors, poets, composers, and performers gradually created classes, and large numbers of these came to expect payment for their work as entertainers. The distinctions too, perhaps clear to many at an earlier time, came to be obfuscated in Alfonso's era. Witness the exchange between Guiraut Riquier, the so-called last of the troubadours, and our Alfonso over such matters, in the "Supplicatio" of Riquier and the response or "Declaratio" of Alfonso (written for him in Provençal by Riquier, as we now believe). There the querulous Riquier is finally declared to be *don doctor de trobar*.[9] What we have to learn from this episode is that, at a time when Alfonso was clearly creating a troubadour persona for his beloved *Cantigas* and was consciously composing in the Occitan style, Riquier's request would receive Alfonso's attention as a matter of great moment. Alfonso's solution is conservative, favoring the tradition of separation of *inventores* and *ioculatori,* and reflecting distinctions to be seen in his own *Cantigas.*

We come to this distinction: there is, on one hand, the art with which the *Cantigas* are being elaborated, and on the other, the representation of that art or style of art in the text and miniatures of the *Cantigas*. In this difference and in its nuancing, we may perceive a process of composition (or of organizing, since I freely admit that Alfonso's is often more the guiding hand than the writing hand) that depends more on maintaining the difference than in stressing the parallels and commonalities forging the link between one kind of troubadour and another. To take a professional troubadour as an example, Guiraut expected his rewards in material coin, so to speak; and his texts, every bit as self-conscious as some of Alfonso's in this same regard, often speak, praisingly or disparagingly, of gained or postponed satisfaction.[10] His reputation, and his earthly well-being, might stand or fall on such things, especially among his fellows, for whom jealousy and the spirit of competition for rewards were professional realities. Alfonso's troubadourship, based on earlier models of love *cansos,* existed in a continuous state of expectation of reward, one that could never be satisfied—not, that is, while he remained alive. And rather than living in a competitive working world, as did real troubadours (and their lesser brethren performers), his mission might broadly be defined as to serve as an example to others. This gap between the secular and the divine becomes increasingly more essential to my "reading" of the *Cantigas,* for it is there dwells the narrative and lyric tension of the story itself.

Having postulated this distinction, at least provisionally, we may now

test it. Alfonso, king and sometimes troubadour, devises for his *Cantigas*—
a collection of a hundred basic units (texts and music, with no illustration
other than the presentation miniature which one would expect)—the persona of an Alfonso.[11] He is named in Prologue A (cast in the third person)
but is not so named in the all-important Prologue B (cast now in the first
person, now speaking as a troubadour). Between the two, somewhere, a
crown is exchanged for more humble headgear, the scepter for the pen, the
rule of a kingdom on earth for the hope of service to the Queen of Heaven.
One, the real Alfonso, controls the development and growth of the other,
the fictional Alfonso, as the idea of the *Cantigas* takes on greater bulk and,
in so doing, becomes ever more permeated with the presence of the two,
the real and the fictional troubadours. This continues until, at the close in
poems 400, 401, and 402, they have clearly merged. We then find ourselves
back at a familiar beginning, only richer for the journey and for the ex-
posure to this facet of the mind of Alfonso X. Time has passed for the
Cantigas (perhaps two decades or more), and time has passed for the
"Alfonso" who undertook them long years ago. The work of composing his
own texts, making his own music, and commissioning such other texts as he
deemed appropriate from those Solalinde termed *los continuadores de la obra
primitiva*[12] was at an end. But why create this dichotomy in the first place? I
suggest that Alfonso uses it as a means of sorting through the levels of
acceptance the term troubadour had gained by the mid- to late-thirteenth
century; and culling out some of the more elevated ones for application to
his own quest, he enriches and expands upon that role. He desires to set
himself apart but also seeks to establish himself as a leader of men and
women, as a model for others to emulate (even professional troubadours).
In setting himself apart, he cultivates Mary's special friendship, fictionalizes
his art, and offers it as a small token, albeit a meritorious service, of his own
devotion. It is a personal response to her loyalty to him. If he fails as a
sinner, he will make up some lost ground as a worthy singer; and this is the
fact that Alfonso never seems to lose sight of in those cantigas that carry the
narrative of his troubadouresque quest for life's highest reward: salvation.

Where this divinized troubadour intersects with the special features of
the traditional *Frauendienst,* service to the lady, is in his alter-ego status as
sinner. It also marks the difference. The professional troubadour may be
unworthy of his lady's notice (or believe that such is the case), but he owns
no wrongdoing. The divinized troubadour in search of salvation, as his
lady's gift to him, must somehow overcome his sin, exculpate himself with
good works and still, in the end, have to throw himself on her mercy, her

bēes, in the hope that his motives will be read as clean ones. The dichotomy between kinds of troubadours, if I have here been reading the story of the *Cantigas* correctly, has been assumed in many previous studies (my own included) to be mere posture-adopting metaphor-making of a superior, even a smug, kind. The initial palinode, as I see it now, carries the additional meaning of having us see that the persona himself is not only changing one set of love objects for another but also protecting a changed self at the same time or, at the very least, a renewed image of a larger self, with greater potential for spiritual growth.

With the palinode, the persona begins a journey, even a limited one, toward better self-knowledge:

> What I want is to make praises of the Virgin
> . . . and therefore do I wish evermore to be
> her troubadour and beg her that
> she grant that I may be her troubadour and that she
> will accept my songs . . .

> O que quero é dizer loor da Virgen
> . . . e por aquest'eu quero seer oy mais
> seu trobador e rogo-lle que me
> queira por seu trobador e que queira
> meu trobar reçeber . . . [Prologue B]

This aspiration bears repeating in cantiga 1: "From this time hence do I desire to speak in song / for my honored Lady" (*Des oge mais quer'eu trobar / pola Sennor onrrada*). It finds its definitive formation in number ten:

> If I can gain the love
> of this Lady whom I accept as my liege
> and of whom I wish to be troubadour,
> all other loves shall I leave to the devil.

> Esta dona que tenno por Sennor
> e de que quero seer trobador
> se eu per ren poss'aver seu amor,
> dou ao demo os outros amores.

The gain compared with losses of the past, expressed here, completes the earlier sentiment of Prologue B: "now I abandon efforts to praise in song / another lady, and think to recover / with [Mary] all that I have squandered on others" (*e ar querrei-me leixar de trobar / des i por outra dona, e cuid'a cobrar / per esta quant'enas outras perdi*). This marvelous contrast between reward and loss, between earthly women and the Virgin, is fruitfully exploited in the now recontextualized opposition Ave/Eva (cantiga 60) and in the alternations of acceptance and rejection (of earthly *domna* and heavenly *Domna*) that give a special cast to the refrains of cantiga 130.

Lest we think that this palinode is meant to be a personal affair between the persona and Mary, we should be proved wrong; on the contrary, it turns out to be rather a public turning point. The troubadour of the *Cantigas* wants his quest to be noticed, for nothing could be better than to have served as a means to an even greater following for this "*Rosa das rosas*":

> Let her give to me such reward as she gives
> to those she loves, and *whoever learns this*
> will more willingly lift his voice in song for her.

> Que me dé gualardon com'ela dá
> aos que ama; e *queno souber*
> por ela mais de grado trobará. [Prologue B]

We might cite one more happy vignette of this generalized picture of the ideal world, hands joined in praise of Mary: "May the crowned Virgin / who is our hope / be praised by us / in song and in dance" (*Cantando e con dança / seja por nos loada / a Virgen corõada / que e noss'asperança*). Over and against this vision, almost utopian in its dimensions, is the richer subtext in which the carefully cultivated difference between the fictionally autobiographical troubadour of the *Cantigas* is dramatically opposed to others who practice the craft:

> Tell me, o troubadours,
> why do you not praise with your song
> the Fairest of the fair?
> If indeed you know how to compose songs,
> why do you not do so
> for her from whom you have access to God?

> Dized', ai trobadores
> a Sennor das sennores
> porque a non loades?
> Se vos trobar sabedes,
> a que por Deus avedes
> porque a non loades? [Cantiga 260]

By now, this has exceeded the limits of a fictional metaphor, used to initiate a particular poem or to set the tone for a collection of this sort. It has become part of a complete (and developing, at this point) narrative story line that never strays far from the goals set out for it in the overall architecture of the compilation, into which it has now been inextricably imbedded. The result is that this second protagonist begins to interest us more and more, and we look for increasing evidence of his developing portrait in the remaining poems. We are not disappointed. In those poems, Mary is seen more as the suitor's ineffably kind benefactor, working her wonders out of an active blend of her love and loyalty, than as a lady waiting to be pleased but somewhat aloof and removed. As Alfonso and Mary exist outside the fiction of the *Cantigas,* so also do they exist inside it: the many visual depictions may be "read" by the viewer as wish fulfillment, as realizations on vellum of a smiling Mary, nodding with frequent approval on the songs of praise of this most faithful *entendedor*-troubadour—shown, unmistakably, crowned.

Alfonso X, king of Castile and León, sings mightily of the pure love he feels for Mary, a love far exceeding the love possible with earth-bound ladies. If the latter love is to be abandoned, it is because the former *is* attainable and lasts *forever.* Even though we are witness to Alfonso's abandonment of the pursuit of other loves (*os outros amores*), and Mary is the substitute for the *domna* sought after by the *canso*-composing troubadours of the Midi, there is also the sense—within the overall scope of the *Cantigas*—that it is also the love of *all* related earthly pursuits that Alfonso seems most strongly to reject. Again, we may usefully read cantiga 300 for a fuller picture of this point of view, in which loyalty, that rarest of qualities, is so much and so fervently valued.

The standard pose of the professional troubadour before his lady requires humility. Still, both walk the same ground. This is not so in the fictionalized case of the *Cantigas*'s persona, however, where the sinner/singer stands before a dweller of paradise. Hence, there is more than *assumed* humility: the original metaphor has taken on the coloration of a spiritual reality. It is about this distinction that Alfonso makes much ado in this spiritual self-portrait, as the *Cantigas*'s troubadour wanders in and around the varied settings of the collection. Once more, we see that a contrast of consequence is allowed to give shape and meaning to the distinction between Alfonso's persona and the real-life situation of the professional troubadour. Balanced against the expected gains and favor of Mary that Alfonso seeks, the more mundane objectives of the secular troubadour pale into insignificance. Even his art passes on to a new plane where special comprehension—*entendimento* and *razon*—is required (Prologue B). The air Alfonso breathes in this idealization is as rare as it is sweet: the object of his affections, while not physically present, exerts a stronger pull on his being. Such troubadours as this one, who deploy their talents to reach for this vastly richer, timeless treasure, sharing as they must in the expectations Alfonso has, will gain lasting (i.e., eternal) life. Alfonso, using his pursuit and wooing as example, clearly sends out his message: "Do as I do."

This then, in part at least, is the troubadour art with which the *Cantigas* were joined and fitted, resulting in a structural edifice in which a divinized *entendedor* could peaceably contemplate his destiny and his relationship with his hostess Mary, whose praises are the major adornment of the several rooms of the edifice. In this mosaic of text, music, and miniature art, what other representations show performing artists? And what relationship do they bear to the self-portrait of the troubadour persona at the center? How did Alfonso, the architect of the edifice, view the professional entertainers other than the fictional Alfonso for whom he had it built? There are twelve cantigas which allow a glimpse of musicians, composers, jongleurs, mimes, and other classes of professional entertainers. Some are laymen, others clerics, some good-hearted, others less well-meaning. What they have in common may be limited to their livelihood and some contact with the Virgin; but that is enough, for the moment, to make them of interest.

Cantiga 8. The figure at the center here is named Pedro de Sigrar: he is identified as a *jograr,* and one sees (even in the miniatures) that "he could sing well, and he played even better" (*mui ben cantar sabia e mui mellor violar*). With these arts, he intoned lays to Mary, which he repeated in all the churches. Like Alfonso, then, his songs are centered around Mary, but his ostensible reward is more modest than the monarch's. Should his songs find acceptance, he desires a wax candle. They do, and it is given.

Cantiga 56. The encounter is with a monk who could read very little (*sabia leer mui poco*), but who composed five psalms in service to Mary so that, we discover, he may earn from her the reward of serving her son (*tal galardon per que podesse veer o seu Fillo piadoso* [31–33]). Upon his death, five roses spring from his mouth, one for each of the songs. Thus is this candid soul rewarded. Note he is not a member of a professional group of entertainers. Note too that he is a composer, and the constancy of his devotion earned him an answer to his prayers.

Cantiga 194. This one tells how Mary rescued a *jograr* from some people who would kill him and steal what he carried with him. This fellow plied well his chosen metier from court to court—*andando pelas cortes*. He sang well—*apost'e sen vergonna* (e.g., songs of a good character, no rib-aldry). Despite this, his host, in cahoots with a confederate, plots to waylay him the next day and relieve him of his earnings. A prayer to Mary is answered and the attack foiled even as it is being carried out. The jongleur goes freely on his way, praising Mary (*dando mui grandes loores aa Virgen groriosa*). We have in this fortunate entertainer a devotee of Mary (it is clear that she is well-disposed toward him); but his goals have not shifted to become comparable to the goals of the persona, second protagonist of these *Cantigas*.

Cantiga 202. The Parisian archdeacon of San Victor made a song of praise (*fez ũa prosa de ssa loor*) and was short a rhyme word. This was his habit: he much enjoyed praising the goodness of Mary and her troubadour qualities of *mesura, prez,* and *valor*. He went before Mary's altar to pray for a rhyme word and was pleased and thankful when it was supplied. One only has to imagine his deep pleasure and surprise when, passing before an image of the Holy Mother, it leaned over and whispered her thanks to him: "Muitas graças, meu sennor."[13]

Cantiga 238. This tells the story of another jongleur who was given to dice-rolling and who spoke ill of God and his Mother when he lost. He is painted black from the outset of the tale. When he blasphemes, he is struck dumb (*nunca mais falou nada*). The devil takes him off. It is important to know that, in addition to his offense, he was not a good practitioner of his art; he did not praise Mary and was given to abusing his artistic gifts.

Cantiga 259. This curious cantiga does indeed deal with two jongleurs, but their art is not the focal point. Aware of their lack of feeling for each other, Mary causes them to be friends and gives them a curative candle (for St. Martial's fire, erysipelas). Their journey is impeded by a bishop, who then contracts the disease and is cured only subsequent to recognizing his error.

Cantiga 279. In this poem, Mary cures a king. From the context, he can be none other than Alfonso. Her intervention is called for and justified by the fact that the ailing king is her *loador* or, even more expressly, her troubadour—as in the refrain "Holy Mary, give succour / and aid to your troubadour, / for it goes ill with him" (*Santa Maria, valed', ai Sennor, / e acorred'a vosso trobador / que mal le vai*). Alfonso is not named, and the cantiga is cast in the third person. No argument can be made for Alfonso's authorship of this composition, but the rubrics used to identify this king, as *vosso loador* and *vosso trobador,* make a search for any other troubadour-king superfluous.

Cantiga 291. A young student from Salamanca winds up imprisoned in Toro and remembers to call upon the Virgin, in whom he has great trust. He writes a song for her then and there, in prison, and sings it. In the event, he is let go (Mary at work behind the scene) and he serves Mary actively ever after, we are told. Even though again the protagonist is not a professional troubadour, the efficacy of turning to Mary, of singing her praises, and staying on that path is the point the composer of these lyrics has in mind. He concludes: "And that's why I've recounted / this happening, that you should take great delight in honoring her" (*E poren vos contei / este feito que ajades gran sabor de a onrrar*). We sense that the form of honor intended by the author of cantiga 291 (perhaps Alfonso, or one of the *continuadores* familiar with his blueprint for the *Cantigas*) might easily have read: *dizer loor* or *trobar*, to sing her praises.

Cantiga 293. Akin to cantiga 238 is this poem in which a *remedador* or mime, who turns a nice profit with his imitations, runs afoul of Mary when—inspired by the devil—he mimics her and her babe in arms. His punishment is a twisted mouth and arm. When he recants, this is undone. Again, we are presented with a professional entertainer who should know better and should use his talents in other, nobler ways.

Cantiga 307. This poem takes place in Sicily during a 40-day sequence of volcanic eruption. One day, in the form of a vision, the Virgin appears to a good man (*bõo ome*) with a curious proposition: "If you wish that an end be made to this calamity, / have a song composed / that is worthy of me, well done in my honor" (*Se tu queres que sse tolla este mal, / un cantar me façan que seja [a]tal / qual a mi conven, ben feit'a mia loor*). This the good man does, first the words and then the music; and then, in good troubadour style, he sings it. Mary keeps her word and the volcanic rocking ceases. Assuming this is not one of Alfonso's compositions, it is easy to see why it must have appealed greatly to him and why he had it recast in Galician-Portuguese for the *Cantigas:* such *loores* are beloved of the Virgin and, when composed in the proper spirit and style, are efficacious in earning her favor.

Cantiga 316. This introduces a cleric from Portugal, Martin Alvitez, a troubadour: rather than of love, he sang of ridicule in his songs (*que sas cantigas fazia d'escarnho mais ca d'amor* [15–16]). When he burns down a rival church through jealousy, the cleric is made blind, a situation later reversed when he completes its reconstruction. What attracts attention is his confession, worth citing in full:

> . . . My Lady, I was foolish
> to sing for another lady, for I have had no relief

from my suffering; therefore, I come before you to swear
that so long as I shall live, I shall no more sing or compose songs
for any other, for it is [now] not necessary;
rather for you will I with all my heart sing all the praise that I can;
and henceforth do I desire to be your troubadour.

. . . Sennor, eu fol
fui de que trobei por outra dona, ca nihũa prol
non ouv'y aa mia coita. Poren te venno jurar . . .
[q]ue enquant'eu vivo seja, nunca por outra moller
trobe nen cantares faça oy mais, ca non mi á mester;
mais por ti direi de grado quanto ben dizer poder,
e des aqui adeante quero ja por ti trobar. [51–58]

Here it is only necessary to remark the conceptual and verbal similarity to the Alfonsine palinode series (Prologue B, cantigas 1 and 10), of which it seems to be a familiar calque. The thematic link too needs to be kept in mind: here is an artist who misused his gifts singing more the songs of *escarnho* than of love. The incident of the miracle narration clearly puts him on the path of Alfonso (in these *Cantigas*); his positive reformation would serve as a model for those others of his fellow poets of secular jests whom Alfonso chides in cantiga 260 (see above, p. 131). The appeal of this account is clear: the links to the frame story of the persona of the narrative are unmistakable. The composition ends with these last words of his speech to Mary, and with the repetition of the refrain. No further words seem called for.

Cantiga 363. This account is important for the identification made in it. A talented singer is imprisoned in Gascony, accused of using his song to criticize society. Thinking that his end is near, he calls on Mary, promising to evermore sing of her love should she avail him in his hour of distress. He is wondrously transported elsewhere and liberated from his incarceration. His days are then consumed in keeping his promise to Mary. While not much is made of his song, it does seem clear that this is yet another case of misapplied talents that find new directions (the glories of Mary's love). The lines of greatest interest would be 27 to 28: "and, lying there, he swore to her that he would, while he drew breath, / sing of her love, *of which we sing*" (*e jurou-ll'ali jazendo, que mentre vivesse / polo seu amor trobasse, de que nos trobamos* [emphasis mine]). Is this *we* Alfonso, speaking in his royal person, or speaking editorially, or even speaking as the self-appointed leader of troubadours (all who praise Mary may be so classed, broadly speaking) seeking only after the one great, eternal *gualardon:* salvation? Whether

Alfonso was himself author or not of 363, it cannot fail to impress itself upon us that once again, in connection with a miracle tale in which a troubadour is featured, the opportunity is taken to assert the leadership that is posited by the very presence of a troubadour persona as a second protagonist in the mosaic that is the *Cantigas*.

Having seen how Alfonso as artist/troubadour is present as the creator/designer/architect of the *Cantigas,* and having seen how Alfonso as artist/troubadour is present as sinner/singer within the *Cantigas,* it may be time for taking stock. First, given the obvious importance of the entire range of troubadour vocabulary, imagery, and formal art to the texture of the *Cantigas de Santa Maria* as a compilation of texts with music, it would be surprising not to have found—among its almost 2,000 miniatures—a generous sampling of these entertainers; *remedadores, jograres, trobadores.* These do appear; they come from Spain, Portugal, France, Italy, Gascony, and Catalonia. They compose, sing, and entertain in other ways, are both lay and clerical, inexperienced and experienced, well-behaved and mischievous, devout and mocking. By and large, they earn their living as performers, though this is not always the case, as we have seen from the dozen cantigas reviewed above.

With one notable exception (no. 279), these *Cantigas* depictions are not truly representative of the rich spectrum of Provençal (high or debased) style present in Alfonso's court and, previously, in the court of his father Fernando III. That is, the troubadours we might expect to see—the Peire Cardenals,[14] the Cerverí de Gironas, the Guiraut Riquiers, all of whom were well-known practitioners of the high troubadour manner, the latter two recognizing in divers texts of their own Alfonso's devotion to Mary—these types of troubadours seem by and large curiously absent. Riquier himself, during the ten years he spent at Alfonso's court, also penned some Marian *loores,* doubtless influenced by his patron's dedication to the *Cantigas.* Can at least a plausible reason be provided by way of justifying this absence? I think so: it seems a role Alfonso was reserving for himself, for his persona, for his *servus Mariae.* He cast himself as the model, the troubadour who would lead other troubadours, the sinner who would turn other sinners onto the upward path toward the greater reward.

The performer as model is such a constant narrative component of the *Cantigas*'s story that it cannot be downplayed by any who would understand the controlling metaphors that provide it with its special organic unity (apart from the very presence of the Virgin, of course). If the very performance of the praise is the important element, then the vision of all mankind joining together in a highly joyful dance of life (in cantiga 409 cited above) serves as a kind of apotheosis of the metaphor of the performer: we can all be (potentially speaking) performers/sinners, working out the means to our salvation, if we but dedicate ourselves.[15] In the story of the *Cantigas,* the tale of one such performer's dedication has been sketched. We have seen, as well, some performers turning from this world to Mary (recall the protagonists of cantigas 291, 316, and 363); these are examples of the troubadours called to task in 260 for not doing so. Especially does cantiga 316 reflect the very same turning away previously expressed in Alfonso's own palinodic sequence from the earliest version (the Toledo MS) of the *Cantigas.*

In all of the inserted performer-type cantigas (excepting 238, the mime or *remedador*), the efforts to please Mary are met with success, in that the Virgin is deeply pleased, grateful, and/or obliged. Sometimes this is owing to the persistence of the performer, already a devotee of Mary. At other times, it is owing to a change in the way the performer's art is used—that is, when he abandons simple displays of virtuosity (as in the composing of *cantigas d'escarnho*) for expression in a more spiritual register.[16] This better employment of one's artistic talent is a rich theme in the *Cantigas,* one Alfonso uniquely exploits. What seems clear, then, is that the choice of performer-centered episodes for the *Cantigas* has much to do with the thematic nucleus centered on the activities of the troubadour persona within. Moreover, it would be easy to make a small series of statements that could apply to the collection as a whole: (1) *Cantar ben* is the same as *loar a Maria;* (2) Mary likes praise (dignified and appropriate, to be sure); (3) to abuse one's artistic gifts is tantamount to devoting one's time to ridicule (*escarnho*) or to *outros amores;* (4) praising Mary—despite the impossibility of ever doing justice to a project almost by definition impossible to achieve, so many are Mary's mercies, or *bẽes*—is rewarding, though requiring a quasi-superhuman effort; and (5) mocking Mary (as did the *remedador*) is inevitably destructive to the one who attempts such acts.

Alfonso is aware of all of this, and thus controls it all from a point above the level of the narrative—as narrator-organizer of the story of the fictional Alfonso-troubadour. His warning is never taken lightly, not even by the persona. In fact, the persona is precisely where the two classes of troubadours meet in the *Cantigas:* the image of the troubadour as a professional is made possible by close adherence to the living (and dead) models Alfonso had before him as prototypes, and whose art and style he was not only adapting and borrowing but also attempting to revitalize. His esteem for the class of performer at the pinnacle of the performance hierarchy, the *don doctor de trobar* (conceded to Riquier as I earlier noted), seems to have been genuine. It inspired him, in this literary actualization of one of his social roles, to cast himself as a professional troubadour, now, however, raised to a spiritual plane in which he could explore the path to salvation through a real service to Mary, a service that is manifest in these same *Cantigas.*

If it has been of any use at all to maintain this distinction between the professional and the occasional troubadour, for the purposes of this discussion, it is this: it has allowed us to perceive more clearly the dual roles I attribute to Alfonso as artist. Alfonso, of course, plays many roles connected to the production of these *Cantigas de Santa Maria.* But the two important roles are both as artist, and we ought not confuse them. The first is as artist-creator, the king who was eminently capable of writing text and composing music. The second is related to the setting down of a literary record of the meaning of the labor invested in the design and elaboration of a specific work of literature: this record is contained within the confines of the work itself, and although literary, the record retains an autobiographical relationship with the work and activity of the artist-creator outside the work. Thus, the fictional persona, also a troubadour, is both created and (within his proper roles) a creator. The persona as creator mainly preoccupies himself with the production of *loores,* or songs of praise: remember that he appears in some, but not a plurality, of the total number of cantigas in the compilation. In those texts, he is both described and graphically depicted in varying attitudes of praise. The presentation miniature depicts Alfonso as composing, perhaps dictating, even while musicians rehearse the music. If this reflects a real scene, as some think, the very self-referentiality of it is never any less strong than in those many more miniatures of the crowned king (troubadour persona) that illustrate the *loores* in the Códice Rico. The effect for Alfonso-the-creator of having created, in his own image, an Alfonso-the-created, is to gain the distance needed for the approach to the daunting task of putting himself in a position of intimacy, or quasi-intimacy, with Mary. One step removed from reality, the persona offers shelter or a defense against assuming too much arrogance, while it simultaneously provides the comfort of maintaining an interior dialogue with himself about the mysteries of faith and the chance of salvation. An idealization it is, that is certain; and it may also be a projection, a hope, a wish, a desire placed thus safely into words (and music).

The many coincidences and the overlap between king and troubadour throughout the *Cantigas* (texts and miniatures) really are a kind of signature. It matters little whether Alfonso was the actual author of each and every one of the *cantigas* in which the story of this second protagonist is told. It does matter that Alfonso chooses to maintain a distinction between his real labor in creating the *Cantigas* and the created image within (with which he may very well have had active, and understanding, collaboration). The story itself reveals that these very *Cantigas* in praise of Mary are the revelation of the persona's hope of the reward of seeing his beloved Mary in paradise. Close examination of the closure poems (400, 401, and 402) shows that these are made more intelligible when read (or heard) in the light of the opening poems, those already alluded to as the palinodic sequence. And what gives them all the extra level of enrichment is the engagement of the persona of the troubadour with the Queen of Heaven: he begs her guidance at one end of his poetic journey, and her grace and understanding at the other.

In the interim, the tension of the relationship is kept acute by the binary opposition of the humility of the sinner and the pride of the singer. In raising the metaphor of the troubadour, his social context (*entorno*), and his professional status to the level of the divine, Alfonso introduces the new element of the sinner into the mix. This is what we scholars have too often overlooked, as we have made our equations between the living troubadour who is also king and the troubadour of the fictional world, through whose guise he is able better to express his own worldly frustration, even as he is engaged in an all-important quest for redress. We should not fail to see how, and to what extent, the *Cantigas de Santa Maria* are truly the work in which Alfonso allows us to peer into the window of his soul and to share with him the experience of the one truth and the one loyalty which for him could never be in doubt.

Nancy Joe Dyer

10. Alfonsine Historiography: The Literary Narrative

In writing about the past, Alfonso X selected sources, determined the linguistic and stylistic medium of presentation, and extended his historiographic works to the general literate lay public, thus demonstrating in the intellectual sphere the same decisiveness and ambition that characterize his legal and political aspirations.[1] Interpreted within the framework of the late medieval formulation of Aristotelian causality,[2] Alfonso X played the dual roles as actor and author of history. He was the *auctor* of historical writings in the sense that he was the motivating agent of the text—that is, the "efficient cause." His sources constituted the "material cause," his literary style and structure were the "formal cause," and his objective in writing would be the "final cause."

Alfonso appropriated the task of writing history from clerical predecessors, some of whom, because of working under royal patronage, exhibited pro-monarchic sympathies in addition to other vested interests. By increasing the variety and number of his sources to an encyclopedic range of narratives and documents from diverse cultural and social perspectives, he augmented the demographic register of people perceived and portrayed to have influenced the course of history.

Innovatively, Alfonso promoted the use of Castilian prose to relate the flow of past events, which he focused toward closure according to his unique sociopolitical vision of universal history and the position of Spain in the scheme, especially Castile. Choice of a selected sociogeographic linguistic variety, "true Castilian" (*castellano drecho*) rather than Latin, insured delivery of his view of history to an intended lay audience (reader or listener) in a medium consonant with the personae of the narrative.

The study of Alfonsine historiography is seriously complicated because Alfonso's historical works, like his personal political ambitions, were terminated without completion by his death. They were left in varying degrees of elaboration, to be reworked and continued by monarchs and minions of different views and talents. The projected *General estoria* of universal scope and the Iberian-focused *Estoria de Espanna* come to us mostly through partially reworked posthumous collections of chronicles, derived from workbooks in varying states of completion prepared under his direction. The earlier portions of the *Estoria de Espanna* (relating the creation, pre-Roman and Roman history, and Gothic and Arabic invasions) had been more polished textually prior to Alfonso's death; later history from the Reconquest to his own time remained less formally elaborated. Fortunately, the inconclusive character of the hundred-or-so chronicle manuscripts provides a means for reconstructing in part the content, intent, and method of elaboration of the original Alfonsine histories.[3]

Writing about "modern" and "contemporary" Spanish history proved to be a significant, if not insurmountable, challenge for the Learned Monarch because of the plethora of divergent sources narrating and interpreting a single event, and because his prime structural framework inherited from the Latin chronicles failed him. Where he failed to dominate his dramatically pre-emplotted and politically charged narrative sources, precisely there do we witness the surprising state of development of Spanish prose narrative. This essay assesses Alfonso's historical works on the basis of treatment of the literary narrative, both as material and formal cause, which advanced his writings beyond the chronicle toward true historical writing. By studying his use and, more importantly but more difficult to show, his deliberate nonuse of extant narrative, we can perceive the complexity of the historiographic task and why a small portion of the *Estoria de Espanna* failed to materialize.

Alfonso's treatment of the reign of Alfonso VIII has been selected for this study partly because of its content—the earlier ruler's hereditary and political ties to Alfonso el Sabio, his popular appeal to the intended thirteenth-century audience and later chronicle consumers, and his appeal to the modern reader. It has been selected also for formal considerations—the unusually complicated beginning of that earlier reign, the availability of primary and secondary source materials, the abundance of textual witnesses to the Alfonsine process, and the fact that it marks the conclusion of the last original workbooks prepared for the *Estoria de Espanna*.[4]

Narrative and Historiographic Modality

From Aristotle to the poststructuralists, medieval Spanish historians not excepted, textual critics have pondered the relationship between historical

writing and literature.[5] The annal originated in the early Carolingian period when the clergy found it necessary to distribute to provincial monks
and priests the exact date of the movable feasts based on the shifting Easter
festival.[6] Systematic annals mentioned only a few memorable events of the
writer's own time. Viewed as a whole, the apparently unrelated listing of
births, deaths, climate, battles, and events presents a curious picture to the
modern reader, but it must represent some cohesion in the writer's mind.
Hayden White observes that "we are likely to be put off by the annalist's
apparent failure to see that historical events dispose themselves to the
percipient eye as 'stories' *waiting to be told.*"[7] When events have no beginning other than the calendar date and have no story conclusion, their
"meaning" derives from inclusion in the list. White questions the validity of
the annal as a type of historical representation, since "it is a product of an
image of reality in which the *social system,* which alone could provide the
diacritical markers for ranking the importance of events, is only minimally
present to the consciousness of the writer, or rather, is present as a factor in
the composition of the discourse only by virtue of its absence." He favors
the Hegelian thesis that a historical account must have a prescribed narrative form and content—that is, a politicosocial order.[8]

The chronicle developed from the annal, following the temporal or-
dering of events but summarizing them, particularly when in the contemporary period more than one account existed. Like the annal, it may appear
not to "conclude" but simply to terminate. "Typically it lacks closure, that
summing up of the 'meaning' of the chain of events with which it deals."[9]
The writing of chronicles from documentary sources entailed a process of
"emplotment," that is, the encoding of the facts as components of specific
kinds of plot structures. "Most historical sequences can be emplotted in a
number of ways so as to provide different interpretations of these events
and to endow them with different meanings. . . . But historical situations
do not have built into them intrinsic meanings in the way that literary texts
do."[10] "Facts" are really story elements which can be suppressed, subordi-
nated, highlighted, and manipulated as one would the elements of a novel
or a play.

Genuine historical writing for White, following a Lacanian formulation, pertains to the "discourse of the real" versus that of the "imaginary" or
"of desire," having a formal coherency (completion), the equivalent of
narrative closure. He distinguishes between narrating (objective recount-
ing of events perceived to exist within or behind evidence) and narrativiz-
ing (subjectively imposing upon events the form of a story in which the
events speak for themselves).[11] Meaning can be derived by subsuming sets

of events into cause-effect paradigms, as a scientific approach, or by encoding them into extant, culturally understood patterns such as a story frame.[12]

Edward W. Said, acknowledging a debt to White, proposes that there
is no way to get past texts in order to apprehend "real" history directly.

> [Said] affirms the connection between texts and the existential actualities of
> human life, politics, societies, and events. The realities of power and author-
> ity—as well as the resistances offered by men, women, and social movement to
> institutions, authorities, and orthodoxies—are the realities that make texts
> possible, that deliver them to their readers, that solicit the attention of critics.
> . . . These realities are what should be taken account of by criticism and the
> critical consciousness.[13]

The Learned Monarch sought to bring meaning to historical events by
artistic and scientific approaches, emplotting events into an effective narrative and explaining their causal relationships. His emplotment of history
was as decisive a social and political strategem as any legal or political move
of his career, motivated in principle by a refined, Aristotelian concept of
order (*por esto fue endereçado el curso del mundo de cada una cosa en su orden*)
which would lead his people to enlightenment (*pora alumbrar los sos entendi-
mientos*), as explained in his authorial prologue to the *Primera crónica
general*. His sources, whether secondary, such as a preconcatenated matrix
or a recently confected Latin chronicle, or primary, such as an epic poem
relative to political unification, appear in his history because he found them
to be more *plausible* than any other choice. Aesthetic and moral considerations ultimately would be subjected to the author's formal and final criteria.

Structure, Narrative Sources, and Demographics of Alfonsine Chronicles

An essential feature of the Spanish chronicle is its traditional open structure,[14] in computing terminology a proclivity for block moves. Each
authority—the Bible, patristic writers, classical and folk literature—dis-
played its own distinctive style of language and unique patterns of content
selection, thereby implying preexisting different ideological and creative
criteria. The presence of an artistically crafted infrastructure, for example a
prosified epic poem or even a traditional legend, might render a historical
work more metaphorical and fictive, in general more literary; but its the-

matic artistic and structural cohesion was subject to the historian's quill. The historians could dilute or distort the form or intent of the infrastructure by stylistic and contextual alterations through reduction (such as deletions of affective references and shift of responsibility for potentially reprehensible action), by interpretive additions, and by contextual displacement.

In the chronistic organizational plan, multiple unifying structural arcs ordered each level of constituent elements of the *Estoria de Espanna,* from its comprehensive metaplan through intermediate dynastic blocks to individual reigns, to minute details of human developmental stages of the protagonists of history. The literary narrative used in the compositional scheme at the lower levels, originating as both individual and traditional creations, already had been brought to narrative closure and now had to be "reopened" to mesh with alternate accounts—some complementary and some contradictory. The literariness of Alfonsine historiography derives in part from the stylistic tension between the aperture of "closed" sources at the lower structural levels, and narrative closure of potentially "open" structures at the metalevel. Alfonso's force as an author derived from his manipulation of the personae of events, the use of sources to empower or marginalize its actors, and his decisions on defining the flow of history.

PRECURSORS OF ALFONSINE HISTORIOGRAPHY

Alfonso X formed part of a continuous tradition of writers about Spain's history, in a trajectory beginning from his oft-cited authority the Roman Paulus Orosius.[15] The earliest peninsular annals, criticized by modern Spanish historiographers for their dry gloominess, constituted notes and mere outlines for subsequent histories.[16] By the close of the twelfth century, preexisting annals formed the vertebral column onto which the Christian writers grafted diverse sources; these include in contemporary periods documentary, literary and folkloric narratives, personal observations and recollections, and progressive infusion of sanguinity into historical personages.

Alfonso's immediate predecessors, both Christian and Arabic, already had begun to transcend the stylistic-modal distance between annalistic lists and narrated history. Lucas de Tuy centralized history into constituent formal blocks constituting the reign of a monarch, marked by an exact beginning and ending, coterminous with accession to the throne and death.

He focused primarily upon an institution or office whose occupant changed through divine intervention, but he included few actual human details, scarcely threading together the strands at the lower structural levels. Rodrigo Jiménez de Rada incorporated more pre-emplotted narrative sources into his chronicle than did his predecessor and, consequently, portrayed more upper nobility and commoners as pivotal in shaping historical events. Although the *cantares* of Castilian counts appear in the *Crónica najerense* around 1150, Lucas de Tuy in 1236 included the legend of the Mora Zaida and a novelesque version of the pilgrimage of Louis VII to Santiago, both of which were extracted from traditional poetic roots. Rodrigo innovatively cited epic sources directly for specific details.[17] This recourse was to reach its apogee after Alfonso's time.

While in the Isidorian tradition the Latin-ecclesiastical historians focused on grandiose events affecting national concerns, their fellow Arabic historiographers were attentive to the individual, even secondary personages of history.[18] Aḥmad b. al-Razī (899–955) even conceived of the history of Spain as the continuation of familial lineages coexisting in the peninsula.[19] In the four decades between the composition of the Latin-ecclesiastical chronicles and the origins of the secularized Alfonsine project, the concept of writing about the recent past again evolved markedly toward greater narrativity and emplotment. Perhaps, as has been suggested, the shift was influenced by the more demographically representative Arabic historiographic models, and perhaps through inclusion of near-contemporary vernacular narratives which often included nonroyal protagonists.

HISTORIOGRAPHIC TEXTS FROM THE ALFONSINE SCRIPTORIUM

ESTORIA DE ESPANNA

The *Estoria de Espanna* was not written in serial progression from one chapter to another but was composed by teams of specialists charged with tasks of translating, chronological sequencing, justifying of content, and stylistic leveling.[20] Assigning tasks to the scribe, compiler, and commentator was done as much from the physical need to facilitate production as to validate Alfonso's individual role as the efficient cause or author of the history. Diego Catalán's magisterial reconstruction of the composition of the *Estoria de Espanna* reveals that Jiménez de Rada's recent *De rebus Hispaniae* of 1243 was translated before 1271 to serve as the backbone of the history; details were fused to this from the slightly earlier parallel narrative of Lucas de Tuy and a mixed range of sources.[21] The *Estoria de Espanna* does not exist in a conclusive manuscript form, but is reflected in dozens of compilations put together from the Alfonsine materials under the direction of Sancho IV, Alfonso XI, and Don Juan Manuel. The reign of Alfonso VIII, shown in the *Primera crónica general* (ed. R. Menéndez Pidal), represents fairly advanced elaboration of that incomplete work. Catalán explains:

> In the royal Castilian chamber there must have remained stored, I believe, together with codices and workbooks from the Alfonsine workshop together with already concluded sections of the *Estoria de España,* fragments still in the course of elaboration (some already far enough advanced, others in initial states of construction); taking advantage of those materials, but without continuing the inconclusive compilatory work, the formulator of the *Primera crónica general* tried to compose a history of Spain without interruptions of continuity.[22]

For Alfonso X, encoding the narrative of power and authority entailed textual criticism and edition. His projected histories would represent, in Said's terms, a "system of forces institutionalized by the reigning culture at some human costs to its various components."[23] To relate a reign, Alfonso must manipulate sources, limiting and subsuming parts of the human side of the ruler's life to those features felt to have affected the course of history. Narrative sources already embued with thematic focus, emplotment, and affective and stylistic color fatally complicated the task. In studying the official history of a monarchy, the modern reader must evaluate narrative elements (including their presence, absence, and variants), respectfully observant of the stated or implied critical evaluations by the authors/editors.

POST-ALFONSINE USE OF COMPILATIONS AND SOURCE MATERIALS

The vernacular chroniclers who continued to mine the Alfonsine compilations and their primary sources after that monarch's death valued traditional narrative for its content and style, at times barely effacing the stylistic contours of the originals. This can be heard particularly in traces of assonant rhyme of epic poetry used as sources in the *Primera crónica general,* the *Crónica de Castilla,* and the *Crónica de veinte reyes.*[24] By 1292 or 1293, the Alfonsine sources again served the author(s) of *Castigos e documentos para bien vivir, ordenados por el rey don Sancho IV*[25] who appropriated the "final cause" but *not* the narratives of the legends such as the tragedies of La Cava and Fermosa.

Less than 40 years after Alfonso's death, Don Juan Manuel studied a different, lost version of the *Crónica general* which he condensed in his *Crónica abreviada.* He planned a *Crónica cumplida,* best seen in the unpublished so-called *Crónica manuelina interpolada.*[26] The third of that work dealing with "modern" history parallels most closely the primitive version (*versión vulgar*) of the *Primera crónica general* (Biblioteca del Palacio Nacional II-429), which is in its Alfonsine redactive state; in the reign of Alfonso VIII, its structural and compositional boundaries relate intimately to the *Crónica ocampiana.*[27]

By the fourteenth century, the vernacular historians working with Alfonsine materials drifted further from the annalistic form, toward the elaborated looser narrative. The compiling phase, once thought to constitute the "efficient cause" of authorship, was overshadowed by the moralistic interpretation of sources, with heavier elaboration of the "final cause." The *Crónica de 1344* and the so-called *Ocampiana* elaborate portions of an already focused and styled Alfonsine matrix, substituting and heavily embroidering into it more novelized accounts. Greater emplotment favored fictionalization of data, and the protagonists began to live personal lives outside their office. Once-marginalized characters—commoners, women, children, Jews—now occupied the stage of history formerly dominated by male monarchs, and new narratives featuring them split into popular ballads. Influenced by the *romances viejos,* the drama and "truth" of the Alfonsine literary narratives were poeticized by the sixteenth-century balladeer Lorenzo de Sepúlveda, who incorporated not only the narratives but the Alfonsine and post-Alfonsine interpretations.[28]

Alfonso VIII in the Literary and Historiographic Tradition

Alfonso VIII of Castile, best remembered in world literature for his cameo role opposite the Jewess of Toledo, ascended the throne a few months before his fourth birthday, following the death of his father, Sancho III, *el Deseado* (the desired).[29] Known as *el rey Niño* (child-king) during his lengthy reign (1158–1214), he later earned the sobriquets *el Noble* (the noble) and *el de Las Navas* (he of the victory at Las Navas) for his acts of piety, such as founding cities, hospitals, and monasteries, and for his military prowess.

Through both Castilian and Leonese grandparents, Alfonso X was the great grandson of Alfonso VIII and was indebted to him for precedents in legal practices.[30]

In the chronicles, the reign of Alfonso VIII was more difficult to narrate in many respects, because of its troubled early years and an unclear, indecisive beginning. Orphaned before the age of four, Alfonso VIII was a pawn between the Laras into whose guardianship he was entrusted and his uncle Fernando II of León; Fernando enlisted the Castro dynasty, bitter enemies of the Laras, to usurp the child's patrimony. When he reached his majority at the age of fifteen as specified in Sancho III's will, the young monarch was to assume full direction of the Castilian empire; yet for a period of time, he still remained under the control of the upper nobility who arranged his marriage to the nine-year-old Eleanor of England, daughter of Henry II and sister of Richard the Lion-Hearted.

The thirteenth-century Latin chronicles cast Eleanor in the pivotal role in his development from *el rey Niño* to *el Noble*. In the vernacular histories, the legend of his relationship with Fermosa, the Jewess of Toledo, leading to grief at her death, was interpreted as prelude to *despertamiento,* or awakening, explaining his repentance, charitable acts, and military excellence. The trajectory of literary narratives relating the early years of Alfonso VIII illustrates stages in the development of Alfonsine and post-Alfonsine historical writing.

El Rey Niño

For the Latin historians, the emplotment of Alfonso's reign was intrinsically more difficult because he was their contemporary, so that living witnesses could question the sequence and interpretation of events. Each writer moreover had biases that channeled his perception of the young monarch and frustrated his effort at compilation. The Alfonsine teams inherited those structural flaws in their secondary sources, and compounded the problem as they worked primary materials into the matrix, undermining their own well-planned effort.

LUCAS DE TUY, *CHRONICON MUNDI*

Less than a quarter-century after the death of Alfonso VIII, the deacon Lucas of the church of León, later bishop of Tuy, completed in 1236 the

Chronicon mundi. He begins his account of Alfonso's reign with the ascent to the throne when Alfonso is three years old. The only allusion to the political discord is clearly pro-Leonese, both by what is stated (that after the death of Sancho III, Fernando II of León cared for the child left under the protectorship of Count Manrique) and by what is omitted. He pointedly does not include stories about how the Leonese monarch took advantage of his brother's death to seize the patrimony of his orphaned four-year-old nephew, hardly a flattering role in any time and culture.

The vicissitudes of Alfonso's minority failed to divert Lucas from his primary objective, a balanced overview of the monarch's military and spiritual reconquest of Spain from Islam. In one sentence, he mentions the wedding, Eleanor's lineage, and the children and initiates a lengthy discussion of the military conflicts with the Muslim ruler, or Miramolin (the caliphal title Amīr al-Mu'minīn). He barely conceals the seams that concatenate sources; these include genealogical lines, lists of cities and monasteries founded, lists of military opponents, and lists of donations. Like Plutarch in his biographies, Lucas describes in general terms the virtues of the young monarch after he comes of age: "For he was great in wisdom, prudent in counsel, vigorous in military action, outstanding for generosity, and strong in the Catholic faith" (*Fuit namque sapientia magnus, consilio providus, armis strenuus, largitate praecipuus et fide catholica roboratus*). The end of Alfonso's reign concludes at his death and interment: "He was splendidly entombed at Burgos, in the monastery of Las Huelgas which he had built; he reigned for fifty-five years" (*Burgis in monasterio de Olgis, quod ipse construxerat, gloriose sepultus est; regnavit annis quinquaginta quinque*).[31] No evidence of historical or literary narrative characterizes Lucas's account of Alfonso VIII, either as a source or at the metalevel structure. Events occur and have beginnings and endings, but neither internally nor through the author's intrusion is meaning added to the events. Subjective commentary had to await another generation of historical writers.

RODRIGO JIMÉNEZ DE RADA, *DE REBUS HISPANIAE*

Jiménez de Rada in *De rebus Hispaniae* (1243) was more thorough in relating the perplexing early years of Alfonso's reign. Since neither inheriting the monarchy a few weeks shy of his fourth birthday nor receiving an impressive coronation on reaching majority at the age of fifteen immediately resulted in Alfonso's autonomy and majestic acts, the Toledan historian was pressed to elect some sequence of events to explain his development from the status of child-king as *Rex puellus* and *Rex parvulus* to *Rex nobilis*. He attempted to rationalize Alfonso's dynamism and success in terms of his own ethical and political values.

The Toledan does not mention that Alfonso VIII's mother, Doña Blanca, died when the infante was nine months of age.[32] In a prehistory of the young monarch's reign, Archbishop Rodrigo detailed the deathbed scene where the moribund Sancho anticipated his own early demise.[33] Clearly concerned about the future of his son and the monarchy, the ailing ruler dictated the protectorship of his infant son to the upper nobility until he would reach the age of fifteen years. Sancho specified members of the Castro and Lara families to guard and tutor the *rrey don Alfonso niño,* thus exacerbating the preexisting tension between the families and later embroiling Fernando II of León.

Subjectivity colors Rodrigo's description of Alfonso's early years. He appears to be clearly touched by the child's beauty, vivacity, and precocity: "from early childhood lively of countenance, retentive of memory, and broad of intellect" (*hic ab infantia vultu vivax, memoria tenax, intellectu capax*).[34] Some of the gratuitous, flattering, descriptive details about Alfonso VIII found in the *De rebus* do not appear in manuscripts of the *Crónica de veinte reyes* or of the *Crónica de Castilla*. Unlike Lucas, the Toledan relates the events of Alfonso's minority with detailed episodes characterized by a stylistically crafted literary narrative, containing minute details about the action, affective reactions (the child's crying, anger of the monarch, fear of the upper nobility), direct and reported discourse, attribution to oral sources (*sic dicitur respondisse*), interpretation by the narrative voice, rhetorical figures, frequent use of sobriquet, and a conclusion.

On Alfonso VIII's early childhood, Rodrigo relates a remarkable chapter in the Lara-Castro feud, in which Manrique de Lara and his nephews disinter the body of Gutierr Fernández de Castro to use as ransom, and the cortes of Castilian nobles meets and determines the outcome.[35] The Toledan's source is not annalistic but clearly a stylistically developed narrative, whose format may have been a historical legend or even an epic poem.[36] Although no evidence of assonance exists, a clear vernacular formula occurs twice in the 1289 post-Alfonsine translation of this portion: "dell una et de la otra part" (*Primera crónica general,* 669a51) and "de la vna et de la otra parte" (669b47–48).[37]

Because of the interrelationship between the reigns of Alfonso VIII of Castile and Fernando II of León and because of his own thinly veiled pro-

Castilian sympathies, the Toledan hesitates and falters in assigning the flow of events to the reign of one monarch or another. His most extensively detailed, sympathetic description of the innocence and beauty of the *Rex puellus,* or tender young king, appears in a chapter entitled "That King Ferdinand gained almost all Extremadura" (*Quod Rex Fernandus obtinuit fere totam Extermaturam*). The archbishop's smoldering anti-Leonese bias surfaces where he narrates Alfonso's recovery of Toledo after twelve years under Leonese domination. He explains that Alfonso's political and spiritual triumphs (the restoration of his *infantaticum,* his good looks, manners, and protection from enemies and seductors) were God's gifts for recovering Toledo from Fernando.

THE *HISTORIA NOBILIARIA* IN ALFONSINE AND POST-ALFONSINE CHRONICLES

The vernacular chronicles under consideration which used the Alfonsine materials (the *Primera crónica general,* the *Crónica de Castilla,* the *Veinte reyes,* the *Ocampiana,* and the *Manuelina interpolada*) begin the narration of the *rey Niño*'s life before the death of Sancho III. They appropriated a single vernacular translation of *De rebus,* which narrates the ruse whereby members of the Castro family kidnapped him under the nose of Fernando II of León and the Laras, and the disinterment of Gutierr Fernández which ultimately motivated the alliance between the Castros and Fernando II of León. The Alfonsine team translated Rodrigo's text directly from Latin; it is not to be confused with the fifteenth-century *Toledano romanzado.*[38] The *Crónica de Castilla* and the *Veinte reyes* lack the rhetorical amplifications found in the 1289 *Primera crónica general,* revealing their close proximity to the original Alfonsine translation.

Always intent upon exact dating of events by year of reign, the *Veinte reyes* notes that in the third year of Alfonso's reign, which would make him about seven, he was still not weaned: "he was not weaned from his nurse's breast" (*non era quito de la teta de su ama*), following the Toledan's "the little one clung to his nurse's breast" (*et qui adhuc a mamillis nutricis parvulus dependebat*) (161). The *Primera crónica general* and the *Ocampiana,* like the Toledan's *De rebus,* do not specify date or age. The first, like its Latin source, says that "he clung to the breasts of his nurses" (*de las tetas du sus amas colgaua*); the *Manuelina interpolada* more colorfully, but probably from a faulty reading, says: "he rode [horseback] on his nurses' breasts" (*de tetas de sus amas caualgaua*).

Toward the end of this story, the vernacular chronicles "open" the shared Alfonsine matrix based on the *De rebus;* that matrix itself evidently was marred structurally, judging by lacunae in the *Primera crónica general* manuscripts (671b27, 55). In this matrix, the chronicles interpolate a literary narrative in which the *rey Niño* becomes a wisp of a background figure, less visible than the upper nobility fighting for his control. Stylistically and thematically, this narrative is similar to the chapter on the disinterment of Gutierr Fernández de Castro included in the *De rebus,* but the narrative is not found in the extant Latin chronicle.

As clearly reflected in the Alfonsine chronicles, this lost *Historia nobiliaria,* clearly pre-emplotted as a coherent and stylistically crafted literary narrative, contained personal and ethical conflicts, characterizations of physical and affective traits (wry humor, paternal instinct, emotional peaks and lows), thematic unity (loyalty, justice), stylistic distinctiveness (dialogue, repetition, rapid concatenations to evoke movement and urgency), perspective (preferential treatment of the Lara dynasty), and mood (a sense of immediacy, tragedy). The clear focus of this lost literary account of the childhood of Alfonso VIII doubtless posed editorial problems for the late thirteenth-century vernacular chroniclers, as it may have for the Toledan previously. Because identical fragments figure in the *Crónica abreviada,* the *Castilla,* and *Veinte reyes,* this *Historia nobiliaria* must have been present in the Alfonsine scriptorium.[39]

The *Ocampiana* and *Manuelina interpolada* chronicles, slightly later than *Castilla* and *Veinte reyes,* announce and justify the inclusion of this source which was *menos atajante* than the Toledan's history. The *Manuelina interpolada* explains:

> And because we feel that much more pertains to it that would not be "complete" if this were not included here, and because we know by proof of these writings that it was like this and is certain, hence we put it here in the history in the reasonable place, neither diminishing nor augmenting the words that Archbishop Rodrigo nor Lucas, bishop of Tuy, nor the other sages and honorable men put here.[40]

Contextually, that introduction implies at least a collected if not unified work. Next, a table of narratives, as part of a scholastic prologue, lists episodes between the Castros and Laras: the trickery of Fernán Ruiz de Castro, the highly dramatic siege of Zorita, and the treason of Dominguillo, to name only a few episodes. This preface to the narrative merits further study in the light of Minnis's work on the prologue and late medieval literary theory. Although the *Veinte reyes* and the *Crónica de Castilla* do not include the prologue or introduce the source by name, they cite its text directly, including discourse and rhetorical figures, suggesting the availability of the narrative body by the end of the thirteenth century.

The absence of the *Historia nobiliaria* from the *Primera crónica general* must be due to the unacceptable or confusing nature of its content, hence its deliberate suppression. Why did the *Crónica de Castilla* and *Veinte reyes,* particularly the latter, favor the *Historia?* Both reflect a democratizing tendency by the portrayal of upper nobility in enhanced political roles; sensing this political danger articulated in the *Historia nobiliaria* and wishing to suppress literary documentation of their nascent power, Alfonso X excluded it from his historical compilation. It simply was not in focus with the essentially pro-monarchic *Primera crónica general.* The bias in the *Historia*'s narratives favors the Lara dynasty, hence its favor with the *Veinte reyes;* but in the *Crónica de Castilla* and the later chronicles, it becomes politically hermaphroditic, favoring occasionally one family, then the other.

The dramatic and poetic potential of the *Historia nobiliaria* narratives caught the attention of Sepúlveda, who cast them into new romances: *Romance del rey don Alfonso y Lope de Arenas* (fols. 142v–45v), and *Romance de el conde don Manrrique y el conde de Castro* (fols. 146–48v). Sepúlveda's early poetic accounts drawn from these legends corroborate the artistic and dramatic merit of the narrative fragments from the lost *Historia nobiliaria* and underscore the political undertones of their content. This may explain why the narratives originally were rejected by the evidently pro-Castro early Alfonsine teams.

EL REY NOBLE, FERMOSA, AND THE DESPERTAMIENTO MOTIF

When Alfonso X selected *De rebus* for the comprehensive organizational framework for the *Estoria de Espanna,* he inherited the Toledan's occasional inexplicable shifts of topic and his implausibly juxtaposed strings of events. The Learned Monarch consulted primary sources for alternate routes to narrative cohesion and "meaning." Following the Toledan in the reign of Alfonso VIII, the *Primera crónica general* and the *Veinte reyes* marginalize Fermosa from the course of history. The *Crónica de Castilla,* the *Crónica abreviada,* the *Manuelina interpolada,* and the *Ocampiana,* however, emplot the story of Alfonso's relationship with Fermosa as pivotal in the true beginning of his reign. In the absence of annalistic record of the events, or specific mention of the affair in either annalistic or chronistic predecessors, factual historical documentation of this illicit relationship remains to be demonstrated. Contributing to the plausibility of an extramarital relationship are the significant difference between his own and his bride's tender ages (fifteen and nine years), the general acceptance by historians that the affair took place immediately following his marriage to Eleanor, the seven-year delay before the birth of the first child, and the premature death of that firstborn son.

DE REBUS HISPANIAE

Rodrigo Jiménez de Rada relates how, precisely fifteen years from Alfonso's birth, the monarch assumed the crown but continued to be under undue influence by the upper nobility, who shortly later arranged his marriage with the nine-year-old Eleanor of England. Subsequently, Alfonso VIII failed to demonstrate political excellence and soon suffered a dramatic defeat by the Moors in 1195 at the battle of Alarcos. Archbishop Rodrigo extracted "facts" relative to this period of Alfonso's life from annals, monastic histories, and perhaps personal recollections; but his attempt to find "meaning" in the facts and to draw them to closure were not successful. Simultaneous with Alfonso's founding the monastery at Burgos with his new bride, he is seen planning revenge for the defeat at Alarcos during a truce with the kingdoms of Navarre and León, ventures hardly compatible. Rodrigo lists and elaborates Alfonso's charitable acts and the death of his infant son, and concludes Book VII of the *De rebus* before the battle of Ubeda or Las Navas in which he himself participated. Structurally, the extant version of the Toledan's history fails, naming Alfonso's children by Eleanor twice; and he does not narrate and elaborate details of the marriage. The legend of Alfonso's liaison with Fermosa does not appear in *De rebus*.

ALFONSINE AND POST-ALFONSINE ACCOUNTS

Alfonso's relationship with the Jewess of Toledo appears in writing for the first time as marginalia in the *versión regia* of the 1289 *Primera crónica general,* and it is incorporated into the text itself in a late fourteenth-century copy.[41] It awkwardly intrudes an unresolved thematic and narrative counterpoint in the chapter based on the *De rebus,* in which Alfonso and Eleanor found the monastery of Las Huelgas in Burgos. The affair is linked with the monarch's defeat at Alarcos, both by its place of interpolation and by intertextual reference in the marginalia. During Alfonso's own lifetime, his dramatic spiritual awakening (*despertamiento*) and repentance were associated with the military defeat at Alarcos in the poetry of Folquet de Marselha, who later would become bishop of Toulouse.[42] The early vernacular marginal mention in the *Primera crónica general* of the seven-year affair explains that the monastery at Burgos was founded for three reasons: service to God, nobility for Alfonso's body and soul, and repentance for his liaison with the Jewess of Toledo. Angered at Alfonso's sin with Fermosa, God sent an angel to Illescas two years after the loss at Alarcos to inform Alfonso that his daughter would inherit his lineage. The angel admonishes Alfonso at Illescas: "for the sin which he committed with the Jewess," abandoning his wife for her, "he was defeated at the battle of Alarcos." When King Alfonso heard this, "he became very sad in his heart, deeply repenting his sins, and from that moment forward he worked to establish the monastery of Burgos and the hospital."[43]

The narrative account of Fermosa's violent beheading at the hands of the advisors, totally absent in the *Primera crónica general* marginalia, constitutes a familiarly grisly motif in popular legend and in the Judeo-Christian tradition. Evidence of a traditional popular legend can be postulated on the basis of other chronicle versions. Just as the Cid epic poem acquired monastic overlays, while the prose legend was convoluted and continued in prose at Cardeña, the account of Alfonso's extramarital conquests attracted monastic interpretation and was used for its contained "truth." The narrative form has disappeared entirely in the *Primera crónica general*'s marginalia, leaving only the moralistic flotsam as witness to its earlier vitality and dramatic cohesion. Alfonso's "no-fault" adultery figures in the earlier *Crónica de Castilla,* where Fermosa is not the temptress or victim but a mutually consenting lover. Later chronicles emphasize antisemitism (Fermosa as a *mala judia* in the *Crónica de 1344* and in *Ocampiana,* and "the sorcery she knew how to do" (*por feitiços quelh ella sabia fazer* in the *Crónica de 1344*). Edna Aizenberg's interesting observations about Fermosa as an object of desire are true of the later chronistic versions;[44] but in the earlier *Crónica de Castilla* account, the story relates true love. Within the trajectory of the Alfonsine and post-Alfonsine chronicles, the once-shadowy paramour acquires powerfully negative dimensions to foil her Christian lover, a conceit for dramatic balance. The interpretive elements that accrued in fourteenth-century handling of Alfonsine texts further mediate to divide us from "reality."

Vernacular chronicles differ significantly among themselves in sequencing and in proportion of detail of the amorous liaison, versus the monastic interpretation and the position of the legend within the text. Unlike the *Primera crónica general,* the late thirteenth-century *Crónica de Castilla,* which in this part reflects most closely the *Estoria de Espanna* materials in the Alfonsine scriptorium, "correctly" positions the legend of his illicit tryst immediately following the wedding to Eleanor, as do the *Ocampiana* and the *Manuelina interpolada.* In these fluent, stylistically embellished narratives, a crazed love causes him to lose control and to abandon governance of his kingdom. The wise counselors enter the king's luxuriously appointed bedroom and engage him in a conversation outside, while others behead Fermosa and her entourage.

In the *Crónica de Castilla* the drama of a vernacular legend overshadows any moralistic interpretation; the Illescas vision contains less detail than even the marginal note in the *Primera crónica general.* The *Crónica de Castilla*'s sister chronicle *Crónica de veinte reyes,* like the *Primera crónica,* the *De rebus,* and the *Crónica abreviada,* does not include the story. The *Manuelina interpolada* and *Ocampiana,* however, based on the amplified, later version of the *Primera crónica general,* interpolate the legend in the same place and with the same detail as the *Crónica de Castilla,* emplotted with sensual detail and affective overtones, following the identical Alfonsine account which predates its moralistic elaboration. Clearly, the presence or absence of the legend in some chronicles relates to ethical, political, and/or social bias and to the intent of the authors of history, not to its availability or perceived validity.

The Fermosa legend in *Castigos e documentos* preserves the later moralized version seen in the *Primera crónica general* marginalia, stripped of its narrative and affective elements. Lorenzo de Sepúlveda drew the historical narrative for his ballads from the Alfonsine version of the *Estoria de Espanna,* involving "all the events and happenings which have happened in our Spain from the time of its settlement to the death of the sainted king don Fernando his father" (*todos los hechos y acontecimientos que en nuestra España han acontecido desde el tiempo de su poblacion, hasta la muerte del sancto rey don Fernando su padre,* 2v–3r). They contain both the narrative and the moral, hence they are related only in gross structural lines to the *Crónica de 1344* and the *Ocampiana.* The *Romance del rey don Alfonso y de la Iudia* mentions the youthful marriage arranged by high nobles of the kingdom (*los grandes de su reynado*), positions the beginning of the affair immediately after the wedding, and again blames the affair on a blind love. These details clearly come from the primitive folkloric tradition, not from the later antisemitic monastic moralization. The ballad also narrates in detail the intrigue of the beheading, including interpretive features of the *Crónica de Castilla* version, not distinguishing between the narrative and the moral, poeticizing both the tryst and the vision at Illescas. Most significantly, the ballad does not directly relate the Fermosa episode to the loss of Alarcos, but more personally to the death of the firstborn son and to the future line of succession through the daughter: "God has taken from you great service because of your evil; no son of yours will remain, only a daughter will receive your inheritance":

> Dios deti gran seruicio
> de tu maldad ha tomado
> no fincara de ti hijo
> mas hija te aura heredado. (145v)

The perception of female firstborn as punishment polarizes the legend toward popular origins and toward a folkloric treatment of the adultery motif.

The Alfonsine chronicles, and the later historical works drawn from them, reveal that the Fermosa legend existed in two stages of development—a popular one emphasizing the tryst and Alfonso VIII's failure to provide a successful heir, and another elaborating the awakening (*despertamiento*) motif with moralistic interpretations linked to the monarch's military failure, accountability, and ultimately successful reign.

Only at the highest structural order, the sequencing of reigns, did Alfonso perpetuate the inherited chronistic mode, presenting events with abrupt beginnings and endings. Within the defined boundaries of a monarch's reign, the Learned Author emplotted the events of history in meaningful sequence and populated the stories with demographically diversified actors, thereby decisively advancing the historiographic modality toward a coherent, unified literary narrative.

Israel J. Katz

11. Melodic Survivals? Kurt Schindler and the Tune of Alfonso's Cantiga "Rosa das rosas" in Oral Tradition

In his last will and testament of 21 January 1284, written in Seville, seventy-four days before his death, Alfonso X decreed that all the *Cantigas* codices be housed in the cathedral of that city, where his body was to be interred, and that the cantigas *de loor* should be sung in the cathedral on the feast days of the Virgin.[1] According to José M. Llorens Cisteró, the king's wish was honored on feast days, not only in the cathedral, during the procession, but also in religious ceremonies at court and in popular festivities (*en algunas celebraciones religiosas de la corte y manifestaciones populares*).[2] By the middle of the fourteenth century, however, interest in the *Cantigas* had begun to decline until they were totally forgotten (*empezaron a decaer en interés hasta quedar completamente olvidadas*).[3]

From John E. Keller's remarks, while not in full disagreement with Llorens Cisteró, one senses the implication that the practice was resumed from time to time and that "even now [cantigas are] sung [at the cathedral of Seville] to musical accompaniment."[4] Thus, any attempt to verify whether or not Alfonso's command was executed *per annum,* through the centuries, would necessitate a laborious and time-consuming perusal of the cathedral's *Actas capitulares,* particularly the entries for the feast days of the Virgin: February 2, March 25, August 15, September 8, October 12, and December 8.[5] Apart from Seville and Toledo where Alfonso held his court, information concerning when, where else, and how Alfonso's *Cantigas* were performed during his reign has to date yielded very little descriptive documentation of musicological significance, except for scanty iconographical evidence.

One has only to view the physical appearance of any one of the extant

Cantigas codices bearing musical notation—ranging from 315 to 485 mm long and from 217 to 326 mm wide, and containing from 160 to 370 leaves of parchment—to realize how unwieldy each was for the solitary singer as well as the clarity of its notation if additional singers were huddled before it. This immediately calls to mind the larger and cumbersome *cantorales,* or choir books, such as those resting on *facistolia* (lecterns or choristers' desks) in the choir loft of the royal monastery of El Escorial, around which several singers stood to sing from the same musical notation, inscribed on huge sheets of parchment. Whether such a group gathered around a *Cantigas* codex, or whether one singer, knowledgeable in reading its notation, taught selected texts and tunes to those gathered around him, remains an enigma. One can add to this problem such further speculations as those pertaining to performance practices, including dancing, with or without the accompaniment of musical instruments like those depicted in several of its miniatures,[6] as well as the manner of accompaniment.

A closer study of the text-tune relationships of both the Marian miracles and the praises sung in her honor may even enable us to differentiate the poetic texts, for which their tunes were created simultaneously, from texts which may have been suited to known melodies of the time taken from either liturgical or secular sources. At the same time, we can take into account their varied formal, modal, cadential, and intervallic structures, ambitus, syllable count, rhythmic features, mensural schemes, and versification.[7] The melodic origins of the *Cantigas* tunes await further investigation.[8] Moreover, considering the fact that the Galician-Portuguese dialect was neither the spoken nor even the written language of most Castilians, it is unlikely that even a handful of sung cantigas would have survived in oral tradition.

Cantiga 10: "Rosa das rosas"

Still, the possible instance of a cantiga tune surviving in oral tradition up to the third decade of the present century appears to have given rise to a few casual notices, even though its sung text is a Castilian translation of the original Galician-Portuguese. I am referring, of course, to Alfonso X's cantiga *de loor* 10, "Rosa das rosas" (Figure 11-1), which appears as no. 263 among the musical notations in Kurt Schindler's *Folk Music and Poetry of Spain and Portugal,* published posthumously by the Hispanic Institute of Columbia University in 1941[9] (Example 11-1b). Schindler collected the cantiga in the town of Ceclavín, in western Cáceres near the Portuguese border, during his short visit there in the late summer of 1932. This was the period of Schindler's second field trip to Spain,[10] during which he transported a Fairchild portable recording apparatus for the purpose of gathering his material on aluminum discs. The label on disc no. 150A, containing "Rosa [de las r]osas," cites Amado Vives Amores as Schindler's informant. Furthermore, in the text portion of his published collection, Schindler identified item 263 as "la Cantiga X del rey Don Alfonso el sabio," yet he questioned whether it was "tradicional en Ceclavín."[11]

Daniel Devoto, in his critical review, was the first to take note of its inclusion in Schindler's magnificent collection. He concluded that the text is traditional (*folklórico*) and relates to its original antecedent, the cantiga, despite the difficulty of proving it (*es [de no establecerse una transmisión no tradicional] folklórico, y cuenta con un antecedente, la cantiga original*).[12] Citing Devoto's reprinted version, Jacques Chailley concurred that "the cantiga 'Rosa das rosas' is preserved in Spanish oral tradition, and in Kurt Schindler's [book] it was collected as a popular song" (*s'est conservé dans la tradition orale espagnole, et a été recueilli comme chant populaire dans Kurt Schindler*).[13] I initially agreed, including in my article not only Schindler's but also four additional modern transcriptions of "Rosa das rosas" for comparative purposes.[14] In a recent critical study of Martin Codax's *Cantigas de amigo*, Manuel Pedro Ferreira included (in the first of three appendixes) a short discussion of "Rosa das rosas," wherein he too expressed a similar view, while, at the same time, suggesting that the cantiga may have had its own manuscript tradition.[15] In support of this last position, Ferreira cited Luis Villalba's published arrangement of "Rosa das rosas" as the "manuscript" source of the Schindler tune, basing his evidence not on the tune, but on the comparison of the text-underlays of their initial strophes.[16] The text for Villalba's setting had been Castilianized by R. de Valle; the deviations in Schindler's text are enclosed in brackets:

> *Rosa entre rosas   Flor de las flores*
> * [de las]*
>
> *Virgen de vírgenes Y amor de amores.*
> *   [Amor]*
>
> Rosa en que el Señor puso su querer
> Flor la más hermosa que se vió nacer
> Virgen que hace dulce todo padecer
> *   [dulces todos los dolores]*
> Amor que hace nuestros sus santos amores.

esta tezéa. e de loór de ſca m̃

comé fremoſa a ḣa za a g̃n poder

oſa das rſas e flor das flores

dona das donas ſeñor das ſeñores

Roſa de beltad é de pareçer....

ꞇ flor dalegria é de prazer

dona en mui piadoſa ſeer....

ſeñor en toller coitas e doores

Roſa das roſas ꞇ flor das flores

dona das donas ſeñor das ſeñores

Figure 11-1. Cantiga *de loor* 10 from To (Biblioteca Nacional, Madrid MS 10.069, f. 20) (facing page) and Escorial B.I.2 (f. 39) (above).

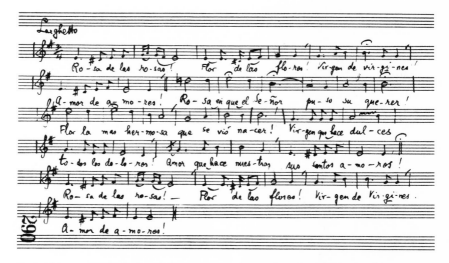

Example II-Ia. Schindler's original notation transcribed from his recording.

Example II-Ib. The notated version as it appeared in Schindler's *Folk Music and Poetry of Spain and Portugal*.

Had Villalba known of the existence of the earliest Castilian version of the text, recently discovered by John Keller,[17] he might have placed it below the original text of his transcription as he had done with R. de Valle's translation. Thus, if both Schindler's and Villalba's text-underlays had agreed closely with the medieval Castilian version, it would have indeed added weight to the speculative opinions registered above for an unbroken chain of oral transmission.

According to Keller, the Castilianized poetic rendition of the original can be considered one of the earliest examples of thirteenth-century Castilian poetry, the first three stanzas of which are almost literal translations from the Galician:

GALICIAN-PORTUGUESE:
Rosa das rosas e Fror das frores
dona das donnas, Sennor das
  sennores.[19]

Rosa de beldad' e de parecer
e Fror d'alegria e de prazer,
Dona en mui piadosa seer,
Sennor en toller coitas e doores.
  Rosa das rosas . . .

Atal Sennor dev' ome muit' amar,
que de todo mal o pode guardar;
e pode-ll' os peccados perdõar,
que faz no mundo per maos
  sabores.
  Rosa das rosas . . .

Devemo-la muit' amar e servir,
ca punna de nos guardar de falir;
des i dos erros nos faz repentir,
que nos fazemos come pecadores.
  Rosa das rosas . . .

Esta donna que tenno por Sennor
e de que quero seer trobador,
se eu per ren poss' aver seu amor,
dou ao demo os outros amores.
  Rosa das rosas . . .

CASTILIAN:[18]
Rrosa de las rrosas e flor de las flores
e dueña de las dueñas, e Señora de las
  señoras.

Rrosa de beldat e de parescer
e flor de alegria e de plazer,
e dueña muy piadosa en nos toller
nuestras cuytas e nuestros dolores.
  Rrosa de las rrosas . . .

  e que es
Atal Señora que devemos mucho amar,
porque de todo mal nos puede
  guardar,
e nuestros pecados nos faz perdonar,
que nos fazemos por malos sabores.
  Rrosa de las rrosas . . .

  e que
La devemos siempre [amar o servir]
que p[ugna] de nos guarir [de falir],
e de los yerros nos faz rrepentir,
que nos fazemos como pecadores.
  Rrosa de las rrosas . . .

  e que
Devemos sienpre trabajar
por todavia su amor ganar,
ca es valiosa e muy celestial,
e non valen nada los otros amores.
  Rrosa de las rrosas . . .

Translations (by Kathleen Kulp-Hill) are as follows:

TRANSLATION OF THE GALICIAN-
PORTUGUESE:
Rose of roses, Flower of flowers,
Lady of ladies, Queen of queens.

Rose of beauty and appearance,
Flower of joy and pleasure,
Lady in being merciful,
Queen in relieving pain and
  suffering.
        Rose of roses . . .

A man should greatly love such a
  Queen,
who can protect him from all
  harm,
and pardon him his sins,
which he basely commits in the
  world.
        Rose of roses . . .

We should devoutly love and
  serve Her,
for She strives to keep us from
  transgression;
She makes us repent of our
  errors,
which we commit as sinners.
        Rose of roses . . .

This lady I have as my Queen,
and Her troubadour I would be.
If I can somehow win Her love,
I consign to the devil all other
  loves.
        Rose of roses . . .

TRANSLATION OF THE CASTILIAN:
Rose of roses, and flower of flowers
Lady of ladies, Queen of queens.

Rose of beauty and appearance
and flower of joy and pleasure,
Lady most merciful in taking away
our cares and our sorrows.

        Rose of roses . . .

        and that she is
A queen such as we should greatly
  love,
because She can protect us from all
  harm,
and She causes to be forgiven the sins
which we commit in our folly.

        Rose of roses . . .

        and that
We should also always love and serve
  Her,
who strives to save us from
  transgression,
and makes us repent of the errors
which we commit as sinners.

        Rose of roses . . .

        and that
We should always endeavor
constantly to win Her love,
for She is powerful and heavenly
and other loves are worth nought.

        Rose of roses . . .

Following my publication of 1974, I was fortunate to acquire an entire set of program notes for the concerts presented by the Schola Cantorum of New York, under Schindler's direction (1912–1926).[20] They were all written by Schindler, with occasional annotations by other authors. Among the programs, the Schola's concert at Carnegie Hall on Wednesday evening, 21 January 1920, which exemplified the kind of programming that made this choral society one of the foremost in the nation, was included the first American performance of "Rosa das rosas." This particular concert was divided in three parts: the first was devoted to Mozart's *Requiem Mass,* the second comprised "Three Ancient Melodies of the Church," and the last was Handel's *Ode on Saint Cecilia's Day.*

Schindler placed "Rosa das rosas" as the third of the "Ancient Melodies," preceded by the Gregorian hymn "Ave maris stella" (from a ninth-century manuscript of the monastery of St. Gall) and the Introit "Rorate caeli" (for the fourth Sunday of Advent). Although mentioning Alfonso's *Cantigas de Santa Maria* as its original source, Schindler did not cite his direct source, that is, Villalba, upon which he based his choral arrangement; nor did he adhere strictly to the original text that was printed on the first page of Villalba's arrangement. Rather he presented his own edited version (variations shown below in bold characters) of the first and last strophes of the original Galician-Portuguese text (compare the versions just given):

Rosa das rosas, et **Flor** das **flores,**
Donna des donnas, Sennor das Sennores.

   Rosa de beldad e de parecer,
   et Flor d'alegria **et** de **placer;**
   Donna en mui piadosa seer,
   Senor en toller **cuitas et dolores.**
Rosa das rosas . . .

   Esta **Donna** que **tengo** por Sennor
   et de que **quiero** seer trobador,
   se **io** per **res** poss' aver **su** amor,
   dono al demo **los otros** amores.

Schindler's own rather free translation was given as:

Rose among roses, O sweetest of flowers,
Chosen of women, to thee bring we homage.

   Rose of beauty, fairest vision,
   Mystic flower of purest joy,
   Holy essence thou of purest joy,
   Victor over pain and woe!

Rose among roses . . .

    To her service I have pledged me
    For to be her troubadour.
    If her love I could but gain me,
    Earthly loves would go for naught.[21]

Schindler also added the following brief description:

> The Tenth Canticle from the "Cántigas de Santa Maria" of the King Alfonso el Sabio. (Spain, XIII Century). This is a song in praise of Saint Mary, of her marvellous goodness and of her great power.
>
> From the illustrated collection, containing poem and melody, in the castle of the Escorial, Madrid, Spain.

Villalba arranged the cantiga for solo, chorus, and piano accompaniment. The opening refrain, which he designated as *tiples,* was to be sung by the sopranos and repeated by the chorus. The sopranos followed, singing the individual strophes to a harmonized piano accompaniment. Schindler, on the other hand, preferred an *a cappella* setting, having the contralto sing the opening refrain, which was repeated by the chorus, singing in octaves. The contralto then sang the two additional strophes that Schindler gave, with the chorus humming the exact harmonization Villalba had written for the piano (Example 11-2).

"Rosa das rosas" was performed again, six years later, at Carnegie Hall on Wednesday evening, 10 March 1926. By some strange coincidence, it was sung at Schindler's final concert with the Schola Cantorum at Carnegie Hall.[22] He had resigned as its founder and musical director owing to a long dispute with the organization's governing board. In the accompanying program guide, Schindler provided a more elaborate, albeit somewhat inaccurate account of the collection from which the cantiga was taken, including comments about its author, whose degree of participation has been widely conjectured:

> King Alfonso the Wise of Castilla and León, who reigned in the middle of the XIII Century in his capital of Santiago de Compostella (the celebrated shrine of Spanish Galicia),[23] was not only a patron of poets and troubadours but also a deeply religious man. During his reign one of the foremost manifestations of mediaeval religious poetry took place: a collection of more than four hundred songs and canticles in praise of the Virgin Mary was issued in magnificent volumes illustrated by exquisite miniature painting. The authorship of the canticles was attributed solely to the King, although we may easily

Example 11-2. Schindler's setting of "Rosa das rosas."

surmise that he was helped by his court of poets and troubadours, among whom he is shown seated in paintings of the period. Only two specimens of the complete collection have been preserved to posterity, one in the library of the Escorial near Madrid, the other at the Vatican in Rome. The text of the canticles (in the old Galician court language, an idiom very nearly related to Portuguese, but retaining a great many traces of pure Latin) has been re-printed in a modern edition,[24] and the illuminated pictures can be seen in photographic reproductions at the Museum of the Hispanic Society of Amer-ica, for which they were ordered by Mr. Archer M. Huntington.[25] Apart from their artistic charm and interest, these pictures represent one of the foremost sources of information regarding the musical instruments of the Middle Ages.

But the most interesting part of the collection is its music, since every canticle is accompanied by a particular melody written in neumatic notation. The deciphering of the 'Neumes' has long been a puzzle to scholars and has given rise to some extraordinary theories and aberrations. The late wizard of Spanish music, Felipe Pedrell, never quite succeeded in finding the key to the code. Julián Ribera, a foremost Arabic scholar of Madrid University, produced and published grotesque and purely theoretical paraphrases of them, but two less known scholars succeeded in reading some of the melodies in most convincing fashion: the late Padre Villalba, who deciphered 'Rosa das Rosas,' and D. Francesch Pujol, who decoded the melody of the "Miracle of the Virgin" [cantiga 139: *Maravillosos et piadosos*].[26]

It is strange that Schindler should level such criticism at Ribera, whose study of the *Cantigas* appeared four years earlier in 1922. It was not until the year after Schindler's comments that Anglés published the first of his articles, dealing with the *Cantigas,* wherein he attacked Ribera's transcrip-tions.[27] I would venture a guess that Schindler picked up the criticism of Pedrell and Ribera from either Gregorio María Sunyol's article of 1924 or Manuel F. Fernández-Núñez's article of 1924–1925.[28] One cannot be sure of Schindler's acquaintance with the two-volume Real Academia Española 1889 edition of the text of the Escorial codex B.I.2,[29] for which Ribera's edition of 1922 constituted the third volume, or with the studies of Pierre Aubry (1907), and of Henri Collet with Luis Villalba (1911).[30] What is certain is that Schindler came upon Villalba's arrangement of cantiga 10 some time in 1917 or earlier.

From the evidence presented above, it appears that Schindler was already familiar with "Rosa das rosas" long before he recorded it in Cáceres. The evidence also explains why he questioned whether it was traditional there. It is also clear that Schindler's informant was acquainted with the Castilian text of Villalba's arrangement. Either he had heard it on repeated occasions or may even have sung it as a member of some chorus, though his tonal memory appears to have faltered with the passage of time. While

Schindler himself seems to have supported the notion that the cantiga survived in oral tradition, I suspect that, had Schindler lived to complete the in-depth musicological study which his collection lacks, he would have attempted to examine the possible transmission of the cantiga through the centuries.

Ferreira's suggestion, linking the cantiga collected in Cáceres with Villalba's arrangement as having its own manuscript tradition, is plausible. However, I would prefer a linkage that was more historically bound, one which can be applied to any of the miracles and cantigas *de loor* that had undoubtedly circulated in this manner—that is, after having been copied from any of the original codices bearing musical notation. Wherever they were circulated, during the generations that followed, there were bound to occur textual and melodic discrepancies owing to the very nature of oral transmission. Doubtless this process also occurred, but exactly when and where it began its gradual to almost total decline are difficult to ascertain. Such questions hinge on the popularity of particular texts and/or tunes as well as events to which they were linked, the verification of which is virtually impossible. Nonetheless, several scholars have noted that *Cantigas* tune variants eventually made their way into regional dance repertoires, or survived as instrumental music or to an even lesser extent as tune contrafacts.[31] Still, with due respect to the conclusions drawn above concerning Schindler's published field notation, Ferreira's alternate suggestion more accurately describes the by no means coincidental relationship between the cantiga Schindler collected in Cáceres and Villalba's arrangement. Inasmuch as a manuscript tradition carries with it the factor of continuity, in our case this factor must be discounted. A more plausible explanation would take into account attempts to resurrect the long-dormant *Cantigas* tradition, which reflected deeply rooted religious sentiments, as a vehicle to arouse nationalistic sentiments as well.

The earliest vocal settings of cantigas can be found among a collection of seventeenth- and eighteenth-century notebooks at the Biblioteca Nacional in Madrid, which contain mainly settings for soprano and continuo that were made by an anonymous composer, and the notebook in which they are found was entitled "Música española" by Francisco Asenjo Barbieri. "Rosa das rosas" is one of eleven cantigas contained therein.[32] In 1855, Mariano Soriano Fuertes published settings for eight of the eleven cantigas, excluding "Rosa das rosas," with continuo accompaniment.[33] The earliest modern musical composition based on a cantiga tune was that of Hilarión Eslava (c. 1861?).[34] From the turn of the century to the early 1930s, there followed arrangements of selected *Cantigas* melodies by Luis Villalba (one being that of the cantiga under discussion), Felipe Pedrell, and Tomás Bretón,[35] including transcriptions of various cantigas made by such renowned musicologists as Pierre Aubry, the Arabist Julián Ribera, Gregorio María Sunyol, and J. B Trend.[36] Trend based most of his transcriptions on those of Aubry, reworking several of them. Thus, by the time Schindler collected "Rosa das rosas," there was a goodly amount of interest in the *Cantigas* repertory, and this undoubtedly prompted Anglés to undertake his monumental study. His transcription of the entire corpus was to become the basis for the present and continued resurgence of cantigas performances throughout the world.[37]

Possible Textual and Melodic Antecedents

Jacques Chailley pointed out Alfonso's literal paraphrase of "Rose des roses et fleurs des fleurs" from the sixth verse of Gautier de Coinci's *Chanson à la Vierge,* "Quant ces floretes florir voi."[38] It is likely that Alfonso was inspired by this verse, which he developed into a full-fledged song in praise of the Virgin and which, together with Prologue B, cantiga *de loor* 1, and the *Petiçon* (cantiga 401), constitutes the strongest grounds for attributing his authorship to these particular examples.

In a recent article I alluded to the ninth-century sequence "Victimae paschali laudes" (Example 11-3c) as a possible source or inspiration for "Rosa das rosas" (Example 11-3a, taken from the Toledo codex, dating from around 1257), whose melodic *incipit* it closely resembles.[39] For the Example 11-3b (taken from Escorial B.I.2), the Argentine musicologist Josué T. Wilkes (1942) found additional melodic similarities in the antiphons "Magnum haereditatis mysterium" (Example 11-3f) and "In patientia vestra" (Example 11-3e),[40] to which I add the antiphon "Juste et pie vivamus" (Example 11-3d). These can be seen in the *Liber usualis.* Even the melodic *incipit* of the thirteenth-century sequence, "Stabat Mater" (Example 11-3g), attributed to the Franciscan Jacopone da Todi (c. 1228–1306) and which also may have been inspired by the earlier ninth-century sequence, is much closer to the Escorial version of "Rosa das rosas" which dates from around 1281.

With regard to the form of the cantiga, Anglés placed "Rosa das rosas" in the category of virelais and mentioned that it was similar in structure to cantiga 64, "Quen mui ben quiser." In his analysis of the refrain and stanzas, he counted, according to the rules of versification, an average of ten syllables per line of verse, save the initial one. Yet a careful reading of the second

Example 11-3. Possible melodic antecedents for "Rosa das rosas."
(a) "Rosa das rosas" (from To).
(b) "Rosa das rosas" (from B.I.2).
Antecedents:
(c) Sequence: "Victimae paschali laudes" (ninth century).
(d) Antiphon: "Iuste et pie vivamus."
(e) Antiphon: "In patientia vestra."
(f) Antiphon: "Magnum haereditatis mysterium."
(g) Sequence: "Stabat Mater" (thirteenth century).

line of the refrain bears out the fact that it contains eleven syllables. Moreover, Anglés used Greek letters to designate the corresponding melody
phrase for each verse.[41]

	RHYME SCHEME	MELODY
Rosa das rosas e Fror das frores	A⁹	α
Dona das donas, Sennor das sennores	A¹¹	β
Rosa de beldad' e de parecer	b¹⁰	γ
e Fror d'alegria e de prazer,	b¹⁰	γ
Dona en mui piadosa seer,	b¹⁰	δ
Sennor en toller coitas e doores	a¹⁰	β

Example II-4 (above and following pages). Schindler's "Rosa das rosas" and comparative transcriptions of To (f. 20) and B.I.2 (f. 39). See Figure II-I.
(a) Schindler, *Folk Music and Poetry,* no. 263 (transposed down a major 2nd).
Codice To:
(b) Ribera, *La música,* 128–29 (transposed down a perfect 4th).[42]
(c) Wilkes, "Cantiga 10," 7–9 (transposed down a perfect 4th).[43]
(d) Anglés, *La música,* 2:18 (transposed down a perfect 4th).[44]
(e) Ferreira, *The Sound,* [186].
Codice B.I.2:
(f) Villalba, *Cántigas,* 2–4.[45]
(g) Aubry, "Iter Hispanicum," 43.[46]
(h) Trend, *The Music,* ex. 13.
(i) Anglés.[47]
(j) Fernandes Lopes, "A música," [67].

Example II-4 (continued).

Example 11-4 (continued).

Example 11-4 (continued).

Example 11-4 (continued).

Example 11-4 (continued).

A more accurate analysis of the musical structure of the cantiga re-quires a subdivision of each verse, as reflected in the musical transcriptions made from the *Cantigas* codices in Example 11-4. The first textual strophe is also problematic, specifically its second and third verses, wherein the division of their lines necessitates six and four syllables per melody phrase. Also notice how the initial melody phrase of the third verse ends on the second syllable of the word *piadosa*.

	POETIC STRUCTURE	MELODIC STRUCTURE
Rosa das rosas		A^{x+w}
e Fror das frores	A^{11} (5+5)	A^{x+y}
Dona das donas.		B
Sennor das sennores.	A^{11} (5+6)	A^{x+z}
Rosa de beldad'		C
e de parecer	b^{10} (5+5)	B′
e Fror d'alegria		C
e de prazer,	b^{10} (6+4)	B′
Dona en mui pia-		E
dosa seer,	b^{10} (6+4)	F
Sennor en toller		B
coitas e doores.	a^{10} (5+5)	A^{x+z}

The only melodic discrepancy that exists between "Rosa das rosas" of the Toledo (To) and Escorial (B.I.2.) codices can be found in the initial melody phrase, above the syllable "ro" (see Example 11-4). In the former codex, the two-note ligature above that syllable is a *podatus* (*b-flat-c;* or *f-g,* transposed down a perfect 4th), whereas in the latter, it is a three-note ligature, *scandius* (*e-f-g*). It is possible, as Josué T. Wilkes suggested, that this was the cause of scribal error, "by mere recollection, not totally exact" (*por simple recordación, no por cierto exacta*), even though two distinct notational systems were employed, the earlier of which the scribe may not have taken care to verify.[48]

To Collet and Villalba's statement that the melodic *incipit* of "Rosa das rosas" is a general formula of plain chant in the Dorian mode ("est une formule générale de plain-chant (Ier mode 'gravis' [the Dorian mode])"), Wilkes responded:

> Rather than a *general formula* that usually comprises but three or four principal tones within the ecclesiastical modality, the tune of the cantiga would have suggested to the composer any one of the melodies from the Christian liturgy.[49]

Yet the most crucial element distinguishing Schindler's example and Ribera's transcription from the others is modality. We have speculated earlier that Schindler's informant may have been acquainted with Ribera's transcription, thus explaining their common modality (D minor, with a raised 7th), which would seem to be more than coincidental. Be that as it may, Ribera's transcriptions of the Toledo codex have continued to provoke criticism, and Wilkes has devoted a major part of his article to condemning Ribera's views on modality.[50]

Of all the literary and scientific works produced under the sponsorship of Alfonso X the Wise, the *Cantigas de Santa Maria* remained his most cherished. The performances of songs from this unique collection, which was compiled, ordered, and lavishly illustrated under his supervision, continue to delight audiences throughout the world. Schindler himself was responsible for such performances; all the same, he was truly excited when he confronted the tune in what he believed to be "oral tradition." Nonetheless, one can only hope that this and other tunes from the collection are still lurking somewhere on the Iberian peninsula.

Jerry R. Craddock

12. The Legislative Works of Alfonso el Sabio

Of the four principal fields cultivated by Alfonso el Sabio—poetry, history, astronomy, and law—it is fair to say that only his contributions to law possess any everyday practical significance outside university departments and other intellectual milieus, where the literati and professional medievalists continue to appreciate and analyze his works. By way of illustration, let me mention a recent court case reported in the Madrid newspaper *El país*.[1] In a small town near Cádiz, a resident had been forbidden to cross a neighbor's patio to reach the main street conveniently. The resulting dispute went to court, where the resident's lawyer brought an *acción de jactancia,* literally a lawsuit for boasting. In layman's terms, he who boasts of possessing a right or privilege may be constrained to prove in court the validity of that right or privilege, the exercise of which allegedly aggrieves another party. In effect, the law places the burden of proof on the defendant. The local court found for the resident-plaintiff, the appellate court found for the neighbor-defendant, and the Spanish Supreme Court agreed to hear the case. The law upon which the resident's lawyer built his case is found in Alfonso el Sabio's legislative masterpiece the *Siete partidas,* or seven parts, of the law.[2]

The text of the law in question says nothing whatsoever about patios or main streets; it considers rather the far more serious case of one person boasting that another is his slave, or of uttering other similar defamatory remarks before witnesses. Such a person may be brought to court and required to prove the truth of his statements; failing to do so, he must repudiate them and thereafter hold his tongue. Alfonso's law code appears to have been rather narrowly concerned with slander at this point; but the legal imagination being what it is, an analogy—farfetched, it seems to me—was drawn between slander and the exercise of property rights. In any case, I carry no brief for the defendant; what seems remarkable is that, after seven centuries, the *Partidas* continues to be living law in Spain, still a functioning part of the fabric of social relations.

Figure 12-1. King Alfonso el Sabio reading in his court. *Cantigas de Santa Maria,*
Patrimonio Nacional.

During his long reign as king of Castile and León, from 1252 to 1284, Alfonso X wished to establish exclusive royal control over all matters legislative and juridical.[3] To accomplish this task, he ordered the composition of two fundamental legal codes. The *Fuero real,* or royal charter, was a model municipal code, granted to the townships of Castile and medieval Extremadura, where it supplanted the existing municipal charters. In León, as well as in the newly conquered southern territories, a certain juridical uniformity already prevailed at the time of Alfonso's accession, since there the fundamental law book was the Visigothic code, the *Forum iudicum,* or in the vernacular *Fuero juzgo*—literally, the charter of the judges. There is no evidence that Alfonso ever attempted to impose the *Fuero real* in those territories. The *Siete partidas* was conceived originally as a uniform code for all of Alfonso's domains, before being redefined in 1274 as a body of general law to be applied principally in appeals to the king's bench or in cases where royal jurisdiction is primary.[4] The titles of both works are the creation of a later age; Alfonso and his jurists referred to the *Fuero real* vaguely and confusingly as the *Libro del fuero* or *Fuero del libro,* with other variants. Late in his reign, it seems likely that Alfonso decided to call his general code the *Setenario,* a title that posterity, however, accorded to a particular fragment, as discussed below.

The *Fuero real* is comprised of four books.[5] A brief prologue explains how the king, at the urgent petition of his subjects, agreed to grant them a charter (*fuero*) so that they might live "rightly," no longer depending on oral precedents (*fazañas*), arbitrary decisions (*alvedríos*), or improper customs (*usos desaguisados*) in their legal disputes. The monarch avers that after taking counsel with his court and with his jurists, he has given the petitioners the charter "written in this book" so that men and women together might be judged according to its provisions; he commands that this charter be observed forever and that no one dare go against it. The first book deals with what might be called public law. Religious orthodoxy and allegiance to the king are enjoined; all citizens are required to maintain and protect the church, in both its officiants and its property, as well as the royal family; there is a title defining and explaining law in general terms. Then the duties and prerogatives of judicial officials are described: the judges (*alcaldes*), the notaries (*escribanos publicos*), the barristers (*vozeros*), and the solicitors (*personeros*). The last two titles of this first book concern the types of legitimate lawsuits and the disposition of property while it is *sub iudice.* The second book is given over to salient points of judicial procedure, such as jurisdiction, initiating a lawsuit, witnesses and proofs, legal documents, types of

defenses, statutes of limitations, oaths, sentences, the conclusion of lawsuits, and appeals.

Book three embraces personal and commercial law, with titles on
marriage, dowry, communal property, legacies and inheritance, orphanage
and tutorships, disinheritance, buying and selling, exchanges, gifts, legal
costs, goods held in trust, loaned and rented property, guarantors and
guarantees, pawns and gages, and debts. Book four covers penal law.
Christians are forbidden to become Jews or Muslims or to embrace heresy.
The title on Jews requires them to be orthodox in their faith, not to
proselytize, and not to nurse Christian children or to have their children
nursed by Christians. No debt to Jews may be secured by a Christian's
body; interest rates are limited to 25 percent annually (if I understand the
passage correctly: *tres por quatro*), and the accumulated interest may not
exceed the value of the capital. The Jewish Sabbath and other holidays are
protected, so that Jews may not be constrained to fulfill any legal obligation
on such days.

The next titles of the fourth book take up insults, involuntary injuries
(*daños*) and willful acts of violence (*fuerzas*), punishments, illegal obstruc-
tion of right-of-way, adultery, incest, intercourse or marriage with nuns or
monks, abandonment of religious orders and pederasty, rape, sequestration
and bawdry, marriage with slaves or freedmen, forgery, theft, the theft of
slaves and the sale of free men into slavery, the protection of escaped slaves,
the regulation of physicians and surgeons, homicide, grave-robbing, the
refusal of military service, and the proper form of accusations and judicial
inquiry (*pesquisa*). The concluding titles are quite heterogeneous and not
particularly penal in nature: adoption, abandonment or repudiation of
children, pilgrimage, and shipwreck salvage. In a minority of *Fuero real*
manuscripts a most interesting title regulating challenges among the nobility concludes the work; in the others, this has been placed, rather reason-
ably, after treatment of accusations (III.4.20).

While the *Fuero real* has a remarkably coherent structure, in comparison with the municipal charters that it was evidently designed to
supplant, it is hard to avoid the impression of some arbitrariness in the
organization of books, titles, and laws. The last seven titles of the first book
are completely germane to the topic of the second book—namely, judicial
procedure. It seems unaccountable that the law governing court costs
(III.14.1), clearly a procedural matter, is buried in the section of titles on
commercial law. If there are laws regulating the Jews, why none for the
Muslims? The concluding hodgepodge of miscellaneous legislation men-

tioned above may represent afterthoughts, strung together when the arche-
type had already been compiled and a fair copy manufactured. But then
why were those laws not redistributed more logically in later copies, as was
done with the title on challenges? (This is said under the risky assumption
that the title on challenges originally came last: in fact, it may have been
inadvertently omitted from its proper place, then appended at the end
when the scribe realized his mistake.) The pairing of abandonment of holy
orders and pederasty in one title (IV.9) seems to reflect no consideration
that the two offenses were similarly heinous. The punishment for the
former is as mild as that for the latter is horrendous. Finally, of all the
multitudinous ways one might physically dishonor another person, why
mention only the action of burying his head in mud (*todo omne que metiere
la cabeça a otro en el lodo,* in IV.3.1)? Surely the Learned King and his jurists
could have come up with a more general provision or at least a longer list.

With regard to this head-burying law, it is possible to imagine that
Alfonso and his jurists did their work with one eye cocked at the municipal
codes, which fixed pecuniary and other punishments for many physical
affronts, some quite absurd. In the *fuero* of Alarcón, for example, "he who
sticks his ass in the face of another and strikes his face with the warmth of a
fart, let him be fined 300 shillings" (*tod aquel que a otro el culo le pusiere en la
faz e con la calor del pedo en la faz le diere, peche .ccc. sueldos*).[6] Was this
horseplay, or serious business which would conceivably lead to the following (retaliatory?) offense: "whoever thrusts a stick up another's ass outside
his house let him be fined 200 maravedies" (*qual quier que a alguno fuera de
su casa el palo por el culo le metiere, peche .cc. morauedis,* in law 291; 1:244)?
Fuera de su casa? Was the practice acceptable indoors? In any case, the
absence of these and many similar provisions here leads one to speculate
that Alfonso rather preferred to avoid the gamier side of village life in his
model code. Still, the inclusion of just one muddy affront in total isolation
from the many that must have existed seems quite mysterious.

The differences in tone and style between the *Fuero real* and the
municipal codes can be fully appreciated in their respective provisions
concerning male homosexuality. The *fuero* of Alarcón, with characteristic
bluntness, states the matter clearly and succinctly, with no roundabout
phraseology: "Let any man found fucking another man be burned" (*todo
aquel omne que fuere fallado fodiendo a otro omne, sea quemado,* in law 285;
1:242). Alfonso can barely bring himself to mention the act and does so
euphemistically, though the penalty he assigns is, if anything, more bar-
baric:

Although it grieves us to speak of a thing that is outrageous [*sin guisa*] to think about and ever so much more outrageous to do, yet because evil sin sometimes happens, such that a man desires another man in order to sin with him against nature, we command: whosoever they might be that commit such a sin, as soon as it is known, that both be castrated before the assembled townsfolk and afterwards on the third day be hanged by their legs until they die, and never be removed thence.[7]

The external history of the *Fuero real* presents numerous difficulties. Some of its manuscripts (as many as forty are extant) bear a colophon declaring that it was completed on 25 August 1255; in others, the date varies as to day and month; but in the majority, the colophon is absent altogether. The prologue in many manuscripts mentions a specific town as the recipient of the code; but in as many others, a vague phrase referring to "many towns and cities" suggests a broad territorial application. Numerous charters granting the *Fuero real* to individual towns, beginning in July of 1256, have been preserved; most scholars are convinced that it was either granted or at least utilized before that time, however, indeed before the date that appears in the colophons mentioned above. A recent theory by Joseph O'Callaghan argues that it was promulgated for all Castile on or near 5 May 1255, and that the charters to individual towns merely confirm the fact that the *Fuero real* was in force.[8]

In 1272 resentment over Alfonso's legislative activity came to a head, and the Learned Monarch was forced to allow numerous towns to revert to the *fueros* in force before his new code was adopted. His great grandson Alfonso XI (1312–1350) not only required various towns to accept the *Fuero real* they had earlier spurned, but he fixed its place in the legal system of Castile and León in his influential *Ordenamiento* of Alcalá of 1348. From this time on, the *Fuero real* grew in importance, while the traditional town charters became relics. The vast majority of its manuscripts were copied at this time or later. It was printed in 1483, with a learned commentary by Alfonso Díaz de Montalvo, and went through many subsequent editions. A goodly portion of its provisions found their way into the general legal digests or *Recopilaciones* of the modern period, from the sixteenth to the early nineteenth century.

Both the external history and the text tradition of the *Siete partidas* are immensely more intricate. To begin with, no fewer than four different, but intimately related, works are associated with the project. The *Espéculo,* fragmentarily preserved in only two manuscripts of the fourteenth and fifteenth centuries, is beyond any reasonable doubt earlier than and a primary source for the *Partidas*. The *Espéculo* appears to be approximately coeval with the *Fuero real;* though it bears no internal chronological indications, its text was utilized in various royal documents during the period from 1258 to 1261. There is good reason to believe that the *Espéculo* was never completed. Though the point remains controversial, Aquilino Iglesia Ferreirós presents compelling evidence for its incomplete nature.[9] His arguments have been corroborated and accepted in the recent critical edition of the text by Gonzalo Martínez Díez.[10] Though it was utilized by some medieval jurists, the *Espéculo* remained virtually unknown after the Middle Ages until the Real Academia de la Historia at Madrid published it in 1836.[11]

The order of subjects treated in the five extant books of the *Espéculo* is similar to that observed in the *Fuero real,* though each is developed in much greater detail. The fairly lengthy prologue casts even stronger aspersions on traditional customary law than did the *Fuero real*. It also enjoins the king's descendants to observe and uphold the laws of the *Espéculo* on pain of God's curse; others who contravene it are to be punished with the immense fine of 10,000 maravedies. A final clause allows the king in consultation with his court to emend and correct the text. The very brief first book includes a title on the nature of law in general, and two titles on the fundamental religious beliefs and duties of all Christians. Book two concerns the king's household and the responsibility of all his subjects to honor and maintain it, while book three is a treatise on military justice, where the king has absolute jurisdiction. The remaining two books cover the duties and obligations of judges and all other public officials, as well as the parties involved in legal proceedings. Book five covers judicial procedure from the initial summons, with regulations on proper defense maneuvers, witnesses, evidence, oaths, up to final judgments and eventual appeals.

It would be hard to exaggerate the differences between the *Espéculo* and the *Fuero real*. The former is insistently didactic, frequently philosophical, and reflects a far more advanced jurisprudence. Each topic regulated is introduced with fully descriptive definitions, often supported by imaginative etymologies of the terms involved. A scholastic love of fine distinctions has induced the compilers to multiply enormously the number of provisions on any given subject. Finally, the reception of Roman law, already evident in the *Fuero real,* is seen here in full swing, particularly in books four and five.

Just to give one example among any number that could be adduced, consider the strictures concerning defamation of the king. The *Fuero real*

(I.2.2) states simply and clearly enough: "let no one curse or denounce the king, nor recount any evil of him or his deeds." In the *Espéculo* (II.1.10), defamation is of two kinds, each of which is further divided into three categories. The first kind touches on the king's good deeds (*por razon de bien*): (1) to deny them, (2) [uncertain because of a lacuna in the text], and (3) not to wish to praise them at the proper time. The second kind involves alleged wrongdoing (*por razon de mal*): (1) to attribute falsely to the king a wrong word or deed, (2) to exaggerate a wrong word or deed the king may have done, and (3) to take delight in speaking evil of the king though with perfect accuracy.

The most plausible reason advanced for Alfonso's failure to complete the *Espéculo* related to a fundamental change in the Learned King's international outlook. In 1256, ambassadors from Pisa persuaded Alfonso to seek the title of Holy Roman Emperor, a forlorn ambition he entertained until his final disillusionment in 1275. This brilliant prospect seems to have been the occasion for a thoroughgoing recasting and restructuring of his general code, perhaps in order to render it more consonant with imperial dignity. The initial product of this revision was the *Libro del fuero de las leyes* of which only a single manuscript remains, containing just the first book. An epigraph on the first folio gives the dates of composition as 23 June 1256 to 28 August 1265.

The content of this first book deals exclusively with general legal principles and canon law. In other words, it is a vastly amplified version of the first book of the *Espéculo*. Thus, it corresponds to the content of the first partida, though with significant differences which have tended to persist, through contamination, in some manuscripts of the *Partidas*. However, the *Libro del fuero de las leyes* agrees with the *Espéculo* in using the word *libro* rather than *partida* to refer to portions of the code, and there is no hint of a seven-part structure. Consequently, it is inaccurate and anachronistic to refer to this work as just another manuscript of the first partida.[12]

The prologue and the first three titles (the nature of law, the nature of Christian faith, and the articles of faith) correspond literally to the respective passages of the *Espéculo*. The prologue has been shorn, however, of all reference to the existence of a model copy of the code kept with the king's court, from which individual exemplars are transcribed and distributed to towns; at the end no pecuniary penalty for failure to observe the code is specified. But the most notable feature is the royal command, broader and more categorical than in the *Espéculo*, that the king's subjects be judged by these laws and by no other law or charter—which on the surface would seem to abrogate even the *Fuero real*. Most commentators have concluded that Alfonso meant only to exclude the direct use of Roman law in the courts of his realm. The fundamental structural difference between the *Libro* and the *Espéculo* can be seen in the last three laws of *Espéculo* I.3 (on the sacraments and statutes of the church), which convert into an extensive treatise on canon law.

The year 1272 appears to have been a genuine watershed in the development of the Alfonsine legislative program. In addition to its importance for the history of the *Fuero real,* this year constitutes a *terminus post quem,* or earliest possible start, for the definitive seven-part format of Alfonso's general code, reflected in its traditional title *Siete partidas.*[13] For this redaction, Alfonso elaborated a two-part introduction. The first attenuates significantly the statement concerning the exclusive validity of the code, by introducing the motif of the mirror of princes:

> For this reason we specifically made this our book so that the kings of our realm might always look in it as in a mirror and see those things which they should correct in themselves, then to correct them and accordingly do likewise with their subjects.

Many commentators have concluded that Alfonso intended to make of the *Partidas* a purely doctrinal treatise; however, various laws in the body of the work continue to demand its exclusive use in law courts.[14]

The purpose of the second part is to extol the virtues of the number seven, by way of introducing and justifying the septipartite structure of the code. The initials of the first word of each partida form an acrostic of the Learned King's seven-letter name: *A-L-F-O-N-S-O.* The first partida presents general legal principles and a treatise on canon law. The second combines the two *Espéculo* books dealing with the king's household and military law. The third merges the last two books of the *Espéculo* (which regulate, we recall, judicial personnel and procedure). The fourth partida takes up matrimonial law and all sorts of personal relations, including feudal obligations between lord and vassal; the fifth contains commercial law; the sixth contains the law of inheritance; and the seventh is a penal code.

Canon law is the basis for the greater part of partidas one and four. Roman law predominates in partidas three, five, and six and is far from absent in seven. The first partida expands title one (the nature of law) of the first (and only extant) book of the *Libro del fuero de las leyes* into two titles, one on the nature of law in general and one on the nature of custom. The revised first title now includes a set of laws (I.1.17–19) allowing for the amendment and repeal of existing laws as well as the introduction of new legislation, among many other significant innovations. The second partida remains the most homegrown of the seven; entire new titles have been added vis-à-vis the second and third books of the *Espéculo*—for example, title twenty-one on knighthood, title twenty-four on naval warfare, and title thirty-one on universities. Though there is much literal carryover from the *Espéculo* to the *Partidas,* it is difficult to find passages that have not been retouched; more often, major rewriting and recasting has occurred.

The didactic and discursive nature of Alfonso's legal discourse in the *Partidas* has lent it a literary significance accorded few law codes. One particularly notable example of elaboration involves the passage quoted above from the *Espéculo,* concerning defamation of the king. In the same law (II.1.10), the legislator adds that no one should wish to hear ill of the king, since "hearing is the entrance for saying"—that is, one tends to repeat gossip. Perhaps inspired by this association of hearing and speaking, Alfonso has incorporated the entire question of defamation into a larger context in the *Partidas* bearing on how subjects should comport themselves with regard to their monarch (II.13), specifically that they should seek his honor at all times with all ten senses, five corporeal (sight, hearing, smell, taste, and touch) and five spiritual (common sense, fantasy, imagination, judgment, and memory). Defamation is associated with the sense of taste (II.13.4–5), since the tongue, the organ of taste, is also used for speech.[15]

There exists a group of *Partidas* manuscripts that lacks any chronological indication whatsoever. I believe they represent an earlier redaction, albeit after 1272, as opposed to the remaining manuscripts which present, at the end of the first part of the prologue, an elaborate chronology carried out with exquisite astronomical exactitude. That chronological statement fixes the dates of composition, in terms of all the major chronological eras known at the time, as between 23 June 1256 (the same initial date as the *Fuero del libro de las leyes*) and seven full years later *(siete años complidos).* Needless to say, the latter bit of chronology is fabulous, concocted to correspond with the seven-part arrangement of the work.

The two groups of manuscripts just mentioned—those that lack the parallel chronology and those that contain it—also differ widely in the first four titles of the first partida. The former group is textually closer to the *Libro del fuero de las leyes,* while the latter reveals a substantial amplification. Neither during Alfonso's reign nor during the remainder of the Middle Ages did any particular one of the redactions of the *Partidas,* including the

Libro del fuero de las leyes, come to be regarded as authentic. As he had done for the *Fuero real,* Alfonso XI in 1348 established the place of the *Partidas* in the legal system of Castile and León by his *Ordenamiento* of Alcalá, stating that they had never had force of law up to that time. When Alfonso Díaz de Montalvo brought out the first edition of the *Partidas* in 1491, he formed a hybrid text that contained the parallel chronology but lacked the amplified portions of the first four titles. As fate would have it, this remained the form in which the code was generally known for centuries, since the renowned jurist Gregorio López, commissioned by Charles I to prepare an authentic text, a task which he accomplished in 1555, perpetuated the hybrid character of Montalvo's edition. López's edition, which included a massive Latin commentary, had exclusive legal authority in all courts of law and, to this day, remains the basic version consulted by civilists and canonists.[16]

The amplified text was reintroduced to the learned public in 1807 by the Real Academia de la Historia, which was roundly denounced for its pains. The base manuscript of the first partida in this edition (chosen for no better reason than it was part of a group of three manuscripts containing the first six partidas, all produced in one scriptorium) just happened to include the amplified portions of the first four titles. Many jurists and theologians regarded these passages, hitherto unknown except to a few antiquarian scholars, as impious and heretical interpolations. Traditionally, academics prefer this edition to that of López; lawyers, despite the authentic character of the latter, were not slow to introduce the 1807 edition into the legal system, with confusing and contradictory results. Finally, in 1860 the Spanish supreme court declared that when the two editions differ, that of López takes precedence. At present in Spain, and perhaps also wherever Spain has exercised dominion, the *Siete partidas* remains in force except insofar as its provisions have been specifically repealed or replaced by later codes.[17]

The second part of the prologue of the *Partidas* begins with the word *Septenario;* I suspect this was also intended as the general title of the work. Posterity, however, attached the label *Setenario* to an incomplete work preserved in two manuscripts and fragmentarily in a composite manuscript of the first partida. I believe the evidence is conclusive that the *Septenario,* long regarded as Alfonso's earliest legal work, represents, in fact, yet another attempt by the Learned King to rewrite the first partida.[18] The text, after an introductory eulogy of Alfonso's father, Fernando III (1217–1252), launches into a radically expanded version of the second part of the prologue of the *Partidas,* and then further amplifies the already amplified first four titles of the first partida with an obsessive, indeed maniacal, concern for the properties of the number seven. The *Septenario* never figured in the legal canon in any way. It was known to scholars and occasionally utilized by them, but it only entered the mainstream of academic concern after Kenneth H. Vanderford published his critical edition in 1945.[19]

As king, Alfonso engaged in constant legislative activity, granting letters patent and privileges of every sort. At frequent intervals, his cortes or parliament was convened and its decisions communicated to municipalities in writing in the form of *cuadernos,* sheets of vellum or paper folded to form four leaves, some of which have been preserved. The king and his advisers (his *curia* and *corte* in the singular, as opposed to plural *cortes* for the parliament) also issued regulations (*ordenamientos*) dealing with judicial matters. In the view of some city fathers, particularly those of Burgos, the *Fuero real* required explanation and amendment. Accordingly, Alfonso, beginning in 1260, issued various provisions which were appended to manuscripts of the *Fuero real* and came to have the title *Leyes nuevas,* or new laws. Finally, a curious collection of bylaws for gambling houses, the *Ordenamiento de las tafurerias,* was allegedly composed in 1276 by a certain Master Roland at the behest of the Learned King. So far as I am aware, its authenticity has not been called into question. All textual witnesses belong to the fifteenth century or later, however, so it is important to establish the accuracy of this attribution.

This survey is sufficient to reveal what an imposing edifice Alfonso left to posterity in his legal works. Our admiration turns to astonishment when we consider that his accomplishments are equally significant in three other fields—poetry, history, and astronomy. Although every historian of the political events, law, or culture of medieval Spain has perforce dealt with Alfonso's legislative works, those works have suffered until quite recently from a dearth of really close textual, source, and analytical studies. In contrast, work on the *Cantigas* and on the histories has advanced much more rapidly in the twentieth century. This neglect may seem hard to understand, since on all sides it is conceded that Alfonso's legislative works are one of the chief glories of Spain's splendid past. I believe that a phenomenon of excessive familiarity was at work in delaying or thwarting serious monographic study. The existence of multitudinous and quite accessible editions, however deficient from the philological point of view, rather precludes the excitement of rediscovery that accompanies the appearance of a *General estoria* or a facsimile of the *Cantigas.* Furthermore, Alfonsine legislation stands apart as a relatively unified corpus, in large part of foreign inspiration, in balancing contrast with the wonderful variety and pictur-esqueness of the municipal codes, with their homely regulations so close to the realities of everyday life and ceaseless conflict with the Moors.[20] Small wonder that the municipal codes were far better studied by twentieth-century scholars, at least before 1980, than Alfonso's legislative works.

This panorama of predominantly perfunctory concern underwent a remarkable change about the time of the recent celebration of the seventh centenary of Alfonso's death on 4 April 1284. The reawakening of interest was already underway and would have gone forward independently of that anniversary; but there is no question that subsequently the pace and quan-tity of work has accelerated dramatically, so that the scholarly production of the 1980s bids fair to eclipse all that has preceded it. Time and space permit only the most general and selective survey of current and recent work on Alfonsine legislation. Items I am unable to include here will be analyzed in a supplement to my recent legislative bibliography,[21] which should go to the printers by mid-1990.

For those in need of a general guide to the subject, there is a competent and well-documented survey of Alfonsine legislation in English by Robert MacDonald. Those undaunted by the monumental prolixity of Aquilino Iglesia Ferreirós will find in him the most ambitious recent attempt at an overall interpretation of Alfonsine legislation. For the *Fuero real,* Antonio Pérez Martín has sketched an all-inclusive survey of outstanding problems. Manuals of Spanish legal history are often inaccurate and out of date with regard to fields like Alfonsine legislation, where controversies are multiple and bibliographic production rapid. A happy exception is Francisco Tomás y Valiente, who presents a balanced summation of the principal theories in circulation.[22]

Of the recent miscellanies devoted to Alfonso X, the most significant are *The Worlds of Alfonso the Learned and James the Conqueror,* edited by R. I. Burns in 1985, and *España y Europa,* edited by Antonio Pérez Martín in 1986. Other worthy, though often uneven, efforts include the exposition catalog *Alfonso X Toledo 1984;* the collection *Estudios alfonsíes,* edited by José Monde-jar and Jesús Montoya in 1985; *La lengua y la literatura en tiempos de Alfonso X,* edited by Fernando Carmona and F. J. Flores in 1985; as well as the special numbers or sections that appeared in *Revista de la facultad de derecho de la Universidad complutense* (1985), *Revista de occidente* (1984), *Historia 16* (1984), *ABC* (1984), and *El país* (1984).[23] With the juridical compilations of J. R. Craddock and L. M. García-Badell, the bibliographical tasks facing those who wish to delve into Alfonsine legislation have been much facilitated. Craddock includes a census of manuscripts and editions.[24] With regard to the *Siete partidas,* we have since 1986 a more complete list of the manuscripts from Antonio García y García, who records over a hundred items, including fragments.[25] The most useful periodical bibliography currently available is the *Noticiero alfonsí,* published since 1982 by Anthony J. Cárdenas at Wichita State University.

A new editorial project directed by Gonzalo Martínez Díez of the University of Valladolid envisages publication of the entire Alfonsine corpus; as of August 1988 the *Espéculo* (1985) and the *Fuero real* (1988) have appeared. The latter includes an exhaustive census of the manuscripts, which number forty or more.[26] Another focus of intense activity is the University of Murcia, where a rival set of editions is planned under the direction of Antonio Pérez Martín and the University of Richmond's Robert MacDonald.[27] The Hispanic Seminary of Medieval Studies at Madison, Wisconsin, has in an advanced state of preparation a concordance of the 1807 edition of the *Partidas.* Individual manuscripts have been the object of recent editions; the *Libro del fuero de las leyes* was brought out under the (pardonable) misnomer of *Primera partida* by J. A. Arias Bonet, also then included in the *Concordances and Texts of the Royal Scriptorium* issued in microfiches by the Hispanic Seminary in Madison by Lloyd Kasten and John Nitti.[28] An extremely important hybrid manuscript of the first partida was edited, with lamentable incompetence, by Francisco Ramos Bossini in 1984; see the brief—and devastating—assessment by Iglesia Ferreirós.[29]

Under the auspices of the Spanish Legal Text series, sponsored by the Hispanic Seminary of Medieval Studies in Madison, Ivy Corfis produced in 1987 a microfiche edition of the *Fuero real* manuscript housed in the Free Library of Philadelphia.[30] Perhaps the finest editorial work recently accomplished involves medieval Portuguese translations of the Alfonsine legal corpus. José de Azevedo Ferreira has editions of the first partida and the *Foro real* to his credit, to say nothing of fragments of the second and third partidas that he has uncovered.[31] Ferreira's 1987 *Fuero real* in two volumes provides a massive paleographic and linguistic study as well as an exhaustive glossary. For an overview of the impact of Alfonsine legislation on Portuguese law, see also his 1986 article; the same scholar's work on the third partida seems well advanced, to judge by his recent progress report.[32]

Some editorial work focuses on portions of the large codes. Dwayne Carpenter included a critical text as part of his thoroughgoing study of the laws concerning the Jews in the seventh partida (VII.24); likewise a critical version accompanies his briefer effort on two laws dealing with the Moors (VII.25.0–1).[33] Craddock regularly uses critically determined texts as a springboard to treatments of individual issues, such as chronology and external history of the Alfonsine codes,[34] the legal responsibility of the king,[35] and the proper title of the *Libro del fuero de las leyes*.[36] This approach—the utilization of all extant textual witnesses rather than available editions—was pioneered by Arias Bonet in his analysis of the regulations on property held in trust contained in the fifth partida (V.3).[37]

Questions of authorship—the identification of the jurists who carried out the actual compilation of the Alfonsine legislative works—have evolved little in recent decades. The one figure securely identified, Jacobo de Junta, "el de las Leyes" (d. 1294), will have all his works edited critically by Jean Roudil of the University of Paris. His *Summa de los nueve tiempos de los pleitos,* a brief procedural manual, appeared in 1986. If all goes well, the *Flores de las leyes* and the *Doctrinal* will soon follow. Both works are important for the text tradition of the *Partidas,* in particular of the third partida.

The external history of Alfonsine legislation has been ventilated in my own works; readers have already been regaled with a synopsis of those views above.[38] For other, often sharply contradictory views, see Alfonso García Gallo,[39] Iglesia Ferreirós,[40] MacDonald,[41] O'Callaghan,[42] and Pérez Martín.[43] It is most unfortunate that García Gallo's immense prestige has lent his utterly topsy-turvy chronology a plausibility and wide acceptance that it does not deserve.

Source studies repeatedly emphasize that, even when Alfonso's sources are known, conclusive textual parallels are often difficult to establish, since his compilers rarely, if ever, adopted them slavishly. Accordingly, Ruggero Maceratini, in his study of likely Roman sources for the *Siete partidas* laws on heresy (VII.26), comes to the following cautious conclusion: "it is possible to attribute to the *Summa [codicis]* of Azo . . . the role of direct, but not literal source."[44] In fact, the whole subject of literal sources must be treated with extreme caution, particularly where one is desirous of deriving from their alleged presence in Alfonso's legal works specific conclusions about the latter's chronology. The late lamented J. A. Arias Bonet reveals with devastating effect the fragility of the claims put forth by Bono and García Gallo, regarding the supposed influence of Salatiel's *Ars notariae* (composed in 1272) on the third partida, and Saint Thomas Aquinas's *De regimine principum* (completed posthumously by an anonymous continuator, circa 1305) on the second partida.[45] For the similarities to, and departures from, the *Corpus iuris civilis* to be detected in the *Siete partidas,* Rafael Zurita Cuenca's outline is most helpful.[46]

The work by historians of law on the Alfonsine legal corpus usually takes one of two forms: (1) some portion of an Alfonsine legislative work is the target for detailed analysis, or (2) some portion of the Alfonsine legal corpus is drawn into the discussion of a specific topic. The latter form has been far more frequent, in line with the often perfunctory attention that has traditionally been paid to Alfonsine legislation. James Powers, however, in his recent work on medieval Hispanic municipal law as it relates to military matters, takes exquisite care to compare at every point the town regulations with the laws of the *Fuero real, Espéculo,* and *Siete partidas;* he thus avoids the temptation to put aside, a priori, the latter three codes as relatively extraneous to the most authentic Hispanic legal traditions. Perhaps the best recent representative of revived interest in the direct approach to the Alfonsine codes is the exceptional work of Jesús Vallejo on procedural law in the *Fuero real.*[47]

Literary and linguistic work on the Alfonsine legislative corpus has never stood in the forefront of scholarly activity. But one can mention the significant contributions of José Antonio Bartol Hernández (1986) on the syntax of adverbial clauses in the *Partidas,* and Rafael Lapesa (1980) on the philosophical basis, structure, style, and vocabulary of the *Setenario.*[48]

A field that constituted a somewhat stagnant intellectual backwater has evolved very quickly to one of the most lively and actively cultivated subspecialties in Hispanic letters. It remains to be seen whether the current frenetic pace can be long maintained.

Anthony J. Cárdenas

13. In Search of a King: An Alfonsine Bibliology

In 1980, Joseph T. Snow presented a bibliographic excursion on *Cantigas* studies, using the geographical metaphor of a *mappa mundi*, uncharted in 1221 at Alfonso's birth and later beginning to take shape as studies appeared. It would seem appropriate to follow suit for Alfonsine studies generally, this time with another analogy, that of a dormant volcano akin to the majestic Mount Saint Helens. Before it literally blew its top, there was a moderate amount of interest in the volcano, but nothing like that which followed the momentous explosion which was felt around the globe. In another study, Snow illustrates with precision the interest in the Alfonsine legacy of the *Cantigas de Santa Maria* by a telling graph, wherein he reports 74 *Cantigas* studies for the pre-1900 period. As he plots subsequent scholarly activity by decade, from 1901 through 1970, there is a gradual increase from twenty studies for the first decade cited to seventy-nine for 1961–1970. In the following decade, 1971–1980, a remarkable rumbling occurs; Snow registers 221 studies in the 1987 *Studies on the Cantigas* discussed below.

Corroborating Snow's findings are James R. Chatham's meticulous bibliographies on dissertations in the United States (cited below) which register twenty-six Alfonsine dissertations for the period from 1876–1966. In a mere fraction of that time, from 1967–1977, the number is nearly duplicated (twenty-five Alfonsine dissertations). The explosion occurs in the 1980s when the entire world celebrates the septicentennial of the anniversary of Alfonso X's death.

Two independent but related publications pertaining to the Alfonsine legacy are part of this eruption. One is the *Bulletin of the Cantigueiros de Santa Maria*, founded in 1987 by John E. Keller. It is a biannual journal seeking to include studies leading to a better understanding of Alfonso's *Cantigas*. The other is the *Noticiero alfonsí*, founded in 1982, a broader-based annual newsletter proposing to include any and all cultural and scholarly interpretations of the Alfonsine legacy since 1 January 1980. The seven volumes printed since 1982 register more than 125 books and more than 600 articles published since 1 January 1980 treating the Alfonsine legacy. The authors of these interpretations are myriad and, like the many scientists who flocked to study Mount Saint Helens once it erupted, bring to the theme a vast array of different, although frequently overlapping, areas of expertise. *Omnis analogia claudicat,* however, and so does this one; for it is their expertise and the many studies they produce which now become the explosion. To establish another analogy from the natural world, in an essay such as this it seems appropriate to meander through the maze of those studies much as a stream might, following what may seem an erratic yet natural course.

Since January 1980, the main point of departure for this examination, scholars have paid tribute to the Learned Monarch in at least twenty-two major conferences from Los Angeles, California, to Murcia, Spain; from Ottawa, Canada, to Bahía Blanca, Argentina; conferences have been held at major research centers throughout the United States and at centers in Ottawa, San Juan, London, Lisbon, and, of course, throughout the rest of the Iberian peninsula. Several of these have produced major anthologies of studies pertinent to the legacy of Alfonso X. The topics they treat are as varied as the Alfonsine legacy itself. This is exemplified by two of the earliest, held in 1981 on opposite coasts of the United States. On 2–4 April 1981, "The Worlds of Alfonso the Learned and James the Conqueror—An International Symposium" took place at and under the auspices of the Center for Medieval and Renaissance Studies of the University of California in Los Angeles. It treated predominantly the historico-political aspects of the reigns of the two rulers, with other studies—Alfonsine language, Alfonsine Jewish collaborators, and manuscript illumination, costume, and castles—rounding out the repertoire. On 19–21 November of the same year, the Spanish Institute in New York hosted the "International Symposium/*Coloquio Internacional* on the *Cantigas de Santa Maria* of Alfonso X el Sabio (1252–1284) in Commemoration of its 700th Anniversary Year–1981." Presentations at this conference treated the literature and language, the iconography, and the music of the *Cantigas*. Both symposia have recently borne fruit in two handsome volumes. The first, *The Worlds of Alfonso the Learned and James the Conqueror: Intellect and Force in the Middle Ages* (Princeton: Princeton University Press, 1985), contains seven chapters felicitously integrated and edited by Robert I. Burns, S.J., who is also author of the first chapter and the excellent epilogue. The other—*Studies on the "Cantigas de Santa Maria": Art, Music, and Poetry* (Madison, Wisc.:

Hispanic Seminary of Medieval Studies, 1987)—comprises twenty-four chapters, including those of the coeditors, Israel J. Katz and John E. Keller, as well as their introduction and a prologue by the latter. It ends with an informative bibliographic epilogue by Joseph Snow treating *Cantigas* studies.

Other volumes resulting from conferences are worth noting: (1) *Cádiz en el siglo XIII* (Cádiz: 1983) contains eleven studies essentially grouped around the theme of Alfonso X and his varied relationship to Cádiz. (2) *Estudios alfonsíes* (Granada: 1985), edited by José Mondéjar and Jesús Montoya Martínez, involves the studies generated in 1984 at the University of Granada on linguistic, lyrical, esthetic, and political aspects of Alfonso's reign. (3) *De astronomia Alphonsi* (1987), edited by Mercè Comes, Roser Puig, and Julio Samsó, contains fourteen studies, including seven presented on the first day (dedicated to Alfonso X), from the Seventeenth International Congress of the History of Science held in August 1985 at the University of California at Berkeley. Two notable conferences of 1984 were: (4) "Alfonso X, jornadas organizadas por el Centro de estudios sociales del Valle de los Caídos" (in press) and (5) "Alfonso X el Sabio: vida, obra, y época," held successively at seven Spanish cities (in press). (6) *La lengua y literatura en tiempos de Alfonso X el Sabio* was edited by Fernando Carmona and F. J. Flores (Murcia: 1986). (7) *Alfonso X y Ciudad Real: conferencias pronunciadas con motivo del VII centenario de la muerte del Rey Sabio, 1284–1984* was edited by Luis Rafael Villegas, et al. (Ciudad Real: 1986). (8) *Homenaje a Alfonso X el Sabio (1284–1984)* includes twelve of the several studies presented at the international congress at Carleton University in Canada and appeared in *Revista canadiense de estudios hispánicos* 9 (1985). (9) *Romance Quarterly* 33 (1986) contains many of the studies on Alfonso presented in his honor at the "Thirty-Seventh Annual Kentucky Foreign Language Conference." (10) The *Homenaje a Alfonso X el Sabio* was edited by Maria B. Fontanella de Weinberg, Graciela R. de Brevedán, et al. (Bahía Blanca, Argentina: 1985). Others—the Harvard conference (see above, ch. 11, n. 8) and the session at Westfield College, for example—are still to be published.

Several journals, in addition to those cited above, have dedicated entire volumes to studies treating the Alfonsine legacy, among them the *Revista de occidente* 43 (1984), *Fragmentos* 2 (1984), *Thought* 60 (1985), *Cuadernos de historia* 16 (1985), *Revista de la Facultad de derecho de la Universidad complutense de Madrid*, monográfico 9 (1985), *Miscelánea medievalia murciana* 13 (1986), and *Revista de musicología* 10 (1987). *Alfonso X Toledo 1984* offers an example of a volume sponsored municipally with the collaboration of the Spanish Ministry of Culture, emerging from the exposition held in Toledo in 1984 and including studies on science, music, law, art, economics, and culture.

A number of recent audiovisual packages have examined Alfonso and his times. The Ministerio de Asuntos Exteriores, with Diodoro Urquía Latorre, for example, produced in 1984 a magnificent audiovisual treat titled "Alfonso X el Sabio" consisting of 195 color slides, sixty-seven minutes of narration on cassette, and an accompanying transcription in a seventy-page booklet. Less ambitious projects of the same ilk include "La España del Rey Sabio" (Madrid: 1984), a thirty-minute cassette tract, pamphlet, and twenty slides; and "Alfonso X el Sabio" (Madrid: c. 1985), a cassette, text, and eighty slides. Finally, Françoise Micheau and Michel Zimmerman have produced teaching units in French (Paris: 1980), consisting of slides, photographs, and occasionally records, with explanatory text. Their unit *Vivre au moyen âge d'après un manuscrit du XIIIe siècle* comprises nine color slides with details from the *Cantigas* (El Escorial codex T.I.1), illustrating scenes from daily life in the Middle Ages. The accompanying text treats the miniatures in the slides not only as works of art but also as documents for an interdisciplinary comprehension of the period.

Providing an even greater visual impact than slides are the Edilán (Editora Internacional de Libros Antiguos) facsimiles of the *Cantigas* in the El Escorial codex T.I.1 (Madrid: 1979), and of the first book of the *Lapidario* in the El Escorial codex H.I.15 (Madrid: 1982). In 1984, Edilán also published, for the Bank of Alicante, the Alfonsine *Privilegios otorgados a la ciudad de Alicante,* a total of thirty-nine folios with a forty-nine-page study by Juan Manuel del Estal, María Luis Cabones, and Francisco Gimeno Menéndez. Also by Estal is the more sober *Documentos inéditos de Alfonso X el Sabio y del infante su hijo don Sancho* (Alicante: 1984) with study, transcription, and facsimiles of several Alfonsine documents. To these must be added the two-volume edition (1: *Estudios introductorios,* 2: *Edición facsímil*) of the *Libros de ajedrez, dados y tablas,* by Vicent García Editores (Valencia: 1987), and the *Fuero real* facsimile (Valladolid: 1979).

Pertinent to this, although not Alfonsine per se, is Julio González's *Reinado y diplomas de Fernando III* in three volumes (Córdoba: 1981–1986), volume one as *Estudio* and volumes two and three as *Documentos 1217–1253,* which bear directly on Alfonso's own reign and chancery inasmuch as Alfonso inherited the chancery and its practices from his father.

Following in this vein is the nascent and blossoming interest of other

Spanish municipalities in their connection with King Alfonso, such as Murcia, Alicante, and Ciudad Real, as well as the monographic work being done by historians in this area, such as Carlos de Ayala Martínez, *La Orden de Santiago en la evolución política del regnado de Alfonso X (1252–1284)* (Madrid: 1983) and his *La monarquía y Burgos durante el reinado de Alfonso X* (Madrid: 1984), or Alfredo Cid Rumbao, *Afonso o Sábio e Ourense* (Orense: 1980).

Ninety-four monographs in the form of dissertations can be found in three meticulously edited compilations by James R. Chatham, et al.: (1) *Western European Dissertations on the Hispanic and Luso-Brazilian Languages and Literatures* (Mississippi State University, 1984); (2) *Dissertations in Hispanic Languages and Literatures* in three volumes, the two U.S. volumes covering *1876–1966* and *1967–1977,* respectively (Lexington: 1970 and 1981), which contain in sequence forty-three, twenty-six, and twenty-five dissertations. Another source for Alfonsine dissertations is David J. Billick's "Graduate Research on Alfonso X," *La corónica* 8 (1979): 67–72 and 9 (1980): 55, together comprising seventy-seven items (sixty-eight and nine, respectively), including both doctoral and master's theses.

Other bibliographies include the oft-cited list in José Sánchez Pérez's *Alfonso X, el Sabio* (Madrid: 1935), 119–76, and Gardiner H. London's in *Boletín de filología española* 6 (1960): 18–31. A sine qua non for *Cantigas* studies is Joseph Snow's monumental compilation *The Poetry of Alfonso X, el Sabio* (London: 1977), with his updates in *La corónica* 11 (1983): 248–57, in *Studies on the Cantigas,* 475–86, and in the *Bulletin of the Cantigueiros de Santa Maria* 1 (1987): 1–10. This same issue of the *Bulletin* contains useful bibliographic studies on aspects of the *Cantigas* by Connie L. Scarborough (miniatures: 41–50), Israel J. Katz (music: 51–60), and a fascinating study, "The *Cantigas de Santa Maria* as a Research Opportunity in History," by Robert I. Burns (11–22).

A concise overview, "Alfonso, prosa y verso," is in "Hispano-Medievalismo," *Revista de la Universidad complutense* 2–4 (1984 [1988]): 171–94. Appropriate sections of *The Year's Work in Modern Language Studies* constitute a bibliographic source not to be overlooked.

Vying in importance with Snow's 1977 *Poetry* is another definitive bibliographic compilation, Jerry R. Craddock's *The Legislative Works of Alfonso X, el Sabio: A Critical Bibliography* (London: 1986). Less ambitious, but useful especially in its coverage of items subsequent to Craddock's bibliography, is Luis María García-Badell Arias's "Bibliografía sobre la obra jurídica de Alfonso X el Sabio y su época (1800–1985)," *Revista de la*

Facultad de derecho de la Universidad complutense de Madrid, monográfico 9 (1985): 288–319, which contains over 500 items. Minor in scope by comparison but nevertheless useful, in that they treat areas largely untouched by the above-cited bibliographies, are Daniel Eisenberg's 76 items in "Alfonsine Prose: Ten Years of Research" and Anthony Cárdenas's 71 items in "A Survey of Scholarship on the Scientific Treatises of Alfonso X, el Sabio," both in *La corónica* 11 (1983): 220–30 and 231–47, respectively. Similar to these is the annual *Westfield College Medieval Hispanic Research Seminary Newsletter* (founded in 1985), with Alfonsine items easily accessible by means of its index. Finally, reference must be made to the Spanish dom of bibliography, José Simón Díaz and his nearly 800 items (nos. 519–1313) treating Alfonso X—bibliographies, codices, editions, and studies—in the third edition (corrected and updated) of his *Bibliografía de la literatura hispánica,* volume two of *Literatura castellana: edad media* (Madrid: 1986).

The 1980s have witnessed new Alfonsine studies not only in the form of articles and books, but also as new editions of Alfonsine works. In addition, several earlier studies and editions have been reprinted. Kenneth Vanderford's edition of the *Setenario* (1945; repr. Barcelona: 1984) is one example. Three editions, five with the Edilán facsimile and the microfiche noted below, of the *Lapidario* have appeared: Diman-Winget, the most reliable (Madison: 1980); Rodríguez M. Montalvo (Madrid: 1981); and for Odres Nuevos, a reprint of María Brey Mariño's modernization of the first book (1968; repr. Madrid: 1980). Walter Mettmann's edition of the *Cantigas* (1959–1972; Vigo: 1981) constitutes another example of these reprints, along with his paperback version for Clásicos Castalia (Madrid: 1986). Another recent version, including profane poems, is *Cantigas,* by Jesús Montoya Martínez (Cátedra: 1988). Montoya Martínez with Juárez Blanquer has also produced the *Historia y anécdotas de Andalucía en las "Cantigas de Santa María" de Alfonso X* (Granada: 1988). Two of the studies accompanying the facsimile editions of the *Lapidario* and the *Cantigas* have been reprinted as monographs: Ana Domínguez Rodríguez, *Astrología y arte en el "Lapidario" de Alfonso X el Sabio* (Madrid: 1984), and José Filgueira Valverde's Spanish prose translation of the *Cantigas* from the Edilán facsimile.

Another useful reprint is Gregorio López's glossed *Las siete partidas* (1555; repr. Madrid: 1985), as is the Real Academia de la Historia 1807 edition of the *Siete partidas* (Madrid: 1972). Other editions of the *Partidas,* complete or partial, have appeared. Notable among them for its thoroughness, and for taking on the plethora of problems any critical edition of the entire *Partidas* would have to confront, is Dwayne E. Carpenter's *Alfonso and the*

Jews: An Edition of and Commentary on "Siete partidas" 7.24 "De los judíos"
(Berkeley and Los Angeles: 1986). Individual codices containing a portion
of the *Partidas* have been edited: Juan Antonio Arias Bonet, *Primera
partida* (Valladolid: 1975), as contained in the British Library codex Add.
20.787; and Francisco Ramos Bossini, *Primera partida* (Granada: 1984), as
contained in the Hispanic Society of America codex HC.397/573. Gonzalo
Martínez Díez's edition of the *Espéculo: leyes de Alfonso X,* vol. 1 (Avila: 1985)
was found deficient by Robert A. MacDonald (*Journal of Hispanic Philology*
10 [1986]: 253–55), who is on the verge of producing his own edition of this
work.

Two editions of Alfonsine Latin works have appeared recently: Emmanuel Poulle, *Les "Tables alphonsines" avec les canons de Jean de Saxe* (Paris:
1984), and David Pingree, *Picatrix: The Latin Version of the Ghāyat al-Ḥakīm*
(London: 1986). Also related to Alfonsine science are the two 1978 editions
of Alfonso's *Canones de Albateni,* one by Georg Bossong (Tübingen) and
the other in the *Concordances and Texts.*

The *Concordances and Texts of the Royal Scriptorium Manuscripts of
Alfonso X, el Sabio* (Madison: 1978), edited by Lloyd Kasten, John Nitti, et
al., is perhaps the most significant current editorial venture in Alfonsine
studies. An eleven-page introductory booklet precedes 110 microfiches containing all the vernacular prose texts extant in bona fide Alfonsine Royal
Scriptorium codices, and even the texts of the *Estoria de Espanna* in the El
Escorial codex X.I.4 and the text of the *Libro del fuero de las leyes* in the
British Library codex Add. 20.787, that is, two texts apparently written
immediately subsequent to Alfonso's reign. These microfiche editions serve
first and foremost as linguistic research tools, and have already begun to
bear fruit in two recent and excellent studies: Jerry R. Craddock's "The
Tens from 40 to 90 in Old Castilian: A New Approach," *Romance Philology*
38 (1985): 425–35, and Ralph Penny's "Derivation of Abstracts in Alfonsine
Spanish," *Romance Philology* 41 (1987): 1–23. These editions constitute the
basis for the soon-to-be-published dictionary of Alfonsine prose of the
Hispanic Seminary of Medieval Studies at the University of Wisconsin.

Reprints and translations have made several important Alfonsine studies readily available to scholarship. Among them are Evelyn S. Procter's
Alfonso X of Castile (1951; Westport, Conn.: 1980), Francisco Rico's *Alfonso el
Sabio y la "General Estoria": tres lecciones* (1972; repr. Barcelona: 1984), and
Antonio Ballesteros Beretta's *Alfonso X el Sabio* (1963; repr. Barcelona: 1984
with the added and welcome indexes of Miguel Rodríguez Llopis). Still
others not only reappear, but reappear translated into Spanish. John E.

Keller's *Pious Brief Narrative,* the fourth chapter of which treats the *Cantigas* (Lexington: 1978), Hans-Josef Niederehe's *Die Sprachauffassung Alfons des Weisen: Studien zur Sprach- und Wissenschaftsgeschichte* (Tübingen: 1975), and Evelyn S. Procter's *Curia and Cortes in León and Castile* (Cambridge: 1980) have metamorphosed into, respectively, an updated *Las narraciones breves piadosas* (Madrid: 1987), *Alfonso X el Sabio y la lingüística de su tiempo* (Madrid: 1987), and *Curia y Cortes en Castilla y León* (Madrid: 1988).

Alfonsine anthologies have proliferated in the 1980s. Antonio G. Solalinde's fundamental anthology in the Colección Austral (Madrid: 1941) was in its seventh printing in 1980. Solalinde's work was essentially reproduced in slightly different form in Margarita Peña's anthology (Mexico: 1973 and 1976). Two other anthologies are Alejandro Bermúdez's *Vivas* (Barcelona: 1983) and Francisco J. Díez Revenga's *Obras de Alfonso X el Sabio (selección)* (Madrid: 1985); the latter is unfortunately sometimes based on very faulty editions, when in fact other more reliable ones are available. Three recent anthologies treat Alfonsine historiography exclusively: Reinaldo Ayerbe-Chaux's selection from the *Estoria de Espanna* (Madrid: 1982), Milagros Villar Rubio's selection from the *General estoria* (Barcelona: 1984), and Benito Brancaforte's *Prosa histórica,* which selects from both Alfonsine histories (Madrid: 1984). Ayerbe-Chaux's and Brancaforte's introductions are outstanding. Brancaforte has the honor of presenting for the first time hitherto unpublished portions of the *General estoria.*

Similar to the marrying of municipal interests to Alfonsine studies is the interest of Galician scholars in Alfonsine works because of their Galician form, which in part accounts for the above-mentioned reprint of Mettmann's edition of the *Cantigas de Santa María* (Vigo, Spain: 1981). Other publications include José de Azevedo Ferreira's editions of the *Primeyra partida* (Braga, Portugal: 1980) and the Galician *Fuero real* (Braga, Portugal: 1982); Ricardo Carballo Calero's *Alfonso X, o Sabio: pequeña antología* (Santiago: 1980), and in collaboration with Carmen García Rodríguez, *Alfonso X o Sabio: cantigas de amor, de escarnio e de louvor* (La Coruña: 1983); Alvaro Cunqueiro's *Cantigas de Santa María* selection (Vigo: 1980); and José Filgueira Valverde's *Alfonso X e Galicia e unha escolma de "cantigas"* (La Coruña: 1980).

It would be fitting to close with a neat synopsis of the many articles treating myriad aspects of the Learned king and his legacy. Their profusion makes this an impossibility, however, and the following closing statements must suffice.

In historiography, Alfonsine studies have concentrated overwhelmingly on the *Estoria de Espanna,* sometimes referred to by Ramón Menéndez Pidal's appellation *Primera crónica general,* almost to the exclusion of the *General estoria.* Notable exceptions are Francisco Rico's 1984 reprint (cited above) and studies by M. Morreale, W. Jonxis-Henkemans, J. González, D. Romano, M. Alvar, J. Dagenais, and A. Cárdenas. D. G. Pattison's *From Legend to Chronicle: A Treatment of Epic Material in Alphonsine Historiography* (Oxford: 1983) seems to have set the tone in the 1980s, since studies examining the relationship between epic and chronicle constitute the most frequent topic in *Estoria de Espanna* research. Another area, prompted principally by Olga Impey, is the study of Dido in the *Estoria de Espanna.* In number, linguistic analyses seem to follow. Miscellaneous themes follow in turn.

In the 1980s, the Barcelona school at the Instituto "Millás Vallicrosa," headed by Juan Vernet, has dominated the topic of Alfonsine science, especially as regards its Arabic sources, with its most prolific member being Julio Samsó. This group's output is matched, if not in quantity, certainly in quality by the work of several individual historians of science who bring a more pan-European perspective to the subject. These include O. Gingerich, B. Goldstein, J. D. North, and D. Pingree. Emmanuel Poulle has concentrated on the Alfonsine *Tablas* and offers important contributions there. N. Roth and D. Romano have pursued the question of Alfonsine Jewish collaborators. G. Bossong has not only edited the *Canones de Albateni* but also provided useful insights into the problem of translation in Alfonso's court, in his masterful *Probleme der Übersetzung wissenschaftlicher Werke aus dem Arabischen in das Altspanische zur Zeit Alfons des Weisen* (Tübingen: 1979).

The dom of Alfonsine legal studies has been Alfonso García Gallo, though Jerry R. Craddock has made serious inroads into his positions. Along with Robert A. MacDonald, Craddock is one of the most meticulous and scholarly of Alfonsine researchers on law. Dwayne E. Carpenter has seriously pursued the Jewish and Moorish question in the *Siete partidas.* This magnum opus of Alfonso, encompassing as it does nearly every aspect of daily life, readily lends itself also as a reference for literary studies treating non-Alfonsine medieval works. For that same reason, its all-encompassing nature, the *Partidas* is the focal point of scholarly investigation regarding Alfonsine law, and other Alfonsine legal treatises are usually examined, if at all, in relationship to it. An important and welcome exception can be found in Jean Roudil's edition of Jacobo de la Junta (*el de las Leyes*), *Summa de los nueve tiempos de los pleitos* (Paris: 1986), and Roudil's plan to edit all of

Jacobo's writings. Finally, apparently because of the stated emphasis of the *Partidas* on linguistic clarity, linguists too have been drawn to it in order to analyze its language.

The least examined Alfonsine treatise of all is his book on games, the *Libro de acedrex & dados & tablas.* Its magnificent assortment of miniatures has been incorporated into the various audiovisual packages cited above, but its text remains grist to be exploited by willing mills. Perhaps the recent two-volume edition of 1987 cited above will encourage further research in this area, as will the new study edition (Madrid: 1987).

Sheer numbers suggest that the most popular area of Alfonsine study is the king's *Cantigas de Santa Maria.* Several reasons account for this. The miniatures of the "Códice Rico" offer an attractive source of investigation; the music itself provides a fascinating field for cultivation; the miracle stories lend themselves to quick literary analysis; and Mettmann's edition of the *Cantigas* makes them accessible for analysis. The topics examined by the *Cantigas* are so varied that a meaningful synopsis is difficult to achieve, and one is best advised to consult the previously cited analyses by Joseph Snow. Before leaving the *Cantigas,* however, it is worth noting that Stephen Parkinson has raised some fundamental and interesting questions concerning the often-touted definitive nature of Mettmann's edition. Parkinson's observations, while they do not detract from the inherent merit of Mettmann's own achievements, are intelligent and pervasive and will lead ultimately to a more accurate understanding and appreciation of Alfonso's Marian achievement and the manner in which it accrued. Finally, Roger Tinnell's *An Annotated Discography of Music in Spain before 1650* (Madison: 1980), which he updates periodically, is a worthy contribution to *Cantigas* studies.

As in the case of the *Acedrex,* the profane poems authored by Alfonso were notable by their near-absence from Alfonsine poetry studies. Although they have been studied effectively by several scholars, they remain fertile Alfonsine literary ground also awaiting further tillage. A new beginning of such studies includes three anthologies featuring the profane works: Carlos Alvar and Vicente Beltrán (Madrid: 1985), Jesús Montoya Martínez (Madrid: 1988), and Juan Paredes Núñez (Granada: 1988).

Assuredly, numerous other studies and other areas of investigation might have been mentioned, but were not—not because they lack merit but because of individual limitations of perspective. For just as one scientist is incapable of analyzing every implication of the Mount Saint Helens explosion, so too is one researcher incapable of encompassing completely the

Alfonsine explosion. It is patent from this limping analogy, however, that Alfonsine studies flourish and deservedly so. Have we, then, drawn closer to a truer picture of this Learned Maecenas? The answer is: most assuredly. But just as miniature depictions of Alfonso vary over the centuries and according to the artist, so too the studies or intellectual depictions of Alfonso reflect the times and the ability of the researcher. Just as Alfonso's essence must rest somewhere within these depictions, so too does the artist's in his sketch and the researcher's in his gloss.

Contributors

Robert I. Burns, S.J., Professor of History at the University of California, Los Angeles, is past president of the American Historical Association's Pacific Coast Branch, of the Academy of Research Historians on Medieval Spain, and of the American Catholic Historical Association, and is currently coeditor of *Viator.* A Guggenheim Fellow and an elected fellow of the Medieval Academy of America, his distinctions include the Medieval Academy's Haskins gold medal, seven national book awards, eight honorary doctorates here and abroad, and from Spain the Premi Catalónia of the Institut d'Estudis Catalans, the Premi de la Crítica "Serra d'Or," the Soci d'Honor of the Acció Cultural del País Valencià, and the Order of the Cross of St. George. His major archival books are *The Jesuits and the Indian Wars of the Northwest* (New Haven 1966), *The Crusader Kingdom of Valencia,* 2 vols. (Cambridge, Mass. 1967), *Islam Under the Crusaders* (Princeton 1973), *Medieval Colonialism* (Princeton 1975), *Jaume I i els valencians* (Valencia 1981), *Muslims, Christians and Jews in Crusader Valencia* (Cambridge, Eng. 1983), and *Society and Documentation in Crusader Valencia* (Princeton 1985).

Anthony J. Cárdenas, Associate Professor of Spanish at Wichita State University, is a member of the Medieval Academy of America, of the Executive Committee of the American Association of Teachers of Spanish and Portuguese, and member of several other organizations pertaining to medievalism in Spain and Spanish literature. He has held grants and awards from the American Philosophical Society, Fulbright, and Ford Foundation. He is editor of the *Noticiero alfonsí,* an international newsletter on the legacy of Alfonso X, el Sabio. He has recently edited the *Libro que es fecho de las animalias que caçan* (Microfiche series, Madison: HSMS, 1987) and collaborated on *Bibliography of Old Spanish Texts* (1975, 1977), the *Concordances and Texts of the Royal Scriptorium Manuscripts of Alfonso X, el Sabio* (1978), and has several articles ranging from studies of literary motifs of Spanish medieval works to those treating codicology. His edition of Alfonso X's *Libro del saber de astrologia* and a *Bibliography of Alfonsine Science* are still in progress.

Jerry R. Craddock, Professor of Spanish and Romance Philology at the
University of California, Berkeley, is currently the prolific editor-in-chief
of the journal *Romance Philology,* and coeditor, with Ivy A. Corfis, Pur-
due University, of the Legal Text Series sponsored by the Hispanic
Seminary of Medieval Studies, Madison, Wisconsin. His doctoral studies
in Romance Philology were carried out at the same institution where he
has taught since 1968. His bibliography is divided between studies on the
historical grammar of the Hispano-Romance languages and treatments
of the chronology and text tradition of the legislative works of Alfonso X
the Learned, the latter published in *Al-Andalus, Anuario de Historia del
Derecho Español,* and various homage volumes.

Nancy Joe Dyer, Associate Professor of Spanish at Texas A&M University,
has received grants from various institutions such as the National Endowment for the Humanities, the American Council of Learned Societies, and the South Central Modern Languages Association to edit
and study lost vernacular literary sources of Alfonsine historiography.
She has dedicated nearly two decades to work on the epic poem of the
Cid prosified in the *Crónica de veinte reyes* (preliminary articles in *Romance Philology, Juglaresca,* and the *Actas de la Asociación internacional de
Hispanistas* [Berlin]; her definitive variata edition is forthcoming). Other
publications deal with the evolution of the adverb in *-mente* in *Primera
crónica general (Hispanic Review),* female decorum in *Castigos e documentos
del rey don Sancho (Studia hispanica medievalia),* Spanish-Arabic code-
switching in the *kharjas (El romancero tradicional),* and foreign language
courseware evaluation (as assistant editor of *Hispania*). At present she is
preparing studies of the language and literary sources of Motolinía's
chronicle of the exploration of New Spain.

Julia Bolton Holloway, Associate Professor and Director of Medieval Studies
at the University of Colorado, Boulder, has received two National Endowment for the Humanities awards and an American Association of
University Women's Founders Fellowship, among other honors. She has
published an edition and translation of Brunetto Latini's *Il Tesoretto*
(New York 1981), *Brunetto Latini: An Analytic Bibliography* (London
1986), *The Pilgrim and the Book: A Study of Dante, Langland and Chaucer*
(Berne 1987), as well as numerous articles on Brunetto Latini, Dante
Alighieri, Geoffrey Chaucer, medieval liturgical drama, and other topics
in *Dante Studies, Lectura Dantis, Comparative Drama, Studies in Iconogra-*

phy, Thought, and elsewhere. She is currently completing *Chancery and Comedy: Brunetto Latini and Dante Alighieri.*

Lloyd Kasten is Antonio G. Solalinde Professor of Spanish and Portuguese, Emeritus, at the University of Wisconsin, Madison. He was the organizer and director of Wisconsin's Luso-Brazilian Center, and for a decade the editor of its *Review.* A Guggenheim Fellow, with an honorary doctorate from The University of the South, he is an elected member of the Hispanic Society of America, the Royal Spanish Academy, and the Academia Norteamericana de la Lengua Española. His seven books, with several others in press, especially center on Old Spanish and on the works of Alfonso the Learned. He has been a pioneer in computer techniques applied to those subjects.

Israel J. Katz taught at McGill and Columbia Universities and at the City University of New York. He specializes in the music of medieval Spain and the musical traditions of the Sephardic Jews. He is editor of *Musica Judaica* and a past editor of *Ethnomusicology* and the *Yearbook of the International Folk Music Society.* Included among his awards are Rockefeller and Ford Foundation grants, Guggenheim Fellowship, and a Comité Conjunto Hispano-Norteamericano grant recommended by the Council for International Exchange of Scholars to undertake bibliographical studies dealing with the traditional folk music of Spain. He has contributed numerous articles and reviews to professional journals, and is the author of *Judeo-Spanish Traditional Ballads from Jerusalem: An Ethnomusicological Study* (New York 1972–75) and coeditor, with John E. Keller, of *Studies on the Cantigas de Santa Maria: Art, Music, and Poetry* (Madison 1987). Katz is currently engaged, under the auspices of the National Endowment for the Humanities, in a collaborative project with the Hispanists Samuel G. Armistead and Joseph H. Silverman on the multi-volume edition of *Judeo-Spanish Ballads from Oral Tradition* (Berkeley 1986–   ). He is also completing a critical edition of Schindler's *Music and Poetry of Spain and Portugal.*

John E. Keller, Professor of Spanish at the University of Kentucky, Lexington, has had a distinguished career here and abroad. Among his honors are the Doctorate of Humane Letters from the Plymouth State College of the University of New Hampshire and the Doctorate Honoris Causa from the University of Granada. King Juan Carlos of Spain has conferred upon him the Gran Cruz de la Orden de Isabel la Católica and the rank of Comendador de la Orden de Alfonso el Sabio. The National Endowment for the Humanities has funded his summer institute for 1990 to offer thirty college teachers guidance for the improvement of teaching medieval Spanish literature to undergraduates. He is a specialist in works sponsored by Alfonso X, particularly the *Cantigas de Santa Maria,* and in the area of medieval Spanish exempla. While a professor at North Carolina, Chapel Hill, he was the associate editor of *Romance Notes* and *Studies in Romance Languages and Literature,* was editor for twenty years of the *Kentucky Romance Quarterly,* and is currently editor of *Studies in Romance Languages* and of the *Bulletin of the Cantigueiros de Santa Maria.* Among his twenty-five books are *Pious Brief Narrative in Medieval Spanish Exempla; Iconography in Medieval Spanish Literature,* co-authored with Richard P. Kinkade; critical editions of *Calila e Digna, Libro de los gatos, Libro de los exienplos por a.b.c.,* and *Barlaam e Josafat*; and he is the author of some eighty articles in journals such as *Speculum, Studies in Philology, Hispanic Review, Hispania,* and *Symposium.* He has lectured at eighty universities—among these Oxford, Coimbra, Madrid, Toronto, and Yale. Currently he is finishing a book titled "The Literature of Recreation in Medieval Spain."

Ellen Kosmer, Professor of Art History at the State College, Worcester, Massachusetts, studied under Walter Cahn at Yale University. Her primary interests are Parisian manuscripts of the thirteenth and fourteenth centuries and iconography of the virtues and vices. A recent National Endowment for the Humanities Fellowship has allowed her to pursue the study of Franco-Italian manuscript illumination at the Angevin Court in Naples. She has published in *Gesta, Art Bulletin,* and *The Journal of the Warburg and Courtauld Institutes.* Active in museum work, she has organized several exhibitions at the College Gallery at the Worcester Art Museum and serves on the board of trustees at the Higgins Armory Museum in Worcester. She is currently involved in research on themes of morality in the visual arts.

Joseph F. O'Callaghan is Professor of History at Fordham University, New York, and former director of its Center for Medieval Studies. He is past president of the American Catholic Historical Association and of the Academy of Research Historians on Medieval Spain. His honors include Spain's Consejero de Honor, Instituto de Estudios Manchegos. Besides his many articles in *Speculum, Tradition,* the *American Historical Review,* and other European and American journals, his several books include *The Spanish Military Order of Calatrava and Its Affiliates* (London 1985), the now standard *A History of Medieval Spain* (Ithaca 1975, 1984), and *The Cortes of Castile-León, 1188–1350* (Philadelphia 1989). He is working on a study of the reign of Alfonso X.

James F. Powers, Professor of History at Holy Cross College, Worcester, Massachusetts, studied under Charles Julian Bishko at the University of Virginia. His interest in the municipal history of the Iberian peninsula during the Central Middle Ages has led to articles in *Traditio* (1970), *Speculum* (1971, 1977, 1987), the *American Historical Review* (1979), *Military Affairs* (1981), and *The Worlds of Alfonso the Learned and James the Conqueror* (1985). His several honors include a Visiting Faculty Fellowship at Harvard University (1976), and he has been a trustee of the Institute of Christian Iberia. Powers was elected President of the American Academy of Research Historians (1986–88) and General Secretary of the Society for Spanish and Portuguese Historical Studies (1988–90). The principal authority on medieval Spanish militias, he has been awarded grants from the Fulbright Committee and the Council for the International Exchange of Scholars in coordination with the Comité Conjunto Hispano-Norteamericano to complete his recently published book, *A Society Organized for War: The Iberian Municipal Militias in the Central Middle Ages, 1000–1284* (1988), and more recently in 1988 for a history of military themes and depiction in Mozarabic, Romanesque, and Gothic art.

Norman Roth, Associate Professor of Jewish Studies at the University of Wisconsin, Madison, has written extensively on the history, literature and poetry, and philosophy of the Jews of medieval Spain. These articles have appeared in journals such as *Sefarad, Speculum,* and *AJS Review,* and in Spanish in *Ciudad de Dios, Anuario de Historia del Derecho Español,* and *Anthologica Annua.* Most recently, he was the recipient of a research grant from the Spanish section of the Comité Conjunto (a joint U.S.-Spain research project) for research in Spanish archives. He is the author of *Maimonides: Essays and Text* (Madison 1986) and for many years has been working on a book on relations between Jews, Muslims, and Christians in medieval Spain.

Joseph T. Snow is Associate Professor of Spanish and Portuguese at the University of Georgia (Athens) and a contributing member of its Medieval Studies Program. He is past president of the U.S. Branch of the International Courtly Literature Society and is the current treasurer of the international organization. He was a student of Lloyd Kasten at Wisconsin's Seminary of Medieval Spanish Studies, and his work there on Alfonso X has led to more than a dozen studies on the *Cantigas* as well as the standard critical bibliography *The Poetry of Alfonso X, el Sabio* (1977), for which a second volume is in preparation. He founded and still edits the special-interest journal, *Celestinesca* (1977–   ) and has published widely in this field. His honors include election as Corresponding Member of The Hispanic Society of America (1987), a year as a fellow at Wisconsin's Institute for Research in the Humanities (1978–79), and visiting appointments at the University of California at Davis (1978), The University of the South (1981), and the University of Chicago (1987), as well as serving as Short-Term Professor at the University of Arizona Center for Medieval and Renaissance Studies (1987). Two projects now under development are a monograph on literary autobiography in Alfonso's *Cantigas* and a volume of studies on the theatrical progeny of Rojas's *Celestina*.

Notes

PREFACE

1. *Thought* 60 (239), December 1985.

CHAPTER ONE

1. Quotations are from the jurist Charles Sumner Lobingier in his extended analysis of Alfonso's code as introduction to the English edition commissioned by the American Bar Association. See *Las siete partidas,* ed. Real Academia de la Historia, 3 vols. (Madrid: Imprenta Real, 1807; repr. Madrid: Atlas, 1972); English transl., Samuel Parsons Scott, same title, 2 vols. (New York: American Bar Association, 1931). The ranking of first or native languages is from the *World Almanac* (New York: Newspaper Enterprise Association, 1984); the figures (in millions) are Mandarin 740, English 403, Russian 277, Spanish 266, and Hindi 264.

2. Various nonuniversity celebrations included an international conference at the Spanish Institute in New York in April 1981, whose proceedings were published as *Studies on the "Cantigas de Santa Maria": Art, Music, and Poetry,* ed. I. J. Katz, J. E. Keller, S. G. Armistead, and J. T. Snow (Madison, Wisc.: Hispanic Seminary of Medieval Studies, 1987). The most spectacular congress was in Spain, linked at seven cities in April 1984; its acta are in press as *Alfonso el Sabio: vida, obra, época.*

3. For further general background see Joseph F. O'Callaghan, *A History of Medieval Spain* (Ithaca, N.Y.: Cornell University, 1975 and 1983), part 4; J. N. Hillgarth, *The Spanish Kingdoms 1250–1516,* 2 vols. (Oxford: Clarendon, 1976–1978), 1: 155–232, 287–311; C. E. Dufourcq and Jean Gautier-Dalché, *Histoire économique et sociale de l'Espagne chrétienne au moyen âge* (Paris: Armand Colin, 1976), expanded in translation with bibliographical notes as *Historia económica y social de la España cristiana en la edad media* (Barcelona: El Albir, 1983), ch. 3; C. J. Bishko, "The Spanish and Portuguese Reconquest, 1095–1492," in *A History of the Crusades,* ed. K. M. Setton, 5 vols. to date (Madison: University of Wisconsin, 1969 et seq.), 3: 417–35; and D. W. Lomax, *The Reconquest of Spain* (London: Longman, 1978).

4. On Alfonso see the chapters by R. I. Burns, J. F. O'Callaghan, J. F. Powers, and R. A. MacDonald in Burns, *Worlds of Alfonso;* the excellent brief review of the king's cultural work by John E. Keller, *Alfonso X, el Sabio* (New York: Twayne Publishers, 1967), chs. 1, 2, 3, and 10; Evelyn S. Procter, *Alfonso X of Castile, Patron of Literature and Learning* (Oxford: Clarendon, 1951), on his patronage; and the ambitious political biography by Antonio Ballesteros Beretta, *Alfonso X el Sabio* (Barcelona: Salvat, 1963; repr. with index, Barcelona: El Albir, 1984). *The Concordances and Texts of the Royal Scriptorium Manuscripts of Alfonso X, el Sabio,* ed. Lloyd Kasten and John Nitti, 2 vols. (Madison, Wisc.: Hispanic Seminary of Medieval Studies, 1978), in 112 microfiches and some 20,000 pages, would fill sixty-seven volumes if in print format. For current books, articles, papers, meetings, and

Alfonsine news of every kind, consult Anthony Cárdenas's annual newsletter, *Noticiero alfonsí* (Wichita State University, 1 [1982] et seq.).

5. *Siete partidas*, pts. 1–2. Keller, *Alfonso X*, ch. 7. See especially MacDonald's article "Law and Politics," in Burns, *Worlds of Alfonso*, 167ff., 173–87, and his objection to the thesis of Alfonso García Gallo on the dating and character of the *Partidas*.

6. The *Cantigas* manuscripts and studies are discussed in this volume, particularly in the chapters by Kosmer and Powers, Keller, Holloway, Katz, and Snow, including the English translation by Kathleen Kulp-Hill (see below, ch. 6, n. 24). Written in Galician, the *Cantigas* has an accent on the initial *a*, now usually omitted in writing.

7. See Hillgarth, *Kingdoms*, 1: 218, and his analysis of Alfonso's work. See also Keller, *Alfonso X*, chs. 4 on *Calila*, 5 on the *Cantigas*, 8 on the scientific works and games, and 9 on the historical works. On use of Castilian, see Kasten below in ch. 3.

8. Keller, *Alfonso X*, 118.

9. Cayetano Socarras, *Alfonso X of Castile: A Study on Imperialistic Frustration* (Barcelona: Hispam, 1976), 11.

10. Ibid., 10–12, 109–12. See also my study in *Viator* 21 (1990), in press.

11. Joaquín Gimeno Casalduero, *La imagen del monarca en la Castilla del siglo XIV* (Madrid: Revista de Occidente, 1972), 11–12, 37–45.

12. Castro, *The Spaniards: An Introduction to Their History* (Berkeley and Los Angeles: University of California Press, 1971), 193–94, 538.

13. Makdisi, *The Rise of Colleges: Institutions of Learning in Islam and the West* (Edinburgh: University of Edinburgh, 1981), 281–91.

CHAPTER TWO

1. Ballesteros, *Alfonso X*; Keller, *Alfonso X*; Evelyn Procter, *Alfonso, Patron*, and her "Materials for the Reign of Alfonso X of Castile, 1252–1284," *Transactions of the Royal Historical Society*, 4th series, 14 (1936): 39–63.

2. See the classic judgment of Juan de Mariana, *Historia general de España* Toledo: 1601), XIII.XX: "While he was contemplating the heavens and looking at the stars he lost the earth and his kingdom." Robert A. MacDonald's forthcoming essay, "The Varying Historical Perspective of Alfonso X of Castile," studies the attitudes of historians toward the king, from his thirteenth-century contemporary Jofre de Loaysa to his twentieth-century biographer Antonio Ballesteros Beretta.

3. See the essays in *Worlds of Alfonso* and in *Alfonso, Emperor*; and Julio Valdeón, "Alfonso X: semblanza de su reinado," *Revista de occidente* 43 (1984): 15–28.

4. *Primera crónica general*, ed. Ramon Menéndez Pidal, 2 vols. (Madrid: Gredos, 1955), 2:772–73 (ch. 1132). Also Julio González, *Reinado y diplomas de Fernando III*, 3 vols. (Córdoba: Monte de Piedad y Caja de Ahorros, 1980–1986).

5. *Setenario*, ed. Kenneth Vanderford (Buenos Aires: Instituto de Filología, 1945; repr. Barcelona: Critica, 1984), 9–10. On Fernando III's desire to conquer North Africa, see *Primera crónica general*, 2: 770 (ch. 1131); on the Leonese imperial idea see Ramon Menéndez Pidal, *El imperio hispánico y los cinco reinos* (Madrid: Instituto de Estudios Políticos, 1950).

6. *Espéculo de las leyes,* II.1.2–5, in *Opúsculos legales del rey don Alfonso el Sabio,* ed. Real Academia de la Historia, 2 vols. (Madrid: Real Academia de la Historia, 1836), 1: 12–14; *Siete partidas,* II.1.5–8 (2: 7–10).

7. *Espéculo,* II.1.13; *Partidas,* III.23.17; Gaines Post, *Studies in Medieval Legal Thought: Public Law and the State 1100–1322* (Princeton: Princeton University Press, 1964), 453–94 ("Rex Imperator" and "Vincentius Hispanus and Spanish Nationalism"); José Antonio Maravall, "Del regimen feudal al regimen corporativo en el pensamiento de Alfonso X," *BRAH* 157 (1965): 220–22.

8. See examples in the royal charters in *MHE,* vols. 1, 2.

9. See O'Callaghan, *Medieval Spain,* 358–81, and Hillgarth, *Spanish Kingdoms,* 1: 286–309.

10. Dwayne Carpenter, *Alfonso X and the Jews: An Edition and Commentary on Siete partidas 7.24 "De los judíos"* (Berkeley and Los Angeles: University of California Press, 1986); Larry Simon, "Jews in the Legal Corpus of Alfonso el Sabio," *Comitatus* 18 (1987): 80–97. See my forthcoming essays, "Alfonso X's Legislation Concerning the Jews" and "The Mudejars of Castile and Portugal in the Twelfth and Thirteenth Centuries."

11. Julio González, *El Repartimiento de Sevilla,* 2 vols. (Madrid: Consejo Superior de Investigaciones Científicas, 1951), and *Repoblación de Castilla la nueva,* 2 vols. (Madrid: Universidad Complutense, 1975–1976); Salvador de Moxó, *Repoblación y sociedad en la España cristiana medieval* (Madrid: Rialp, 1979), 349–69.

12. Manuel González Jiménez, *En torno a los orígenes de Andalucía: La repoblación del siglo XIII* (Seville: Universidad de Sevilla, 1988), and *La repoblación de la zona de Sevilla durante el siglo XIV: estudio y documentación* (Seville: Universidad de Sevilla, 1975); Manuel González Jiménez and A. González Gómez, *El libro del Repartimiento de Jerez de la Frontera: estudio y edición* (Cádiz: Instituto de Estudios Gaditanos, 1980).

13. Juan Torres Fontes, *La reconquista de Murcia en 1266 por Jaime I de Aragón* (Murcia: Diputación, 1967), and *Repartimiento de Murcia* (Madrid: Consejo Superior de Investigaciones Científicas, 1960) and *Repartimiento de Lorca* (Murcia: Academia Alfonso X el Sabio, 1977).

14. Peter Linehan, "The Politics of Piety: Aspects of the Castilian Monarchy from Alfonso X to Alfonso XI," *RCEH* 9 (1985): 385–404, and "Pseudo-historia y pseudo-liturgia en la obra alfonsina," *España y Europa, un pasado jurídico común,* ed. Antonio Pérez Martín (Murcia: Instituto de Derecho Común, 1986), 259–74; Joseph F. O'Callaghan, "The *Cantigas de Santa Maria* as a Historical Source: Two Examples (nos. 321 and 386)," *Studies on the Cantigas,* 387–93.

15. *Espéculo,* II.1.10–11; II.2.1–6; II.3.1–3; II.4.1–7; II.14.5–9; II.15.1–13; II.16.7; *Partidas,* II.13.17–18; II.14.1–4; II.15.1.

16. Evelyn Procter, "The Castilian Chancery during the Reign of Alfonso X, 1252–1284," *Oxford Essays in Medieval History presented to Herbert Edward Salter* (Oxford: Clarendon, 1934), 104–21.

17. For the Ordinance of Zamora see *CLC,* 1:87–94; Aquilino Iglesia Ferreirós, "Las cortes de Zamora de 1274 y los casos de corte," *AHDE* 41 (1971): 945–72; Miguel Angel Pérez de la Canal, "La justicia de la corte de Castilla durante los siglos XIII al XV," *Historia, instituciones, documentos* 2 (1975): 383–481.

18. Robert A. MacDonald, "Problemas políticos y derecho alfonsino considerados desde tres puntos de vista," *AHDE* 53 (1984): 25–53, and "El *Espéculo* atribuido a Alfonso X, su edición y problemas que plantea," *España y Europa, un pasado jurídico común*, 611–53, and "Law and Politics: Alfonso's Program of Political Reform," in *Worlds of Alfonso*, 150–202; Joseph F. O'Callaghan, "Sobre la promulgación del Espéculo y del Fuero real," *Estudios en homenaje a don Claudio Sánchez Albornoz en sus 90 años*, 4 vols. (Buenos Aires: Instituto de Historia de España, 1985), 3: 167–80; Alfonso García Gallo, "Nuevas observaciones sobre la obra legislativa de Alfonso X," *AHDE* 46 (1976): 609–70; Aquilino Iglesia Ferreirós, "Alfonso X el Sabio y su obra legislativa: algunas reflexiones," *AHDE* 50 (1980): 531–61, and "Cuestiones alfonsinas," *AHDE* 55 (1985): 94–149.

19. *Ordenamiento de Alcalá* 1348 (LXIV), *CLC*, 1: 511–12; Jerry R. Craddock, "La cronología de las obras legislativas de Alfonso X el Sabio," *AHDE* 51 (1981): 365–418, and his *The Legislative Works of Alfonso el Sabio: A Critical Bibliography* (London: Grant and Cutler, 1986).

20. *CAX*, ch. 1 (in *BAE*, 3–4). Miguel Angel Ladero Quesada, "Las transformaciones de la fiscalidad regia castellano-leonesa en la segunda mitad del siglo XIII (1252–1312)," *Historia de la hacienda española. Homenaje al profesor García de Valdeavellano* (Madrid: Instituto de Estudios Fiscales, 1982), 321–68.

21. Wladimir Piskorski, *Las cortes de Castilla en el período de tránsito de la edad media a la moderna 1188–1520*, tr. Claudio Sánchez Albornoz (Barcelona: 1930; repr. Barcelona: El Albir, 1977), 196–97, no. 1. Evelyn Procter, *Curia and Cortes in León and Castile 1072–1295* (Cambridge, England: Cambridge University Press, 1980), 118–51; Joseph F. O'Callaghan, "The Beginnings of the Cortes of León-Castile," *American Historical Review* 74 (1969): 1503–1537, and "The Cortes and Royal Taxation during the Reign of Alfonso X of Castile," *Traditio* 27 (1971): 379–98, and *The Cortes of Castile-León 1188–1350* (Philadelphia: University of Pennsylvania Press, 1988).

22. Joseph F. O'Callaghan, "Alfonso X and the Castilian Church," *Alfonso, Emperor*, 417–29; Peter Linehan, *The Spanish Church and the Papacy in the Thirteenth Century* (Cambridge, England: Cambridge University Press, 1971), 101–221; José Manuel Nieto Soria, *Las relaciones monarquía-episcopado castellano como sistema de poder (1252–1312)*, 2 vols. (Madrid: Universidad Complutense de Madrid, 1983).

23. O'Callaghan, "Alfonso X and the Castilian Church," 420–21, nn. 5–8, and "The Ecclesiastical Estate in the Cortes of León-Castile, 1252–1350," *Catholic Historical Review* 67 (1981): 191–93.

24. *CAX*, chs. 25–26, in *BAE*, 22–23; *Les registres de Nicholas III*, ed. Jules Gay (Paris: Bibliothèque des écoles françaises d'Athènes et de Rome, 1898), nos. 739–41, 743, pp. 338–40; Peter Linehan, "The Spanish Church Revisited: The Episcopal *Gravamina* of 1279," *Authority and Power: Studies in Medieval Law and Government presented to Walter Ullmann on his Seventieth Birthday*, ed. Brian Tierney and Peter Linehan (Cambridge, England: Cambridge University Press, 1980), 141–47; O'Callaghan, "Alfonso X and the Castilian Church," 423–26.

25. *CAX*, ch. 1, in *BAE*, 4; *CLC*, 1: 85–86.

26. *CAX*, chs. 23–40, 47, in *BAE*, 19–31, 35; *CLC*, 1: 85–86; O'Callaghan, "The Cortes and Royal Taxation during the Reign of Alfonso X of Castile," 384–88.

27. *Fuero real*, in *Opúsculos legales*, 2: 1–169; *El fuero viejo*, ed. Ignacio Jordán del

Asso and Miguel de Manuel y Rodríguez (Madrid: Joaquín Ibarra, 1771), prologue, 2; O'Callaghan, "Sobre la promulgación del Espéculo y del Fuero real," 167–80.

28. *MHE*, 1:89–100, nos. 3–4; Aquilino Iglesia Ferreirós, "El privilegio general concedido a las Extremaduras en 1264 por Alfonso X: edición del ejemplar enviado a Peñafiel en 15 de abril de 1264," *AHDE* 53 (1983): 456–521; James Powers, "Two Warrior Kings and their Municipal Militias: The Townsman-Soldier in Law and Life," *Worlds of Alfonso*, 95–117.

29. Joseph F. O'Callaghan, "Paths to Ruin: The Economic and Financial Policies of Alfonso the Learned," *Worlds of Alfonso*, 41–67; Julius Klein, "Los privilegios de la Mesta de 1273 y 1278," *BRAH* 64 (1914): 202–29, and *The Mesta, A Study in Spanish Economic History 1273–1836* (Cambridge, Mass.: Harvard University Press, 1920); Miguel Angel Ladero Quesada, "Aspectos de la política económica de Alfonso X," *Revista de la Facultad de derecho de la Universidad complutense de Madrid* (1985): 69–82.

30. The poet Gil Pérez Conde, recording his past services to the king, mentioned an instance "en Toledo, / quand' i filhastes corõa," *Cantigas de escarnho e de mal dezir dos cancioneiros medievais galego-portugueses*, 2nd edn., ed. Manuel Rodríguez Lapa (Coimbra, Portugal: Galaixa, 1970), 261, no. 167.

31. *MHE*, 1: 5–8, 154–55, nos. 4, 71. Pedro Fernández del Pulgar, *Historia secular y eclesiástica de la ciudad de Palencia*, 4 vols. (Madrid: 1679), 2: 344–45; Antonio Ballesteros, "El itinerario de Alfonso el Sabio," *BRAH* 108 (1936): n. 1.

32. *MHE*, 1: 151, no. 69. Carlos de Ayala Martínez, *Directrices fundamentales de la política peninsular de Alfonso X (relaciones castellano-aragonesas de 1252 a 1263)* (Madrid: Universidad Autónoma de Madrid, 1986).

33. Charles F. Fraker, "The *Fet des Romains* and the *Primera crónica general*," *Hispanic Review* 46 (1978): 199–220, and "Alfonso X, the Empire, and the *Primera crónica*," *BHS* 55 (1978): 95–102.

34. Pedro Marín, *Los miráculos romanzados*, cited by Gregorio de Balparda, *Historia crítica de Vizcaya y sus fueros*, 3 vols. (Madrid: Artes de la Ilustración, 1924), 2: 537, no. 387. Ballesteros, *Alfonso X*, 118–19, 793–810, 819–27; Ayala Martínez, *Directrices*, 41–44, 59–85, 129–42.

35. *CAX*, chs. 7, 19, in *BAE*, 7, 14; Antonio Brandão, *Crónica de D. Afonso III*, ed. A. Magalhães Basto (Pôrto, Portugal: Livraria Civilização, 1945), 186–87, 191, 256–57, 369–73, nos. 18–20; Ballesteros, *Alfonso X*, 74–76, 386, 420–24.

36. *CAX*, ch. 18, in *BAE*, 13; *Anónimo de Sahagún*, ed. Romualdo de Escalona, *Historia del real monasterio de Sahagún*, chs. 74–75, pp. 360–62; Thomas Rymer, *Foedera, conventiones, litterae et cujuscunque acta publica inter reges Angliae et alios quosvis imperatores, reges, pontifices, principes*, 2nd edn., 20 vols. (London: J. Tonson, 1704–1735), 1: 503–10; Ballesteros, *Alfonso X*, 92–96.

37. *MHE*, 1: 155–60, 164–66, nos. 72–75, 79–80. *CAX*, chs. 5, 19, in *BAE*, 6–7, 13–14; Antonio Ballesteros, "La toma de Salé en tiempos de Alfonso el Sabio," *Al-Andalus* 8 (1943): 89–128; Ambrosio Huici, "La toma de Salé por la escuadra de Alfonso X," *Hespéris* 39 (1952): 41–52; Rachel Arié, *L'Espagne musulmane au temps des Naṣrides (1232–1492)* (Paris: E. de Boccard, 1973), 61–68.

38. *CAX*, chs. 10–12, in *BAE*, 8–12; Toribio Mingüella, *Historia de la diócesis de*

Sigüenza, 3 vols. (Madrid: Revista de Archivos, Bibliotecas y Museos, 1900–1913), 1: 599–601, no. 225; see notes 12–13.

39. Antonio Ballesteros, *Alfonso X, emperador-electo de Alemania,* Discurso de entrada en la Real Academia de la Historia (Madrid: Real Academia de la Historia, 1918); Socarras, *Imperialistic Frustration;* Carlos Estepa Díaz, "El 'fecho del imperio' y la política internacional en la época de Alfonso X," in *Estudios alfonsíes. Lex-icografía, lírica, estética y política de Alfonso el Sabio,* ed. José Mondéjar and Jesús Montoya (Granada: Universidad de Granada, 1985), 189–206, and "Alfonso X y el fecho del imperio," *Revista de occidente* 43 (1984): 43–54.

40. *CAX,* ch. 17, in *BAE,* 12–13; Jofre de Loaysa, *Crónica de los reyes de Castilla, Fernando III, Alfonso X, Sancho IV y Fernando IV (1248–1305),* ed.-tr. Antonio García Martínez (Murcia: Academia Alfonso X el Sabio, 1961), ch. 7, p. 68; Bruce Gelsinger, "A Thirteenth-Century Norwegian-Castilian Alliance," *Medievalia et Humanistica,* n.s., 10 (1981): 55–80.

41. Robert L. Wolff, "Mortgage and Redemption of an Emperor's Son: Castile and the Latin Empire of Constantinople," *Speculum* 29 (1954): 45–84; *MHE,* 1: 154–55, no. 71.

42. *CAX,* chs. 22, 59, in *BAE,* 18–19, 47–49; Fernández del Pulgar, *Palencia,* 1: 344–45; Ballesteros, *Alfonso X,* 683–87, 717–32.

43. *CAX,* chs. 61–65, in *BAE,* 48–52; Ballesteros, *Alfonso X,* 744–69; Arié, *Naṣrides,* 68–75.

44. Jofre de Loaysa, *Crónica,* 90–91, chs. 19–21; Ballesteros, *Alfonso X,* 785–827; Robert MacDonald, "Alfonso X and Succession: A Father's Dilemma," *Speculum* 40 (1965): 647–54; Eloy Benito Ruano, "El problema sucesorio de la Corona de Castilla a la muerte de don Fernando de la Cerda," in *VII Centenario del infante don Fernando de la Cerda: jornadas de estudio* (Ciudad Real: Instituto de Estudios Manchegos, 1976), 217–26; Marta López Ibor, "El pleito de sucesión en el reinado de Alfonso X," *Revista de occidente* 43 (1984): 55–65; Jerry R. Craddock, "Dynasty in Dispute: Alfonso X el Sabio and the Succession to the Throne of Castile and León in History and Legend," *Viator* 17 (1986): 197–219.

45. *CAX,* chs. 67–68, in *BAE,* 83; *MHE,* 2: 113, no. 228. Fidel Fita, "Dos obras inéditas de Gil de Zamora," *BRAH* 5 (1884): 146.

46. *CAX,* chs. 69–74, in *BAE,* 53–58; Ballesteros, *Alfonso X,* 853–56, 875–85.

47. *CAX,* ch. 75, in *BAE,* 59–60; Antonio Ballesteros, "Burgos y la rebelión del infante don Sancho," *BRAH* 119 (1946): 151–53; O'Callaghan, "The *Cantigas de Santa María* as an Historical Source," 393–97, on the cortes of 1281.

48. *CAX,* chs. 75–76, pp. 60–61; Jofre de Loaysa, *Crónica,* 102, ch. 28.

49. *MHE,* 2: 59–63, 67–70, nos. 198, 202–3; Luis Suárez Fernández, "Evolución histórica de las hermandades castellanas," *Cuadernos de historia de España* 16 (1951): 6–78.

50. *CAX,* ch. 77, in *BAE,* 63–66; *MHE,* 2: 110–34, nos. 228–29. Georges Daumet, "Les testaments d'Alphonse le Savant, roi de Castille," *Bibliothèque de l'école des chartes* 67 (1905): 70–99.

51. Roger B. Merriman, *The Rise of the Spanish Empire in the Old World and the New,* 4 vols. (New York: Macmillan, 1918–1934), 1: 112.

52. II.15.5.

CHAPTER THREE

1. See above, ch. 1, n. 4.

2. *Diccionario crítico etimológico castellano e hispánico,* ed. Joan Corominas and José A. Pascual, 5 vols. (Madrid: Gredos, 1980–1983).

3. Victor R. B. Oelschläger, *A Medieval Spanish Word-List: A Preliminary Dated Vocabulary of First Appearances Up To Berceo* (Madison, Wisc.: University of Wisconsin Press, 1940).

4. Many additional definitions may be found in Herbert Allen Van Scoy, *A Dictionary of Old Spanish Terms Defined in the Works of Alfonso X,* ed. Ivy Corfis (Madison, Wisc.: Hispanic Seminary of Medieval Studies, 1986).

5. Ed. by A. G. Solalinde, et al. (Madrid: Molina, 1930, for part 1; Madrid: Consejo Superior de Investigaciones Científicas, 1957, for part 2), part 2, 1: 425.

CHAPTER FOUR

1. There are four extant manuscripts of the *Cantigas.* Two are in the Biblioteca de San Lorenzo el Real at the El Escorial palace near Madrid: MS T.I.1, called the Códice Rico, the most lavishly illustrated version and the subject of this article, and MS B.I.2 (formerly j.b.2), which has 40 miniatures illustrating musicians playing a wide variety of instruments. The third is in Madrid, Biblioteca Nacional MS 10.069, often referred to as To(1) or Toledo since it was originally in the cathedral there. The fourth is in Florence, Biblioteca Nazionale, MS Banco Rari 20 (formerly MS II.I.213). The definitive editions of the *Cantigas* discuss these manuscripts and their textual relationships: *Cantigas de Santa Maria,* ed. Walter Mettmann, 4 vols. (Coimbra, Portugal: University of Coimbra, 1959–1972). The manuscript in Florence is illustrated; in both format and style, its miniatures are closely related to the Escorial MS T.I.1, and both manuscripts appear to have been produced in the same workshop. See Antonio García Solalinde, "El códice florentino de las 'Cantigas' y su relación con los demás manuscritos," *RFE* 5 (1918): 143–79. See also Ramón Menéndez Pidal, "Los manuscritos de las 'Cantigas': cómo se elaboró la miniatura alfonsí," *Boletín de la Real academia española* 150 (1962): 23–51; he also discusses the Florentine codex. See also below, ch. 11, n. 1.

2. Keller has written most extensively on the *Cantigas,* although his focus is literary. He has provided some discussion of the miniatures; see, for example, his *Alfonso X,* and also Keller and Richard P. Kinkade, *Iconography in Medieval Spanish Literature* (Lexington: University Press of Kentucky, 1984), 6–40, with further bibliographic references. See too his "The Art of Illumination in the Books of Alfonso X (Primarily in the Canticles of Holy Mary)," *Alfonso, Emperor,* 388–406. Menéndez Pidal, in his 1962 article cited above in note 1, does discuss the question of foreign influences, citing a number of possibilities including German and Islamic art. Reproductions of the miniatures of Escorial MS T.I.1 are easily available. An early edition of the miniatures in black and white is that of José Guerrero Lovillo, *Las cántigas, estudio arqueológico de sus miniaturas* (Madrid: Consejo Superior de Investigaciones Científicas, 1949). See also Matilde López Serrano, *Cántigas de Santa María de Alfonso X el Sabio, rey de Castilla* (Madrid: Editorial Patrimonio

Nacional, 1974), and *Cantigas de Santa María: edición facsímil del códice T.I.1 de Biblioteca de San Lorenzo el Real de El Escorial, siglo XIII*, 2 vols. (Madrid: Editorial Nacional de Libros Antiguos, 1979).

3. For a good general discussion of literary patronage, see Erich Auerbach, *Literary Language and its Public in Late Latin Antiquity and in the Middle Ages*, trans. R. Manheim, Bollingen Series, vol. 74 (Princeton: Princeton University Press, 1965), 2. For patronage of Louis IX see *Le siècle de Saint Louis* (Paris: Archives Nationales de France, 1970) by various authors, published to commemorate the seventh centennial of Louis' death. For a discussion of patronage in the reign of Philippe le Bel, see Ellen Kosmer, "A Study of the 13th-Century *Somme Le Roi*, B. M. MS Add. 54180" (Ph.D. diss., Yale University, 1973), and also her "Gardens of Virtue in the Middle Ages," *Journal of the Warburg and Courtauld Institutes* 41 (1978): 302–7. For Italian manuscripts and patronage, see *Federico II e l'arte del duecento italiano: atti della III settimana di Studi di storia dell'arte medievale dell'università di Roma*, 2 vols. (Rome: University of Rome, 1980), vol. 2.

4. Robert Branner, *Manuscript Painting in Paris during the Reign of Saint Louis* (Berkeley and Los Angeles: University of California Press, 1977), provides an extensive discussion of manuscript production during this period. On the court style in general, see *Transformations of the Court Style, Gothic Art in Europe, 1270 to 1330*, exhibition catalogue, Department of Art, Brown University at the Museum of Art, Rhode Island School of Design, Providence, Rhode Island, 2–27 February 1977. See also P. Verdier, P. Brieger, and M. F. Montpetit, *Art and the Courts: France and England from 1259 to 1328* (Ottawa: National Gallery of Canada, 1972).

5. Two leaves are in Paris (BNM, MS/n.a. lat. 2294) and one leaf is privately owned. See S. C. Cockerell and M. R. James, *A Book of Old Testament Illustrations . . . in the Pierpont Morgan Library, Cambridge, Roxburghe 1927, and reprinted with facsimile illustrations in color* (New York: Braziller, 1970).

6. New York, Pierpont Morgan Library, MS 619. Erlangen Universitätsbibliotek, Cod. 1, perg. Lambeth Palace Library, MS 3. See Walter Cahn, *Romanesque Bible Illustration* (Ithaca, N.Y.: Cornell University Press, 1982), who reproduces a number of full-page miniatures with compartmentalized scenes, e.g., 137, 141, 145, 153.

7. See especially fols. 10 and 22 of the *Bible*, and *Cantigas*, nos. 46, 51, 63, and 129.

8. *Shah Abbas Bible*, fols. 9v, 10, 13, 21, 24, 24v, 30v, 33, 39, 41. *Cantigas*, nos. 28, 51, 99, 129, 181.

9. *Cantigas*, nos. 165, 181. *Bible*, 3v, 10v, 27v.

10. *Cantigas*, nos. 63, 165, 181. For a discussion of the evolution of riding style see Ramón Menéndez Pidal, *Cantar del mio Cid*, 4th edn., 2 vols. (Madrid: Espasa-Calpe, 1969), 2: 582–84; Jaime Oliver Asín, "Origen árabe de 'rebato,' 'arrobda,' y sus homónimos," *Boletín de la Real academia española* 15 (1928): 372–89. The Spanish barb horse is also discussed in James F. Powers, *A Society Organized for War: The Iberian Municipal Militias in the Central Middle Ages, 1000–1284* (Berkeley and Los Angeles: University of California Press, 1988), 160–61. It has been suggested that the artists of the *Cantigas* also exploit the color of the horses in an interesting manner—employing dapple gray, light brown, and darker chestnut brown, always in that order—to indicate the nearest horse of a group, the next distant, and the most

distant, starting the series over again if there are more than three in a group. This was first indicated in an unpublished paper by Theresa Vann of Fordham University (1984). One can surmise that color used in this way is a device to clarify the crowded scenes created by the tight frames of the *Cantigas*. Although the *Shah Abbas Bible* in at least one place (fol. 44v) does display horses in this color arrangement, a particular color order seems nowhere established in the equestrian scenes. The more open space and less constricting borders of the *Shah Abbas Bible* would probably have obviated the need to attempt such techniques.

11. Menéndez Pidal, "Los manuscritos de las 'Cantigas,'" 23–51.

12. Rome, Biblioteca Angelica, MS 1474, *Balneum Raynerii;* and Biblioteca Vaticana, MS Pal. Lat. 1071, *De arte venandi cum avibus.* François Avril and Marie-Thérèse Gousset, *XIIIe siècle,* vol. 2 of *Manuscrits enluminés d'origine italienne* (Paris: Bibliothèque Nationale, 1984), 151ff., with extensive bibliography. See also W. F. Volbach, "Le miniature del Codice Vatic. Pal. Lat. 1071, De arte cum avibus," *Rendiconti della pontif. accad. di Roma di archeologia* 15 (1939): 170ff. H. Toubert, "Influences gothiques sur l'art frédéricien: le maître de la Bible de Manfred et son atelier," in *Federico II e l'arte,* 2: 59–76. C. M. Kauffmann, *The Baths of Pozzuoli, A Study of the Medieval Illuminations of Peter of Eboli's Poem* (Oxford: Oxford University Press, 1959). A later copy of this manuscript can be found in Spain in the University of Valencia library, no. 2.396. See James F. Powers, "Frontier Municipal Baths and Social Interaction in Thirteenth-Century Spain," *American Historical Review* 84 (1979): 658. The University Library catalogue misattributes this manuscript to Arnau de Vilanova.

13. The authors would like to acknowledge the use of English translations of the *Cantigas de Santa Maria,* provided in typescript form by Kathleen Kulp-Hill of the University of Northern Iowa. See ch. 6, n. 24 below.

CHAPTER FIVE

This chapter, as its new title indicates, represents a considerable revision of the original version in *Alfonso, Emperor.*

1. For the "congress" see Steinschneider, *Die hebraeischen Übersetzungen des Mittelalters und die Juden als Dolmetscher* (Berlin: Komissionsverlag des bibliographischen Bureaus, 1893; repr. Graz: Akademische Druck, 1956), 561–62. A popular account focusing on early translation at Toledo, and scarcely mentioning the Jews, is Alfonso Gamir, "Toledo School of Translators," *Journal of the Pakistan Historical Society* 14 (1966): 85–92. Similarly popular though not without merit is Juan Vernet, though he deals more with early scientific developments in Islamic Spain than with translation as such: "Les traductions scientifiques dans l'Espagne du Xe siècle," *Les cahiers de Tunisie* 18 (1970): 47–59. L. P. Harvey's essay is merely an expression of indignation at the lack of appreciation of Islam found in the *Primera crónica,* and it has absolutely nothing to do with his title: "The Alfonsine School of Translators: Translations from Arabic into Castilian Produced under the Patronage of Alfonso the Wise of Castile (1221–1252–1284)," *Journal of the Royal Asiatic Society* (1977–1978): 107–17. It is incredible that Jacob L. Teicher could have written that the existence of a "school" of Hebrew translators "has not even been suspected hith-

erto," in light of the splendid work of Steinschneider and the admirable summaries of Sarton. See Teicher, "The Latin-Hebrew School of Translators in Spain in the Twelfth Century," *Homenaje á J. M. Millás Vallicrosa*, 2 vols. (Barcelona: Consejo Superior de Investigaciones Científicas, 1956), 2: 403–4; and George Sarton, *Introduction to the History of Science*, 3 vols. (Baltimore: Carnegie Institution, 1927–1931), e.g., vol. 2, pt. 1: 349 and pt. 2: 721. When the less developed version of this study was published (see preface above), it was impossible to obtain a copy of José Gil's doctoral thesis. It has now appeared in a revised form and contains some, but by no means all, of the information here. See his "The Jews in the Toledo School of Translators" (Ph.D. diss., Catholic University of America, 1974), revised and translated as *La escuela de traductores y sus colaboradores judíos* (Toledo: Instituto Provincial de Investigaciones y Estudios Toledanos, 1985). The same judgment applies to David Romano, "Le opere scientifiche di Alfonso X e l'intervento degli ebrei," *Oriente e occidente nel medioevo: filosofia e scienze*, in the *Atti dei convegni* 13 (Rome: Accademia Nazionale dei Lincei, 1971), 677–710. A good summary of the translators and their activity can also be found in Muñoz Sendino's edition of *La escala* (see note 3 below), 163–72. Pilar León Tello has a section on Jewish translators and authors, but it is based on outdated and largely incorrect secondary literature: *Los judíos de Toledo*, 2 vols. (Madrid: Consejo Superior de Investigaciones Científicas, 1979), 1: 65–75. The 1985 Berkeley symposium *De astronomia Alphonsi regis*, ed. Mercè Comes, Roser Puig, and Julio Samsó (Barcelona: University of Barcelona, 1987), contains no reference at all to the subject, or any awareness of the 1981 UCLA conference.

2. Even the late historian of the Jews in Christian Spain, Yitzhak (Fritz) Baer, virtually ignored the translators and Jewish scientists; see his *A History of the Jews in Christian Spain*, 2 vols. (Philadelphia: Jewish Publication Society of America, 1966).

3. In *La escala de Mahoma*, ed. José Muñoz Sendino (Madrid: Ministerio de Asuntos Exteriores, 1949), 15.

4. "El literalismo de los traductores de la corte de Alfonso el Sabio," *Al-Andalus* 1 (1933): 155–87. This great scholar, fluent in both Hebrew and Arabic and an accomplished scientific historian, was fully qualified to make such a judgment. Cf. also Gil's criticism of Claudio Sánchez Albornoz for attempting to deny the value of Jews as translators, arguing that there were more Christians than Jews in Spain! To this Gil replies: "Certainly, but what was the work of these Christians? Where are their translations? If one compares the effort realized by the Jews with that of the Christians, that of the latter was minimal. Furthermore, the Christians were collaborators with the Jews and not the opposite" (Gil, *Escuela de traductores*, 57, n. 3).

5. Menéndez Pidal, "Cómo trabajaron las escuelas alfonsíes," *NRFH* 5 (1951): 367. Although he wrote this after Muñoz had published his edition of the *Escala*, where he made the remarks cited in note 4, in general, Menéndez's conclusions should be carefully checked in light of Gerold Hilty's analysis in his edition of *El libro conplido en los judizios de las estrellas por Aly aben Ragel*, or ʿAlī ibn Abī al-Rijāl (Madrid: Real Academia Española, 1954).

6. *España en su historia; cristianos, moros y judíos* (Buenos Aires: Editorial Losada, 1948), 494; cf. the note on 495–96 on the scientific vocabulary created by

Jewish translators. Herbert Van Scoy's dissertation noted there has since been published; see his *Old Spanish Terms,* above in ch. 3, n. 4.

7. Juan Manuel, *Libro de la caza,* ed. J. Gutiérrez de la Vega in his *Biblioteca venatoria,* 5 vols. (Madrid: M. Tello, 1877–1899), 3: 4; also ed. J. M. Castro y Calvo (Barcelona: Consejo Superior de Investigaciones Científicas, 1947), 11: "Otrosi fizo traslador toda le ley de los judios et aun el su *Talmud* et otra sciencia que han los judios muy escondida, a que llaman *Cabala.* Et esto fizo porque parezca manifestamente por la su ley que toda ella es figura de esta ley que los cristianos habemos; et que tambien ellos como los moros estan en gran error et en estado de perder las almas."

8. *Lapidario,* ed. José Fernández Montaña (Madrid: Imprenta de la Iberia, J. Blasco, 1881). On the author and his possible identity see George Darby, "The Mysterious Abolays," *Osiris* 1 (1936): 251–59, and his "Ibn Waḥshīya in Medieval Spanish Literature," *Isis* 33 (1941): 433–38. In the latter, Chaldean on 433 almost always means Syriac. *El libro de Calila e Digna: edición crítica,* ed. John E. Keller and A. White Linker (Madrid: Consejo Superior de Investigaciones Científicas, 1979).

9. José Amador de los Ríos erroneously has 1241 in his *Historia crítica de la literatura española,* 7 vols. (Madrid: J. Rodríguez, et al., 1861–1865), 3: 630. He describes the *Lapidario* on 630–31.

10. Translation by Evelyn Procter, "The Scientific Works of the Court of Alfonso X of Castile: The King and His Collaborators," *MLR* 40 (1945): 12–29. On her explanation of the word *indio* there, which should actually be *iudio,* see Yaakov Malkiel and María Rosa Lida-Malkiel, "The Jew and the Indian: Traces of a Confusion in the Hispanic Tradition," in *For Max Weinreich on His Seventieth Birthday, Studies in Jewish Languages, Literature and Society* (The Hague: Mouton, 1964), 203–8. Cf. also *Mishlei Sendebar, the Tales of Sendebar,* ed. and trans. Morris Epstein (Philadelphia: Jewish Publication Society, 1967), 388, n. 2; and King Alfonso's *El libro de los engaños,* ed. John E. Keller (Chapel Hill: University of North Carolina Press, 1953; rev. edn. 1959); also ed. Emilio Vuolo (Naples: Liguori, 1980), 1. If the *Lapidario* was translated from a *Hebrew,* not Arabic, version (which is entirely possible), then the confusion of "India-Iudia" is understandable; whereas the Arabic word for India is *Hind.*

11. See the discussion by Gerold Hilty, "El *Libro conplido en los judizios de las estrellas,*" *Al-Andalus* 20 (1955): 6 (with notes 2, 3) and 30–1. His claim (8, n. 2) that the title of *alfaquim (alfaqi)* was given only to Jews is not correct, as Muslims also had this title (Romano, "Intervento degli ebrei," 688, n. 61, also makes this mistake). As far as I can determine, the study of this promised there by Hilty was never written. Details on this title will be in my book on relations between Jews, Christians, and Muslims in Spain.

12. On the confusion this has caused various writers, see Hilty, "El *Libro conplido*": n. 3.

13. Ibid., 22. Baer had already suggested the identity but wrongly assumed that Mosca was the same as Moses; see his *Die Juden im christlichen Spanien: Urkunden und Regesten,* 2 vols. (Berlin: Akademie für die Wissenschaft des Judenthums, 1929–1936), 2: 59–60; see also his *Jews in Christian Spain,* 1: 120. Yehudah certainly was not a "rabbi of the Toledo synagogue," as Gil claims in his "Escuela de traductores," 62. There is an edition of the astronomical treatise by Yehudah b. Solomon (whose

family name apparently should be read Ibn Mosca, not Motqa), *Mishpaṭei kokavim, otot ha-shamayim* (Warsaw: 1886), extremely rare. This has been overlooked by bibliographers; a copy is in the National Library at Jerusalem. Maimonides knew this family and refers to the "aged" Ibn Mosca, perhaps the father of our Yehudah, and also seems to indicate that Ibn Mosca was related to the famous Ibn al-Fakhkhar family of Granada (letter to Ibn Tibbon in *Qoveṣ teshuvot ha-Rambam ve-iggrotav,* ed. A. Lichtenberg [Leipzig: 1859], 2: 27a).

14. Yehudah b. Solomon states that his grandfather was "Zira" Ibn Susan, which is a printer's error for Ziza (*Mishpaṭei kokavim,* 16). On Ziza see Heinrich Brody, "'Al shushan 'edut" (Hebrew), in *Ṣiyyonim, qoveṣ le-zikhrono shel Y.N. Ṣimḥoni* (Berlin: Eschkol, 1929), 48 n. Yehudah b. Solomon was born in 1219 and was a student of Meir Abulafia.

15. Millás Vallicrosa suggested *tabulae* or *traductor* in *Las traducciones orientales en los manuscritos de la Biblioteca central de Toledo* (Madrid: Consejo Superior de Investigaciones Científicas, 1942), 182. Cf. his *Estudios sobre Azarquiel* (Madrid and Granada: Consejo Superior de Investigaciones Científicas, 1943–1950), 452.

16. Hilty, *Libro conplido,* 47–48 n., and on the Millás Vallicrosa theory, p. 17. Cf. Sarton, *Science,* 2: pt. 2, 842 and Millás, *Traducciones,* 158–59. The Spanish manuscript of the translation is not extant, but see the *Escala,* 92ff., on a manuscript of a Latin translation which the editor thought was copied from the Spanish.

17. In addition to Hilty's article and edition, see the important observations on this work in the *Escala,* 85ff., and by Steinschneider, *Hebraeischen Übersetzungen,* 585.

18. "A Study and Edition of the Royal Scriptorium of *El libro del saber de astrologia* by Alfonso X, el Sabio," 4 vols. (Ph.D. diss., University of Wisconsin, 1974), 1: xxvi, cf. xxiii–iv. This edition is cited here throughout, as obviously superior to *Libros del saber de astronomia,* ed. Manuel Rico y Sinobas, 5 vols. (Madrid: E. Aguado, 1863–1867). Francisco Vera gives the number of treatises as twenty-four, but he counts parts of books as whole separate books. However, he is almost correct in saying that seventy-five percent of the *Libro del saber* was composed and/or translated by Jews; the exact figure is somewhat higher. See his *Los judíos españoles y su contribución a las ciencias exactas* (Buenos Aires: El Ateneo, 1948), 156.

19. On him, and with reference to Yehudah's translation, see Steinschneider, "Zur Geschichte der Uebersetzungen aus dem Indischen in's Arabische . . ." *Zeitschrift der deutschen morgenlandischen Gesellschaft* 24 (1870): 349–50.

20. Cf. O. J. Tallgren, "Sur l'astronomie espagnole d'Alphonse X," *Studia orientalia* 1 (1925): 344.

21. Abraham Zacut, *Sefer yuḥasin ha-shalem,* ed. Herschell Filipowski (London: 1857, repr. Jerusalem: 1963), 222. Hilty also cites a manuscript of Zacut's astronomical tables and translates the passage ("El *Libro conplido*": 26). The work he cites is not currently available to me, but Hilty certainly seems correct in saying that Zacut erred there and referred actually to the *Libro de la ochava sphera* and to the *Libro conplido (Libro conplido* edn., introduction, lxi). This is all the more surprising since in the chronicle Zacut clearly mentions the author of the work, as well as Yehudah as the translator, so it is obvious that he is referring to the *Libro de la ochava sphera.* Incidentally, Hilty's reference may be the source of Gil's confusion (*Escuela de traductores,* 65) that Ibn al-Rijāl was called "Zacuto"!

22. Cf. Antonio Ballesteros Beretta, "Burgos y la rebelión del infante don Sancho," *BRAH* 119 (1946): especially 119–21.

23. *Libro del saber,* Cárdenas edn., 2: 185 (fol. 24).

24. See Sarton, *Science,* 2, pt. 2, 836. Cf. also the description of the work in José Soriano Viguera, *Contribución al conocimiento de los trabajos astronómicos desarrollados en la escuela de Alfonso X el Sabio* (Madrid: A. Fontana, 1926), 41–50. There is, however, no justification for the claim that Alfonso himself wrote the prologue, which clearly was written in each case by the translators.

25. *El libro del saber,* Cárdenas edn., 1: xxxvii–xl.

26. *El libro conplido,* Hilty edn., 39–40.

27. Baer, *Die Juden,* 2: 51. The document was first edited in *MHE,* 1: 13ff. and then by Julio González, *Repartimiento de Sevilla* (in ch. 2 above, n. 11), 2:113, 118, 233, and passim.

28. On these see Norman Roth, "Two Jewish Courtiers of Alfonso X Called Zag (Isaac)," *Sefarad* 43 (1983): 75–85. For conditions of the Jewish community of Toledo in general during this period, see his "New Light on the Jews of Mozarabic Toledo," *AJS Review* (Association for Jewish Studies) 11 (1986): 189–220.

29. Sarton, *Science,* 1: 370; 2: pt. 1, 442. J. A. Sánchez Pérez points out that chapter three of the book gives a date corresponding to 1066–1067 of the Common Era, whereas Abū Saʿīd died in 1058. See the "Nota preliminar" to King Alfonso's "El libro de las cruces," edited by Sánchez Pérez in *Isis* (below in ch. 7, n. 91), p. x. And see most recently on this work Julio Samsó, "La primitiva versión árabe del Libro de las cruces," in *Nuevos estudios sobre astronomía española en el siglo de Alfonso X,* ed. Juan Vernet (Barcelona: Consejo Superior de Investigaciones Científicas, 1983), 149–61.

30. *El libro de las cruzes,* ed. Lloyd A. Kasten and Lawrence B. Kiddle (Madrid: Consejo Superior de Investigaciones Científicas, 1961), 1, col. b. The *explicit,* on the other hand, states: "e fue su [Yehudah] companero en esta translacion Maestre Johan Daspa" (168). Undoubtedly Hilty is correct (*contra* Menéndez Pidal, "Escuelas alfonsíes," 369, 371) in seeing that "Maestre Johan" of the prologue is the same as "Maestre Johan Daspa" of the *explicit.* We need not, however, make too much out of the term "companero" here. On the possibility of ch. 59 (Sánchez Pérez edn., 124; Kasten and Kiddle edn., 160) being an interpolation, composed entirely by Yehudah, see Samsó, "Primitiva versión": 150.

31. *El libro conplido,* 55–60.

32. Ibid., 46. Regarding what Hilty wrote on 47, it should be mentioned that, while it is true that there is a tendency to call almost every medieval Jew "rabbi," there is nothing in the fact that Yehudah was a doctor which precludes his also having been, or had the title of, a rabbi. The argument ought rather to be that none of the treatises in which his name appears refers to him as such.

33. Ibid., n. 3, drawing from the documents in Angel González Palencia, *Los mozárabes de Toledo en los siglos XII y XIII,* 3 vols. (Madrid: Instituto de Valencia de Don Juan, 1926–1930). Hilty's table is on p. 15. Muñoz Sendino considered "Judá ben Moisés [*sic*] ha-Cohen" and "Judá ben Moisés ben Mosca" two different people (perhaps including even a third!) in his edition of *Escala,* 172.

34. See Sarton, *Science,* 2: pt. 2, 837 and the list of editions of the Latin translations on 840, with a bibliography of studies on 841.

35. *BNM,* 3306, fols. 34v–35.

36. *Libro conplido:* 42.

37. Hilty, ibid. Sarton, *Science,* 2: pt. 2, 837. Millás, *Traducciones,* 227–30.

38. Cf. Millás, ibid., and his *Azarquiel,* 407–15.

39. Millás, *Azarquiel,* 15ff. The peculiarities of Arabic pronunciation in al-Andalus, however, do not affect the spelling of the name.

40. Madrid, Real Academia de la Historia, MS Heb. 7, fols. 27–28 and 30–39, described by Francisco Cantera Burgos in *Sefarad* 19 (1959): 12. This is not, of course, the Hebrew manuscript of the translation of the tables mentioned above. This *RAH* manuscript is obviously at least fifteenth century, not fourteenth as Cantera suggested (10, 13).

41. Amador de los Ríos in his *Historia social, política y religiosa de los judíos de España y Portugal* (Madrid: T. Fortanet, 1875) erroneously referred to him as "Rabbi Isahak Aben Zagut Metolitolāh" (1: 448–49)!

42. Isaac Israeli, *Yesod ʿolam,* 2 vols. in 1, ed. Baer Goldberg and Loeb Rosenkranz (Berlin: 1777 and 1847; latter as repr. Jerusalem: 1970), fols. 11b and 12a. In the 1777 edition, fol. 70b, the first section quoted here is lacking altogether and the section on the solar eclipse gives his name as "Isaac ben Sir"; but see the corrections following p. 48 of the 1847 edition. On the other hand, the earlier edition gives the date of the solar eclipse as 1266, which seems to me more correct than 1263. The title *ḥazzan* does not mean "precentor" in medieval Spain, as Sarton says (*Science,* 2: pt. 2, 843), but rather a teacher and/or reader of the Scriptures in the synagogue. Thus, his Spanish title "rabi" (rabbi) is correct. Isaac Israeli again cites investigations of Isaac b. Sīd on the solstice of the Hebrew month of Tishrei, 1265 (fol. 30a, or fol. 82b of the 1777 edition). At the end of Rico's edition of *Libros del saber* (2: 222) appear certain calculations for Seville, which led Ballesteros (*Alfonso X,* 308–9) to conjecture that Isaac lived in that city, but this is not necessarily so.

43. Zacut, *Sefer,* 221–22.

44. Roth, "Zag," 81, n. 29 for details.

45. *Astrolabio* in Alfonso's *Libro del saber,* 2: 270–384.

46. Cf. Soriano Viguera's *Contribución,* 52–74.

47. In *Libro del saber,* 2: 384, 422, 461.

48. In *Libro del saber,* 2: 459 and 471.

49. A. Wegener, "Die astronomischen Werke Alfons X," *Bibliotheca mathematica,* series 3, 6 (1905): 150. Heinrich Suter, *Die Mathematiker und Astronomen der Araber und ihre Werke* (Leipzig: B. G. Teubner, 1900), 124; the usually reliable Suter was incorrect here.

50. *La ciencia árabe en la edad media* (Madrid: Instituto de Estudios Africanos, 1954), 69. He confused the *Lamina universal* with the *Laminas de cada una de las siete planetas,* which is by al-Zarqāllah.

51. *Libro del saber,* Cárdenas edn., 1, cl, n. 9; Millás, "Un ejemplar de azafea árabe de Azarquiel," *Al-Andalus* 9 (1944): 112.

52. In *Libro del saber,* IV: 892 (fol. 166v). See Millás Vallicrosa, *Estudios sobre la*

historia de la ciencia española (Barcelona: Consejo Superior de Investigaciones Científicas, 1949), 66–67 and plate at 80.

53. Both forms appear in the text, but *armellas* with more frequency.

54. In *Libro del saber,* 3: 743 to 847 (fols. 132v to 152v).

55. In *Libro del saber,* IV: 1000 (fol. 198). This work is the strange "Fabrica y usos del instrumento del levamento que en Arabigo se llama atazin" ("The construction and use of the instrument of elevation called in Arabic *atazin*") to which Sarton refers as being in an Italian translation in a Vatican manuscript (*Science,* 2: pt. 2, 843). He attributed it either to Samuel ha-Levi or to Isaac b. Sīd. Given the strange title he had for the work, it is not surprising that he was unable to find it in the *Libro del saber.* See most recently on the *Ataçir* Mercè Viladrich and Ramon Martí in Vernet, *Nuevos estudios,* 75–100.

56. In *Libro del saber,* IV, 913 (fol. 172).

57. Ibid., respectively 988 (fol. 177), 966 (fol. 185), and 988 (fol. 195). On the water clocks of "Azarquiel" in Toledo, see the interesting story in Millás, *Azarquiel,* 7ff. The *Libro de las armellas* was an extremely important work, and was utilized as late as the fifteenth century by the German astronomer Johann Müller Regiomontanus ("of Königsberg") for the construction of his astronomical instruments (Vera, *Judíos,* 132).

58. Millás, "Una nueva obra astronómica alfonsí: el tratado de cuadrant 'sennero,'" *Al-Andalus* 21 (1956): 77–92.

59. Respectively in fols. 1–93 and 94–135; see Millás, "Obra": 59–61, 63.

60. Steinschneider, *Hebraeischen Übersetzungen,* 986.

61. See index to Baer, *Jews in Christian Spain,* s.v. "Abulafia," and his Hebrew article on "The Life and Times of Todros Abulafia," *Zion* 2 (1936): 19–55.

62. Baer, *Jews in Christian Spain,* 1: 362–63. The literature on the synagogue, now a national monument in Spain, is vast. See generally Francisco Cantera Burgos, *Sinagogas de Toledo, Segovia y Córdoba* (Madrid: Consejo Superior de Investigaciones Científicas, 1973), and Don A. Halperin, *The Ancient Synagogues of the Iberian Peninsula* (Gainesville: University of Florida Press, 1969), 49–55; both works have photographs.

63. In *Libro del saber,* 976 (fol. 189).

64. Steinschneider, *Catalogus librorum hebraeorum in bibliotheca bodleiana* (Berlin: A. Friedlaender, 1852–1860 and various reprint editions), col. 2747 (no. 7406.2); cf. also Steinschneider, *Hebraeischen Übersetzungen,* 657, 737, 740, 972. On Shem Tov see Sarton, *Science,* 2: pt. 2, 1085 and 1096, and on our Abraham 844.

65. Procter, "Scientific Works," 23. Procter was not correct in saying that Steinschneider and Sarton have no basis for calling him Abraham of Toledo, however, for Abraham Ibn Waqar in fact lived in Toledo. Procter did not know, apparently, of the Ibn Waqar name or realize that this was our Abraham.

66. Juan Manuel, "Tratado sobre las armas," in *Biblioteca de autores españoles* (Madrid: M. Rivadeneyra, 1846–1880), series 1, vol. 51: 262. Edited also from the manuscript by Antonio Giménez Soler in his *Don Juan Manuel, biografía y estudio crítico* (Zaragoza: 1932), 688.

67. *Jews in Christian Spain,* 1: 126.

68. This work was first mentioned by Steinschneider, *Catalogus,* col. 2747. The

manuscript of an "Astrolabio" by one "Habraham magister" discussed by the editor Muñoz (*Escala*, 22) is possibly a work by Abraham Ibn 'Ezra.

69. *Escala*, 18 and n. 2, where the prologue is cited; cf. Procter, "Scientific Works," 15, 18 (prologue), 22; Sarton, *Science*, 2: pt. 2, 844.

70. Sarton, ibid., is somewhat misleading; it is the translation by Fernando, not the one by Abraham, which is included in the *Libro del saber*, 2: 601 (fol. 106v).

71. Procter, *Alfonso, Patron*, 125. See Castro, *España*, 497.

72. Millás, *Ciencia española*, 104–5; cf. his *Azarquiel*, 462ff.

CHAPTER SIX

1. *European Literature and the Latin Middle Ages*, trans. Willard R. Trask (New York: Pantheon Books, 1953), 417.

2. *A Literary History of Spain: The Middle Ages* (London: Barnes and Noble, 1971), 208–9.

3. Hardison has made two films in color of the *Misteri d'Elx*, which have been shown at many universities. They present the history of the legend of the Lady of Elche, preparations made for the drama-opera, and the entire representation, including the machinery required for depicting the Assumption of the Virgin. His valuable *Christian Rite and Christian Drama in the Middle Ages: Essays in the Origin and History of Modern Drama* (Baltimore: Johns Hopkins University Press, 1965) is a classic. See too Gonzalo Gironés's book-length "Los orígenes del Misterio de Elche," *Marian Library Studies* n.s. 9 (1977): 19–188, and the symposium *Món i Misteri de la festa d'Elx*, with its companion volume by M. T. Vicens, *Iconografia assumpcionista* (Valencia: Generalitat, Conselleria de Cultura, 1986). A summary background and bibliography is in D. J. Viera, *Medieval Catalan Literature: Prose and Poetry* (Boston: Twayne, 1988), ch. 10, "Medieval Catalan Theater."

4. Urban Tigner Holmes, Jr., *A History of Old French Literature from the Origins to 1300* (New York: F. S. Crofts, 1937) is the most substantial history of this literature to be found. Holmes includes virtually all works in Old French, and his extremely sage criticism has not been bested.

5. Antonio Ubieto, et al., *Introducción a la historia de España*, 10th edn. (Barcelona: Editorial Teide, 1974), 46–47, treats Byzantine occupation of the area from Alicante to the Algarve, including the Balearic Islands, which lasted some seventy years. The Byzantines came to the aid of Athanagild in his struggle with Agila, and this assistance and occupation paralleled a period of the life of Isidore of Seville. This cultural enclave, the last flickering of Greco-Roman civilization in the West, meant a great deal to the production of Isidore's *Etymologiae*.

6. Curtius, *Literature*, 417.

7. *Partidas*, I.6.34. The translation is by Samuel Parsons Scott, *Las siete partidas* (see above, ch. 1, n. 1); since Scott's English version is so difficult to obtain, I refer the reader to his excerpts on drama in my *Alfonso X, el Sabio*, 124–26. On church plays, see Richard B. Donovan's essential *Liturgical Drama in Medieval Spain* (Toronto: Pontifical Institute of Mediaeval Studies, 1958). And see Humberto López Morales, *Tradición y creación en los orígenes del teatro castellano* (Madrid: Ediciones Alcalá, 1968).

8. Procter, *Alfonso, Patron,* 50–52.

9. *Literary History,* 207–8. Cf. Donovan, *Liturgical Drama,* ch. 6.

10. Ibid., 209.

11. Guerrero Lovillo, *Las cántigas, estudio arqueológico* (above in ch. 4, n. 2), 93. Domínguez, "Iconografía evangélica en las *Cantigas de Santa Maria,*" in *Studies on the Cantigas,* 56. On the Códice Rico see above, ch. 4, nn. 1 and 2, and below, ch. 11, n. 1.

12. Presilla, "The Image of Death and Political Ideology in the *Cantigas de Santa Maria,*" in *Studies on the Cantigas.*

13. Kinkade, "Sermon in the Round: The *Mester de Clerecía* as Dramatic Art," in *Studies in Honor of Gustavo Correa* (Potomac, Md.: Scripta Humanistica, 1986), 27–36. Pächte, *The Rise of Pictorial Narrative Art in Twelfth-Century England* (Oxford: Clarendon, 1962), 31. John E. Keller and Richard P. Kinkade, *Iconography in Medieval Spanish Literature,* 16–17.

14. Keller and Kinkade, *Iconography,* 17.

15. *Alfonso X,* 92–93.

16. Ibid.

17. Ballesteros Beretta, *Alfonso X,* 1053, quotes from the king's will (my translation): "Likewise we order that all the books of the *Songs of Praise of Holy Mary* be in that church where our body shall be interred, and that they be sung on the feast days of Holy Mary. And if that one who inherits legally and by our will what is ours should wish to own these books of the *Songs of Holy Mary,* we order that he therefore make good compensation to the church from whence he removes them so that he may have grace without sin."

18. Presilla, "Political Ideology," 403ff.

19. "The Central Role of the Troubadour Persona of Alfonso X in the *Cantigas de Santa Maria,*" BHS 56 (1979): 305–15; and below, ch. 9 by Snow.

20. *European Literature,* 417.

21. "Iconografía evangélica," 54 (my translation).

22. Guerrero Lovillo, *Cántigas,* 22–23.

23. *Old French Literature,* 246.

24. Filgueira Valverde, "Introducción histórica-crítica, transcripción, versión castellana y comentario de las *Cantigas de Santa Maria*" (Madrid: Edilán, 1979), 35–264. Kulp-Hill kindly allows scholars, who request it, the translations of cantigas they need for their articles or books. Her address is Department of Modern Languages, University of Northern Iowa, Cedar Falls, Iowa 50614.

25. "Iconografía evangélica," 58.

26. This and all English verses from the *Cantigas* are by Kulp-Hill (see n. 24 and text), based on the critical edition of the poems by Walter Mettmann (above, ch. 4, n. 1).

27. "Iconografía evangélica," 64.

28. Connie L. Scarborough, "Visualization vs. Verbalization in ms. T.j.1 of the '*Cantigas de Santa Maria*'" (Ph.D. diss., University of Kentucky, 1963).

29. "Iconografía evangélica," 57.

CHAPTER SEVEN

1. Margo Ynes Corona de Ley, "The Prologue in Castilian Literature between 1200 and 1400" (Ph.D. diss., University of Illinois, 1976; Ann Arbor: University Microfilms, 1988), 10. My thanks to Kathleen L. Kirk for improving the style of this study; remaining infelicities and errors are mine alone.

2. Antonio G. Solalinde, "Intervención de Alfonso X en la redacción de sus obras," *RFE* 2 (1915): 283–88.

3. All translations within the text are mine unless otherwise indicated. Here I translate from the Alfonsine text in Solalinde's "Intervención" (285–86) whose full context follows (emphasis mine). "Dell escruiuir destas palabras auedes oydo enel començamiento deste capitulo, como dixo Nuestro Sennor que el las escriuirie; e aqui dize en el XXXIIII° capitulo dell Exodo que las mando escriuir a Moysen; e auredes otrossi enel libro que a nombre Deuteronomio . . . que diz que Nuestro Sennor que el mismo las escriuio. E ssemeia que son contrallas estas razones. E sobresta contralla fabla maestre Pedro e departe desta guisa: Diz que todo es bien dicho, et que podemos entender e dezir que compuso Nuestro Sennor las razones delos mandados, e que ouo ell auctoridad e el nombre dend, por que las mando escriuir, mas que las escriuio Moysen; assi como dixiemos nos muchas uezes: *el rey faze un libro, non por quel el escriua con sus manos, mas porque compone las razones del, e las emienda et yegua e enderesça, e muestra la manera de como se deuen fazer, e desi escriue las qui el manda, pero dezimos por esta razon que el rey faze el libro.* Oatrossi quando dezimos el rey faze un palacio ol alguna obra, non es dicho por quelo el fiziesse con sus manos, mas por quel mando fazer e dio las cosas que fueron mester para ello. E qui esto cumple, aquel a nombre que faze la obra, e nos assi ueo que usamos de lo dezir."

4. Francisco Rico, *Alfonso el Sabio y la "General estoria": tres lecciones* (Barcelona: Ariel, repr. 1984), 99.

5. "Nos Rey don Alfonso el sobredicho ueyendo la bondat desta açafeha que es generalmientre para todas las ladezas. & de como es estrumenten muy complido & mucho acabado. & de como es caro de sennalar. & que muchos ombres non podrien entender complidamientre la manera de como se faz por las parablas que dixo este sabio que la compuso; Mandamos figurar la figura della en este libro. Et mandamos sennalar con tinta prieta todos los cercos que son llamados almadarat . . . Et otrossi por que sean estos cerculos mas connosçudos & mas departidos delos otros; fiziemos tinnir lo que a entre ell uno & ell otro dellos con acafran. Et mandamos fazer otrossi los cercos que son llamados en arabigo almamarrat que uan de un polo del mundo al otro con uermeion. & los cercos de las longuezas que son en par zodiago. & en so derecho. Et otrossi los cercos de las ladezas que uan del un polo delos signos al otro. Et estas dos maneras de cercos so[n] al zodiaco; como los otros dos primeros al eguador. Et destas quatro maneras son todos los cercos que a en la faz de la Lamina. Et por que se fazen muchos & se semeian los unos alos otros; fiziemoslos sennalar con colores departidas segund es dicho." *Liber del saber de astrologia,* fol. 109. With minor modifications, I cite all Alfonsine texts as found in the *Concordances and Texts of the Royal Scriptorium Manuscripts of Alfonso X* (above in ch. 1, n. 4).

The treatises (with title abbreviations used in this study indicated within parentheses) contain the prologues examined, and follow: *Canones de Albateni (Albateni); Estoria de Espanna,* part I *(EE I); General estoria,* part I *(GE I); Lapidario* (same); *Libro conplido en los iudizios de las estrellas (Iudizios); Libro de las formas e [de las] ymagenes (Formas); Libro de las cruzes (Cruzes); Libro de las leyes (Leyes); Libro del quadrante sennero (QS); Libros de ajedrez, dados e tablas (Acedrex); Libro del saber de astronomia (Libro del saber, LSA).* Not included in this study is the text of the so-called *Picatrix* because it is incomplete at the beginning, the *Tablas de Zarquiel,* the second part of the *Estoria de Espanna,* and the fourth part of the *General estoria.*

My rationale for the title for Alfonso's treatise on games is as follows. Although Alfonso provides no official title for his treatise on games, it seems (at risk of sounding unduly punctilious) that the title *Libro de acedrex & dados & tablas* most closely reflects what Alfonso would have called it, if we can trust Alfonso's written text: "mandamos fazer este *libro* en que fablamos en la manera daquellos que se fazen mas apuestos assi como *acedrex & dados & tablas* (iv 13–16, emphasis mine). This title respects the unity of the treatise (*libro,* not *libros*) and its thirteenth-century form (both orthography and polysyndeton). *Formas,* strictly speaking, refers to itself as "libro delas formas & delas ymagenes" (lri–2, emphasis mine). Also, the correct title is not *Libros del saber de astronomia* but *Libro del saber de astrologia.* I have clarified this in my study "A New Title for the Alfonsine Omnibus on Astronomical Instruments," *La corónica* 8.2 (1980): 172–78. For the *Iudizios,* I follow Gerold Hilty's designation (see below), which is the correct one. For the three treatises found within the *LSA,* I use the titles taken from their texts: *Libro de la espera (Espera); Libro de la açafeha (Açafeha);* and *Libro del quadrante (Quadrante* or *Q).*

6. *Libros del saber de astronomia,* Rico y Sinobas edn. (above in ch. 5, n. 18), 1:7, as cited in Solalinde, "Intervención": 287. "Et despues lo endreço et lo mando componer este rey sobredicho; et tollo las razones que entendio eran soueianas et dobladas, et que non eran en castellano drecho; et puso las otras que entendio que complian, et quanto en el lenguaje endreçolo el por si se."

7. Procter, "Scientific Works of the Court of Alfonso" (see ch. 5, n. 10), 22.

8. George E. McSpadden, "The Spanish Prologue before 1700" (Ph.D. diss., Stanford University, 1947; Ann Arbor, Mich.: University Microfilms, 1976), 21.

9. Sarton, *History of Science,* 2, part 2: 835.

10. "Los prólogos de Alfonso X serían probablemnte [*sic*] obra personal suya." Alberto Porqueras Mayo, "Notas sobre la evolución histórica del prólogo en la literatura medieval castellana," *Revista de literatura* 11 (1957): 188. This statement becomes less satisfactory when "probablemente" is changed to "siempre" in the reprint in his *El prólogo como género literario* (Madrid: Consejo Superior de Investigaciones Científicas, 1957), 80.

11. De Ley, "Prologue in Castilian Literature," 90.

12. Ballesteros, *Alfonso X,* 58–59.

13. Keller, *Alfonso X,* 31; E. N. van Kleffens, *Hispanic Law until the End of the Middle Ages* (Edinburgh: Edinburgh University, 1968), 149.

14. Charles Faulhaber, *Latin Rhetorical Theory in Thirteenth- and Fourteenth-Century Castile* (Berkeley and Los Angeles: University of California Press, 1972), 98–99.

15. *Setenario* (Vanderford 1984 edn.), xvi–xvii; also Van Kleffens, *Hispanic Law,* 164–65, and Procter, *Alfonso, Patron,* 50. See, however, Craddock's incontrovertible evidence arguing against this notion and for the *Setenario* as the last Alfonsine legal bequeathal: "El Setenario: última e inconclusa refundición alfonsina de la primera *Partida," AHDE* 56 (1986): 441–66.

16. Van Kleffens, *Hispanic Law,* 178–79, who calls him "de las Leyes" and ultimately "de la Junta," whereas Jean Roudil in his edition of the *Summa de los nueve tiempos de los pleitos,* vol. 1 of his *Jacobo de Junta "el de las Leyes"* (Paris: Klincksieck, 1986, p. 13), reverses the order and calls him "Jacobo de la Junta—le futur 'el de las Leyes.'"

17. Roudil claims that Jacobo arrived sometime before the death of Fernando III (*Summa de los nueve tiempos,* 18). Alfonso García Gallo in his "El 'Libro de las leyes' de Alfonso el Sabio: del *Espéculo* a las *Partidas*" (*AHDE* 21–22 [1951–1952]: 425) finds it odd that, if Jacobo was a resident in Spain about this time, his name does not appear among those mentioned in the 1253 *Repartimiento* of Seville as being a part of Alfonso's court; Jacobo, however, is mentioned with distinction in the 1257 *Repartimiento* in Murcia.

18. *Partidas,* II.7.10 (Real Academia edn., 2: 52): "Et esto es leer et escrebir que tiene muy grant pro al que lo sabe para aprender mas de ligero las cosas que quisiere saber, et para poder mejor guardar sus poridades."

19. *Partidas,* II.5.16 (Real Academia edn., 2: 36–37): "Acucioso debe el rey seer en aprender los saberes, ca por ellos entenderá las cosas de raiz; et sabrá mejor obrar en ellas, et otrosi por saber leer sabrá mejor guardar sus poridades et seer señor dellas, lo que de otra guisa non podrie tan bien facer, ca por la mengua de non saber estas cosas haberie por fuerza de meter otro consigo que lo sopiese, et poderle hie avenir lo que dixo el rey Salomon, que el que mete su poridat en poder de otro fácese su siervo, et quien la sabe guardar es señor de su corazon; lo que conviene mucho al rey."

20. Procter, *Alfonso X,* 4.

21. González, *Reinado y diplomas de Fernando III* (see ch. 2 above, n. 4), 2: 67, item 55.

22. *Hispanic Law,* 148.

23. "Por que entiendo que es pro del myo regno e de mi tierra otorgo e mando que aya escuelas en Salamanca," in Cándido Ajo G[onzález] y Sáinz de Zúñiga, *Historia de las universidades hispánicas,* 10 vols. (Madrid: Consejo Superior de Investigaciones Científicas, 1957–1975), 1: 436.

24. "Et yo con gra[n]d sabor que he quel estudio sea mas auançado e mas aprovechado cate aquellas cosas que me ellos pedieron e oue mi conseio e mi acuerdo con los obispos e con arçidianos e con otros clerigos buenos, que conmigo eran sobre ellas e auido el consejo aquello quelos entendieron que era pro e onrra de mi e de mios Regnos e delos escolares e toda la tierra aquello fis yo e mande e toue por bien" (Ajo, *Universidades hispánicas,* 1: 438–39).

25. Anthony J. Cárdenas, "Foral Statutes and the 'Educational Code' of Alfonso X: A Study of Sources" (tentative title), forthcoming.

26. The first educational code of its kind according to Hastings Rashdall, *The*

Universities of Europe in the Middle Ages, ed. F. M. Powicke and A. B. Emden, 3 vols. (Oxford: Oxford University Press, 1936), 2: 79.

27. See Anthony J. Cárdenas, "Alfonso X and the *Studium Generale,*" *Indiana Social Studies Quarterly* 33 (1980): 65–75.

28. *GE IV,* fol. 169v79–92, in the *Concordances and Texts.*

29. "Un trattato di *Ars dictandi* dedicato ad Alfonso X," *Studi mediolatini e volgari* 15–16 (1968): 12. Faulhaber concurs (*Latin Rhetorical Theory,* 103).

30. Procter, *Alfonso X,* 12–13.

31. Ibid., 3: "ut omnes possent evidentissime intueri et intelligere quoquomodo illa, que sub lingue latine phaleris et figura tecta et secreta, etiam ipsis sapientibus, videbantur."

32. Ibid.

33. "Ya cuando empezó a reinar Fernando III avanzaba con vigor la lengua romance; aparecía con frecuencia creciente, y con más o menos integridad en los documentos particulares, e iba irrumpiendo en los mandatos reales; durante su época acabaría imponiéndose en la última década" (González, *Reinado y diplomas de Fernando III,* 1: 19).

34. "Castilian Chancery," 106.

35. Ibid., 108.

36. Anthony J. Cárdenas, "The Literary Prologue of Alfonso X: A Nexus between Chancery and Scriptorium," *Alfonso, Emperor,* 456. Henceforward, I borrow heavily from this study without citing it further.

37. Procter, "Castilian Chancery," 108–9.

38. *Reinado y diplomas de Fernando III,* 1: 517.

39. See also Juan Manuel del Estal, *Documentos inéditos de Alfonso X el Sabio y del infante su hijo don Sancho* (Alicante, Spain: Universidad de Alicante, 1984), 2: 209. The cover of his work sports a color reproduction of one of these *ruedas.*

40. "Castilian Chancery," 106–8.

41. Procter admits to knowing of "only one event thus mentioned—the knighting by Alfonso X of his brother-in-law Edward of England which is commemorated in privileges from October 1254 to December 1255" ("Castilian Chancery," 108).

42. In "Alfonso X and the *Studium Generale,*" I have discussed at length the theoretical nature of the *Siete partidas* as manifested in its Educational Code (II.31.1–11), as compared to the practical *fueros académicos* issuing from Alfonso's chancery. Stanley G. Payne, *A History of Spain and Portugal,* 2 vols. (Madison, Wisc.: University of Wisconsin Press, 1973) 1: 80, briefly but adequately discusses the ideal nature of the *Siete partidas.*

43. Ajo, *Universidades hispánicas,* 1: 440–41. "Conoscida cosa sea a todos los omes que esta carta vieren como nos d. Alfonso por la gracia de Dios, Rey de Castiella, de Leon, de Toledo, de Gallisia, de Sevilla, de Cordoba, de Murcia, de Jahen, é Señor de toda la Andalucia en uno con la Reyna Doña Violante, mi muger é con mis fijos la Inffante Doña Berenguella e la Inffante Doña Beatris . . . Fecha la carta en Burgos por mandado del Rey veintiocho días andados del mes de Deziembre en era de mill é docientos e noventa é dos años. Et yo [el] sobredicho Rey Don Alfonso, regnante en uno con la Reyna Doña Violante mi muger, é con mis

fijas la Infante Doña Berenguella é la Infante Doña Beatris en Castiella, en Toledo, en Leon, en Gallisia, en Sevilla, en Cordoba, en Murcia, en Hajen [*sic*], en Baeza, en Badalloz, é en el Algarve, otorgo este privilegio et confirmolo é mando que vala, el año que Don Odoarte fijo primero é heredero del Rey Enrrique de Anglaterra recebio caballeria en Burgos del Rey don Alfonso el sobredicho . . . Johan Perez de Cuenca la escribio el año tercero que el Rey regno." I have reproduced the text exactly as found, though there are several questionable transcriptions within.

44. "Començamos este libro en el nombre del padre. & del spiritu sancto" (*Leyes*, fol. 1r29–30, in the *Concordances and Texts*).

45. "Laores & gracias rendamos a dios padre" (*Iudizios*, fol. 1r1–2, in the *Concordances and Texts*).

46. "En el nombre de dios" (*Iudizios*, fol. 1v13, in the *Concordances and Texts*).

47. "Dixo Mahomat fijo de Gerber Albatheni que la primera cosa en que deue omne començar en cada libro es de loar a Dios & alauarlo" (*Albateni*, fol. 2r66–71, in the *Concordances and Texts*).

48. "En el nombre de Dyos. Este es el libro de las cruzes en los judizios de las estrellas que esplano Oueydalla" (*Cruzes*, fol. 4v25–28, in the *Concordances and Texts*).

49. Preambles occur with the following distributions: *Cruzes*, 1v55–68; *Leyes*, 1r65–1v3; *Formas*, 1r1–5; *QS*, 136r1–6, 13–21, 28–38; *Acedrex*, 1v13–16; *Iudizios*, 1r44–49; *GE I*, 1r59–66; *EE I*, 1v27; *Lapidario*, 1r2–76; *LSA: Espera*, 24r6–10; *Açafeha*, 106v10–11; *Quadrante*, 166v52–57. The only exception is *Albateni*, for reasons discussed below.

50. "Castilian Chancery," 108.

51. Ibid., 107.

52. "Et por esto nos don alfonsso el sobredicho. Mandamos a Rabiçag de Toledo nuestro sabio el sobredicho" (*Quadrante sennero*, fol. 136r38–40, in *Concordances and Texts*).

53. "Fablado auemos fasta aqui eneste libro en las maneras de las equaciones de las planetas. Et por qual razon fue fecha cada una dellas" (*Quadrante sennero*, fol. 136r7–13, in *Concordances and Texts*).

54. Millás, "Nueva obra astronómica" (ch. 5 above, n. 58), 59–92, though at 63 Millás does register its unity. The *Concordances and Texts* and Georg Bossong's edition of *Los "Canones de Albateni"* (Tübingen: Max Niemeyer Verlag, 1978, p. 6) also mention its unity.

55. "El muy noble Rey don Alfonso Rey despanna" (*Cruzes*, fol. 2r20–21, in *Concordances and Texts*).

56. "Et de Badaioz" (*Iudizios*, fol. 1r28, in *Concordances and Texts*).

57. "Del Algarue" (*Iudizios*, fol. 1r28, in *Concordances and Texts*).

58. "Castilian Chancery," 108.

59. *Cruzes*, fol. 202r73–78, in *Concordances and Texts*.

60. "Et fue acabado de trasladar el segundo anno que el noble Rey don Ferrando su padre gano la cibdat de Seuilla" (*Lapidario*, fol. 1v23–24, in *Concordances and Texts*).

61. "Mando fazer" (*GE I*, fol. 1r16, in *Concordances and Texts*).

62. "Mandolo trasladar" (*Cruzes*, fol. 2r68, in *Concordances and Texts*).

63. "Mandamos fazer este libro" (*Acedrex*, fol. 1v14, in *Concordances and Texts*).

64. "Mandamos ayuntar" (*EE I*, fol. 2v24, in *Concordances and Texts*).

65. *GE I*, fol. 1r52, 59, 60, 63, in *Concordances and Texts*.

66. "Por mandado de" (*Iudizios*, fol. 1r41 and *Açafeha*, fol. 106v22, in *Concordances and Texts*).

67. Procter, "Scientific Works," 22; Hilty, "El *Libro conplido*" (ch. 5 above, n. 11), 39; Romano, "Opere scientifiche," 677–711, especially 687–89.

68. "Aqui se comiença el libro delos Canones de Albateni que mando escreuir el muy noble Rey don Alfonso a quien Dios de uida & salud por mucho tiempo" (*Albateni*, fol. 1r1–10, in *Concordances and Texts*).

69. Bossong, *Canones*, 6.

70. Zacarías García Villada, *Paleografía española*, 2 vols. (Barcelona: El Albir, [1923] 1974), 2: plate 56. I am grateful to John J. Nitti for bringing this to my attention, though the discussion is mine and does not necessarily reflect his views.

71. *Documentos inéditos,* 105, 107–9, 112, 113, passim.

72. "Scientific Works," 24–25.

73. Procter, *Alfonso X,* 86, 90, 101.

74. Dagenais, "A Further Source for the Literary Ideas in Juan Ruiz's Prologue," *Journal of Hispanic Philology* 11 (1986): 32–34.

75. "Muchos de los maestros, quando quieren leer sus libros en las escuelas, demandauan en los comienços dellos unas tantas cosas e otros más, los unos .v. cosas, et los otros VI, e ay otros que aun más" (*GE I*, p. 465a, in Rico, *Alfonso el Sabio,* 180).

76. Quain, "The Medieval *Accessus ad auctores*," *Traditio* 3 (1945): 215: "vita auctoris, titulus operis, intentio scribentis, materia operis, utilitas, et cui parti philosophiae supponatur."

77. *Alfonso el Sabio,* 178, also generally 167–88; see also Anthony J. Cárdenas, "Alfonso X: Incest and the Scholastic Method," *Romance Notes* 23 (1982): 93–98.

78. Rico, *Alfonso,* 97–120.

79. "Que, de 'todos los altos reyes' modernos que cabía citar, Alfonso (¿quién si no?) sólo mencione explícitamente a su bisabuelo Barbarroja y a su tío Federico II: es decir, a los dos grandes emperadores de la casa de Suabia, de donde emanaban sus propios derechos y ambiciones imperiales" (*Alfonso el Sabio,* 113–14).

80. "Alfonso X, the Empire and the *Primera crónica*," *BHS* 55 (1978): 95. See also his critic, Benito Brancaforte, edition, *Alfonso X el Sabio, prosa histórica* (Madrid: Cátedra, 1984), 22–24.

81. Fraker, "Empire," 101.

82. Fraker, "*Fet*" (in ch. 2 above, n. 33), 202.

83. Fraker, "*Fet,*" 211–12.

84. Ibid., 213.

85. "Desde luego, es un hecho que una porción importante de las que cabría tratar de 'digresiones' (glosas, meditaciones y *obiter dicta* que no constituyen propiamente una nota explicativa del relato) alude a temas que encajarían a maravilla en cualquier tratado *de regimine principum*" (*Alfonso el Sabio,* 100).

86. "Porque delos fechos delos buenos tomassen los omnes exemplo pora fazer

bien. Et delos fechos delos malos que reçibiessen castigo por se saber guardar delo non fazer" (*GE I,* fol. ir, in the *Concordances and Texts*).

87. "De arauigo en lenguaie castellano por que los omnes lo entendiessen meior; et se sopiessen del mas aprouechar" (*Lapidario,* fol. iv18–19, in the *Concordances and Texts*).

88. *Lapidario,* fol. iv27–44, in the *Concordances and Texts.*

89. John Horace Nunemaker, "Obstetrical and Genito-Urinary Remedies of Thirteenth-Century Spain," *Bulletin of the History of Medicine* 15 (1944): 162–79.

90. See Hilty, Procter, and Romano (n. 67 above) for an elucidation of Yhuda's identification and role in the Alfonsine venue; and see ch. 5 above, pp. 61ff.

91. "El *Libro de las cruzes* es un trabajo astrológico con el deliberado propósito de reunir únicamente los juicios de la astrología judiciaria que más pueden afectar a la persona de un rey y a la política de su reino." Sánchez Pérez, preface to *Libro de las cruzes,* ed. Lloyd A. Kasten (Madrid: Consejo Superior de Investigaciones Científicas, 1959), x. See also Sánchez Pérez, "El *Libro de las cruzes:* una obra astrológica que don Alfonso X, rey de España, mandó traducir del árabe," *Isis* 14 (1930): 78.

92. Friedrich Heer, *The Medieval World* (New York: New American Library of World Literature, 1961), 299.

93. "Estas figuras tantas & de tal manera. & las pusso alli o entendio que serie meior. Et dioles uertud & fuerça por que se podiessen los ombres ayudar dellas en sos fechos. & ennas cosas que ouiessen gran mester. tan bien en saber lo que era passado; comolo que auia de uenir. Ca esto es cosa que cobdicia mucho ell alma del ombre. saber las cosas que an de seer enante que sean" (*Libro de la espera,* fol. 15v56–63, in *Concordances and Texts*).

94. Keller's *Alfonso X* (21–23, 34–37) and Payne's *Spain* (80–81) both give an idea of some of the political problems Alfonso had to face.

95. Snow, "Troubadour *persona* of Alfonso X," 305–16; and his "A Chapter in Alfonso X's Personal Narrative: The *Puerto de Santa Maria* Poems in the *Cantigas de Santa Maria,*" *La corónica* 8 (1979): 10–21.

96. "King Alfonso's Virgin of the Villa-Sirga, Rival of St. James of Compostela," *Middle Ages–Reformation–Volkskunde: Festschrift for John J. Kunstmann* (Chapel Hill, N.C.: University of North Carolina Press, 1959), 81.

97. "Por que toda manera de alegria quiso dios que ouiessen los omnes en si naturalmientre por que pudiessen soffrir las cueytas & los trabaios quandoles uiniessen; por end los omnes buscaron muchas maneras por que esta alegria pudiessen auer complidamientre" (*Acedrex,* fol. 1r2–12, in the *Concordances and Texts*).

98. "Mugieres que non caualgan & estan encerradas . . . & otrossi *Los omnes que son uieios & flacos.* o los que han sabor de auer sus plazeres apartadamientre por que non reciban en ellos enoio nin pesar; o los que son en poder ageno assi como en prision o en catiuerio o que uan sobre mar" (*Acedrex,* fol. 1r39–47, emphasis added; in the *Concordances and Texts*).

99. "Scientific Works," 12.

100. Lynn Thorndike and Pearl Kibre, *A Catalogue of Incipits of Mediaeval Scientific Writings in Latin,* 2nd edn. rev. (Cambridge, Mass.: Medieval Academy of America, 1963) offers entries in 41 columns for the *Alfonsine Tables;* see index column 1729.

101. Poulle, "Les *Tables alphonsines* sont-elles d'Alphonse X?" in *De astronomia Alphonsi regis* (ch. 5 above, n. 1), 51–69.

102. The lack of entries corroborates this in the *Bibliography of Old Spanish Texts,* compiled by Charles B. Faulhaber et al. (Madison, Wisc.: Hispanic Seminary of Medieval Studies, 1984).

103. Procter, "Scientific Works," 12.

CHAPTER EIGHT

1. Miguel Asín Palacios, *La escatología musulmana en la Divina commedia,* 3rd edn. (Madrid: Instituto Hispano-Arabe de Cultura, 1961). Germán Sepúlveda, *Influencia del Islam en la Divina comedia* (Santiago de Chile: Instituto Chileno-Arabe de Cultura, 1965). Enrico Cerulli, *Il "Libro della scala" e la questione delle fonti arabospagnole della Divina commedia* (Città del Vaticano: Biblioteca Apostolica Vaticana, 1949); and his *Nuove ricerche sul Libro della scala e la conoscenza dell'Islam in occidente* (Città del Vaticano: Biblioteca Apostolica Vaticana, 1972). An early version of our present chapter appeared in *Alfonso, Emperor* but has been thoroughly recast and revised during a year of work in European archives. I wish to thank the National Endowment for the Humanities for a 1983 summer stipend and the American Association of University Women for the 1987–1988 Founders Fellowship to work in Europe. I also wish to thank Professors Spurgeon Baldwin, Robert I. Burns, Kenneth Brown, Anthony J. Cárdenas, Alan Deyermond, Jaime Ferreiro Alemparte, John Geary, John E. Keller, Anthony Luttrell, Robert MacDonald, and others who have most courteously aided a non-Hispanist.

2. Robert Davidsohn, *Geschichte von Florenz,* trans. as *Storia di Firenze* by Giovanni Battista Klein (Florence: Sansoni, 1977), 2: 687–89; Archivio di Stato di Firenze, MS 225, fol. 9; Ricordano Malispini, *Storia fiorentina* (Florence: 1816; repr. Rome: Multigrafica, 1976), 139. The treaties are in Archivio di Stato di Siena (ASS), 20 April 1254, original diplomatic document, copied in *Caleffio vecchio,* fol. 330v, ed. Giovanni Cecchini (Florence: Olschki, 1935), 2: 779, no. 567; Archivio di Stato di Firenze (ASF), 25 August 1254, Capitoli di Firenze 29, fols. 189–91, published in *Documenti dell'antica costituzione del comune di Firenze. Appendice: parte prima, 1251–1260,* ed. Pietro Santini (Florence: Olschki, 1952), 75–78.

3. Davidsohn, *Firenze,* 2: 617–18.

4. Escorial, MS *Tresor* L.II.3, fol. 25v; ed. Francis J. Carmody, *Li livres dou tresor* (Berkeley: University of California Press, 1947), 80–81 (from second redaction manuscripts): "Vient une devision entre les princes de alemaine car luns esleirent a roi et a enpereor monseignor anfons rois de chastelle et despaigne, li autres esleurent li cuent ricart de cornoaille frere au roi dengleterre." The remainder of this chronicle account deserves consultation, as it gives in full the context of these events written by a participant.

5. Davidsohn, *Firenze,* 2: 666–67.

6. Ibid., 2: 687–88.

7. *Cronica,* 4 vols. (Florence: Magheri, 1823; repr. Rome: Multigrafica, 1980), 2: 99–100 (VI.lxxiv): "Nel detto anno, essendo d'assai tempo prima per gli elettori

dello'mperio eletti per discordia due imperadori, l'una parte (ciò furono tre de' lettori) elessono il re Alfonso di Spagna, e l'altre parte degli elettori elessono Ricciardo conte di Cornovaglia e fratello del re d'Inghilterra; e perchè il reame di Boemia era in discordia, e due se ne faceano re, ciascuna diede la sua boce alla sua parte. E per molti anni era stata la discordia de' due eletti, ma la Chiesa di Roma più favoreggiava Alfonso di Spagna, accioch'egli colle sue forze venisse ad abattere la superbia e signoria di Manfredi; per la qual cagione i guelfi di Firenze gli mandarono ambasciadori per sommuoverlo del passare, promettendogli grande aiuto accioché favorasse parte guelfa. E l'ambasciadore fu ser Brunetto Latini, uomo di grande senno e autoritade;* ma innanzi che fosse fornita l'ambasciata, i Fiorentini furono sconfitti a Montaperti, e lo re Manfredi prese grande vigore e stato in tutta Italia, e'l podere della parte della Chiesa n'abassò assai, per la qual cose Alfonso di Spagnia lasciò la'mpresa dello'mperio, e Ricciardo d'Inghilterra no la seguio." The asterisk designates a variant in *Rerum italicarum scriptores,* ed. Lodovico Antonio Muratori, 25 vols. in 28 (Milan: 1723–1751), XIII, col. 204: "il quale fece molti Libri."

8. Ed. Julia Bolton Holloway (New York: Garland, 1981), 8–9, lines 113–34.

9. Fols. 11, 50v (twice), 65v, 74v. The illumination showing Brunetto with King Alfonso is on fol. 1v; it is reproduced by Holloway in *Alfonso, Emperor,* 473, and in her edition of the *Tesoretto,* 154. *Il libro di Montaperti (an. MCCLX),* ed. Cesare Paoli (Florence: Vieusseux, 1889), 34, 123, 148 (twice), 172.

10. I am currently editing these texts, thirteen of which are extant in Italy; all demonstrate a chancery context. Three examples are: Florence, Riccardian 1538; Biblioteca Vaticana, Chig. L.VII, 267; and Verona, Bibl. Capitolare, DXIX. For Pier delle Vigne see A. Huillard-Breholles, *Vie et correspondence de Pierre de la Vigne, ministre de l'empereur Frédéric II* (Paris: Plon, 1864); Pier delle Vigne, *Epistolarium quibus res gestae ejusdem imperatoris aliaque multa ad historiam ac jurisprudentiam spectantia continentur libri VI,* ed. J. Rudulph Iselms (Basel: Schard, 1740).

11. There was an Arabic genre, the "Book of Treasures," such as that written by Job of Edessa in A.D. 814; see F. E. Peters, *Aristotle and the Arabs* (New York: New York University Press, 1968), 70; Miguel Asín Palacios, *La escatalogía musulmana en la "Divina commedia,"* 3rd edn. (Madrid: Instituto Hispano-Arabe de Cultura, 1961), 384. See also M. Jourdain, *Récherches critiques sur l'âge et l'origine des traductions latines d'Aristote et sur des commentaires grecs ou arabes employés par les docteurs scholastiques* (Paris: Fantin, 1819). Because of one (late, paper) Venetian manuscript ascription of the translation into Italian to Bono Giamboni rather than to Latini, editors from the nineteenth century ascribed that text to Bono rather than Brunetto. The ascription is no longer accepted by Giamboni scholars; see Emilio Cecchi and Natalino Sapegno, *Storia della letteratura italiana* (Milan: Garzanti, 1965), 1: 605–15, and Cesare Segre and Mario Marti, *Prosa del duecento* (Milan: Ricciardi, 1959), 311. Manuscript study also shows that the *Tesoro* was produced by Latini himself.

12. Madeleine Dillay, "Une source latine de Brunetto Latini," in *Recueil des travaux offert à M. Clovis Brunel* (Paris: Société de l'Ecole des Chartes, 1955), 366–86. Alfraganus, *Il libro dell'aggregazione delle stelle: secondo il codice Mediceo laurenziano Plut. 29. cod. 9, contemporaneo di Dante,* ed. Romeo Campani (Città di Castello: Lapi, 1910). Jaime Ferreiro Alemparte, "Hermann el Alemán, traductor del siglo XIII en Toledo," *Hispania sacra* XXXV (1983): 9–48. See also the work of Asín Palacios (381–87), Cerulli, and Sepúlveda above in n. 1.

13. Goetz, "Brunetto Latini und die arabische Wissenschaft," *Deutsches Dante Jahrbuch* 21 (1939): 105; Latini, *Tresor* (Carmody edn.), xvii. Carmody, who belongs to the "debunking" school of scholarship, claims that there is no evidence in Brunetto's work of his visit to Spain: "Les ouvrages de Latini ne montrent aucune influence des lettres espagnoles, aucune connaissance du pays; du *Tesoretto* nous savons seulement que Latini a passé près de Roncevaux et par Montpellier."

14. *La cancelleria della repubblica fiorentina* (Rocca S. Casciano: Capelli, 1910), 35–48. Marzi is perhaps incorrect here, as the Primo Popolo did not centralize power, and we witness a rotation of notaries functioning in this manner, Latini not being the most prominent of them.

15. Manuscripts demonstrating this are Riccardian 1538 in Florence and Biblioteca Vaticana, Chig. L.VII.267, both of which include Latini's own letter as chancellor, written in Pier delle Vigne's style, addressed to Pavia on the occasion of the Florentines' murder of the Pavian abbot Tesoro of Vallombrosa. The Sicilian chancery, from the brilliant Norman tradition, combined Byzantine Greek bureaucracy with that of the Arab world, the chancellor being termed "logothete" and the system capable of functioning multilingually, sensitive to and thereby controlling all cultures in its midst. See Ernst Kantorowicz, *Federico II imperatore,* trans. Gianni Pilone Colombo (Milan: Garzanti, 1976).

16. Ferreiro Alemparte, *Hermann,* 24, quotes Alfonso X's *Partidas,* II.1.6: "e señaladamiente Aristotels en el libro que se llama Politica."

17. Florence, Biblioteca Nazionale, Mag. II.IV.127.

18. Especially true of the manuscripts in London, British Library, Addit. 30024, fol. 226v; 30025, fol. 72v; and in Carpentras, Bibl. Municipale, 269. See Julia Bolton Holloway, "Brunetto Latini and England," *Manuscripta* 31 (1987): 11–21, esp. 18.

19. "Bonacursius latinus de florencia dilecto filio Bornecto notario, ad excellentissimum dominum Alfonsum romanorum et hispanorum regem iamdudum pro comuni florentie destinato, salutem, et paterne dilectionis affectum. Mestam flebilis epistole paginam, quam forte videbis lituris multipliciter maculatam, defluens ab instrinsecus diluvium lacrimarum quas nec debebam nec poteram continere, scribentis faciem, pectus, et cartulam proluebat"; "te et alios guelfos et populares bannis perpetuis supponentes"; in D. Donati, "Lettere politiche del secolo XIII sulla guerra del 1260 fra Siena e Firenze," *Bullettino senese di storia patria* 3 (1896): 223, 230–32. Brunetto's father, "Bonaccursus Latinus de Lastra, imperiali auctoritate judex et notarius," compiled the *atti* of the *vescovado* of Fiesole (Davidsohn, *Firenze,* 3: 211).

20. Friedrich Wilhelm Schirrmacher, *Geschichte Castiliens im 12. und 13. Jahrhundert,* ed. Friedrich Wilhelm Lembke (Gotha: F. A. Perthes, 1881), 2: 476; *Tresor* (Carmody edn.), xv. Lodovigo Frati, "Brunetto Latini speziale," *Giornale dantesco* 22 (1914): 207–9. The Bonaccorsi family are later found as bankers at the court of King Robert of Naples, the Villani family associated with them, until the 1312 bankruptcy and expulsion from the kingdom; see Romolo Caggese, *Roberto d'Angiò e i suoi tempi* (Florence: Bemporad, 1922), 581–89 and passim. This may explain why both Latini and Villani chronicle not only Florentine but also Neapolitan and Sicilian history.

21. Arch. Seg. Vat., Instr. Miscell. 99 (Arras, 15 September, and Paris, 26 Octo-

ber 1263), published in M. Armellini, "Documento autografo di Brunetto Latini relativo ai ghibellini di Firenze scoperto negli archivi della S. Sede," *Rassegna italiana* 5 (1885): 360–63. Hans Foerster, *Mittelalterliche Buch und Urkundschriften auf 50 Tafeln mit Erlaüterungen und vollständiger Transkription* (Bern: Haupt, 1946), 64–65, plate XXXV. Bruno Katterbach and Carolus Silva-Tarouca, "Epistolae et instrumenti saeculi XIII," in *Exempla scriptorum edita consilio et opere procuratorum bibliothecae et tabularii Vaticane,* fasc. 2 (Rome: Biblioteca Apostolica Vaticana, 1930), 20, plate 21. Westminster Abbey Muniment 12843, unpublished (Bar-sur-Aube, 17 April 1264). Davidsohn, *Firenze,* 2: 607–9, 701, 741, 754; 3: 30.

22. Davidsohn, *Firenze,* 2: plate 33, reproduces the sculpture in Rome's Palazzo dei Conservatori. The letter occurs in *Tresor,* 3: 77 (Carmody edn., 396–97).

23. Davidsohn, *Firenze,* 2: 754; 3: 30. E. Jordan, *De mercatoribus camerae apostolicae saeculo XIII* (Paris: 1909), notes that the Florentine bankers named in the Brunetto documents—Thomas Spiliati, Hugo Spina, and others—are associated with Arras (25–30, 97).

24. Julia Bolton Holloway, *Brunetto Latini: An Analytic Bibliography* (London: Grant and Cutler, 1987), 20–32.

25. Paris, Bibl. Nat., lat. 6556, a Latin Alfraganus, written in Bolognan *libraria* typical of Brunetto's book-production workshop, speaks (fol. 2v) of *Asaph ebreum,* an *alfaquín* or Jewish court physician associated with its translation. Can anyone recall him as associated with Alfonso's court or another such manuscript ascribed to him? For Alfraganus in Dante (taught him by Latini) see Paget Toynbee, "Dante's Obligations to Alfraganus in the *Vita nuova* and *Convivio,*" *Romania* 24 (1895): 413–32; M. A. Orr (Mrs. John Evershed), *Dante and the Early Astronomers,* intro. Barbara Reynolds (London: Wingate, 1956 [1st edn. 1913]). See also my previous version in *Alfonso, Emperor,* which discusses Alfraganus material in greater depth.

26. In Berthold Weise's preface to his second edition of the *Tesoretto* (Strasbourg: Heitz and Mundel, 1909), Biblioteca Romanica, vols. 94–95. Mario Schiff, however, in *La Bibliothèque du Marquis de Santillane* (Paris: Bouillon, 1905), does not give any *Tesoretto* manuscripts, though citing other Latini manuscripts in Madrid. The librarians of the Biblioteca Nacional in Madrid note that thousands of their manuscripts are uncatalogued, and it could be among these.

27. For information on *Tesoretto* manuscripts, see *Il tesoretto* (Holloway edn.), xxviii–xxxv; and Holloway, *Brunetto Latini: Bibliography,* 16–19.

28. Madrid, Bibl. Nac., 10124, in Bolognan *libraria* with careful corrections to text, and a miniature. An awkward study of Latini manuscripts is Concetto Marchesi, "Il compendio volgare dell'Etica aristotelica e le fonti del VI libro del 'Tresor,'" *Giornale storico della letteratura italiana* 42 (1903): 1–74, who believed Latini's source manuscript was Laurenzian Gadd. 87, inf. 41, and assumed the manuscript's date to be 1243. Although 1243 was the date of its original translation which is repeated in this manuscript copy, the colophon to the whole manuscript, written in the same hand, gives 1313.

29. Taddeo Alderotti was an Averroist professor of medicine; see N. G. Siraisi, *Taddeo Alderotti and His Pupils: Two Generations of Italian Medical Learning* (Princeton: Princeton University Press, 1981), 77–82 and passim. An especially fine manuscript of Taddeo's *Consilia medicina* (Biblioteca Vaticana, lat. 2418, fol. 93) includes

material by Avicenna with Averroës's commentary and an illumination of a physician in a red gown examining a urinal. Its script is Bolognan *libraria*.

30. Paris, Bibl. Nat., 16581, giving Hermann the German's Latin translation of Aristotle's *Ethics* is written in Bolognan *libraria;* it has careful annotations to the text in a hand like Brunetto Latini's in holograph legal documents. Bibl. Nat., lat. 12954, has a note on its flyleaf in Brunetto Latini's hand that "this book [*Iste liber*] contains the book of Seneca and the book of Aristotle's Ethics." The texts are in Bolognan *libraria*, the *Ethics* noting that it was translated from Arabic into Latin by Taddeo, 9 April 1244. A third such text is at Arras. Thus, Brunetto had access to both translations into Latin in France.

31. Pier delle Vigne's style, also mocked by Dante in *Inferno*, XIII, employed outrageous biblical puns. Brunetto's letter puns upon Tesoro's name, bidding the Pavians not to lay up their treasure (*tesoro*) on earth but in heaven. He puns also upon *livres* as both books and money in the title *Li livres dou tresor*, and within it in the letter to Charles of Anjou. Dante puns upon Brunetto's name, having him browned and cooked beneath the flames of hell. See Bibl. Vat., Chig. L.VII, 267, fol. 111v–113, a manuscript having associations with Brunetto's son, notary to Robert of Sicily. See Chig. L.VII, 249, fol. 44–45v, and Riccardian 1538 for letter.

32. *Convivio*, I.10.70; *Paradiso*, XII, 83. Excellent discussions of Dante's *Vita nuova* and use of Averroism in connection with Brunetto Latini are to be found in Francesco Novati, "Il notaio nella vita e nella letteratura italiana delle origini," in *Freschi e minii del dugento* (Milan: Cogliati, 1925); Domenico de Robertis, *Il libro delle "Vita nuova,"* 2nd edn. (Florence: Sansoni, 1970). Guido Cavalcanti was also an Averroist and also Brunetto Latini's student.

33. Antonio García Solalinde, "El códice fiorentino de las Cantigas y su relación con los demás manuscritos," *RFE* 5 (1918): 143–79. John E. Keller and Richard P. Kinkade, "Iconography and Literature: Alfonso Himself in Cantiga 209," *Hispania* 66 (1983): 348–52 and plate. The manuscript was originally Palatine, then Magliabechian, today Banco Rari 20.

34. Arch. Seg. Vat., A. A. Arm. 1–18, n. 167, published in Katterbach and Silva-Tarouca, "Epistolae et instrumenta," table 22a. Other documents in Instr. Misc. 87, 1257/1268: "Articuli proposti a procuratoribus Alphonsi regis Castellae coram Clem. IV, ad probandum eius electionem in Regem Romanorum a nonnullis Electoribus Imperii facta an. 1257, contra Riccardum, fratrem Regis Angliae, qui ab aliis Electoribus inauguratus fuerat. Exemplar membr. 9 paginorum"; Instr. Misc. 56, 23 March 1276: "Innocentius PP V concedit Regi Castellae et Legionis ecclesiasticarum decimarum . . . pro subsidio contra Saracenos. Bulla orig. carens plumbo."

35. I was unable to see Biblioteca Colombina 5-1-6 (formerly, Vitrina VI?), which I had thought was French but is Castilian, as it is in restoration in Madrid. Spurgeon Baldwin tells me it is possibly thirteenth century. He and Charles Faulhaber appear to think there are two separate manuscripts, but the librarian insists these are the same one. The Real Academia Sevillana de Buenas Letras 13-3-18, is copied from it; it is late, and its ink is bleeding badly from current dampness, making much of its text illegible.

36. Frati, "Brunetto": 207–9.

37. ASF, *Liber Fabarum* I, fol. 49v, *Consulte della repubblica fiorentina dell' anno*

MCCLXXX al MCCXCVIII, ed. Alessandro Gherardi (Florence: Sansoni, 1896), I, 109.

38. They are to be found in the Isidore del Lungo appendix in Thor Sundby, *Della vita e delle opere di Brunetto Latini,* trans. Rodolfo Renier (Florence: Le Monnier, 1884), 200–77, extracted from *Consulte della repubblica* (Gherardi edn.), which in turn published the *Libri fabarum* from the Archivio di Stato di Firenze.

39. Villani, *Cronica,* 2: 22; 8: x. Filippo Villani, "Brunetto Latini rettorica," in *Le vite d'uomini illustri fiorentini* (Florence: Magheri, 1826), 32. I do not present them here, but other lives of Brunetto appear in archival manuscripts which also mention the Spanish embassy.

40. Ernesto Monaci, *Crestomazia italiana dei primi secoli* (Rome: Editrice Dante Alighieri, repr. 1955), 290–91. See Bibl. Vat., 3793, for *tenzoni* of Palamidesse Bellindoti, Guglielmo Beroardi, Rustico di Filippo, Brunetto Latini, and others.

41. Michele Amari, *La guerra del Vespro Siciliano,* 2 vols. (Paris: Baudry, 1845), 1: 200, gives Bartholomew of Neocastro's account in which a Ser Bonaccorso, one of Brunetto's banker relatives, goes so far as to fell the king "with a good shot from a ballista" artillery engine (*con bel tiro di mangano*) from the walls as the king seeks refuge in the church of Santa Maria in Messina, while a Latini *Tesoro* manuscript notes and praises this same Bartholomew of Neocastro's presence during the Sicilian Vespers; and a collection of Pier delle Vigne and Brunetto Latini letters (Bibl. Vat., Chig. L.VII, 267) includes the letter written from the commune of Palermo to that of Messina, couched in the most ringing rhetoric concerning freedom. It is of interest that Brunetto, the Ciceronian republican, should have associations both with Gianni di Procita, the Mario Savio of the Vespro Siciliano, and with Dante's relative, Giano della Bella, who played out a similar role in Florence. The square in Palermo where the Sicilian Vespers revolt commenced is next to that of Garibaldi's Risorgimento uprising.

42. Amari, *Altre narrazione del Vespro Siciliano scritte nel buon secolo della lingua* (Milan: Hoepli, 1887), 23–229, which publishes the Biblioteca Nazionale's *Tresor,* VIII, 1375.

43. San Daniele del Friuli, Biblioteca Communale, 238, fol. 42. Folio 45 discusses *il re de raona,* the king of Aragon; it elsewhere mentions the presence of Henry, brother of Alfonso el Sabio, "li romani et donno arrigo il filgliolo del re di castello il qualera sanatore di roma," who had been created such by Charles of Anjou in 1266 when in exile from Spain because of his treachery to Alfonso, but who then fought against Charles, receiving Conradin in Rome. See Steven Runciman, *I Vespri siciliani: storia del mondo mediterraneo alla fine del tredicesimo secolo,* trans. Pasquale Portoghese (Milan: Rizzoli, 1976); Amari, *Altre narrazione;* "Due croniche del Vespro in volgare siciliano del secolo XIII," ed. Enrico Sicardi, in *Raccolta degli storici italiani,* ed. Lodovico Antonio Muratori (Bologna: Zanichelli, 1917), 3–29; these accounts deserve comparison with that of Giovanni Villani.

44. Instr. Misc. 157–60, 592, 1276, 1278. See also Charles-Joseph Hefele, *Histoire des conciles,* trans. H. Leclercq, 10 vols. in 20 (Paris: Letouzey, 1907–1938), 6: 1, 153–270.

45. Isidoro Carini, *Gli archivi e le biblioteche di Spagna in rapporto alla storia d'Italia in generale e di Sicilia in particolare* (Palermo: Statuto, 1884), 2: 45–46;

register of Peter II, letter from Gi(ov)anni di Procida to Alfonso el Sabio (Alcira, 18 January 1281), fol. 115, another to Don Sancho (Valencia, 1 April 1282), fol. 117; (19 May 1282), fol. 118, etc.

46. In Barcelona: Arxiu d'Història de la Ciutat, MS Gremis 1/129; Biblioteca de Catalunya, MS 357; and Biblioteca Episcopal del Seminar Conciliar, MS 74 (with chronicle including Sicilian Vespers). Madrid, Biblioteca Nacional, MS 10.264. El Escorial, 234 (lost). Gerona, Archivo Catedral, 60. Further associations between Aragon, Sicily, and Florence can be gleaned from such documents as Rome, Biblioteca Angelica, B.VIII, 17; Palermo, Qq.G1, fols. 1–141v (where the lost Neapolitan Angevin archives, burnt in 1944, can be partly retrieved through copies of material relevant to Aragon and Sicily made by interested individuals, in the first instance by "Nicolas Cardinal Aragonie"); and the Bibliothèque Mazarine copy of the first printed edition of the *Tesoro* as splendidly illuminated with the arms of Aragon.

47. Barcelona, Biblioteca Episcopal del Seminar Conciliar, MS 74. Though dated as late as 1416, the manuscript copies faithfully conventions one finds in contemporaneous Brunetto Latini manuscripts: capitalization of *Rey* (King), yellow wash applied to small capitals, alternate red and blue of large ones, the careful inclusion of material concerning Alfonso of Castile, Conradin's death at Palermo, the Sicilian Vespers, and "Rey Carlo" (fols. lv–lviiii). It is also explicitly written to teach "Rey Don Jaime" Aragonese history and is bound with the third part of the *Tresor* in Catalan: "Assi comença lo libre del tresor de Mestre brunet lati qui parla de le ensenyaments de bona parleria." Beautifully written out in Brunetto Latini's manuscript style, it is of great interest. This Catalan text of *Tresor* III is published as *Libre dels enseynaments de bona parleria,* ed. Juan Codina y Formosa, 2 vols. (Barcelona: Real Academia de Buenas Letras, 1902–1903), 1: 181–85, 246–50, 315–23, 377–80; 2: 52–55, 94–103, 157–68, 203, 216, 279–87, 427–35, 475–83. The Aragonese chronicle likewise deserves publication. Curt J. Wittlin has published two of three volumes of the *Llibre del tresor: versiò catalana de Guillem de Copons,* 2 vols. (Barcelona: Barcino, 1971–1976), Els Nostres Clàssics, A (102, 111) of the Biblioteca de Catalunya, MS 357; it is reviewed by Francisco J. Hernández, *RCEH* 2 (1977–1978): 315–21. The Castilian version still lacks a complete edition.

48. Arch. Seg. Vat., Instr. Misc. 56 (23 March 1276): "Innocentius PP. IV concedit regi Castellae et Legionis ecclesiarcum decimarum . . . pro subsidio contra Saracenos. Bulla orig. carens plumbo."

49. See her "Brunetto Latini als Lehrer Dantis und der Florentiner (Mitteilungen aus Cod. II.VIII.36 der Florentiner National Bibliothek)," *Archivio italiano per la storia della pietà,* 2 (1959): 171–89; also in her *Politics and Culture in Medieval Spain and Italy* (Rome: Edizione di Storia e Letteratura, 1971), 515–61. Besides giving parts of the *Ethics* and the *Politics,* this manuscript also has astronomical material, a horoscope (there is a tradition that Brunetto cast Dante's), and the notarial formulary the *Sommetta* (which is dated around 1286–1287).

50. Fol. 75rv: "Como lo papa scrive a li Re et a le Reine [*rubric*]. [Paragraph sign] Gregorio vescovo servo di servi di dio Al preclaro et amato figliuolo lodoyco Re di francia. Al preclaro et amato figliuolo Anfonso Re di castella. Al preclaro et amato figliuolo Adoardo Re dinghilterre. Al preclaro et amato Jacomo Re dara-

gone . . . Al preclaro et amato figliuolo Karolo. Re di sicilia." He adds that, when writing to queens, the forms are changed from masculine to feminine.

51. "Come lo papa scrive a Vescovi et a li arcivescovi [*rubric*]. Gregorio vescovo. Al venerabile frate in xpo. R. archivescovo di Pisa. Al venerabile frate in xpo. O. vescovo di Luccha."

52. *The Spread of Italian Humanism* (London: Hutchinson, 1964), 35. Pier delle Vigne had similarly been chancellor and professor, establishing the tradition; see Armando Petrucci, *Notarii: documenti per la storia del notariato italiano* (Milan: Guiffre, 1958), 17. The contemporary tradition that Brunetto was Dante's teacher, stated by Dante himself, was debunked by Vittorio Imbriani, "Che Brunetto Latini non fu maestro di Dante," *Studi danteschi* (Florence: Sansoni, 1891), 335–80; but this was most ably countered by Novati in "Il notaio nella vita," 269–76, and in *Le Epistole, conferenza letta de Francesco Novati nella Sala di Dante in Orsanmichele* (Florence: Sansoni, 1905).

53. Verona, Bibl. Capitolare, DVIII.

54. The Biblioteca de Palacio MS has: "Questo libro si chiama il tesoro maggiore il quale fu composto per ser Burnecto latini di firençe. Scripsit anno mcccxxxiii." See Spurgeon Baldwin, *The Medieval Castilian Bestiary* (Exeter, England: University of Exeter, 1982). *Catálogo de los manuscritos catalanes, valencianos, gallegos y portugeses de la biblioteca de El Escorial,* ed. E. J. Zarco Cuevas (Madrid: Tip. de Archivos, 1932). Charles Faulhaber, "Retóricas clásicas y medievales en bibliotecas castellanas," *Abaco* 4 (1973): 151–300. A. R. D. Pagden, "The Diffusion of Aristotle's Moral Philosophy in Spain, ca. 1400–ca. 1600," *Traditio* 31 (1975): 287–373. Francisco López Estrada, "Sobre la difusión del 'Tesoro' de Brunetto Latini en España," *Gesammelte Aufsätze zur Kulturgeschichte Spaniens* 16 (1960): 137–52 (which only discusses the manuscript in the Real Academia Sevillana de Buenas Letras, 13-3-18).

55. Ferreiro Alemparte, "Hermann el Alemán," 17: "Aqui comiença el libro del tesoro que fabla di muchas nobles cosas, el qual fiso e compuso el muy noble e muy virtuoso rrey don Alfonso de Castilla el qual se partio en tres libros o partes." It should be noted that the Salamancan manuscripts did not originate there but were given to the university from the royal collection, with the bookplate of the Emperor Napoleon as ruler of Spain. Biblioteca Nacional MS 3380 does have a Salamanca connection but is an odd forgery, purporting to have been written by Alfonso VI in 1065.

56. Ferreiro Alemparte, "Hermann el Alemán," 15 (Real Academia Sevillana de Buenas Letras, 13-3-18): "Aqui comiença el libro del thesoro que traslado maestre Brunete de latyn en rromance frances, et el muy noble don Sancho fijo del muy noble Rey don Alfonso . . . mando trasladar de frances en lenguaje castellano a maestre Alfonso de Paredes fissico del jnfante don Ferrandod . . . e a Pascual Gomez escriuano del Rey sobre dicho e fabla de la nobleza de todas las cosas."

57. Alan Deyermond and John K. Walsh, "Enrique de Villena como poeta y dramaturgo: bosquejo de una polémica frustrada," *NRFE* 28 (1979): 57–85. A. Labandeira Fernández, "Un cronista español del siglo XV entre la ciencia de Brunetto Latini y la nobleza de Suero de Quiñones," *RABM* 79 (1976): 73–95. Antonio Torres-Alcalá, *Don Enrique de Villena* (Washington: Catholic University Press, 1983).

58. Marvin B. Becker, "The Communal Paideia and Emerging Humanism," *Florence in Transition* (Baltimore: Johns Hopkins University Press, 1967), 34, 35, 42, 60, mentions Brunetto Latini and speaks throughout of the importance of Cicero and Aristotle in Italian communes, not stressing that it was Latini who translated these two authors into the Italian vernacular precisely for the purposes of communal government. My work on Brunetto Latini was greatly shaped by Quentin Skinner, *The Renaissance* (Cambridge: Cambridge University Press, 1978), vol. I, in his *Foundations of Modern Political Thought.* My thanks to Professor Southern for his gift of "Dante and Islam," *Relations between East and West in the Middle Ages,* ed. Derek Baker (Edinburgh: Edinburgh University Press, 1973), 133–45, and to Professor Aaron Sayvetz for his "On the Alfonsine Astronomical Tables," *Romance Quarterly* 33 (1986): 343–47.

CHAPTER NINE

1. See particularly Solalinde, "Intervención de Alfonso X en la redacción de sus obras," in ch. 7 above, n. 2. This classic article should be complemented by Gonzalo Menéndez Pidal, "Como trabajaron las escuelas alfonsíes" (above in ch. 5, n. 5), 363–80.

2. Both versions can be found in *Alfonso X, el Sabio. Antología,* ed. A. G. Solalinde (Madrid: Espasa-Calpe, 1941); reprinted many times since, e.g., as no. 169 in Colección Austral (Madrid: Espasa-Calpe, 1965).

3. The beautiful Escorial manuscript was published in full-size, eight-color facsimile in 1979 (see above, ch. 4, n. 2); it is now out of print and rare.

4. Snow, "The Troubadour Persona of Alfonso X" (see above, ch. 6, n. 19), 314.

5. Two such studies are Snow, "Alfonso's Personal Narrative," 10–21; and "Self-Conscious References and the Organic Narrative Pattern of the *Cantigas de Santa Maria,*" in *Medieval, Renaissance and Folklore Studies in Honor of John Esten Keller* (Newark, Del.: Juan de la Cuesta, 1981), 53–66.

6. This major point is discussed in all its ramifications in J. T. Snow, "Alfonso X y/en sus *Cantigas,*" *Jornadas de estudios alfonsíes* (Granada: Universidad de Granada, 1985), 71–90.

7. In addition to the pioneering studies of Milá y Fontanals, Gonzalo Menéndez Pidal, and C. Michaëlis, the modern scholar will want to consult the valuable companion-volumes of Carlos Alvar, *La poesía trovadoresca en España y Portugal* (Madrid: Cupsa [Planeta], 1977), and *Textos trovadorescos sobre España y Portugal* (Madrid: Cupsa [Planeta], 1978).

8. For the full text, see the edition by Fidel Fita, "Biografías de San Fernando y de Alfonso el Sabio por Gil de Zamora," *BRAH* 5 (1884): 308–28.

9. These very important texts of Riquier have been studied usefully by V. Bertolucci Pizzorusso, "La supplica de Guiraut Riquier e la risposta di Alfonso X di Castiglia," *Studi mediolatini e volgari* 14 (1966): 9–135, and E. Vuolo, "Per il testo della supplica de Guiraut Riquier ad Alfonso X," *Studi medievali,* 3rd series, 9 (1968): 729–806.

10. See Alvar, *La poesía,* 181–258.

11. This early version, known as *To* or *Tol* (for Toledo, and actually in the Biblioteca Nacional in Madrid), establishes the framing story. For all quotations

from the *Cantigas,* I will be citing the texts from Mettmann's edition (see above, ch. 4, n. 1). All English translations are my own.

12. See A. G. Solalinde, "El códice florentino de las *Cantigas* y su relación con los demás manuscritos," *RFE* 5 (1918): 176.

13. For an absorbing account of how a statue of Mary was imagined to have done the same for an unnamed king (Alfonso?), see cantiga 295.

14. Author of a notable paean to Mary, the "Vera vergena, Maria," in *Anthology of the Provençal Troubadours,* ed. R. T. Hill et al., 2nd edn. (New Haven: Yale University Press, 1973), I: 209–10.

15. See J. T. Snow, "Alfonso X y la *Cantiga* 409: un nexo posible con la tradición de la *Dança de la muerte,*" in *Studies in Honor of Lloyd A. Kasten* (Madison, Wisc.: Hispanic Seminary of Medieval Studies, 1975), 261–73.

16. This posture was suggested by A. da Costa Pimpão, *Idade média,* vol. 1 in his *Historia da literatura portuguesa,* 2nd edn. (Coimbra, Portugal: Atlântida, 1959), 71–72, as motivation for Alfonso X's famous criticism of Pero da Ponte: "vos non trobades come Proençal, mais come Bernart de Bonaval." Alfonso, the thinking goes, having achieved the transition to the plane of the spiritual troubadour, following a trend among the latter-day Provençal poets, is chiding Pero, a famed older poet, for preferring to continue composing in the secular vein of the more popular and raucous genres of verse-making. If this proves to be an appealing reading of this line, it will give added support to what the Alfonso persona is expressing also in the embedded narrative of the *Cantigas.*

CHAPTER TEN

1. The manuscripts selected for this study are: *Primera crónica general,* in Biblioteca de El Escorial, X-I-4, and in Biblioteca del Palacio Nacional II-429 (ant. 2-E-4); *Crónica de Castilla,* in Bibliothèque Nationale, Paris, 12; *Crónica de veinte reyes,* in Biblioteca de El Escorial, Y-i-12; *Crónica manuelina interpolada,* Biblioteca Nacional, Madrid, 6441; *Crónica ocampiana,* Biblioteca del Palacio Real, Madrid, 1877. Some of the microfilm and typescripts of the manuscripts used in this study were provided by the Cátedra-Seminario Menéndez Pidal in Madrid. With research grants and travel money from Texas A&M University and the American Council for Learned Societies, I consulted all the original manuscripts in the summers of 1978, 1984, and 1986.

Four published chronicle texts were particularly consulted: (1) *Primera crónica general,* ed. Ramón Menéndez Pidal (as above in ch. 2, n. 4); quotations from this edition cite page, column, and line, for example (685b42–47). (2) *Crónica geral de Espanha de 1344,* ed. Luis Filipe Lindley Cintra, 3 vols. (Lisbon: Academia Portuguesa da História, 1951–1961). (3) *Las quatro partes enteras de la Crónica de España que mando componer el serenissimo rey don Alonso llamado el sabio,* ed. Florian de Ocampo (Zamora, Spain: 1541). (4) *Crónica abreviada,* in Don Juan Manuel, *Obras completas,* ed. José Manuel Blecua, 2 vols. (Madrid: Gredos, 1983), 505–817, esp. 781–94.

For a study of Alfonso's material conquest, see R. A. MacDonald, "Law and Politics: Alfonso's Program of Political Reform," in *Worlds of Alfonso,* 150–202.

2. A. J. Minnis, *Medieval Theory of Authorship: Scholastic Literary Attitudes in the Later Middle Ages* (London: Scolar Press, 1984), 5. See also Rita Copeland's review article, "Literary Theory in Later Middle Ages," *Romance Philology* 41 (1987): 58–71, esp. 64–65.

3. Diego Catalán, "El taller historiográfico alfonsí: métodos y problemas en el trabajo compilatorio," *Romania* 84 (1963): 358. Diego Catalán, "Poesía y novela en historiografía castellana de los siglos XIII y XIV," in *Mélanges offerts à Rita Lejeune*, 2 vols. (Gembloux, Belgium: J. Duculot, 1966), 1: 423–41.

4. Catalán, "Taller," 362–63, 365.

5. For an excellent review of the evolution of the relationship between historical narrative and literature, see Lionel Gossman, "History and Literature: Reproduction or Signification," in *The Writing of History: Literary Form and Historical Understanding,* ed. Robert H. Canary and Henry Kozicki (Madison, Wisc.: University of Wisconsin Press, 1978), 3–39. A checklist of works on Alfonsine historiography is included in Daniel Eisenberg's "Alfonsine Prose: Ten Years of Research," *La corónica* 11 (1983): 220–30.

6. Harry Elmer Barnes, *A History of Historical Writing,* 2nd edn. rev. (New York: Dover Publications, 1963), 64.

7. Hayden White, "The Value of Narrativity in the Representation of Reality," *Critical Inquiry* 7 (1980): 10 (emphasis in original).

8. Ibid., 13–15 (emphasis in original).

9. Barnes, *Historical Writing,* 65 (annals). White, "Narrativity," 20 (quote).

10. White, "The Historical Text as Literary Artifact," in *Writing of History,* 48. In contemporary perspective, this question is treated differently by Roger G. Seamon, "Narrative Practice and the Theoretical Distinction between History and Fiction," *Genre* 16 (1983): 197–218. A fuller exposition of White's model, a culmination of his earlier *Metahistory* (1973) and *Tropics of Discourse* (1978), is his *The Content of the Form: Narrative Discourse and Historical Representation* (Baltimore: Johns Hopkins University Press, 1987).

11. White, "Narrativity" 7.

12. White, "Historical Text," 49.

13. Edward Said, *The World, the Text and the Critic* (Cambridge, Mass.: Harvard University Press, 1983), 4.

14. Ramón Menéndez Pidal, "Tradicionalidad de las Crónicas Generales de España," *BRAH* 136 (1955): 131–97. Diego Catalán, "Don Juan Manuel ante el modelo alfonsí," in *Don Juan Manuel Studies,* ed. Ian Macpherson (London: Tamesis, 1977), 28, esp. n. 38.

15. Diego Catalán, "España en su historiografía: de objeto a sujeto de la historia," in Ramón Menéndez Pidal, *Los españoles en la historia* (Madrid: Espasa-Calpe, 1982), 16–37.

16. E. Benítez Ruano, "La historiografía en la alta edad media española," *Cuadernos de historia de España* 17 (1952): 97.

17. Ramón Menéndez Pidal, *Reliquias de la poesía épica española,* 2nd edn. (Madrid: Gredos, 1980), xliii, xliv, xlix.

18. Ramón Menéndez Pidal, *La España del Cid,* 7th edn. (Madrid: Espasa-Calpe, 1966), 5.

19. Diego Catalán, *Crónica del moro Rasis,* Fuentes Cronísticas de la Historia de España, vol. 3 (Madrid: CSMP/Gredos, 1975), xxix–xxx; also in Catalán, "España," 31.

20. Gonzalo Menéndez Pidal, "Como trabajaron las escuelas alfonsíes," *NRFH* 5 (1951): 363–80; Antonio G. Solalinde, "Intervención de Alfonso X en la redacción de sus obras," *RFE* 2 (1915): 283–88.

21. Diego Catalán, *De Alfonso X al conde de Barcelos* (Madrid: Gredos, 1962), 91–92.

22. Catalán, "Taller," 357–58. My translation.

23. Said, *World,* 52.

24. For what follows, consult the list of manuscript and source citations above in n. 1.

25. Ed. Agapito Rey, Humanities Series, vol. 24 (Bloomington: Indiana University Press, 1952).

26. Catalán, "Juan Manuel," 28, esp. n. 38.

27. Ibid., 38–39.

28. Lorenzo de Sepúlveda, *Romances nuevamente sacadas de las historias antiguas* (Antwerp: Casa de Iuan Steelsio, 1551).

29. For a biographical study of Alfonso VIII, see Julio González, *El reino de Castilla en la época de Alfonso VIII,* 2 vols. (Madrid: Consejo Superior de Investigaciones Científicas, 1960).

30. MacDonald, "Law," 151, 170.

31. *Chronicon mundi,* in *Crónica de España,* ed. Julio Puyol (Madrid: Real Academia de la Historia, 1926), 409, 414 (quotations). Scholars who pursue this subject may be interested in the curious fact that the earliest Castilian translation of the *Chronicon mundi* has a lacuna where the reign of Alfonso VIII should appear.

32. Doña Blanca's death appears in the *Crónicas navarras,* ed. Antonio Ubieto Arteta, Textos medievales, vol. 14 (Valencia: Anubar, 1964), 42.

33. Rodrigo Jiménez de Rada, *De rebus Hispaniae,* in his *Opera,* ed. F. A. (Cardinal) de Lorenzana, 3 vols. (Madrid: Vidua Ioachimi Ibarra, 1782–1793), 3: 158–59. I am indebted to Professor Diego Catalán and the Seminario Menéndez Pidal in Madrid for a xerox copy of this work.

34. *De rebus,* 159a.

35. Ibid., 160b.

36. Georges Cirot, "Anecdotes ou légendes sur l'époque d'Alphonse VIII," *Bulletin hispanique* 29 (1927): 253.

37. For a study of this formula, see B. Dutton, "Fórmulas épicas en la literatura hispánica," in *Juglaresca,* ed. M. Criado de Val (Madrid: Edi 16, 1986), 144–45.

38. Diego Catalán, "El Toledano Romanzado y las estorias del fecho de los godos del s. XV," in *Estudios dedicados a James Homer Herriott* (Madison, Wisc.: University of Wisconsin Press, 1966), 9–10.

39. *Primera crónica general,* end of section 991. *Crónica abreviada,* chs. 199–203 in Blecua edn., 2: 782–83.

40. Fol. 15v: "E porque tenemos que le pertenesçe mucho que (fueron); non podia ser conplida si esto non y fuese puesto. E porque sabemos por prueuas destas escripturas que esto fue asi e que es çierto, por ende ponemoslo aqui en la estoria en

los logares convenibles, non menguando nin cresçiendo ninguna de los rrazones que el arçobispo don Rodrigo, nin de don Lucas Obispo de Tuy, nin los otros sabios e omes honrrados y pusieron."

41. This manuscript is Biblioteca Nacional, Madrid, 10134 bis (ant. Ii, unnumbered) described in Catalán, *De Alfonso X*, 42–43, nn. 15–16.

42. Carlos Alvar, *La poesía trovadoresca en España y Portugal* (Barcelona: Planeta/Real Academia de Buenas Letras de Barcelona, 1977), 78.

43. *Primera crónica general*, 685b42–7: "por el peccado que feziste con la judia et dexauas la reyna tu muger por ella, quisotelo Dios calomiar . . . et por esso fuste uençudo en la batalla de Alarcos. . . . Quando el rey don Alfonso ouo oydo esto, fico muy triste en so coraçon, repentiendose mucho de sus peccados, et de alli adelante puso de facer el monesterio de Burgos et el ospital."

44. Edna Aizenberg, "*Una judia muy fermosa:* The Jewess as Sex Object in Medieval Spanish Literature and Lore," *La corónica* 12 (1984): 187–94.

CHAPTER ELEVEN

1. Alfonso's text reads: "Otrosi mandamos, que todos los libros de los *Cantares de loor de Sancta Maria* sean todos en aquella iglesia do nuestro cuerpo se enterrare, e que los fagan cantar las fiestas de Sancta Maria. E si aquel que lo nuestro heredare con derecho e por nos, quisiere haber estos libros de los *Cantares de Sancta Maria,* mandamos que faga por ende bien et algo a la iglesia onde los tomare porque los haya con merced e sin pecado." See Alfonso X, *Antología* (ed. A. G. Solalinde, Madrid: Espasa-Calpe, 1942, Colección Austral, vol. 169), 236.

The books to which Alfonso referred comprise the four extant codices of *Cantigas de Santa Maria* (see above, ch. 4, n. 1). Two of them are located at the Biblioteca de San Lorenzo el Real at El Escorial near Madrid (B.I.2 [formerly j.b.2] and T.I.1 [formerly T.j.1], respectively), a third at the Biblioteca Nacional, Madrid (B.N. MS 10.069), and the fourth at the Biblioteca Nazionale, Florence (MS Banco Rari 20). Alfonso had the latter version prepared as a gift to his cousin, Louis IX of France (Keller, *Alfonso X,* 69). All but the Florentine codex bear musical notations; however, only its staff lines had been inscribed, examples of which can be seen for cantigas 1 and 14 in two plates supplied by Solalinde in his description of this codex. See Solalinde, "El códice florentino de las *Cantigas* y su relación con los demás manuscritos," *RFE* 5 (1918): insert between 152–53.

The cantigas *de loor,* which are the songs sung in praise of the Virgin Mary, begin with cantiga 1, after which, commencing with cantiga 10, they constitute every tenth cantiga throughout the remainder of the collection. These have been studied by Joseph T. Snow in his "The *Loor* to the Virgin and Its Appearance in the *Cantigas de Santa Maria* of Alfonso X, el Sabio" (Ph.D. diss., University of Wisconsin, 1972). In Codex B.I.2, each of the cantigas *de loor* bear the miniatures of the instrumentalists as their initial vignettes.

2. José M. Llorens Cisteró, "La música," in El *"Códice Rico" de las Cantigas de Alfonso el Sabio,* supplementary volume to the facsimile edition of the Escorial manuscript (see above, ch. 4, n. 2), 321–96, opinion on 331.

3. Ibid.

4. Keller, in *Studies on the Cantigas* (see above, ch. 1, n. 2), 11.

5. Robert Stevenson undertook an investigation of the cathedral's *actas capitulares catedralicias* for the years 1478 through 1606 by extracting information linking the musical life of the incipient cathedral of Mexico with that of the cathedral of Seville, upon which it was modeled (cf. *La Música en la Catedral de Sevilla, 1478–1606: Documentos para su estudio,* 2nd. edn. [Madrid: Sociedad Española de Musicología, 1985]). In his extractions, no mention is made of musical performances, even for the few entries coinciding with the feast days of the Virgin.

6. Codex T.I.1, fol. 5, cantiga 8 (panels 1–5, depicting the minstrel Pedro Desigrad); cantiga *de loor* 100 (panel 6, depicting angels singing, while a consort, comprising instruments of Eastern origin, accompanies them); cantiga 194 (panel 2), cantiga *de loor* 120 (panel 1), and Codex B.I.2, fol. 29v.

7. Ismael Fernández de la Cuesta studied both the intervals and ambitus of the *Cantigas* melodies in his "La interpretación melódica de las *Cantigas de Santa María,*" in *Studies on the Cantigas,* 155–88. Gerardo V. Huseby, in "The 'Cantigas de Santa Maria' and the Medieval Theory of Modes" (Ph.D. diss., Stanford University, 1982), studied their modes. The controversies concerning their rhythm were taken up by J. M. Llorens Cisteró, in "El ritmo musical de las *Cantigas de Santa Maria:* estado de la cuestión," *Studies on the Cantigas,* 203–21. Huseby added a further contribution, "Musical Analysis and Poetic Structure in the *Cantigas de Santa Maria,*" in *Florilegium Hispanicum: Medieval and Golden Age Studies Presented to Dorothy Clotelle Clarke,* ed. John S. Geary, et al. (Madison, Wisc.: Hispanic Seminary of Medieval Studies, 1983), 81–101. For a classic study regarding their versification, see Dorothy Clotelle Clarke, "Versification in Alfonso el Sabio's *Cantigas,*" *Hispanic Review* 23 (1955): 83–98.

8. See my article, "Higinio Anglés and the Melodic Origins of the *Cantigas de Santa Maria,*" in *Alfonso X the Learned King—An International Symposium, Harvard University, 17 November 1984,* ed. Francisco Márquez Villanueva (Cambridge, Mass.: Studies in Romance Languages Series, Harvard University, 1989), 46–75.

9. *Folk Music and Poetry of Spain and Portugal,* with an introduction on Kurt Schindler and his Spanish work (in English and Spanish) by Federico de Onís (New York: Hispanic Institute, 1941). Onís, then chairman of the Spanish department at Columbia University, supervised the final editing of Schindler's field notations. Concerning its publication, see my article "The Posthumous Publication of Kurt Schindler's *Folk Music and Poetry of Spain and Portugal* (New York, 1941)," in *Libraries, History, Diplomacy, and the Performing Arts; Essays in Honor of Carleton Sprague Smith,* ed. Israel J. Katz (Stuyvesant, N.Y.: Pendragon, forthcoming).

10. The second field trip took place between July 1932 and December 1933, under the auspices of Columbia University. The first trip, which took place between the fall of 1928 and fall of 1931, was unsponsored.

11. Schindler, *Folk Music and Poetry,* 18.

12. Devoto, "Sobre la música tradicional española," *RFE* 5 (1943): 344–66, esp. 352, n. 1. Reprinted in Devoto, *Las hojas (1940–1949)* (Buenos Aires: Aldabahor, 1950): 24–48, esp. 36, n. 18.

13. *Les Chansons à la Vierge de Gautier de Coinci (1177/78–1236),* ed. Jacques Chailley (Paris: Huegel, 1959), 45, n. 1.

14. Katz, "The Traditional Folk Music of Spain: Explorations and Perspectives," *Yearbook of the International Folk Music Council* 6 (1974): 64–85, esp. 78. The other transcriptions were made by (1) Pierre Aubry, "Iter Hispanicum. Notices et extraits de manuscrits de musique ancienne conservés dans les bibliothèques d'Espagne. III. Les Cantigas de Santa Maria de don Alfonso el Sabio," *Sammelbänder der internationalen Musik-Gesellschaft* 9 (1907): 32–51, esp. 43; (2) Julián Ribera Tarragó, *La música de las Cantigas: estudio sobre su origen y naturaleza,* with photographic reproductions of the text and in modern transcription, volume three of *Las Cantigas de Santa Maria,* Real Academia Española edn. (Madrid: Revista de Archivos, 1922), 127–28; (3) John Brande Trend, *The Music of Spanish History to 1600* (Oxford: Oxford University Press, 1926), 206 (after Aubry); and (4) Higinio Anglés, taken from Gustave Reese, *Music in the Middle Ages* (New York: W. W. Norton, 1940), 247.

15. Manuel Pedro Ferreira, *The Sound of Martin Codax: On the Musical Dimension of the Galician-Portuguese Lyric (XII–XIV Century)* (Lisbon: Unisys, Imprensa Nacional—Casa da Moeda, 1986), bilingual edition, 190. Facing Schindler's transcription (which he transposed down a major 2nd), Ferreira provided his own of cantiga 10, from the Toledo codex, which he presumed to be the oldest of the extant codices.

16. Luis P. Villalba Muñoz, *Cántigas a la Inmaculada Virgen María: cantiga X de el rey D. Alfonso el Sabio* (Madrid: Ildefonso Alier, 190?).

17. Keller, "An Unknown Castilian Lyric Poem: The Alfonsine Translation of *Cantiga X* of the *Cantigas de Santa Maria,*" *Hispanic Review* 43 (1975): 43–47. Keller discovered the poem among the Castilian prosifications of the first twenty-six cantigas, which, according to recent investigations, could have been made during the reign of Sancho IV (1284–1295), by Sancho himself, or by Alfonso's nephew, Juan Manuel (1282–1348/49), or perhaps much later. For a discussion of the prosifications, see Anthony Cárdenas, "A Study of Alfonso's Role in Selected *Cantigas* and the Castilian Prosifications of Escorial Codex T.I.1," in *Studies on the Cantigas,* 248–68.

18. Compare Keller's textual transcription with that of José Filgueira Valverde, *Alfonso X el Sabio. Cantigas de Santa María* (Madrid: Editorial Castalla, 1985), 352. For modern Castilianized versions, see Angel del Río, *Antología general de la literatura española* (New York: Holt, Rinehart and Winston, 1960), 1: 50–51, and Filgueira Valverde, *Alfonso: Cantigas,* 29. See also the instructive comments on the text by Augusto J. Magne, "Afonso X, o Sábio. Excerptos anotados," *Revista da lingua portuguesa* 8/44 (1926): 55–110, esp. 68–69.

19. The text is taken from Walter Mettmann, *Alfonso X, el Sabio. Cantigas de Santa Maria (cantigas 1 a 100)* (Madrid: Editorial Castalia, 1986), 84–85. Mettmann, "Die altportugiesische Marienlyrik vor 1300," in *Grundriss der romanischen Literaturen des Mittelalters,* ed. H. H. Jauss (Heidelberg: Carl Winter, 1968), 18, cites *Sennor* and *Sennor das Sennores* among the most traditional names and Marian epithets and refers to the phrases of the first textual strophe "Rosa das rosas, etc." as Hebrew superlatives.

20. This was given to me as a gift by Hugh Ross, Schindler's successor at the Schola Cantorum.

21. For other free as well as literal English translations, see (1) Robert Eisenstein, *Program notes* for the Folger Consort's program "A Medieval Tapestry" presented at Corpus Christi church (New York, Sunday, 27 November 1983), 5; (2) Kathleen Kulp-Hill, *Cantigas* (see above, ch. 4, n. 13), 109; (3) Lorraine Noel Finney, in Reese, *Music in the Middle Ages*, 248; (4) *Medieval Lyrics of Europe*, ed. Willard R. Trask (New York: World Publishing Co., 1969), 130; and (5) Américo Castro, *The Structure of Spanish History*, trans. Edmund L. King (Princeton: Princeton University Press, 1954), 362.

22. Officially, his final concert with the Schola Cantorum took place ten days later at the high school auditorium in Summit, New Jersey.

23. This certainly is not true. During Alfonso's reign (1252–1284), there was no fixed capital. Seville, however, was the most favored city of the court.

24. He is referring here to *Las Cantigas de Santa Maria de Alfonso el Sabio*, ed. Leopoldo Augusto de Cueto, Marqués de Valmar, 2 vols. (Madrid: Real Academia Española, 1889).

25. Schindler was ignorant of the existence of the four extant *Cantigas* codices. At the Hispanic Society, the former work can be seen in a photographic copy under the call name *Cantigas de Santa Maria* MS T.j.1 (Escorial thirteenth century). It is the only *Cantigas* codex for which photocopies exist. The latter, the Vatican compilation, to which Schindler alluded, may be that of the *Cancioneiro de Vaticana* (Vatican MS 4803), which does not contain any of the *Cantigas de Santa Maria*, but rather fifteen of Alfonso's cantigas *profanas* (nos. 61–79), some of which are cantigas *de mal-dezir* or *mal-decir*, i.e., "cántigas en las que se maldice de algo, sino cántigas escritas con palabras obsenas, género que cultivaban la mayoría de los trovadores gallego-portugueses, incluso el piadoso D. Alfonso X el Sabio" (Eugenio López Aydillo, *Las mejores poesías gallegas* [Madrid: Imprenta Artística Española, 1914], 173, n. 9). There are no photographic reproductions of this work at the Hispanic Society. See also Francisco Márquez Villanueva, "Las lecturas del deán de Cádiz en una *cantiga de mal dizer*," in *Studies on the Cantigas*, 329–54.

26. Schindler created an eight-part setting *a cappella*, with soprano and baritone as narrators, to open the first Spanish concert of the New York Schola Cantorum at Carnegie Hall, Tuesday evening, 15 January 1918. The arrangement was based on Pujol's transcription, which was printed in Lluís Millet's article, "The Religious Folk-Song of Spain," printed in the *Actas* of the Third National Congress of Sacred Music, held in Barcelona in November 1912. Schindler's arrangement, according to the program notes (p. 3) of 10 March 1926 was also "sung in Madrid by a chorus of four hundred voices under the direction of Padre Nemesio Otaño on the Tercentenary of the death of Saint Ignacio de Loyola." Had this been the occasion, the year should have been 1856, for Ignacio died in 1556. Pujol's transcription of the tune can also be found in Trend, *Music of Spanish History*, 205.

27. See Anglés, "Les 'Cantigues' del rey N'Anfós el Savi," *Vida cristiana* (Barcelona) 14 (1926–1927) nos. 109–16: 1–64.

28. Sunyol, "Cantigues de Montserrat del rei Anfós X, dit 'el Savi'," *Analecta montserratensia* 5 (1924): 361–417. Fernández Núñez, "Las canciones populares y la tonalidad medieval, aclaraciones a la obra *Las Cantigas de Santa María* escrita por D. Julián Ribera," *La Ciudad de Dios* 138 (1924): 273–83, 343–52; 139 (1924): 33–38,

97–110, 353–60; 140 (1925): 102–13; 141 (1925): 426–35; 142 (1925): 422–34; and 143 (1925): 134–45, 209–21: reprinted as a booklet (El Escorial: Monasterio de Escorial, 1924–1925). The article of Fernández Núñez, which contains a more vehement attack, is poorly documented.

29. See Cueto, above in n. 24.

30. For Aubry see above, n. 14. Collet and Villalba, "Contribution à l'étude des *Cantigas* d'Alphonse le Savant d'après les codices de l'Escurial," *Bulletin hispanique* 13 (1911): 270–90.

31. Discussed in Katz, "Anglés and Melodic Origins," 61–63.

32. The call number for the notebook is M. 3881/8. "Rosa das rosas" can be found on folio 3r. It is unfortunate that I was unable to photocopy the melody. See the commentary of Anglés and José Subirá, *Catálogo musical de la Biblioteca nacional de Madrid*, 1: *Manuscritos* (Barcelona: Instituto Español de Musicología, 1946), 281–83. See also Anglés, *La música*, 2: 16–17, n. 2.

33. Soriano Fuertes, *Historia de la música española desde la venida de los fenicios hasta el año 1850* (Madrid: Martín y Salazar, 1855), 1: 109ff. and the *apéndice musical*. He claimed to have taken them from the so-called *Cancionero de Marialva*, which belonged to D. Francisco Contiño, Conde de Marialva, and which to date has not been located. See Anglés/Subirá, *Catálogo musical*, 1: 281–83, and Anglés, *La música*, 2: 16–17, n. 2.

34. Hilarión Eslava, *Cantiga 14 del rey don Alfonso el Sabio, parafraseada con coros y orquesta* (Madrid: Fétis, [1861?]). Joseph Snow, *The Poetry of Alfonso X, El Sabio: A Critical Bibliography* (London: Grant and Cutler, 1977), no. 31, who did not see this composition, cites (Antonio) Palau (y Dulcet), *Manual [del librero hispano-americano*, 2nd edn. (Barcelona: A. Palau, 1948)], 1: 206, where it is listed as item 7136. Snow (no. 71) also suggested that Felipe Pedrell's *Seis cantigas, transcriptas y harmonizadas con acompañamiento de órgano o harmonio. Textos originales y versiones en castellano* (Barcelona: Vidal Llimona y Boceta, 1905–191?) "probably appeared first, singly, in the review *Salterio Sacro Hispano,* ca. 1882–83."

35. See Villalba above in n. 16. Pedrell, *Cancionero musical popular español* (Madrid: J. Fernández Arias, 1914), 1: nos. 145–48; 3 (Valls, Spain: Eduard Castells, 1920): nos. 1–4. For information concerning Bretón's settings, see Julián Ribera Tarragó, "Valor de la música de las *Cantigas*," in *Discursos leídos ante S. M. el Rey y la real familia (23 de noviembre de 1921) . . . para conmemorar el VII centenario del nacimiento del rey don Alfonso el Sabio* (Madrid: Tipografía de la Revista de Archivos, Bibliotecas y Museos, 1921), 7–20. Bretón's arrangements, based on Ribera's transcriptions, were interspersed among the various discourses presented during the evening. These arrangements were not published.

36. See Aubry and Ribera above in n. 14; see Sunyol above in n. 28, and Trend, *Music of Spanish History,* mus. exs. 9–14.

37. Anglés, *La música de las Cantigas de Santa María del rey Alfonso el Sabio,* facsimile with transcriptions and study, 3 vols. (Barcelona: Diputación Provincial, 1943–1964). Volume two (1943) contains the musical transcriptions.

38. However, it was Elias F. Dexter who undertook the first serious study of Alfonso's sources for his *Cantigas,* among which was *Les Miracles de la Sainte Vierge* of Gautier de Coincy (1177/1178–1236). See Dexter's "Sources of the 'Cantigas' of

Alfonso el Sabio" (Ph.D. diss., University of Wisconsin, 1926). See also Walter Mettmann, "Os *Miracles* de Gautier de Coinci como fonte das *Cantigas de Santa Maria*," *Homenagen Luciana Stegagno Picchio* (in press). Peter Dronke observes that "only in the twelfth century [such] expressions . . . as 'flos florum', 'rosa rosarum' became a common currency in hymns." See Dronke, *Medieval Latin and the Rise of European Love-Lyric* (Oxford: Clarendon Press, 1965), 186.

39. Katz, "Anglés and Melodic Origins," 53–54.

40. Wilkes, "La XI cantiga de Alfonso el Sabio y su armonización por Julián Ribera," *Revista del profesorado* [Buenos Aires] (June 1942): 109–24, esp. 118 and 120, respectively. Wilkes confused the numbering of "Rosa das rosas," referring to it as cantiga 10 when discussing the Escorial codices and as 11 for the Madrid ([*sic*] Toledo). Wilkes was following Ribera's enumeration. He also discussed the notational differences between the Escorial and Toledo codices and elaborated on the relationship of the *Cantigas* tunes to the Gregorian modes. Wilkes was both a composer and a musicologist. In the latter capacity, he was known for his study on medieval modes and Gregorian chant. It is surprising that Gerardo V. Huseby, in his exhaustive study "The *Cantigas de Santa Maria* and the Medieval Theory of Modes," does not make reference to Wilkes's work. See also Wilkes, "Cantiga 10," in *Joya de canciones españolas,* prologue and selection by Ernesto Mario Barreda (Buenos Aires: Asociación Patriótica Española, 1942), 17–19.

41. Anglés, *La música,* 19 (transcription). The text follows Mettmann's arrangement; see his *Cantigas (1 a 100),* 84–85. Anglés differentiated the rhyme schemes between the refrain and strophe by employing upper and lower case letters, respectively. The superscript numbers designate the syllable count in their respective lines of verse. In my analysis of the tune, given under the heading *Melodic structure,* the upper case letters correspond to the melody phrase, while the superscript letters designate subdivisions in the phrase. Their coordination with the melody can be seen in Example 11–4.

42. Ribera's transcription was printed without a text underlay.

43. The Castilian version was made by Ernesto Mario Barreda.

44. In Anglés's transcription of To and B.I.2, their differences are reflected in the transposition (To is a 4th higher) and in bars 2, 8, and 19.

45. E. López Chavarri duplicated Villalba's transcription in his *Historia de la música* (Barcelona: Hijos de Paluzíe, 1921), 1: facing p. 156.

46. The first two measures of Pedrell's arrangements indicate that he used Aubry's transcription; see Higinio Anglés, *Catàleg dels manuscrits musicals de la Col·lecció Pedrell* (Barcelona: Institut d'Estudis Catalans, 1920), 79.

47. See Anglés above in n. 46. Anglés's transcription of the cantiga 10 from B.I.2 was subsequently utilized by: (1) Reese, *Music in the Middle Ages,* 247, who obtained it from Anglés's unpublished paper, "La notación mensural de la música monódica de la corte española del siglo XIII ofrece soluciones nuevas, hasta hoy totalmente desconocidas, para la interpretación estético-rítmica de las melodías de los trovadores," a discourse delivered by proxy to the American Musicological Society of New York, September 1939; (2) José María Lamaña, *Canciones de la Andalucía medieval y renacentista (siglos XIII–XVI) para canto y piano* (Madrid: Unión Musical Española, 1968), 1, who transposed it up a major 2nd, with minor

alterations; (3) Venancio G. Velasco, *Rosa das rosas (cantiga de Santa María)* (Madrid: Unión Musical Española, 1973), who employed it in his arrangement for guitar, transposed up a major 3rd and renotated in a strict 6/4 meter; and (4) Mariano Pérez Gutiérrez, "Rosa das rosas (armonización modal)," Op. 56, (unpublished manuscript dated 1967), who arranged it for mezzo-soprano solo and four-part chorus, *a cappella*. It should also be noted that the portion accompanying the text "Rosa de beldad' e . . . et de prazer" in Anglés's transcriptions (Example 11-4, d and i) duplicates that made earlier by Friedrich Ludwig: see Guido Adler, *Handbuch der Musikgeschichte,* 2nd edn. (Frankfurt am Main: Hess, 1930), 1: 213.

48. Wilkes, "La XI cantiga," 118.

49. Ibid. "Más que una 'fórmula general' que por lo común no comprende sino tres o cuatro sonidos capitales dentro de la tonalidad eclesiástica, el tema de la Cantiga se diría sugerido al compositor por alguna de las melodías de la liturgia cristiana."

50. See Wilkes, "La XI cantiga," 118.

CHAPTER TWELVE

1. 13 May 1988, page 30. Joseph Snow of the University of Georgia kindly brought this article to my attention. Barbara De Marco, the assistant editor of *Romance Philology,* and Dr. Paula Rodgers of the University of California at Davis read a draft of this chapter and suggested numerous useful improvements.

2. III.3.46.

3. I find Aquilino Iglesia Ferreirós the most persuasive and plausible overall presentation of Alfonsine legislation and have adopted here the substance of his basic points of view, though considerable differences remain between us in matters of detail. See his "La labor legislativa de Alfonso X el Sabio," *España y Europa* (ch. 2 above, n. 14), 275–599; but see the important review by Carlos Petit, *AHDE* 56 (1986): 1087–92.

4. On this point see Iglesia Ferreirós's 1971 paper (*LWAX,* C357).

5. Literal quotes are taken from the recent edition by Ivy A. Corfis, *El fuero de Burgos: European MS 245 Philadelphia Free Library* (Madison, Wisc.: Hispanic Seminary of Medieval Studies, 1987). Otherwise, I cite the more accessible 1836 edition (*LWAX,* Bb13).

6. *Fuero* of Alarcón, law 286, in *Les Fueros d'Alcaraz et d'Alarcón,* ed. Jean Roudil, 2 vols. (Paris: Klincksieck, 1968), 1: 243.

7. *Siete partidas,* IV.9.2, my translation. For a commentary on this law, see John Boswell in *LWAX,* C118.

8. O'Callaghan's article is above in ch. 2, n. 18. His case rests in large part on an interpretation of a passage in the prologue of the *Espéculo,* where Alfonso supposedly refers to the distribution of copies of the *Fuero real.* On a purely linguistic level, the passage in question cannot, I believe, bear the construction O'Callaghan puts on it. The passage refers to copies of the *Espéculo*—which, it would seem, were in fact never produced, as noted below.

9. "*Breviario,* recepción y *Fuero real:* tres notas," in *Estudios jurídicos: homenaje al profesor Alfonso Otero* (Santiago de Compostela: Universidad de Santiago, 1981),

148–51; his *"Fuero real y Espéculo,"* *AHDE* 52 (1982): 180–84; and especially his "Labor legislativa," 409–63.

10. *Leyes de Alfonso X,* vol. 1: *Espéculo,* in collaboration with J. M. Ruiz Asencio (Avila, Spain: Fundación Sánchez Albornoz, 1985), 31–39.

11. *LWAX,* Ba1.

12. On these points see my "How Many *Partidas* in the *Siete Partidas?*" in *Hispanic Studies in Honor of Alan D. Deyermond: A North American Tribute,* ed. J. S. Miletich (Madison, Wisc.: Hispanic Seminary of Medieval Studies, 1986), 83–92.

13. As maintained in *LWAX,* C195, C197.

14. For example, III.4.6.

15. On the ten senses in the *Partidas,* see Herriott in *LWAX,* C342.

16. *LWAX,* Bh1 (1st edn.) and Bh7 (López edn.).

17. On the continuing legal validity of the *Partidas* in Spain and the Americas, North and South, see *LWAX,* C33, C670, and G. C. Barragán, *La obra legislativa de Alfonso el Sabio* (Buenos Aires: Abeledo-Perrot, 1983), especially his ch. 3, "Las *Partidas* en America," 65–112. On the 1860 decision, see *LWAX,* C569.

18. Craddock, "El *Setenario:* última e inconclusa refundición alfonsina de la primera *Partida,"* *AHDE* 56 (1986): 441–66.

19. *LWAX,* Bg1; and ch. 2 above, n. 5.

20. See now the superb treatment by James F. Powers, *A Society Organized for War: The Iberian Municipal Militias in the Central Middle Ages, 1000–1284* (Berkeley and Los Angeles: University of California Press, 1988).

21. *LWAX.*

22. MacDonald, "Law and Politics: Alfonso's Program of Political Reform," and his "Problemas políticos," both above in ch. 2, n. 18. Iglesia Ferreirós, "Labor legislativa," 275–599. Pérez Martín, "El *Fuero real* y Murcia," *AHDE* 54 (1984): 55–96. Tomás y Valiente, *Manual de historia del derecho español,* 4th edn. (Madrid: Tecnos, 1983).

23. Catalog for the exposition at the Museo de Santa Cruz (Madrid: Dirección General de Bellas Artes y Archivos, 1984). *Estudios alfonsíes: lexicografía, lírica, estética y política de Alfonso el Sabio,* above in ch. 2, n. 39. *La lengua y la literatura,* Congreso Internacional, Murcia, 5–10 March 1984 (Murcia, Spain: Universidad de Murcia, 1985). "Alfonso X el Sabio: VII centenario," *Revista de la Facultad de derecho de la Universidad complutense,* monograph 9 (1985). "Alfonso X y su época," *Revista de occidente* 43 (1984), extraordinary no. 9. "Informe: Alfonso X el Sabio, VIII centenario," *Historia 16,* 9 (1984), no. 96: 45–70. "Setecientos años del rey Sabio," *ABC,* 4 April 1984. "1284–1984: septimo centenario de la muerte de Alfonso X el Sabio," *El país,* 4 April 1984. I have not yet been able to see M. B. Fontanella de Weinberg, et al., *Homenaje a Alfonso el Sabio* (Bahía Blanca, Argentina: Departamento de Humanidades, Universidad Nacional del Sur, 1984); or *Cádiz en el siglo XIII,* Actas, VII Centenario de la muerte de Alfonso X el Sabio (Cádiz, Spain: Universidad de Cádiz, 1983). What appeared to be the premier conference of the centenary, "Alfonso X el Sabio: vida, obra, época," has not yet been favored with a volume of *actas* (see *AHDE* 54 [1984]: 771–72).

24. Craddock, *LWAX.* García-Badell, *"Bibliografía sobre la obra jurídica de*

Alfonso X el Sabio y su época (1800–1985)," Revista de la Facultad de derecho de la Universidad complutense, monograph 9 (1985): 287–319.

25. "La tradición manuscrita de las *Siete partidas,"* in *España y Europa,* 655–99.

26. *Espéculo* above in n. 10; reviewed by R. A. MacDonald, *Journal of Hispanic Philology* 10 (1986): 253–55. *Fuero real,* vol. 2 of *Leyes de Alfonso X,* ed. G. Martínez Díez, J. M. Ruiz Asencio, and César Hernández Alonso (Avila: Fundación Sánchez Albornoz, 1988).

27. On MacDonald's editorial labors, see his "Notas sobre la edición de las obras legales atribuidas a Alfonso X de Castilla," *AHDE* 53 (1983): 721–25; and his *"Espéculo* atribuido" above in ch. 2, n. 18.

28. Arias Bonet, in *LWAX,* Bh38. *Concordances* in *LWAX,* Bh39 (see above, ch. 1, n. 4). See too the comparative review article by J. R. Craddock, "A New Medium for Lexical and Textual Research: The HSMS Microfiche[s]," *Romance Philology* 39 (1986): 462–72.

29. Ramos, *Primera partida (MS. HC. 397/573) Hispanic Society of America* (Granada: Caja General de Ahorros y Monte de Piedad, 1984). Iglesia Ferreirós, in *AHDE* 55 (1985): 953.

30. Above in n. 5.

31. *Primeyra partida: édition et étude* (Braga, Portugal: Instituto Nacional de Investigação Científica, 1980). *Fuero real: edição, glossário e concordância da versão portuguesa* (Braga, Portugal: Universidade do Minho, 1982). *Foro real,* 2 vols. (Lisbon: Instituto Nacional de Investigação Científica, 1987).

32. "A obra legislativa de Afonso X em Portugal," *Diacrítica: revista do Centro de estudos portugueses* (Braga, Portugal: Universidade do Minho), 1 (1986): 15–21. "Subsídios para uma edição da *Terceira partida* de Afonso X," *Boletim de filologia* 29 (1984): 101–18.

33. *Alfonso and the Jews* (see above, ch. 2, n. 10), and his "Alfonso el Sabio y los moros: algunas precisiones legales, históricas y textuales con respecto a *Siete partidas* 7.25," *Al-Qanṭara* 7 (1986): 229–52.

34. *LWAX,* C195 and C197.

35. *LWAX,* C196.

36. "How Many *Partidas?"* (see above, n. 12).

37. *LWAX,* Bh35, C40.

38. *LWAX,* C195 and C197; see also "How Many *Partidas?"*

39. *LWAX,* C274, C276; his "La obra legislativa de Alfonso X: hechos e hipótesis," *AHDE* 54 (1984): 97–161; and his "La problemática de la obra legislativa de Alfonso X," *Boletín del ilustre Colegio de abogados de Madrid* 5 (1984): 9–18.

40. "Alfonso X, su labor legislativa y los historiadores," *Historia, instituciones, documentos* 9 (1982): 9–112. *"Fuero real,"* above in n. 9. *Privilegio general,* above in ch. 2, n. 28, and "Cuestiones alfonsinas," in n. 18. "Labor legislativo de Alfonso," above in n. 3.

41. "Notas sobre la edición" above in n. 27; and his "Problemas políticos," and "Law and Politics," above in ch. 2, n. 18.

41. Besides the three articles in n. 40 here, see his *"Espéculo* atribuido," above in ch. 2, n. 18.

42. "Sobre la promulgación," above in ch. 2, n. 18.

43. "El *Fuero real*"; see also his "El estudio de la recepción del derecho común en España" in *I Seminario de historia del derecho: derecho privado: nuevas técnicas de investigación,* ed. Joaquín Cerdá y Ruiz-Funes and Pablo Salvador Coderch (Bellaterra: Universidad Autónoma de Barcelona, 1985), 241–325.

44. "La posizione giuridica dell'eretico nelle *Siete partidas:* contributo allo studio delle fonti della partida 7 tit. 26," *Studi senesi* 97 (1985): 223–46, my translation.

45. Arias Bonet, "Sobre presuntas fuentes de las *Partidas,*" *Revista de la Facultad de derecho de la Universidad complutense,* monograph 9 (1985): 11–23. José Bono, *Historia del derecho notarial español,* part 1, vol. 1 (Madrid: Junta de Decanos de los colegios notariales de España, 1979). García Gallo, "Obra legislativa" and "Problemática" above in n. 39.

46. "Titulos de las *Siete partidas* y del *Corpus iuris civilis,*" *Revista de la Facultad de derecho de la Universidad complutense,* monograph 9 (1985): 129–55.

47. For Powers, see above, n. 20. Vallejo, "*Fuero real* 1,7,4: pleitos de justicia," *Historia, instituciones, documentos* 11 (1985): 1–32; and his "La regulación del proceso en el *Fuero real:* desarrollo, precedentes y problemas," *AHDE* 55 (1985): 495–704.

48. Bartol, *Oraciones consecutivas y concesivas en las "Siete partidas"* (Salamanca: Universidad de Salamanca, 1986). Lapesa, "Símbolos y palabras en el *Setenario* de Alfonso X," *NRFH* 29 (1980): 247–61; reprinted in the Vanderford edition of the *Setenario* (see above, ch. 2, n. 5), and in Lapesa's *Estudios de historia lingüística española* (Madrid: Paraninfo, 1985), 226–38.

Index

For the policy of omitting many medieval accents and Anglicizing certain names, see the Preface.

University of Pennsylvania Press
MIDDLE AGES SERIES
Edward Peters, General Editor

Edward Peters, ed. *Christian Society and the Crusades, 1198–1229*. Sources in Translation, including The Capture of Damietta by Oliver of Paderborn. 1971

Edward Peters, ed. *The First Crusade: The Chronicle of Fulcher of Chartres and Other Source Materials*. 1971

Katherine Fischer Drew, trans. *The Burgundian Code: The Book of Constitutions or Law of Gundobad and Additional Enactments*. 1972

G. G. Coulton. *From St. Francis to Dante: Translations from the Chronicle of the Franciscan Salimbene (1221–1288)*. 1972

Alan C. Kors and Edward Peters, eds. *Witchcraft in Europe, 1110–1700: A Documentary History*. 1972

Richard C. Dales. *The Scientific Achievement of the Middle Ages*. 1973

Katherine Fischer Drew, trans. *The Lombard Laws*. 1973

Edward Peters, ed. *Monks, Bishops, and Pagans: Christian Culture in Gaul and Italy, 500–700*. 1975

Jeanne Krochalis and Edward Peters, ed. and trans. *The World of Piers Plowman*. 1975

Julius Goebel, Jr. *Felony and Misdemeanor: A Study in the History of Criminal Law*. 1976

Susan Mosher Stuard, ed. *Women in Medieval Society*. 1976

Clifford Peterson. *Saint Erkenwald*. 1977

Robert Somerville and Kenneth Pennington, eds. *Law, Church, and Society: Essays in Honor of Stephan Kuttner*. 1977

Donald E. Queller. *The Fourth Crusade: The Conquest of Constantinople, 1201–1204*. 1977

Pierre Riché (Jo Ann McNamara, trans.). *Daily Life in the World of Charlemagne*. 1978

Edward Peters, ed. *Heresy and Authority in Medieval Europe*. 1980

Suzanne Fonay Wemple. *Women in Frankish Society: Marriage and the Cloister, 500–900*. 1981

Edward Peters. *The Magician, the Witch, and the Law*. 1982

Barbara H. Rosenwein. *Rhinoceros Bound: Cluny in the Tenth Century*. 1982

Steven D. Sargent, ed. and trans. *On the Threshold of Exact Science: Selected Writings of Anneliese Maier on Late Medieval Natural Philosophy.* 1982

Benedicta Ward. *Miracles and the Medieval Mind: Theory, Record, and Event, 1000–1215.* 1982

Harry Turtledove, trans. *The Chronicle of Theophanes: An English Translation of* anni mundi *6095–6305 (A.D. 602–813).* 1982

Leonard Cantor, ed. *The English Medieval Landscape.* 1982

Charles T. Davis. *Dante's Italy and Other Essays.* 1984

George T. Dennis, trans. *Maurice's Strategikon: Handbook of Byzantine Military Strategy.* 1984

Thomas F. X. Noble. *The Republic of St. Peter: The Birth of the Papal State, 680–825.* 1984

Kenneth Pennington. *Pope and Bishops: The Papal Monarchy in the Twelfth and Thirteenth Centuries.* 1984

Patrick J. Geary. *Aristocracy in Provence: The Rhône Basin at the Dawn of the Carolingian Age.* 1985

C. Stephen Jaeger. *The Origins of Courtliness: Civilizing Trends and the Formation of Courtly Ideals, 939–1210.* 1985

J. N. Hillgarth, ed. *Christianity and Paganism, 350–750: The Conversion of Western Europe.* 1986

William Chester Jordan. *From Servitude to Freedom: Manumission in the Sénonais in the Thirteenth Century.* 1986

James William Brodman. *Ransoming Captives in Crusader Spain: The Order of Merced on the Christian-Islamic Frontier.* 1986

Frank Tobin. *Meister Eckhart: Thought and Language.* 1986

Daniel Bornstein, trans. *Dino Compagni's Chronicle of Florence.* 1986

James M. Powell. *Anatomy of a Crusade, 1213–1221.* 1986

Jonathan Riley-Smith. *The First Crusade and the Idea of Crusading.* 1986

Susan Mosher Stuard, ed. *Women in Medieval History and Historiography.* 1987

Avril Henry, ed. *The Mirour of Mans Saluacioune.* 1987

María Rosa Menocal. *The Arabic Role in Medieval Literary History.* 1987

Margaret J. Ehrhart. *The Judgment of the Trojan Prince Paris in Medieval Literature.* 1987

Betsy Bowden. *Chaucer Aloud: The Varieties of Textual Interpretation.* 1987

Felipe Fernández-Armesto. *Before Columbus: Exploration and Colonization from the Mediterranean to the Atlantic, 1229–1492.* 1987

Michael Resler, trans. *EREC by Hartmann von Aue.* 1987

A. J. Minnis. *Medieval Theory of Authorship.* 1988

Uta-Renate Blumenthal. *The Investiture Controversy: Church and Monarchy from the Ninth to the Twelfth Century.* 1988

Robert Hollander. *Boccaccio's Last Fiction: "Il Corbaccio."* 1988

Ralph Turner. *Men Raised from the Dust: Administrative Service and Upward Mobility in Angevin England.* 1988

David Anderson. *Before the Knight's Tale: Imitation of Classical Epic in Boccaccio's "Teseida."* 1988

Charlotte A. Newman. *The Anglo-Norman Nobility in the Reign of Henry I: The Second Generation.* 1988

Joseph F. O'Callaghan. *The Cortes of Castile-León, 1188–1350.* 1988

William D. Paden. *The Voice of the Trobairitz: Essays on the Women Troubadours.* 1989

William Chester Jordan. *The French Monarchy and the Jews: From Philip Augustus to the Last Capetians.* 1989

Edward B. Irving, Jr. *Rereading* Beowulf. 1989

David Burr. *Olivi and Franciscan Poverty: The Origins of the* Usus Pauper *Controversy.* 1989

Willene B. Clark and Meradith T. McMunn, eds. *Beasts and Birds of the Middle Ages: The Bestiary and Its Legacy.* 1989

Richard C. Hoffmann. *Land, Liberties, and Lordship in a Late Medieval Countryside: Agrarian Structures and Change in the Duchy of Wrocław.* 1989

Robert I. Burns, S.J., ed. *Emperor of Culture: Alfonso X the Learned of Castile and His Thirteenth-Century Renaissance.* 1990